MARTIN LUTHER KING, JR.
AND THE CIVIL RIGHTS MOVEMENT

Edited by David J. Garrow

A CARLSON PUBLISHING SERIES

We Shall Overcome

THE CIVIL RIGHTS MOVEMENT
IN THE UNITED STATES
IN THE 1950'S AND 1960'S

Edited with a Preface by David J. Garrow

IN THREE VOLUMES

Volume One

CARLSON
Publishing Inc

BROOKLYN, NEW YORK, 1989

For copyright holders for individual articles, please see the Acknowledgments at the end of Volume Three.

Library of Congress Cataloging-in Publication Data

We shall overcome : the Civil Rights Movement in the United States in
   the 1950s and 1960s / edited with a preface by David. J. Garrow.
         p.   cm. —(Martin Luther King, Jr. and the Civil Rights
   Movement ; v. 4-6)
     Includes bibliographies and index.
     1. Afro-Americans—Civil rights. 2. Afro-Americans—Civil rights–
   –Southern States. 3. Civil rights movements—United States–
   –History—20th century. 4. Civil rights movements—Southern States–
   –History—20th century. 5. King, Martin Luther, Jr., 1929-1968.
   6. United States—Race relations. 7. Southern States—Race
   relations. I. Garrow, David J., 1953-   . II. Series.
   E185.61.W33   1989
   323.1'196073'09045—dc20   89-9962
   ISBN 0-926019-02-3 (alk. paper)

The index to this book was created using NL Cindex, a scholarly indexing program from the Newberry Library.

For a complete listing of the volumes in this series, please see the back of Volume Three.

Printed on acid–free, 250–year–life paper

Manufactured in the United States of America.

Contents of the Set

Volume One

Volume Two

Volume Three

Preface

The fifty-two articles contained in these three volumes comprise a very wide-ranging and very high-quality set of analyses concerning the southern black freedom struggle of the 1950s and 1960s. In many instances these articles in their original form have been little-cited or hard to obtain, but their breadth of coverage—ranging chronologically from two early overview analyses by August Meier and Elliott Rudwick and Charles Smith and Lewis Killian's important 1958 study of the under-appreciated Tallahassee (Fla.) bus boycott, to Richard Lentz's valuable analysis of press coverage of the 1968 Memphis sanitation strike—offers many valuable contributions to the historiography of the southern civil rights struggle.

Three major themes and substantive emphases can be traced through this rich corpus of first-rate articles on the southern movement. One is the especial importance that indigenous local protest efforts played during those years, local efforts that oftentimes did not draw extensive contemporaneous coverage in the national press and that have likewise generally not received sufficient scholarly attention in later years. Smith and Killian's valuable report on the Tallahassee boycott is but one important example of how local protests that were extremely significant at the time have been under-appreciated by subsequent history; Carl Graves' excellent but obscure article on the earliest sit-ins, John Ricks' *Journal of Southwest Georgia History* article on the Albany Movement of 1961-1962, and James Ely's important study of the Danville, Virginia, protests of 1963 are additional, notable examples. One particularly nice strength of these volumes is the presentation of a number of valuable analyses concerning black activism in Selma, Alabama, in the years prior to 1965, when Selma became internationally famous; Harris Wofford's lengthy unpublished 1953 paper is an especially important addition to the historical record of one of the southern movement's most important locales. Jerry DeMuth's and John Fry's 1964 pieces on Selma, and the extensive but hard-to-find 1965 *Ramparts* coverage of the Selma demonstrations are also important reports on a particularly significant local struggle.

Such an appreciation of the significance of crucial local movements is also reflected in a number of August Meier's important pieces that are reprinted here, as well as in broader overview analyses such as Anne Braden's substantial 1965 *Monthly Review* essay. Secondly, however, much of Meier's work, as well as other valuable overview pieces, such as Kenneth B. Clark's significant 1965 article from *Daedalus*, draw particular attention to the special roles that both the Student Nonviolent Coordinating Committee (SNCC) and the Southern Christian Leadership Conference (SCLC) played in stimulating the southern movement. In particular, some of Meier's work, along with significant contemporaneous analyses such as Louis Lomax's important 1960 article from *Harper's* and Staughton Lynd's 1963 piece from *Commentary*, identify and acknowledge the important organizational tensions that existed between SNCC and SCLC on the one hand and especially the National Association for the Advancement of Colored People (NAACP) on the other. Such tensions often manifested themselves in local movements, such as in Albany, but the region-wide importance of both SNCC and SCLC was quite considerable, wholly apart from the tactical and generational tensions that often existed between the two of them and the NAACP, and, sometimes, between the two of them themselves.

With regard to SNCC, two important participant/observer accounts—Diane Nash's 1961 essay on the sit-ins and Freedom Rides, and Julius Lester's insightful 1966 retrospective article—and one conceptually and analytically important scholarly piece, by Emily Stoper, appear in these volumes. With regard to SCLC, Randall Kryn's previously unpublished paper on James Bevel, and Adam Fairclough's much broader analysis, as well as Ewell Reagin's little-known piece, all offer material of value. Bridging specific organizational focuses, both Bayard Rustin's justly famous 1965 and 1966 essays in *Commentary*, and Vincent Harding's two lengthier 1968 papers offer profoundly important analyses and explanations regarding the evolution that the movement, and particularly SNCC in one way and Dr. Martin Luther King, Jr., and SCLC in another, underwent between the early and the late 1960s.

Third, and distinct from indigenous local initiatives and from the organizational roles and tensions involving SNCC, SCLC, and other regional or national groups, are the protest dynamics and interrelationships that linked black-led efforts in the South to the federal government in Washington and other potential allies outside the region. Two dramatically-different and substantively significant but little-cited contemporaneous articles by Justice

Department civil rights attorneys—Burke Marshall and Thelton Henderson—offer instructive perspectives from the Washington side of the equation; Howard Zinn's 1964 essay, as well as other commentators here such as Kenneth Clark and August Meier, offer more critical movement perspectives on the interrelationship between southern activists and their sometimes-allies in Washington.

Additionally, three particularly insightful and instructive interpretive articles—those by Jan Howard from 1966, by Howard Hubbard from 1968, and by Neil McMillen from 1977—offer significant analyses of the public protest dynamics that black demonstrations in the south, and media coverage of them, generated for both the elite political audience in Washington and for the mass audience of Americans all across the country. While in the years after 1978 such an understanding and appreciation of the movement's protest dynamics and their political impact became very widely shared among scholars and students of the southern movement, explicit description and articulation of those political dynamics before that time had been relatively uncommon. Howard in particular, and Hubbard and McMillen as well, all offered significant insight that later scholars were able to build and expand upon, especially with regard to the strategy and tactics employed by Dr. King and SCLC in particular.

Lately, in the decade between the late 1970s and late 1980s, a predominant amount of the most provocative and at times insightful analyses of the southern black freedom struggle's development and evolution was provided by sociologists rather than by historians or scholars from additional disciplines. Much of sociology's active interest in using the history of the southern movement to enrich and inform analytical work concerning social protest movements more broadly began with significant scholarly articles published by Aldon Morris and Doug McAdam in the *American Sociological Review*. Although those contributions drew qualifications and partial rebuttal—most importantly from long-time movement scholar Lewis Killian, also writing in the *American Sociological Review*—the application of sociology's "resource mobilization" perspective has been perhaps the most conceptually and analytically enriching development in civil rights scholarship over the past decade or decade-and-a-half. As the "mature" version of resource mobilization analysis has focused more scholarly attention than previously was the case on the often-overlooked indigenous resources—both organizational and institutional as well as material or financial—of southern black communities, evolving scholarship on the southern movement, and especially on the state of black activism in the South during the 1950s, has more and more recognized and acknowledged the pre-eminent importance of local, grass roots people and institutions, over and above the stimulating or mobilizing roles played by external organizations, actors, and developments. This trend will no doubt mature and deepen, enriching our scholarly understanding of early movement activism, and it may well increasingly be coupled with more and more sophisticated analyses of the relationships that existed between external supporters of the movement and different movement organizations. The work of Herbert Haines—both his *Social Problems* article that is reprinted here, and his subsequent book, *Black Radicals and the Civil Rights Mainstream, 1954-1970* (University of Tennessee Press, 1988)—is a particularly significant reflection of the new and insightful directions such analyses may take.

All in all, the articles presented in these three volumes offer a very substantial amount of insight regarding all three of the major emphases that civil rights movement historiography has reflected over the past several decades: the increasing appreciation of the importance of local, indigenous black activism in creating the southern movement; the pre-eminent significance of SNCC and SCLC, and the organizational tensions their activism generated, in the mobilization and maturation of a region-wide civil rights struggle; and the complicated, ambiguous, and multi-layered relationships that developed between those southern movement activists on the one hand and a potentially supportive federal government on the other. As scholarly work on the southern movement continues to develop and hopefully expand during the decade of the 1990s, the articles contained in these three volumes, as well as in the other volumes of Carlson Publishing's series on *Martin Luther King, Jr., and the Civil Rights Movement*, can make a very significant contribution to strengthening the quality of future work by displaying and disseminating the breadth and depth of scholarly insight that work in the movement has already generated.

David J. Garrow

We Shall Overcome

DE FACTO LEADERSHIP AND THE CIVIL RIGHTS MOVEMENT: PERSPECTIVE ON THE PROBLEMS AND ROLE OF ACTIVISTS AND LAWYERS IN LEGAL AND SOCIAL CHANGE*

NORMAN C. AMAKER**

> *It was the people who moved their leaders, not the leaders who moved the people. Of course, there were generals, as there must be in every army. But the command post was in the bursting hearts of millions of Negroes. When such a people begin to move, they create their own theories, shape their own destinies, and choose the leaders who share their own philosophy.*[1]

1

1965 was the year I first visited Southern University law school. As a lawyer for the NAACP Legal Defense Fund,[2] I had been involved during the previous few years in a number of school desegregation cases filed in the federal district court in Baton Rouge, including the Baton Rouge school desegregation case.[3]

---

* This article was originally presented as a lecture at the Southern University School of Law on April 2, 1980 as part of the lecture series, "The Legal Parameters of Leadership." It is printed here with the author's editing and footnotes.

The author wishes to express his appreciation for the research assistance of Ms. Patricia Needham, Loyola University of Chicago Law School, Class of 1982.

** Professor of Law, School of Law, Loyola University of Chicago, Chicago, Illinois.

1. M. KING, WHY WE CAN'T WAIT 144 (1964).
2. The NAACP Legal Defense Fund was incorporated separately from the National Association for the Advancement of Colored People (NAACP) for tax purposes in 1939 to carry on the legal work begun initially by the legal committee of the Association in the 1930's. For the last four decades, it has been the pre-eminent legal organization working to combat racial discrimination in the United States.
3. Davis v. East Baton Rouge Parish School Board, 214 F. Supp. 624 (E.D. La. 1973). This case was filed originally on February 29, 1956. More than four years later, on May 25, 1960, an injunction first issued enjoining segregation in the schools. However, it was not until 1963, after I had begun work on the case by filing and arguing a "Renewed Motion for Further Relief", that an order was issued requiring the submission of a plan of desegregation pursuant to which initial desegregation occurred at the beginning of the 1963 school year — eight years after the case started!

1965 was notable in other ways. It was a very significant year. It was the mid-point, perhaps even the high point, of the "civil rights" decade — a decade that saw the greatest amount

---

The Baton Rouge School case was the first school desegregation case I argued. The argument remains notable because as soon as I completed it, the judge — without taking the case under submission — began reading his opinion from the bench. It obviously had been prepared beforehand. As reported, the judge (E. Gordon West) called the *Brown Case (Brown v. Board of Education of Topeka*, 347 U.S. 483 (1954)), "one of the truly regrettable decisions of all times", 214 F. Supp. at 625, and after excoriating, "[i]ts substitution of so-called 'sociological principles' for sound legal reasoning" as "almost unbelievable" went on to say that, "the trouble that has directly resulted from this decision in other communities has been brought about not by the citizens and residents of the community involved, but by the agitation of outsiders [presumably like me] from far distant states. . . ." *Id.*

This was the first but not the last time that a southern based federal district judge before whom I appeared in a school desegregation case had already prepared his opinion and proceeded to read it from the bench. It would happen to me again in Dallas in August 1964 after a hearing in the Dallas School Desegregation Case (*Bell v. Folsom*, 10 RACE REL. L. REP. 1173 (N.D. Tex. 1964), *rev'd sub nom Britton v. Folsom*, 348 F. 2d 158 (5th Cir. 1965).

I mention these experiences and quote Judge West's comments to point up the kind of problems resulting from the attitude of some members of the federal judiciary faced by civil rights lawyers of the period. The nature of these problems is a major theme of this article.

Beyond these examples, the reader should also understand the pervasive, continuing nature of the problems associated with school desegregation suits. These suits literally were on the cutting edge of drastic social change in all the communities in which they were filed beginning with the original group of *Brown* cases filed in the trial courts beginning in 1950. There was great resistance to this change and it was manifested not only by the defendants but quite often — as in the case of Judge West — by the judges before whom the cases were brought. This combined resistance meant that plaintiffs' lawyers were constantly required to file additional legal proceedings, e.g., a "Renewed Motion for Further Relief", in case after case irrespective of when it had begun in order to secure even initial compliance with the law as settled in *Brown*. It was and has remained for three decades, a wearying, time and resource consuming process which explains why school desegregation suits though begun about the time of the *Brown* cases or shortly thereafter, are still in court today. *See, e.g.,* Northcross v. Board of Education of Memphis City Schools, 611 F.2d 624 (6th Cir. 1979), *cert. denied* 447 U.S. 911 (1980) (case filed 1960 - attorneys' fees question still in litigation). As late as January, 1979, certiorari was denied by the Supreme Court from an appeal in the Baton Rouge school case vacating and remanding on questions of one-race schools and teacher reassignment. East Baton Rouge Parish School Board v. Davis, 439 U.S. 1114 (Jan. 15, 1979). And the *Brown* case itself has recently been reopened as a new generation of plaintiffs filed suit in federal district court in Topeka, Kansas in November 1979. New York Times, Nov. 30, 1979, §A at 20, col. 1-2.The other school desegregation cases, cited at 303 F. Supp. 1224 (E.D. La. 1969), included: *Dunn v. Livingston Parish School Board; Williams v. Iberville Parish School Board; Thomas v. West Baton Rouge Parish School Board; Boyd v. Pointe Coupée Parish School Board; Carter v. West Feliciana Parish School Board; George v. Davis, Pres., East Feliciana Parish School Board;* and *Charles v. Ascension Parish School Board. Hall v. St. Helena Parish School Board,* 233 F. Supp. 136 (E.D. La. 1964) was also included.

of social ferment ever manifested in the conduct of people on a massive scale motivated by their intense desire for simple justice. In that year, the National Association for the Advancement of Colored People (NAACP) which had been barred from Alabama, resumed operation there.[4] It was the year in which a crucial aspect of that social ferment, the voting rights demonstrations that occurred in Selma and other communities in Alabama, took place[5] — events which were marked by the courage of leaders and their followers, by violence and by death;[6] events in which I was deeply involved and will discuss. It was the year in which the Voting Rights Act[7] that resulted from those demonstrations was passed. Those events, and others that I will mention, resulted from this massive social ferment with important consequences on several levels.

3

On one level this upsurge of action, conscience and spirit which came to be known as the civil rights movement produced from its ranks persons who became authentic de facto leaders. In communities of varying size across the country, particularly here in the South, emerged individuals who at the time of their emergence were not particularly well-known, sometimes even in their own communities, but who led the way in articulating the concerns of that time and helping others push forward toward realization of their shared goals. Very few communities did not have such individuals. Among such persons in this community were men like Raymond Scott,[8] Depuy Anderson,[9] Acie Belton,[10] and of course, Johnnie Jones.[11] Many such persons, because of their activity, rose

---

4. *See* p. 237 *infra.*
5. *See* p. 272 *infra.*
6. *See* note 175 *infra.*
7. P.L. 89-110, 79 Stat. 437, 42 U.S.C. § 1973 *et seq.* (1976).
8. Scott, a tailor in Baton Rouge though never a plaintiff in a suit seeking desegregation, assisted those who were by providing transportation, money, tutorial assistance for desegregating school children and other needed help.
9. Anderson was the named plaintiff in *Anderson v. Martin,* 375 U.S. 399 (1964). He was then, and is now, a practicing dentist who was instrumental in desegregating the state and local dental associations even though his own membership has continually been rejected.
10. Belton was also a plaintiff in *Anderson v. Martin,* 375 U.S. 399 (1964). At the time, he was a laborer working for the Esso Corporation in Baton Rouge.
11. Johnnie Jones was born in Laurel Hill, Louisiana on November 30, 1919 and was graduated from Southern University's Law School in 1953. Soon after his admittance to the Louisiana bar, he became counsel to a group of black citizens in Baton Rouge who, a few years prior to Martin Luther King's successful boycott of the buses

to prominence not only in their own communities but in their region and their state. The martyred Medgar Evers[12] from Mississippi comes to mind, as does the late Fannie Lou Hamer,[13] also from that state. From Alabama, people like the

---

in Montgomery, Alabama, launched a similar boycott in Baton Rouge which, however, was not sustained. One of the few black lawyers in Louisiana during the 1950's and early 1960's, he was the local attorney-typically the person of initial contact of local blacks complaining of racial discrimination — in most of the cases supported by the NAACP Legal Defense Fund in Baton Rouge and the surrounding area during this period. He was the attorney in *Anderson v. Martin* 375 U.S. 399 (1964) (one of my earliest assignments at the Fund) which proscribed Louisiana's attempt to place racial designations on the ballots bearing the names of candidates for elective office and in the early "sit-in" cases arising from Baton Rouge and the surrounding area during this period. *See* p. 232 *infra*. He was also with me in the Baton Rouge school desegregation case (*see* note 3 *supra*) and later in the case brought against the Fun Fair Amusement Park (see note 125 *infra*). Subsequently, he was appointed as assistant parish (county) attorney of East Baton Rouge Parish embracing Baton Rouge and was later elected to the Louisiana House of Representatives. He is still practicing law in Baton Rouge. Jones, a small, wiry man of great courage, became for me a respected friend and colleague.

12.   Medgar Evers was born Sept. 11, 1922 in Decatur, Mississippi, one of four children. After graduation from Alcorn A & M College in Mississippi, he organized an NAACP chapter in Mound Bayou where he was selling insurance. In 1954, after the Supreme Court's decision in *Brown* (*see* note 3 *supra*), he applied for admission to the University of Mississippi law school and was rejected. In December 1954, he was invited to become the NAACP's first paid field secretary in Mississippi.

Constantly in danger because of his activities and a frequent target of assaults and threats, he was killed from ambush in the early morning hours of June 12, 1963. He was thirty-seven years old. The previous day, Governor George Wallace of Alabama "stood in the schoolhouse door" in a vain effort to block the admission of two black students to the University of Alabama and that night, a few hours before Evers' assassination, President Kennedy made a nationwide address on behalf of Blacks' civil rights, the first address of its kind by an American President. See text accompanying notes 96, 97, *infra*.

13.   Fannie Lou Townsend Hamer was the youngest of twenty children of black sharecroppers. She was born October 6, 1917 in rural Montgomery County, Mississippi. After marriage in the early forties, she secured a job as a timekeeper on a plantation until she was fired in 1962 for attempting to register to vote. She soon became involved, as a field secretary for the Student Non-violent Coordinating Committee (SNCC) in voter registration and the formulation of welfare programs in Mississippi.

After suffering a terrible and humiliating beating while jailed in June 1963 for her activities, she became the following year one of the founders of the Mississippi Freedom Democratic Party which challenged the regular Mississippi Democratic National Convention in 1964. She later ran unsuccessfully for Congress and continued to challenge the exclusion of blacks from the political process in Mississippi. The citation accompanying her honorary degree from Atlanta's Morehouse College in 1969 said: "[Y]ou have little formal education and your speech is full of errors of grammar and diction; but you tell your story with a passionate power that is intensified by pain, and you are a natural leader with the capacity to guide and inspire your fellow sufferers." Fannie Lou Hamer died in 1977.

stalwart Amelia Boynton[14] from Selma and the courageous
Fred Shuttlesworth[15] from Birmingham. Then too, there are
individuals who rose to national even international prominence like the late Dr. Martin Luther King, Jr.[16] Others who
emerged from this time became household names years later
like former United Nations ambassador, Andrew Young.[17] Beyond their own emergence as leaders in fact of the most important and far-reaching social movement of our era, they also

---

14. Amelia Boynton, a sturdy, handsome woman of medium brown complexion,
owned a store in Selma during the 1960's. A soft-spoken, intelligent woman of quiet
strength, she was one of those who spearheaded the voting drive in Selma during
1963-65 (*see* below at 271) and her home and place of business served as a headquarters of the movement. She was born Amelia Plats, August 18, 1911 in Savannah,
Georgia and received a B.S. degree from Tuskegee Institute (Alabama) in 1931. Wid-
owed in 1963, the year that I met her, she has since remarried and is now living in
Tuskegee Institute. She frequently lectures around the country on her experience and
has published an autobiography depicting her role in the civil rights movement, A
BOYNTON, BRIDGE ACROSS JORDAN (1979).

15. Fred Suttlesworth, a native Alabamian (born in Montgomery, March 18,
1922) was one of the premier social and political activists of the civil rights movement. He was educated in Alabama at Selma University and Alabama State College
and was the founder of the Alabama Christian Movement for Human Rights in Birmingham, Alabama in 1956. This organization in conjunction with the Southern
Christian Leadership Conference spearheaded the Birmingham demonstrations of
1963. *See* p. 241 *infra*.

I first met Fred Shuttlesworth in Montgomery, Alabama in 1961 where he had
been arrested for taking part in the protest demonstrations at Southern bus terminals
known as the "Freedom Rides." This was my initial exposure as a lawyer to the representation of civil rights demonstrators. During the Birmingham movement of 1963,
I worked very closely with Fred and came to admire both his great physical courage
and mental toughness. His crusading activities in Birmingham (*see* p. 237 *infra*)
made him my most prolific "client". (I was the frequent recipient of phone calls from
him during the course of several years asking, "Norman, how's my neck doing?").
Since 1966, he has pastored a Baptist Church in Cincinnati, Ohio.

16. Among the many sources documenting the life and work of Martin Luther
King are L. BENNETT, WHAT MANNER OF MAN (1964); R. MILLER, MARTIN LUTHER
KING, JR. (1968); J. WILLIAMS, THE KING GOD DIDN'T SAVE (1970); D. LEWIS, KING: A
CRITICAL BIOGRAPHY (1970); and J. BISHOP, THE DAYS OF MARTIN LUTHER KING
(1971). His own thoughts and feelings are in STRIDE TOWARD FREEDOM (1958) and
WHY WE CAN'T WAIT (1964).

I first met Martin in Birmingham in 1963 and worked with him there and later in
Selma as recounted here. Like so many others across the nation, those who knew him
and those who did not, I miss him very much.

17. The entire country now knows what those of us who worked with Andy during the movement discerned: that he is one of the most intelligent, most capable men
in America. On the personal level, he is also one of the genuinely nice and decent
people around. The most unusual "honorarium" I ever received for making a speech I
got from Andy in 1965: a mason jar of Georgia Moon corn liquor.

Books written about Andy are: ANDREW YOUNG AT THE UNITED NATIONS (L.
Clement, ed. 1977); G. CARPOZI, JR., ANDREW YOUNG: THE IMPOSSIBLE MAN (1978);
and J. HASKINS, ANDREW YOUNG: MAN WITH A MISSION (1979).

provided an example for others in their own time — and later — concerned with other problems which they began to address at least initially, by adoption of the methods used in the civil rights movement. I think particularly here of the thrust of leadership on behalf of the rights of the poor, of the movement for women's rights and the protests concerning the Vietnam War later in the decade.

On another level, leadership of the civil rights movement produced significant legal as well as social change. Attention was focused on problems long unattended that needed solutions. The movement's leaders confronted a host of problems connected with their roles as leaders. In turn, their problems and reactions to them — their own and that of others — created problems of a unique nature for those of us who, as lawyers, were assisting them, advising them, and representing them. Their activities, that of their followers and their lawyers exposed not only problems of the larger social order, but also problems of the legal system — its lack of responsiveness, the inadequacy of then existing remedies, and the narrow interpretation of existing laws. Of necessity, the roles of lawyers and the courts and inevitably that of the law schools came under scrutiny and were redefined.[18]

---

18. One manifestation of the redefining process that resulted is the relatively larger numbers of black (and other minority) students who entered predominantly white law schools after 1965, the first year which showed any marked increase over the then prevailing pattern. That pattern has been described in generally accurate terms as "the 'one black per class' quota which characterized . . . the more liberal law schools until the early sixties." Bell, *Black Students In White Law Schools: The Ordeal and The Opportunity*, U. OF TOLEDO L. REV. 539, 541 (1970). The general accuracy of that description by Professor Bell, a friend and colleague at the Legal Defense Fund, is attested to by his experience at the University of Pittsburg Law School (class of 1957) and by my own at Columbia University Law School (class of 1959). The increased numbers resulted from active recruitment programs not theretofore undertaken in conjunction with the relaxation to some degree of traditional admission standards and the provision of financial aid and tutorial assistance. An important part of the effort was the formation in 1968 of The Council on Legal Education Opportunity (CLEO), supported by the organized bar, the Association of American Law Schools (AALS) and the Law School Admission Council (LSAC), to assist minority and economically and educationally disadvantaged students enter the more than 140 accredited law schools in the United States. The CLEO program is described in *All About CLEO* (1978) published by the organization from its Washington, D.C. headquarters. Other sources descriptive of the process, direction and significance of the changes occurring (ever so slowly) in American law schools and increased minority admissions are, *Symposium: Disadvantaged Students and Legal Education Programs For Affirmative Action*, 1970 U. OF TOLEDO L. REV. nos. 2 and 3 (1970) (passim); Gellhorn, *The Law Schools and the Negro*, 1968 DUKE L.J. 1069 (1968);

So it is instructive — and important — for us to look back now at this distance of more than a decade in an attempt to define and evaluate these problems and their solution so that we may better understand our own time and our roles. Looking back at this remove permits us to put in perspective what that time of ferment and change has meant. That perspective instructs us both as to opportunity and to limits, as to reach and to grasp. Though the full meaning of this period cannot yet be fully appreciated, it nevertheless presents for us the challenge of de facto leadership today and serves as a continuing point of reference for those who would assay leadership roles in solving the continuing problems of social, political and legal responsiveness to all that is good, fair, just and humane.

What I propose then, is to place in context and examine an aspect of that massive social ferment that I know best because of my first-hand involvement with it — the relationship between the social action movement of that era and the litigation occasioned by it, litigation that was both product and producer of significant social change and far-reaching legal

7

Symposium: Minority Students in Law School, 20 BUFFALO L. REV. 423 (1971); *Special Report of the Proceedings of the American Association of Law Schools, Section on Minority Admissions,* 4 BLACK L.J. 453 (1975); *Rutgers L. Rev.* 857 (1979); W. LEONARD, BLACK LAWYERS — THE MINORITY STUDENT AND THE LAW (1977). A more generalized discussion of minority admissions is BAILEY AND HAFNER, MINORITY ADMISSIONS (1978).

Another aspect of the slowly changing face (literally) of white American law schools is that of faculty and administration. Beginning around 1968, law schools began actively seeking minority faculty. The process accelerated through the 1970's (when I entered full-time teaching). The pace of change here, however, has been even slower than that of student admissions (I am once again repeating my law school student experience as the only black). A Minority Groups Section was formed in the AALS during the '70s and has published for the past several years a *Directory of Minority Law Faculty Members.* The most recent edition counted 352 persons which included 27 administrators, 44 teacher-administrators and 4 teaching fellows (1978-79 school year). More recent figures compiled from the 1979 *Directory of Law Teachers* (published by the A.A.L.S. in conjunction with the West Publishing Co.) and published in the Association's June 1980 Newsletter give the totals (including administrators) as 324 for the 1979-80 school year. Since entirely accurate data is hard to come by, the numbers may understate the total slightly but they are very small compared with the total number of teachers in American law schools which the Newsletter gives as 5,226. Thus even making adjustment for slight error, the figures are less than 10% of the total. Yet they do reflect change however glacial: at the midpoint of the 1960's there were fewer than 10 black law professors teaching outside the traditionally black law schools. The situation of law school deans is hardly worth mentioning: there is one at Duquesne in Pittsburgh, Ronald Davenport; another at DePaul in Chicago, Elwin Griffith; and since January 1981, Derrick Bell at the University of Oregon.

change. I propose to demonstrate in this era of the quest for "relevance", just how relevant to the concerns and issues of today are the problems confronted and the solutions adopted during that time. I propose to do this by examining some pivotal events, events in which, to one degree or another, I was involved with others who were the kind of leaders that I have mentioned.

I begin with a brief look at the early part of the decade and the de facto leadership of students like yourselves and what resulted from it. The student protest movement at the beginning of the period was the spur to much of what followed. Two incidents are illustrative.

The first incident occurred in Montgomery, Alabama, the scene of the successful bus boycott four years earlier led by Martin Luther King. In late February 1960, there was a sit-in at a lunch counter in the Montgomery County Courthouse. It was the first recorded student protest in the State of Alabama.[19] The protest was against the exclusion of blacks from the lunch counter which was open to all whites. The protestors were students from the predominantly black Alabama State College in Montgomery, a tax-supported college. It was led by a young man who as a result of it emerged as one of the de facto leaders of the student movement, Bernard Lee,[20] who subsequently became one of the closest aides to Dr. King. Because they protested, the students were expelled from school without notice or an opportunity for a hearing. They filed suit in a federal district court which rejected their arguments that they were entitled to such notice and hearing before being expelled.[21] The district court was reversed on appeal[22] and the

---

19. Trial transcript dated August 22, 1960 in *St. John Dixon et al. v. Alabama State Board of Education* (Civ. No. 1634-N, M.D., Ala.) at 79.

20. *Id.* at 73. Bernard Lee, who I also met initially in Montgomery during the Freedom Rides (*see* note 15 *supra*) was one of a number of SCLC (Southern Christian Leadership Conference) staff who came out of the student protest movement of the early sixties. Like many of the other SCLC staff aides, I came to know and work closely with him during the Birmingham episodes of 1963. Though it is difficult now it seems, to meet anyone who was not a "close aide" of Dr. King, Bernard accurately fit that description generally traveling with Martin wherever he went. I knew him as a very young (weren't we all), aggressive, spirited man who associated with people with ease.

Lee was born in Norfolk, Virginia in 1935 and attended Virginia State College (Petersburg, Va.) and Morris Brown (Atlanta) as well as Alabama State. He is in business in Atlanta and has retained his connection with SCLC.

21. Dixon v. Alabama State Board of Educ., 186 F. Supp. 945 (M.D. Ala. 1960).

8

appeals court decision upholding their right to procedural due process, stands today as the leading case in this area, a precedent which by emphasizing constitutional guarantees against unfair disciplinary action, paved the way for student protests on other issues later in the decade and subsequently.[23]

Another aspect of student led protests and consequent legal development can be seen as a result of sit-in demonstrations in this city led by students from this University. The students whose names appear of record in the leading U. S. Supreme Court decision growing out of the early sit-in movement were Janette Hoston, John Garner and Mary Briscoe. A little more than a month after Bernard Lee, St. John Dixon — the named plaintiff in the case — and the other Alabama State students went to the Montgomery County courthouse (but in the same month in which they were expelled, March 1960), these three students and others went to "white" lunch counters at Sitman's Drug Store, the Greyhound Bus Station and the S.H. Kress store here in Baton Rouge. They sat down at these counters, requested service and were refused. They continued to sit after being refused and were arrested at each location by the same Baton Rouge police officer for "disturbing the peace." The record of the trial of their cases in

9

---

22.   Dixon v. Alabama State Board of Educ., 294 F.2d 150 (5th Cir. 1961), *cert. denied* 368 U.S. 930 (1961).

23.   Once the right to education is extended, due process requires a hearing before a student can be expelled, 294 F.2d 150, or suspended Goss v. Lopez, 419 U.S. 565 (1975) (suspension of high school students). *But see* Board of Curators, University of Missouri v. Horowitz, 435 U.S. 78 (1978) (no hearing required when the student is dismissed for academic as opposed to disciplinary reasons). Procedural due process requirements for students include reasonably clear and narrow rules for suspension, *Soglin v. Kaufman*, 418 F.2d 163 (7th Cir. 1969), and adequate notice, a definite charge, and an opportunity to present one's own side of the case with all necessary protective measures, *Esteban v. Central Mo. State College*, 415 F.2d 1077 (8th Cir. 1969). *See Esteban v. Central Mo. State College*, 277 F. Supp. 649, 651 (W.D. Mo. 1967) for a complete list of procedural safeguards for students.

The substantive rights of students to protest have included: the right of students to wear black armbands in anti-war protests as long as they are not disruptive, Tinker v. Des Moines Ind. Comm. School Dist., 393 U.S. 503 (1969); the right of assembly and free speech, Edwards v. South Carolina, 372 U.S. 229 (1963); the right of protesting students to adequate protection from politically motivated assault by a bystander, Jones v. Board of Regents of University of Arizona, 436 F.2d 618 (9th Cir. 1970); and the right to wear buttons carrying a message of protest, Burnside v. Byars, 363 F.2d 744 (5th Cir. 1966). *But see* Blackwell v. Issaquena County Board of Education, 363 F.2d 749 (5th Cir. 1966), decided the same day as *Burnside*, affirming the right of the school to prohibit wearing buttons where distribution of buttons in hall of school caused disruption and confusion.

which they were convicted contains remarkably candid testimony by the arresting officer that they were disturbing the peace only "by the mere presence of their being there."[24]

The legal problem created by their arrests was brought to Johnnie Jones who in turn brought the problem to us at the Inc. Fund[25] just as Montgomery's leading black attorney, Fred Gray,[26] had brought the problem posed in the *Dixon* case. The problem we had to face in this early protest period a few years before it was solved by legislation[27] growing out of events I will discuss in a moment, was what arguments could be successfully made for overturning the students' convictions in light of the state of the law at that time which gave them absolutely no right to be served at these counters and was very unclear as to whether their refusal to move was protected under then available legal theories. This, after all, was conduct now beginning to occur on a broad scale, that had not been attempted to any great degree before in this country. The available legal precedents were from free expression cases decided in other contexts all involving clearly defined "state

10

---

24. The arresting officer was Captain Weiner. The statement appears in the record filed with the United States Supreme Court in *Mary Briscoe v. State of Louisiana* (No. 27, Oct. Term 1961) at 38.

25. The separately incorporated NAACP Legal Defense and Educational Fund (*see* note 2 *supra*) is often referred to by those who have been associated with it in this shorthand fashion.

26. Fred Gray was the first local Inc. Fund "cooperating lawyer" I worked with in the South. It was the spring of 1961 and my first trip to the region (Montgomery, Alabama) as a lawyer. The case, growing out of the "Freedom Rides", was *Lewis v. Greyhound Corp.*, 199 F. Supp. 210 (M.D. Ala. 1961), in which the federal district judge, Frank Johnson, later enjoined Alabama and Montgomery officials. It was the first of many lawsuits in which I was associated with Fred in Montgomery and its environs.

Gray was born in Montgomery, Dec. 14, 1930. After graduating from Alabama State College in that city, he took his law degree at Western Reserve in Cleveland, Ohio at a time when blacks could not attend the University of Alabama. In addition to being one of the South's premier civil rights lawyers, he has also been the City Attorney for Tuskegee, Alabama, County Attorney for Macon County (which includes Tuskegee), an attorney for Tuskegee Institute and General Counsel of the Alabama State Teachers Association. He served in the Alabama House of Representatives from 1970 to 1974, the first black elected since Reconstruction. During the 1970's, he was the lawyer who secured damages from the United States and the State of Alabama for several black men who had been exposed without their knowledge to syphillis by experiments conducted on them in the 1930's. *Pollard v. United States*, 69 F.R.D. 646 (M.D. Ala. 1976) (att'y fee ques.) A man with a fine legal mind, great courtroom composure and an acute sense of justice (he is also a minister and evangelist), Fred became one of my close friends during the years of our association in the sixties.

27. The Civil Rights Act of 1964, 42 U.S.C. §2000a et seq. *See* p. 257 *infra.*

action"[28] which, except for the arrests and convictions, was not readily apparent here. Moreover, the facilities at which the sit-ins occurred were not state owned as was the courthouse in the *Dixon* case.[29]

The students' convictions reached the Supreme Court in 1961, and though the argument that there was unconstitutional state action because of the arrests and convictions was made, the Court seized on other arguments in unanimously overturning the convictions, the principal one being that since the protests were peaceful, there was no evidence that the

11

---

28. The following cases upholding the free expression interest asserted all involved state statutes, municipal ordinances, or other official conduct directed at the expression involved: *Stromberg v. California*, 283 U.S. 359 (1931) (flag display); *Lovell v. Griffin*, 303 U.S. 444 (1938) (distribution of literature); *Schneider v. State*, 308 U.S. 147 (1939) (same); *Hague v. C.I.O.*, 307 U.S. 496 (1939) (right to hold lawful meeting); *Cantwell v. Connecticut*, 310 U.S. 296 (1940) (solicitation for religious, charitable or philanthropic purposes); *Thornhill v. Alabama*, 310 U.S. 88 (1940) (labor picketing); *A.F. of L. v. Swing*, 312 U.S. 321 (1941) (same); *Largent v. Texas*, 318 U.S. 418 (1943) *Niemotko v. Maryland*, 340 U.S. 268 (1951) (holding of meeting in public park); *Staub v. Baxley*, 355 U.S. 313 (1958) (solicitation of organizational membership).

Clearly, none of these cases involved black protest against racial discrimination. Later decisions during the decade would address this question directly(*see* notes 29 & 30 *infra*) but they were yet to be decided.

29. It was precisely the absence of "state action" in the traditional sense of state ownership or overt state regulation or control that presented the problem for civil rights lawyers of how successfully to argue against the convictions of protestors in what came to be known collectively as the "sit-in" cases. The sit-ins occurred on property that was, at least in the formal sense, "private" even though the facilities in question were open to all the white public. The Supreme Court had never accepted the argument that mere licensing by the state of private proprietorships serving the public was "state action". *See* the dissent of the first Mr. Justice Harlan in the *Civil Rights Cases*, 109 U.S. 3, 41 (1883); nor has that position been accepted yet. *See* Moose Lodge v. Irvis, 407 U.S. 163 (1972). The Court moreover did not seem inclined to extend the doctrine of *Shelley v. Kraemer*, 334 U.S. 1 (1948) (judicial enforcement of racially restrictive private housing covenants unconstitutional state action) to the convictions of sit-in protestors who were frequently charged under state law for criminal trespass on private property. Unlike *Shelley*, where the motive was obviously racial, these proprietors could argue their right to refuse service to anyone deemed objectionable to them and claim their right to the state's protection of their personal decision.

Eventually, a majority of the "sit-in" cases were decided by the Supreme Court favorably to the protestors by the Court's acceptance of arguments which either expanded the state action principle to include these cases. *See, e.g.*, Lombard v. Louisiana, 373 U.S. 267 (1963) (highly publicized statements of local officials that sit-ins would not be permitted was unconstitutional "state action"); Robinson v. Florida, 378 U.S. 153 (1964) (state board of health regulations requiring segregated toilets sufficient to mandate owner's exclusion policy and hence void the convictions) or by application of "due process" principles as in *Garner*, (*see* note 30 *infra* and accompanying text).

"mere presence" of the students disturbed the peace.[30] These cases, though not responsive to more fundamental questions of the overriding fact of racial discrimination and its stultifying effects, nevertheless were important in crystallizing a simple but crucial aspect of due process of law: that people ought not to be convicted of crime if there isn't any evidence to support the crime charged. This evident principle was applied here for the first time to a group of black students and their leaders whose only "crime" was their protest of racial segregation.

The "no evidence" principle[31] as it came to be known surely was — and is today — an important principle, but as I have said, the decision left in place the basic evil. There, thus, remained the next set of problems for de facto leaders, lawyers and the legal system, and on their resolution depended the resolution of some of these fundamental questions at the core of the problems of our society.

I turn then to look at this next set of problems in the context of a series of events which I will describe in somewhat greater detail. They are probably the best known, they certainly contain the most dramatic elements and demonstrate

---

30. Garner v. Louisiana, 368 U.S. 157 (1961). Justice Harlan, in a separate concurrence, also mentioned the vagueness of the statute as applied to the facts of the case, another of the "due process" arguments made. *Id.* at 185. Justice Douglas was alone in responding to the argument that the arrests and convictions were unconstitutional state action because they supported the pervasive state custom of segregation. *Id.* at 176. For other decisions in "sit-in" cases overturning the convictions on due process grounds, *see Taylor v. Louisiana*, 370 U.S. 154 (1962) and *Barr v. City of Columbia*, 378 U.S. 146 (1964) (both following *Garner's* "no evidence" approach); *Bouie v. City of Columbia*, 378 U.S. 347 (1964) (application of the statute deprived defendants of fair warning).

31. The "no evidence" principle was given birth the year prior to *Garner* in *Thompson v. City of Louisville*, 362 U.S. 199 (1960), in which the Court held there was no evidence of the loitering or disorderly conduct charged to a man who was merely "shuffling his feet" to jukebox music at a bus stop cafe. (Thompson's name was Sam and the case became known as the case of "Shuffling Sam.") Subsequent to *Garner*, the principle was applied in two other sit-in cases, *(see* note 30 *supra)*, and has been used by the Court in other contexts to reverse convictions of contributing to the delinquency of a minor ("no evidence" of wilful contribution by defendant who sold sexually suggestive button to 14 year old girl), Vachon v. New Hampshire, 414 U.S. 478 (1974); revocation of parole based on arrest when parolee was involved in traffic accident), Douglas v. Buder, 412 U.S. 430 (1973); and vagrancy conviction where defendant was only sitting on bench at 4:25 A.M., Johnson v. Florida, 391 U.S. 596 (1968). The "no evidence" principle, however, has been specifically rejected by the Supreme Court as an improper and inadequate test to use in evaluating a conviction under due process attack for insufficient evidence. *See,* Pilon v. Bardenkircher, 444 U.S. 1 (1979).

most clearly the nature of de facto leadership problems and the problems faced by lawyers in turn. In terms of their impact on society and the subsequent development of legal rules, they have had the most far-reaching of consequences. I am referring to the dramatic events that occurred in Birmingham, Alabama, in 1963.

Some background is necessary to place them in perspective and to carry through the theme I am developing of the relationship between leadership in the social action arena and legal consequences. The events of 1963, in Birmingham, were the culmination not only of much that had gone before in that community, but were also a reflection of the overall situation regarding race relations in the State of Alabama and the Nation as a whole — including the nonresponsiveness of the political and judicial systems.[32]

Until June 1, 1956 — which incidentally was the same year in which the Montgomery boycott led by Dr. King ended with desegregation of the city's buses — the NAACP's southern regional headquarters covering 58 branches in 7 states was located in Birmingham.[33] But on June 1, pursuant to an injunction issued by an Alabama state court, the NAACP was barred from further operation in the State.[34] (The injunction was not dissolved until 1964 and effectively barred the NAACP from operating until 1965, the year which I have described as the pivotal midpoint of the civil rights decade).[35] As

13

---

32. A perspective on the situation throughout the nation at the beginning of 1963 is in Why We Can't Wait (*see* M. King, *supra* note 1, at 5-13). Accounts of the situation in Birmingham and Alabama prior to 1963 can be found at *Id.* at 39-43; A. Westin & B. Mahoney, The Trial of Martin Luther King 10-15 (1974) [hereinafter cited as Mahoney]; C. Morgan, A Time to Speak 25-122 (1964). In the ensuing pages, I will be referring frequently to the accounts of the Birmingham movement and its consequences contained in the books written respectively by King and Westin and Mahoney. The latter in several places has drawn heavily on my own recollection of the events described obtained through interviews with me.

33. Mahoney, *supra* note 32, at 15.

34. *Id.* at 16. The injunction was issued in *Alabama ex rel. Patterson v. NAACP,* 1 Race Rel. L. Rep. 707 (1965) (Circuit Ct. Montgomery). A contempt judgment was also entered for the NAACP's non-compliance with a court order requiring it to produce records of the organization. Alabama ex rel. Patterson v. NAACP, 1 Race Rel. L. Rep. 917 (1956) (Circuit Ct., Montgomery). This aspect of the State's attack on the NAACP was overturned by the Supreme Court on due process grounds i.e., protection of the members' right to association. NAACP v. Alabama, 357 U.S. 449 (1958); NAACP v. Alabama, 360 U.S. 240 (1959), reh. denied, 361 U.S. 856. *See also* Bates v. Little Rock, 361 U.S. 516 (1960). *Cf.* Shelton v. Tucker, 364 U.S. 479 (1960).

35. Mahoney, *supra* note 32, at 16. After an extended course of proceedings in

a consequence of the legal ban on the NAACP, the Alabama Christian Movement for Human Rights was formed that June by Fred Shuttlesworth, then pastor of a Birmingham church, who had been the membership chairman of the State NAACP.[36] Fred Shuttlesworth, who I eventually came to know well and count among my friends today, is among the clearest examples of de facto leaders of the dominant social movement of those times. His problems were numerous and certainly instructive for us. They were literally life-threatening.

For example, in 1956 shortly after the NAACP ban and the founding of the Alabama Christian Movement, the Supreme Court of the United States upheld the ban on racial segregation of the buses in Montgomery[37] — that was in December 1956. Shuttlesworth then announced that he and other members of the Christian Movement planned to ride in the front of the buses in Birmingham on December 26, the day after Christmas. On Christmas night, as a result of this announcement, Shuttlesworth's home was bombed. He escaped injury.[38] On December 26, when Birmingham's Blacks rode the buses as announced, 21 of them were arrested.[39] The following year in September 1957, Shuttlesworth was beaten by a mob, wielding chains and wearing brass knuckles, after he tried to enroll his daughter in an all-white Birmingham public school. (His wife was also stabbed in the hip on this occasion and one of the children was also injured).[40] The beating however did not deter him from subsequently filing a school desegregation suit against the Birmingham schools and establishing at that point, a few years prior to 1963, the nexus between leadership-directed social action and legal action.[41]

14

---

both state and federal courts for eight years, the Supreme Court finally ordered the injunction vacated, *NAACP v. Alabama,* 377 U.S. 288 (1964) and the Alabama Supreme Court complied with its direction, *NAACP v. Alabama,* 277 Ala. 89, 167 So. 2d 171 (1964). By this time, change had begun as a consequence of the events of the previous year described herein. For detailed treatment of the NAACP litigation, *see* Osborne, *Freedom of Association: The NAACP in Alabama* in PRITCHETT AND WESTIN eds., THE THIRD BRANCH OF GOVERNMENT 142-203 (1963).

36. MAHONEY, *supra* note 32, at 16.

37. Browder v. Gayle, 352 U.S. 903 (1956), *aff'd.,* 142 F. Supp. 707 (M.D. Ala. 1956).

38. MAHONEY, *supra* note 32, at 17.

39. *Id.*

40. *Id.*

41. *Id.* The suit filed by Shuttlesworth however, itself created problems. Ala-

Between 1957 and 1962, the efforts of Shuttlesworth and members of his organization continued to create problems for him and them. The Alabama Christian Movement held weekly meetings in churches which were monitored by Birmingham city detectives who not only took notes and made tape recordings of what was said and who said it, but also searched persons as they left the meetings.[42] A member of the Christian Movement, another indigenous de facto leader, the Rev. Charles Billups,[43] was, during this period, tied to a tree and beaten by members of the Ku Klux Klan.[44] Shuttlesworth was continually subjected to a series of arrests and convictions for, among other things, inciting disobedience, blocking the sidewalks, disorderly conduct, and the like. Indeed, I know of no one who donned the mantle of de facto leadership in this

15

---

bama, along with several other southern states, had adopted so-called pupil place-ment laws in response to the *Brown* school desegregation decisions. These laws con-tained a number of subjective criteria which, though ostensibly affording a basis for complying with those decisions, were in fact intended and used to limit school deseg-regation. The Alabama law contained more than a dozen such criteria. Among them were (1) the psychological qualification of the pupils; (2) the possibility or threat of friction or disorder among the pupils or others; (3) the maintenance or severance of established social or psychological relationships with the pupils and teachers. These laws, in short, were "almost as far-reaching in modifying and limiting the integration of schools as the original [*Brown*] decision had been in attempting to eliminate segre-gation." KING, *supra* note 31, at 6.

The Shuttlesworth suit unfortunately attacked the pupil placement laws on their face rather than as applied. The Alabama federal district court upheld the facial va-lidity of the laws, *Shuttlesworth v. Birmingham Board of Education*, 162 F. Supp. 372 (N.D. Ala. 1958) and on direct appeal, the United States Supreme Court affirmed "on the limited ground on which the district court rested its decision." 358 U.S. 101 (1958). The tactical mistake was quickly evident as the lower federal courts, now armed with the Supreme Court's affirmance of the *Shuttlesworth* decision, approved pupil placement laws and the Supreme Court refused review of those decisions. *See, e.g.,* Covington v. Edwards, 264 F.2d 780 (4th Cir. 1959), *cert. denied* 361 U.S. 840 (1959); Holt v. Raleigh City Board of Educ., 265 F.2d 95 (4th Cir. 1959), *cert. denied* 361 U.S. 818 (1959).

42. MAHONEY, *supra* note 32, at 17.

43. Billups, a Birmingham minister, was a defendant with Shuttlesworth in one of the Birmingham sit-in cases that went to the U.S. Supreme Court (*Shuttlesworth and Billups v. City of Birmingham*, 373 U.S. 262 (1963) *see* note 45 *infra*). He was also one of the most active and involved of the cadre of local ministers engaged in the protest demonstrations in 1963. In one notable incident on a Sunday afternoon, he was leading a group of demonstrators when Birmingham firemen were ordered to turn on their fire hoses to stop them. Billups ordered the group to kneel and pray. He led them in prayer and the firemen refused to turn on the hoses.

In 1968, his dead body was found in an automobile in Chicago. Chicago Tribune, Nov. 8, 1968 at 10, col. 6.

44. MAHONEY, *supra* note 32, at 17.

period — with the possible exception of Martin Luther King himself — who was arrested and convicted more often than Fred Shuttlesworth. The number of those convictions all of which were eventually overturned on appeal — again the partnership of legal action — is imposing.[45]

We come then to 1962 and the beginning of events which were to dominate national headlines in the next year and fully expose the related problems of de facto leadership, social action, legal effect and legal response. Early that year the action of Birmingham's local leaders intersected the problems of the student movement of which I have spoken. Black students at Talladega College in Talladega, Alabama protested in that community, and at Miles College in Birmingham students began boycotting local merchants who refused to entertain Negro patronage.[46] The State of Alabama, once again, successfully used the state court injunction to thwart the Talladega protest.[47] The Alabama Christian Movement joined the student initiated boycott in Birmingham in 1962.[48] But, in the end, it was unsuccessful exposing again at this point two major recurring problems of leadership: the lack of planning and organization and the failure of response to initiatives by those intended to benefit from them. As events later showed, these

16

---

45. Shuttlesworth v. City of Birmingham, 394 U.S. 147 (1969)(arrest and conviction for "parading without a permit" growing out of events described below at 250); Shuttlesworth v. City of Birmingham, 382 U.S. 87 (1965) (arrest and conviction for loitering and refusal to obey a police officer); Abernathy et al. v. Alabama, 380 U.S. 447 (1965) (arrest and conviction for sit-in at bus station lunch counter); Shuttlesworth v. City of Birmingham, 376 U.S. 339 (1964) (interference with police officer); Shuttlesworth v. City of Birmingham, 373 U.S. 262 (1963) (arrest and conviction for aiding and abetting criminal trespasses in connection with sit-ins at department stores); In Re Shuttlesworth, 369 U.S. 35 (1962) (arrest and conviction for disorderly conduct involving bus station demonstrations). *See also* New York Times Co. v. Sullivan, 376 U.S. 254 (1964) (reversal of libel judgment based on newspaper ad critical of public official). *But see,* Walker v. City of Birmingham, 388 U.S. 307 (1967) (conviction of contempt for defiance of injunction against protest march on Good Friday 1963 upheld).

Cases involving Shuttlesworth as a plaintiff are *Shuttlesworth v. Birmingham Board of Education,* 162 F. Supp. 372 (N.D. Ala. 1958), *aff'd,* 358 U.S. 101; *Shuttlesworth v. Connor,* 291 F.2d 217 (5th Cir. 1961); *Shuttlesworth v. Gaylord,* 202 F. Supp. 59 (N.D. Ala. 1961), *aff'd sub nom, Hanes v. Shuttlesworth,* 310 F.2d 303 (5th Cir. 1962); *Shuttlesworth v. Dobbs Houses,* 7 RACE REL. L. REP. 835 (N.D. Ala. 1962). *See also Lewis v. Greyhound Corp.,* 199 F. Supp. 210 (M.D. Ala. 1961).

46. KING, *supra* note 1, at 44; MAHONEY, *supra* note 32, at 19.

47. State ex rel Gallion v. Gray, 7 RACE REL L. REP. 449 (Cir. Ct. Talladega County, Alabama, April 28, 1962).

48. KING, *supra* note 1, at 44: MAHONEY, *supra* note 32, at 20.

problems were solved by the time of the 1963 demonstrations.

The Alabama Christian Movement was an affiliate of the Southern Christian Leadership Conference formed by Dr. King in 1957.[49] Plans were made to hold the SCLC Convention in Birmingham in September 1962.[50] Because of this, the Alabama Christian Movement succeeded initially in securing the promise of several merchants to remove their separate "white" and "colored" signs and to open their facilities to blacks and whites alike without segregation.[51] The signs were taken down during the Convention but reappeared shortly after as a consequence of the threats of the Police Commissioner, Eugene "Bull" Connor, to revoke their licenses.[52] Obviously another problem of de facto leadership was manifested here: that of the inability to hold gains once made as a consequence of counteraction by recalcitrant opposing forces in the community. Thus, it was that as 1962 drew to a close, the efforts by Shuttlesworth and his followers to change the racial situation in Birmingham, efforts which had consumed more than half a decade with all their attendant problems, were unsuccessful.

Because these efforts had been unavailing and there was no apparent likelihood that they would succeed, plans were then made by the Southern Christian Leadership Conference in cooperation with the Alabama Christian Movement to launch a full scale program of direct action protests in Birmingham early in 1963, at the beginning of the Easter season.[53] During the months following the SCLC Convention several strategy meetings occurred to devise tactics for carrying out the action program. Problems that had to be considered included such things as the training of demonstrators in the philosophy and practice of nonviolent protest, decisions as to objectives, the targets of the protests, and arrangements for providing money for bail that would be needed as a consequence of the arrest of demonstrators.[54]

17

---

49. KING, *supra* note 1, at 44; MAHONEY, *supra* note 32, at 31.
50. KING, *supra* note 1, at 45; MAHONEY, *supra* note 32, at 20.
51. KING, *supra* note 1, at 45-46; MAHONEY, *supra* note 32, at 20.
52. KING, *supra* note 1, at 47; MAHONEY, *supra* note 32, at 21.
53. Accounts of the planning for "Project C" as it was called ("C" for Birmingham's Confrontation) are in KING, *supra* note 1, at 47-50 and MAHONEY, *supra* note 32, at 48-51.
54. KING, *supra* note 1, at 52.

Other problems also intruded. The original timetable for the demonstrations had to be postponed because toward the end of 1962, Birmingham voters had voted to change the City's form of government from the then existing commissioner form to the mayor-council form. One expected effect of this change was the replacement of the dominance of the virulently racist Police Commissioner, Bull Connor.[55] The problem resulting from the vote was that the elections were scheduled for March 1963, the same time as the projected start of the campaign. Those who would take part in the demonstrations were already trained and ready to move, and delay might cause some of them to lose their resolve. On the other hand, King and Shuttlesworth and their associates did not want to risk interfering with an election, the likely result of which would be the replacement of Bull Connor. Connor's removal from office was an important objective for the long run success of whatever was achieved by the protests.[56] Hence another problem: timing, important as it is, cannot always be achieved as planned. When the election did occur in March 1963, its results were inconclusive, forcing a run-off for April 2, and again postponing the start of the campaign.[57] But as soon as the results of that election were in and the Birmingham commission system was voted out, the movement commenced and the demonstrations began the following day, April 3.[58]

Timing, though thrown off, still remained critical. The objective, as I said, was to put the demonstrations in motion during the Easter shopping season when they were likely to be most effective. Between April 3 and April 6, a carefully planned program of sit-in demonstrations, at selected targets in the city, occurred resulting in the arrest of 35 persons. On Saturday, April 6, there was a march on City Hall and during this first week, the movement expanded to church kneel-ins, library sit-ins, and a march on the county building for voter registration.[59] At an early point, a local member of the Alabama Christian Movement went to City Hall and asked for a permit to picket. She was told by Commissioner Connor, "You

---

55. *Id.* at 49.
56. Id.; MAHONEY, *supra* note 32, at 50.
57. KING, *supra* note 1, at 50; MAHONEY, *supra* note 32, at 50-51.
58. KING, *supra* note 1, at 53; MAHONEY, *supra* note 32, at 50-51.
59. KING, *supra* note 1, at 66-67.

will not get a permit in Birmingham, Alabama to picket. I will picket you to the City Jail."[60]

Accounts of the first week of the Birmingham movement indicate that Connor, who had refused to accept the results of the vote and continued in office while challenging it in court,[61] showed initial restraint in the face of the demonstration activities. Those accounts reveal that, in part, this restraint was an adoption of tactics used successfully by the police chief of Albany, Georgia the previous year which by and large thwarted a similar protest movement in that city.[62] There was, however, another reason: on Wednesday, April 10, the city officials, as had been done with the NAACP and the Talladega student protests, resorted to what they conceived as their ultimate weapon — a state court injunction barring further protests.[63] The injunction was issued around 9 p.m. and was served on King, Shuttlesworth, and other named leaders of the movement shortly after 1 a.m. on the morning of April 11.[64] It was precisely at that time that I was flying to Birmingham from New York to begin my long personal involvement in these critical events.

On the afternoon of April 10, our office received a call from Rev. Shuttlesworth requesting that someone be sent to Birmingham to work with local attorneys there and coordinate the representation of the persons arrested and the procedures for securing their release on bond. I was detailed to go and because of the urgency of the call, I was asked to leave that

19

---

60. *See* Record in *Walker v. City of Birmingham*, U.S. Sup. Ct., Oct. Term 1966, No. 249 at 355 (hereinafter cited as Record) (also quoted in MAHONEY, *supra* note 32, at 66 and 122). The testimony is that of Lola Hendricks given during the contempt trial. *See* p. 254 *infra*.

61. MAHONEY, *supra* note 32, at 65.

62. KING, *supra* note 1, at 67.

63. The use of the injunction as a means of thwarting protest was widespread during this period. State court injunctions were obtained as follows: *City of Danville v. Campbell*, 8 RACE REL. L. REP. 434 (Corp. Ct. Danville, Va., 1963); *City of Jackson v. Salter*, 8 RACE REL. L. REP. 433 (Chancery Ct., Hinds County, Miss. 1963); *State ex rel Flowers v. Zellner*, 8 RACE REL. L. REP. 848 (Circuit Ct., Dekalb Cty., Ala. 1963); *State ex rel Flowers v. Robinson*, 8 RACE REL. L. REP. 848 (Cir. Ct., Etowah Cty. Ala. 1963); *Town of Plaquemine and Parish of Iberville v. C.O.R.E.*, 8 RACE REL. L. REP. 862 (Cir. Ct., Iberville Parish, La. 1963).

Federal court injunctions were also obtained: *Clemmons v. C.O.R.E.*, 201 F. Supp. 737 (E.D. La. 1962); *Griffin v. C.O.R.E.*, 221 F. Supp. 899 (E.D. La. 1963); *Town of Clinton and Parish of East Feliciana v. C.O.R.E.*, 9 RACE REL. L. REP. 1131 (E.D. La. 1963); *Kelly v. Page*, 9 RACE REL. L. REP. 1115 (M.D. Ga. 1963).

64. MAHONEY, *supra* note 32, at 71-72, 76.

evening so that I could begin work the next morning in Birmingham. I took a 12:15 a.m. flight on the morning of April 11, from Newark Airport and arrived in Birmingham at approximately 2:00 a.m. local time. I was met there by a man sent by Fred Shuttlesworth. On the ride in from the airport, I was informed of the latest crisis: the injunction had been served on most respondents during the night and thus, the question of what to do about it became the point of immediate focus.

20

When I arrived at the A.G. Gaston Motel,[65] the headquarters of the movement where King and his Southern Christian Leadership Conference (SCLC) staff were housed,[66] I was shown a copy of the injunction and the complaint upon which it was based. The complaint alleged the course of demonstrations that had occurred to that point and asked that the named respondents, which included King, Shuttlesworth, Rev. Ralph Abernathy (King's closest friend and principal lieutenant), Rev. Wyatt E. Walker (then SCLC staff director), some local ministers and all those acting with them, be enjoined from any further protest demonstrations. The injunction was issued *ex parte,* there having been no opportunity afforded any of the persons named for a hearing prior to its issuance.[67]

---

65. The Gaston Motel is on 5th Avenue North between 15th and 16th Streets in Birmingham's black area. In 1963 (before passage of the Civil Rights Act of 1964), it was the best motel for blacks in the city and the hub of all movement activity. A restaurant and lounge is part of the establishment; it was in the restaurant that I first met and talked with Martin Luther King at lunch on April 11 after the press conference in the motel's courtyard. *See* p. 249 *infra.*

Across the street from the motel is A. G. Gaston Building, an office building which housed the law office of Arthur Shores (*see* note 81 *infra*) out of which I worked during the Birmingham campaign. Both the motel and the office building were owned by Arthur G. Gaston, Sr., Birmingham's wealthiest black and one of the wealthiest men in the city. Gaston was among those in Birmingham's black community who had opposed the Birmingham demonstrations. *See* MAHONEY, *supra* note 32, at 50. For King's account of the opposition to the movement and the steps he took to counteract it, see KING, *supra* note 1, at 62-66. Opposition of this sort has frequently been one of the problems of leadership.

66. Room 30, in the southwest corner of the motel on the second level was the room in which Martin stayed. As the only suite in the motel, it was the room in which meetings were held including that of Good Friday morning (*see* p. 250 *infra*). Situated almost directly above the motel's office, it was the target of the bombing that occurred on Saturday night, May 11 which destroyed the office (*see* p. 256 *infra*).

67. The issuance of such an injunction is part of the traditional equitable powers of the courts and is specifically provided for in the Federal Rules of Civil Procedure (Rule 65). Because issuance of such an order is contemplated as the rare, exceptional case, stringent safeguards generally attend their issuance. *See* Fed. R. Civ.

I read it through that evening, and after a few hours sleep, discussed it with my New York office later that morning. That discussion revealed the first of many serious problems relating to the issuance of the injunction — it had been issued by a state court. Even though it was clear that we could not expect relief from the Alabama state courts, which as I have said had used this tactic before, the law with respect to the right to remove a state proceeding of this nature to a federal district court was unclear but seemed to be against us.[68] Even if the injunctive proceeding was removed, there was scant likelihood that we could get any relief from the local federal district court either,[69] and at that time, an unfavorable decision in a

21

Pro., 65(b). Indeed, five years after the Birmingham *ex parte* order and a year after its decision in the case that resulted from its issuance (*see* note 162 *infra*) the Supreme Court held that such an order was violative of the First Amendment. Carroll v. President and Commissioners of Princess Anne, 393 U.S. 175 (1968).

68.   The civil rights removal provision of the federal judicial code is 28 U.S.C. §1443(1) which is based on section 3 of the first federal civil rights Act, the Act of April 9, 1866. The removal statute speaks of the removal to a federal district court of:

[C]ivil actions or criminal prosecutions, commenced in a State court

(1) Against any person who is denied or cannot enforce in the courts of such state a right under any law providing for the equal civil rights of citizens of the United States. . . .

There were obvious interpretive difficulties (including classification) in seeking to apply this statute to effect removal of the already issued injunction to the federal court. Moreover, in a series of restrictive rulings in criminal cases involving Negro defendants made between 1880 and 1906, the Supreme Court had practically rendered the removal remedy useless: *Virginia v. Rives,* 100 U.S. 313 (1880); *Neal v. Delaware,* 103 U.S. 370 (1881); *Bush v. Kentucky,* 107 U.S. 110 (1883); *Gibson v. Mississippi,* 162 U.S. 565 (1896); *Smith v. Mississippi,* 162 U.S. 592 (1896); *Murray v. Louisiana,* 163 U.S. 101 (1896); *Williams v. Mississippi,* 170 U.S. 213 (1898); *Kentucky v. Powers,* 201 U.S. 1 (1906). Later in the decade, the Court would have its first opportunity since this period to reconsider these rulings. *See* notes 160-61 *infra.* For an excellent treatment of civil rights removal jurisdiction written before these later cases, see Amsterdam, *Criminal Prosecutions Affecting Federally Guaranteed Civil Rights: Federal Removal and Habeas Corpus Jurisdiction To Abort State Court Trial,* 113 U. PA. L. REV. 793 (1965).

69.   The Birmingham federal judges at the time were Seybourne Lynne, Harlan Grooms and Clarence Allgood. Lynne and Allgood, the most recent appointment, were Southern democrats whose decisions in civil rights cases reflected their own predilections and the prevailing attitude of the region; they could not be expected to render any favorable decision. Grooms, a republican appointment, had a somewhat better record but in a situation where the law was not clear as here, he could not be expected to break any new ground. As it turned out, the judge who handled the cases that were brought to the federal court, was Judge Allgood who in no way disappointed our expectations. *See* City of Birmingham v. Croskey, 217 F. Supp. 947 (N.D. Ala. 1963) (removal denied).

The Southern federal judiciary—at least at the district court level—would remain a serious problem for civil rights lawyers for many years (*see* note 3 *supra*). The case removed from a state to a federal district court could not be appealed.[70] The other possibility for federal court relief from the injunction, an affirmative action seeking to enjoin the state proceeding, seemed also not to hold much promise of success.[71] Consequently, we decided to defend the injunctive proceeding in the state court even though we realized that we would lose there and at every appellate level in the state judicial system.

One of the things that civil rights lawyers of that period

22

exceptions were notable because they were men like Grooms in Birmingham and Frank Johnson in Montgomery. For a general assessment of the deep south federal judiciary in the early sixties, see Comment, *Judicial Performance in the Fifth Circuit*, 73 YALE L.J. 90 (1963).

70.   Act of March 3, 1887, ch. 373 §2, 24 Stat 553 as amended, Act of Aug. 13, 1888, ch. 866 §2, 25 Stat 435. Before the Civil Rights Act of 1964, this enactment was part of the judicial code (28 U.S.C. §1447 (d)) which was amended by the Act. *See* note 158 *infra*-and accompanying text.

71.   *Ex Parte Young*, 209 U.S. 123 (1908) upheld an injunction when the state proceeding was brought subsequent to the federal proceeding, both proceedings dealt with the same issue (constitutionality of a railroad rate-setting law) and the defendant in the federal suit (the state's attorney general) sought enforcement of the statute as plaintiff in the state suit. But in cases in which a state proceeding was begun first and the state defendants then sought a federal injunction against those proceedings, such an injunction was refused. *See, e.g.,* Fenner v. Boykin, 271 U.S. 240 (1926); Spielman Motor Sales Co. v. Dodge, 295 U.S. 89 (1935); Beal v. Missouri Pacific R.R. Co., 312 U.S. 45 (1941); Watson v. Buck, 313 U.S. 387 (1941); Douglas v. City of Jeannette, 319 U.S. 157 (1943).

In these cases, the Supreme Court articulated the principle that a federal injunction of state proceedings would not issue unless there was a showing of the danger of irreparable loss that would be both "great and imminent." Aside from the question of whether an already issued ex parte injunction would classify as a "proceeding," there was the further question of whether the Birmingham respondents could show such great and imminent irreparable loss within the standards articulated in the Supreme Court cases, particularly when a motion to dissolve the injunction could be made in the state court that issued it. The only case growing out of civil rights protest activity in which such showing was made is *Dombroski v. Pfister*, 380 U.S. 479 (1965), subsequent to Birmingham.

But *Dombroski* has been confined to its own facts (bad faith prosecution with "chilling effect" on First Amendment rights) as later cases have refused injunctive relief—Cameron v. Johnson, 390 U.S. 611 (1968) (no injunction against anti-picketing statute); Younger v. Harris, 401 U.S. 37 (1971) (no injunction against prosecution under syndicalism statute when issue of unconstitutionality can be raised in state proceeding); O'Shea v. Littleton, 414 U.S. 488 (1974) (no injunction against alleged discriminatory practices of local officials where plaintiff's injury was conjectural); Kugler v. Helfant, 421 U.S. 117 (1975) (indictment of municipal judge based on grand jury testimony). *But see* Wooley v. Maynard, 430 U.S. 705 (1977). The doctrine requiring federal court abstention absent a special showing of imminent and irreparable harm applies whenever the federal plaintiff has an opportunity to present the federal claims in the state court proceeding. Juidice v. Vail, 430 U.S. 327 (1977); Moore v. Sims, 442 U.S. 415 (1979).

quickly came to learn was that the primary reason for defending cases in state courts was to make a record in which federal constitutional claims were made and preserved for ultimate review by the United States Supreme Court, which by now, since its decision in *Brown v. Board of Education*,[72] had begun to render favorable decisions in the area of civil rights.[73] Even so, there was at this time a great deal of uncertainty as to the limits the Court would impose on protest demonstrations of this kind; the law on this question was still being made.[74] Even more problematic was the question of what the court would do in a situation in which, beyond the question of the right to protest, was the further question of continued protest in defiance of a state court injunction.[75] That question was ultimately resolved unfavorably, but I am getting ahead of my story.

So, you see, all the actors in the drama were at risk. Neither the leaders and members of the movement nor those

23

---

72.   347 U.S. 483 (1954).

73.   *See* Muir v. Louisville Park Theatrical Association, 347 U.S. 971 (1954)(auditorium); Holmes v. City of Atlanta, 350 U.S. 879 (1955) (golf course); Mayor and City Council of Baltimore City v. Dawson, 350 U.S. 877 (1955) (beach); Browder v. Gayle, 352 U.S. 903 (1956) (buses); New Orleans City Park Improvement Ass'n v. Detiege, 358 U.S. 54 (1958); Watson v. City of Memphis, 373 U.S. 526 (1963); Wright v. Georgia, 373 U.S. 284 (1963); City of New Orleans v. Barthe, 376 U.S. 189 (1964) (parks and playgrounds); Burton v. Wilmington Parking Authority, 365 U.S. 715 (1961) (parking garage); Turner v. City of Memphis, 369 U.S. 350 (1962) (airport); Johnson v. Virginia, 373 U.S. 61 (1963) (courthouse).

74.   *See* Edwards v. South Carolina, 372 U.S. 229 (1963); Fields v. South Carolina, 375 U.S. 44 (1963); Henry v. Rock Hill, 376 U.S. 776 (1964). These cases, by reversing the convictions, upheld the protests involved but subsequent cases in the decade would evidence a serious split on the Court regarding such activity. *See* Cox v. Louisiana, 379 U.S. 536 (1965); Brown v. Louisiana, 383 U.S. 131 (1966); Adderley v. Florida, 385 U.S. 39 (1966).

75.   There were three Supreme Court cases involving state court injunctions. In one of them, *Howat v. Kansas*, 258 U.S. 181 (1922), the Court had upheld a contempt conviction for defiance of the injunction. In a second case, *Thomas v. Collins*, 323 U.S. 516 (1945), the criminal contempt conviction had been reversed but the case involved a single labor organizer who had made a single speech before a single assemblage after being ordered not to do so without a labor organizer's permit required by a statute. The third case, *In Re Green*, 369 U.S. 689 (1962), overturned the contempt conviction but the decision was based on the doctrine of federal preemption by the national labor laws. There were also three decisions involving federal court injunctions, one of them issued by the Supreme Court. In these cases, the Court upheld the contempt. In Re Debs, 158 U.S. 564 (1895); United States v. Shipp, 203 U.S. 563 (1906); United States v. United Mine Workers, 330 U.S. 258 (1947). Finally, three other cases even older than *Debs* seemed of little precedential value either way. Ex Parte Rowland, 104 U.S. 604 (1881); In Re Ayers, 123 U.S. 443 (1887); In Re Burrus, 136 U.S. 586 (1890).

of us who were their lawyers were able to predict with any certainty what the outcome would be, socially, politically, or legally. But the one thing on which we all agreed was that the risks, whatever they were, were risks that had to be taken.

This became very clear in the days that followed. After talking with my office on the morning of April 11, I began drafting a response to the complaint upon which the injunction was based and a motion to dissolve the injunction itself. In light of what I have said, we felt that there was no choice other than to proceed in the state courts. I recall though, that when I showed my initial draft to Fred Shuttlesworth later that day he responded with disdain and disapproval because we had decided to challenge the injunctive proceeding in a state rather than a federal court. One of the problems for the lawyers of the movement was trying to explain to our clients the nature of the legal problems we faced and why we felt we had to proceed as we did. After all, a man like Fred Shuttlesworth and many others, knew full well the kind of treatment they and other blacks received at the hands of state courts in the South and understandably looked with a measure of scorn on a lawyer's decision to deal with those courts. There was also, it should be frankly stated, some measure of distrust on the part of protest leaders who in many instances were literally laying their lives on the line for what they believed, distrust of the legal system as a whole and distrust of the ability of the few black lawyers who would take civil rights cases in this period[76] to cope with it on their behalf. Beyond this or perhaps because of it, the distrust went even deeper; there

---

76. At this time, there were only sixteen black lawyers in all of Alabama; nine of them in Birmingham, the state's largest city. Of those in Birmingham, some would not take a civil rights case since these cases challenged the prevailing political and social system. During this period and in the succeeding years, I worked with only five of those who were practicing in Birmingham in 1963. (One of them, Oscar W. Adams, Jr. was sworn in as the first black justice of the Alabama Supreme Court on October 17, 1980). Others would be added to the bar later in the decade. One of them, U.W. Clemon, was sworn in in the summer of 1980 as the first black federal judge in the State's history.

The small number of blacks at the bar and the even smaller number available to civil rights clients was one reason why involvement of "outside" lawyers like me and my colleagues at the Inc. Fund was necessary. In Alabama, during this period, there was only one white lawyer, Charles Morgan, Jr., who dared active, public involvement with black civil rights cases. He paid the price by being ostracized and eventually was forced to leave Alabama. He has written of his experience in two books, A TIME TO SPEAK (1964) and ONE MAN, ONE VOICE (1979).

was the feeling that not only could black lawyers not do very much for the cause, but that many would not; that they elevated their own professional and social standing and economic interest above the interest of their black brothers and sisters, and that, as a general proposition, they were more interested in the fees they would receive rather than in the results achieved for their clients. Indeed, it was this latter reason that prompted the call from Shuttlesworth to our office; we were told that the black lawyers who had been approached in Birmingham were reluctant to act without assurance of the payment of their fees and that it simply was not possible for the movement to pay the fees that were requested. In time, I think it is fair to state, these problems dissipated; the movement leaders developed a measure of trust and eventually came to believe not only in our commitment to our shared goals but also in our ability to achieve at least some of them.

The issuance of the injunction created the most difficult decision that King, Shuttlesworth and other movement leaders ever had to face. On the one hand, obedience to the injunction meant the end of the protest; on the other hand defiance of it surely meant a certainty of jail and/or fines and, perhaps even more importantly, an erosion of the still limited but necessary support of whites of apparent goodwill, of the media, and of the federal government.[77] The decision, however, was theirs alone to make and I did not try, nor would I have succeeded had I tried, to make it for them. I could only advise as to what the state of the law was and predict what the results of defiance would be. I could neither in good conscience urge them to go ahead in face of the injunction; nor equally in good conscience could I urge them to stop and let the movement peter out with all that would have meant to a black community that had too often seen its initiatives thwarted. At about the time that I was beginning to start work on drafting the response to the injunction, Dr. King and the other leaders were holding a press conference in the courtyard in the A.G. Gaston Motel announcing that they would not obey it.[78] I recall standing on the balcony overlooking the courtyard as the press conference was held. Later that night, I

25

---

77. *See* MAHONEY, *supra* note 32, at 60-61, 86-87.

78. *Id.* at 77-80. The press release issued at the press conference created yet another problem (*see* p. 254 *infra*). It is in the *Record* at 409-10 and is quoted in MAHONEY, *supra* note 32, at 78-79.

attended my first of the many "mass meetings" that were held on a nightly basis at which King, Abernathy and others spoke and King stated: "Injunction or no injunction, we're going to march tomorrow."[79] Thus, the die was cast.

The next morning, Good Friday, April 12, after I had completed in rough form a draft of our opposing papers, I met with King, Shuttlesworth, Abernathy and approximately a score of others in room 30 of the Gaston Motel, King's and Abernathy's suite. I will never forget the agonizing over the decision that had already been made and its possible consequences. All that I did or could do was to tell these brave, proud men what they might expect, but this they knew full well without my saying so. The Good Friday March, so important for its symbolic value, was scheduled to begin early that afternoon from a north side church.[80] In the motel room that Friday morning, we all circled and joined hands while prayer was said. Dr. King and Abernathy changed into their "jail clothes," the denim shirt and work pants which, like the overalls worn by their followers, symbolized the movement. They then proceeded to the church. I went across the street to the office of the Dean of the Alabama black attorneys, Arthur Shores,[81] and asked his secretary to begin typing the draft of

---

79. MAHONEY, *supra* note 32, at 81; *Record* at 242, 244, 407. I heard the statement while seated on the platform at the church. It was an exciting thing to hear and I was filled with anticipation of what would happen the following day.

80. There seems to be general agreement that the march originated at the 16th street Baptist Church (where later in the year, a bombing killed four children). *See* MAHONEY, *supra* note 32, at 83; Brief for Petitioners at 16, Walker v. City of Birmingham, No. 249 Oct. Term 1966; Walker v. City of Birmingham, 388 U.S. 307, 310 (1967). However, Martin King in his book says that the march began from the Zion Hill Church, KING, supra note 1 at 72. Further confusing the question of location is a reference in MAHONEY, *supra* note 32, at 81 to the "Zion Hill (Sixteenth Street) Baptist Church" but the churches are not at the same location. Since, when the march occurred, it was only my second day in town, I do not have any independent recollection of which church it was.

81. Shores is a short, dark-skinned compact, well-muscled man who looks as if he could have been a boxer. He was born in Birmingham and was in his early fifties when I met him there. He had been educated at Talladega College in Talladega, Alabama and the University of Kansas. After teaching school and serving as a school principal in the thirties, he was admitted to the Alabama Bar in 1937 and was recruited by Thurgood Marshall for work on the NAACP's (and later Inc. Fund) cases in the thirties and forties. By the time of the Birmingham demonstrations, he had become noted as *the* civil rights lawyer in the city and his home had been bombed several times because of his work (and would be bombed again later that year). Toward the end of 1968, he was elected to the Birmingham City Council. Now in his late seventies, his career is one deserving of the plaudits of younger generations of black

our papers. I then proceeded to the church where final words were said inside as I stood outside in the crowd and watched as the demonstrators came out of the church and were soon arrested. The pictures of King and Abernathy being grabbed from behind by the collars of their shirts and their belts, and being pushed into the police paddywagons were widely circulated as stark testimony of the nature of the problems faced by these leaders.

After King was taken to jail, he was placed in solitary confinement, cut off from communication with his followers from the outside. One small advantage of my role as a lawyer was that even the State of Alabama in this period, nominally at least, respected the right of a lawyer to consult with his client in jail. Since members of the movement were not permitted to see him, I was asked to go to the jail that evening to see if I could talk to him and at least verify that he was not being mistreated. As long as I live, I will not forget that Friday evening. When I arrived at the jail around 7:30 p.m., I asked to see Dr. King and was told that I could not talk to him except through a glass screen which opened onto the reception area of the jail. Under no circumstances, I was told, would I be permitted to go inside the jail and talk to him face to face. But I had been instructed by the leaders of the movement to insist upon doing just that. There then ensued for several hours what only could be described as a Mexican stand-off. Care was taken that I was not told I could not see him at all, but that he would be brought to the front and we could communicate in the way I mentioned. I continued to insist that this arrangement was not acceptable, that I had the right to enter through the jail gates and talk to him confidentially. Bull Connor had instructed his jailers that this would not occur and my instructions were that it must occur. In the end, Connor's instructions prevailed and I left the jail that evening about 11 p.m. without seeing Martin at all.[82]

The next morning, Saturday, is equally vivid if not more so. I went with Arthur Shores and another black attorney, Or-

27

---

lawyers for whom his work paved the way.

82. During these hours, I was told several times that I could effect Martin's release immediately on bail. But I had firm instructions from Martin's principal lieutenants, Wyatt Walker and Andy Young, that Martin must not be bailed out until they were ready to have him come out of jail.

zell Billingsley,[83] to Connor's office to ask that any of the three of us be permitted to visit privately with Martin in jail and I related the problem of the previous evening. I reminded him (very respectfully) of the importance of the right to counsel in our system and why it was necessary for counsel to be able to confer privately in order to afford that right. All the while of course, I was seething inwardly. But obviously, more than my own feelings were at stake. The offshoot of the conversation was Connor's agreement to pemit us to enter the jail and talk with Martin twice each day while he was incarcerated. We were reminded though, as I had been told by the jailer many times the previous night, that he could be released on $300 bond at any time. The Movement people, however, felt it important that he remain in jail to focus the attention of the media and national public opinion on the Birmingham situation. Therefore, my instructions were not to bail him out until they gave the word. Of course Connor knew this so it did not have to be said, so we gingerly side-stepped that point. But I still remember him saying to me, words to the effect that since I was one of the Movement's lawyers from "New Yawk", hence an outsider, I did not understand how things were done in Birmingham, but that if I followed the lead of these "boys" (referring to Shores and Billingsley) I would get along all right. Connor called the jail and directed that I be permitted to see Dr. King. What followed next has never left me! I immediately went to the jail, identified myself, and asked to see him. The jailer directed one of his subordinates "to go get that nigger King and open up the door and let this nigger in." Again an occasion even more enraging than earlier, of inward seething and the biting of one's tongue — the problems of leadership!

Beginning that day, Saturday, April 13, until the following Friday I visited Martin King in jail each day checking on his condition and that of Ralph Abernathy whom I also saw, taking messages from the outside and relaying instructions.

---

83. Orzell Billingsley, Jr., now a municipal judge in Roosevelt City, Alabama (on the outskirts of Birmingham) and also still practicing law in Birmingham was the other local attorney with whom I worked during the demonstrations. After the marches of Good Friday and Easter Sunday, he and I handled the cases of the scores of demonstrators who were being arrested daily (*see* p. 253 *infra*). He is a cousin of Arthur Shores and was born in Birmingham Oct. 23, 1924. His undergraduate degree is from Talladega; his law degree from Howard University in 1950.

28

Surely it was a curious role for a lawyer but these were curious and unique times. It was during the course of that week while I was going back and forth to visit Martin Luther King in jail that he composed the now famous "Letter From A Birmingham Jail."[84] It was I to whom was given the initial draft to take to Wyatt Walker and Andy Young for reproduction and circulation.

Events now began to move swiftly. On Easter Sunday, April 14, the day after my initial visit to Martin, the second march was held in the face of the injunction. As a consequence of this march, other Movement leaders were also arrested. During that day, having purchased on Saturday a pair of blue overalls for myself,[85] I put them on and took statements from people who had been involved in the demonstrations, which I turned into affidavits in support of the motion to dissolve the injunction I filed the next morning, Monday, April 15.

29

On that morning I went with Arthur Shores to the chambers of Judge William H. Jenkins in the Birmingham County Courthouse to present the motion and request an immediate hearing on it. Even though the city's attorneys did not file their motion to have King and the others held in contempt of court until later that day, I was told that the court would not consider any motion to dissolve the injunction before considering the question of whether it had been violated and, accordingly, a hearing on that question was set for the following Monday, April 22. During that week, the week of April 15, demonstrations continued and further arrests were made and it became my task to oversee, on a daily basis, the process of representing the groups of defendants. In that process what quickly became the accepted manner of treatment of the cases was developed. Each morning, when those arrested the previous day were bought to court, a petition containing their names (some of which I had to get right on the spot in the courtroom — other problems, meeting your client for the first time in court) was filed seeking removal of the cases to the federal district court despite the fact that, as I have said, the standards for removing cases such as these to the federal dis-

---

84. KING, *supra* note 1, at 77-100 (ch. 5).
85. This did not go unnoticed. It was my way of showing solidarity with the movement's activists, further lessening the gulf between them and their lawyers.

trict court were unclear and in any event there could be no appeal from the district judge's order remanding the case back to the state court for trial.[86] But this method of dealing with the cases not only bought time and postponed the date of trial, it also meant that the defendants — as long as bail money remained available which was another problem that caused worry but was eventually solved[87] — would be free to participate in demonstrations again, a principle that I labeled, "Liberate, then litigate." Of course from the standpoint of the state judicial system, release on bond and postponement of the trials by removal, had the effect of not tying up both the jail and the courts interminably. So this pattern was repeated throughout the week, and subsequently.

30

At the beginning of the following week, on the morning of April 22, the trial of King and the other Movement leaders who had been arrested in the Good Friday and Easter Sunday marches commenced. It was an attention grabbing spectacle and from the beginning we knew what the outcome would be. A serious problem, however, that we had to confront was the question of whether or not the court would find the contempt to be civil or criminal. The problem was posed by the press release issued at the press conference the Thursday before the Good Friday march and the statements made at the mass meeting that night. The City's motion asked the court to hold King, Abernathy, Walker, and Shuttlesworth in civil contempt unless they publicly recanted. If the motion were granted, there was the likelihood of indefinite incarceration. The problem was very real because we had been told by them that under no circumstances would they retract anything they had said at the press conference or at the mass meeting. If on the other hand the court held the contempt criminal, the penalty under Alabama law was only five days in jail and a $50 fine.[88] Thus the task for us was how to deal with the possibility of civil contempt.

The solution found was imaginative. We knew that not only did King and the others not want to spend, as Martin put it to me in Room 30 on the morning of the Good Friday March, "the rest of my life in jail," but we also knew that the

---

86. *See* note 70 *supra.*
87. *King, supra* note 1, at 70, 74.
88. Code of Alabama, Title 13 §9 (1958).

city of Birmingham and the state of Alabama did not want to
put him and the others in jail for the rest of their lives — that
was the importance of the media attention that had focused
public opinion on the Birmingham Movement. On the other
hand of course, the court felt that its authority had to be vindicated. So the question was how to save face on both sides.
What we did was to file a most unusual legal document which
we labeled simply, "Statement of Counsel" which in essence
said that the respondents to the contempt proceeding never
intended violation of the law (but avoided saying they did not
intend to violate the injunction) but rather felt that what they
had done accorded with the law under the federal constitution
which of course we knew the State of Alabama followed and
would follow in this case.[89] It was a remarkable document because it did not apologize or recant but at the same time said
to the state court that "we respect law and we know that you
do too." The document apparently achieved its goal for when
the court's decision was announced on Friday, April 26, the
finding of contempt was criminal, not civil, and the court de-
ferred the serving of the sentence until May 16 and granted
bond in the meantime.[90]

After the trial, I flew back to New York and spent the
weekend preparing papers seeking a further stay of the sentence pending appeal from the Alabama Supreme Court, an
argument which I successfully presented to that court the following Monday. In the meantime, the Movement continued,
but now in its next phase there was a serious escalation of
problems. The week following the contempt conviction there
occurred what came to be known as "Ḋ Day," a day on which
large numbers of persons, including school children, were arrested in demonstrations all over Birmingham.[91] The day after
"D Day," May 3, the situation peaked and the spectacle of the
use of police dogs and fire hoses on the demonstrators flashed
all over the nation. At this point, the business community in-
tervened and a week later a peace pact was announced which
seemingly achieved the demonstration's goals. Facilities were
to be open to blacks, nonsegregated hiring would begin, and a
bi-racial committee was formed to deal with the total

31

---

89. *See Record, supra* note 78, at 418-19.
90. City of Birmingham v. Wyatt Tee Walker, (Cir. Ct. Jefferson County).
91. KING, *supra* note 1, at 104.

situation.

That announcement occurred on Friday, May 10.[92] The next day, Saturday the 11th, I was in Birmingham where I had been all week, again processing the cases by having them removed to the federal court as I've indicated. Late that afternoon, I rode to the airport with Martin to discuss some matters with him since he was returning to Atlanta to preach in his pulpit the following Sunday, Mother's Day. I recall returning to my room at the motel after having dinner, and while relaxing on my bed and watching television, I was literally jolted out of bed by a loud explosion. My first reaction was that the motel had been bombed. I was right. Members of the Klan, infuriated by the peace pact, had planted a bomb directly under Room 30 where Martin had stayed until that very afternoon. I remember jumping off the bed, throwing on a pair of trousers and running out into the courtyard where I saw people milling around in the air filled with acrid smoke. I embraced one woman who was wandering around in a daze with tears streaming down her face. I went into the motel office underneath Room 30 and found that it had been wrecked by the explosion. Word of the bombing and the earlier bombing that night of the home of Martin's brother, A.D. King, had circulated through the Birmingham black community, and during the next several hours a confrontation of varying dimension occurred between the Birmingham police, George Wallace's Alabama state troopers who had been sent to the scene, and members of the black community. I, along with some members of the Movement, tried to assay the role of peacemaker that night, walking into alleys, asking people not to throw rocks and other missiles, and at one point locking arms trying to hold back the surge of the crowd. The Birmingham police rolled out a huge white armored tank on the sidewalk across the street from the motel and the state troopers surrounded the area. The scene became very ugly and continued into the wee hours of Sunday morning. Matters had gotten out of control.

The next morning, cut off from all communication because the bombing had destroyed the motel's switchboard, I was interviewed by a local member of the FBI in my motel room. After the interview, in the early afternoon I left the

---

92. *Id.* at 112; MAHONEY, *supra* note 32, at 148.

motel to walk to the home of a friend to get something to eat since all the eating facilities had also been shut down at the motel. About a block away from the motel as I attempted to walk down a path in a nearby park,[93] I was surrounded by approximately a dozen state troopers with their shotguns leveled at me and I was ordered to spreadeagle against a tree. As you might imagine, many thoughts went through my mind, but remembering the lessons of a lifetime I made no quick or sudden moves and kept my hands in plain sight — in the language of Oscar Brown, Jr., "I was cool."[94] A Birmingham police captain whose attention had been attracted, walked over, recognized me, vouched for me to the state troopers and offered me a ride out of the area.[95] He first took me to the office of the police chief who furnished me a pass that permitted me to move freely around the city the rest of the day. That night President Kennedy spoke deploring the situation in Birmingham and announced that he had ordered federal troops into the city. A month later he delivered a major nationwide address proposing a comprehensive federal civil rights law[96] which was enacted the following year after his assassination and became the Civil Rights Act of 1964.[97]

Thus, there is a direct link between the development of law and the combination of leadership-directed efforts toward social change and lawyer-directed efforts toward legal change and the confrontation by both groups of the myriad of problems I have described. The Civil Rights Act of 1964 is the direct legacy of the Birmingham events. It is not only the clearest example of legislative response to activist leadership in the social arena, but in its subsequent development through years of litigation by lawyers facing up to and attempting to solve problems spawned by its language and history and of courts grappling with these problems, is among the most sig-

---

93. Kelly Ingraham Park, made famous then as the scene of much of the demonstration activity and confrontations with the Birmingham police and firemen with water hoses.

94. "But, I Was Cool" (Kicks Music Co.) from the album "Sin and Soul", Columbia Records (1973).

95. It was Captain G. V. Evans who had earlier given an affidavit in support of the City's petition for injunction. *See Record, supra* note 78, at 39-41.

96. June 11, 1963. The speech was delivered a few hours before Medgar Evers' assassination (*see* note 12 *supra*). The President's message to Congress was sent June 19.

97. P.L. 88-352, 78 Stat. 244, 42 U.S.C. §2000 et seq. (1976) (July 2, 1964).

nificant causes of legal and social change today. Its two most important titles relating directly to the Birmingham movement for open access and jobs are Title II,[98] banning discrimination in what the Act calls a "place of public accommodation,"[99] and Title VII,[100] which outlaws discrimination in employment on grounds of race, color, national origin, sex, and religion. Another part of the Act of nearly equal importance — some might rightly say of equal importance — is Title VI,[101] which outlaws discrimination in any "program or activity receiving Federal financial assistance."[102] The force of the proposition I'm asserting can be demonstrated by considering each of these titles and developments under them in turn.

First, Title II. Because of the Birmingham movement, Congress, nearly a century after the decision in the *Civil Rights Cases of 1883*[103] in which the Supreme Court held that congress could not outlaw racial discrimination in privately operated facilities open to the public on the basis of its power under the 13th and 14th Amendments to the Constitution, used its plenary power under the Commerce Clause[104] to achieve this result, a possibility suggested in those cases.[105] Discrimination based on race, color, religion, or national origin was proscribed in establishments serving the public and "affecting" interstate commerce as defined in the Act,[106] as well as in establishments of any kind in which discrimination is supported by "state action,"[107] a concept also traceable to the Court's decision in the Civil Rights Cases.[108] The establishments covered include inns, hotels, motels, and other facilities providing lodging to transients;[109] restaurants, cafeterias, lunchrooms, lunch counters and similar eating places;[110] gaso-

---

98. 42 U.S.C. §2000a et seq. (1976).
99. §201(a), 42 U.S.C. §2000a (1976).
100. 42 U.S.C. §2000e et seq. (1976).
101. 42 U.S.C. §2000d et seq. (1976).
102. §601, 42 U.S.C. §2000d (1976).
103. 109 U.S. 3 (1883).
104. U.S. Const., Art. I, §8, Cl. 3.
105. 109 U.S. 18, 19 (opinion of the Court); 109 U.S. 61 (dissenting opinion of Mr. Justice Harlan).
106. §201(c), 42 U.S.C. §2000a(c) (1976).
107. §201(d), 42 U.S.C. §2000a(d) (1976).
108. 109 U.S. at 11, 13, 14, 17, 18.
109. §201(b)(1), 42 U.S.C. §2000a(b)(1) (1976).
110. §201(b)(2), 42 U.S.C. §2000a(b)(2) (1976).

line stations;[111] movie houses, theaters, concert halls, sports arenas and the like[112] and any establishment located within one of these facilities[113] or in which any of these facilities is located.[114] The Act was upheld by the Supreme Court soon after its passage[115] and there then remained the necessity of solving some interpretive problems arising from its language and history. I mention three key problems which had they been resolved differently, would not have resulted in the legal protection available today.

The first is that of what meaning would be given to the language of Section 201(b) (2) of the Act,[116] proscribing discrimination by eating places "principally engaged in selling food for consumption on the premises." The language was clear enough as applied to establishments in which patrons customarily entered and consumed their food or drink, either seated or standing, where it was purchased. But what of the large number of drive-in or walk-up places across the nation in which on many occasions, food is bought at the window or brought to the car or other vehicle permitting the purchaser to drive away and eat it elsewhere? Are these places "principally engaged in selling food for consumption on the premises?"

This issue was raised in a South Carolina case, *Newman v. Piggie Park Enterprises, Inc.*,[117] in which the black plaintiffs were turned away from a drive-in restaurant. The Fourth Circuit Court of Appeals held that the word "principally" was intended to exclude places, such as bars, where food service was only incidental to some other business and the phrase "consumption on the premises" was designed to exclude grocery stores and the like but to embrace places where ready-to-eat food was sold. It continued:

> When a substantial minority of American citizens are denied restaurant facilities — whether sit-down or drive-in — that are open to the public, unquestionably interstate commerce is bur-

35

---

111. *Id.*

112. §201(b)(3), 42 U.S.C. §2000a(b)(3) (1976).

113. §201(b)(4), 42 U.S.C. §2000a(b)(4) (1976).

114. *Id.*

115. *See* Heart of Atlanta Motel, Inc. v. United States, 379 U.S. 241 (1964); Katzenbach v. McClung, 379 U.S. 294 (1964).

116. 42 U.S.C. §2000a(b)(2) (1976).

117. 377 F.2d 433 (4th Cir. 1967).

dened . . . It was this evil the Congress sought to eliminate to the end that *all* citizens might freely and not inconveniently travel between the states. We think the Congress plainly meant to include within the coverage of the Act all restaurants, cafeterias, lunchrooms, lunch counters, soda fountains, and *all other facilities* similarly engaged as a main part of their business in selling food ready for consumption on the premises. . . .[118]

The second important problem arose in the same case, but was decided only on appeal from the Court of Appeals' decision that had reversed the district court on the "consumption on the premises" issue. The Appeals court had upheld the denial of attorney fees despite the provision of Title II that allows attorney fees to be awarded to "the prevailing party as costs" in suits to enforce its provisions.[119] The issue was whether the successful plaintiffs in the action could be awarded such fees absent some showing of bad faith by the defendant. The Supreme Court, reversing the Court of Appeals, ruled favorably on the attorney fees question. The Court's language is instructive because it not only decided the issue under the Civil Rights Act of 1964 but for subsequent legislation as well:[120]

A Title II suit is . . . private in form only.

When a plaintiff brings an action under that Title, he cannot recover damages. If he obtains an injunction, he does so not for himself alone, but also as a 'private attorney general' vindicating a policy that Congress considered of the highest priority. If successful plaintiffs were routinely forced to bear their own attorneys' fees, few aggrieved parties would be in a position to advance the public interest by invoking the injunctive powers of the federal courts. Congress therefore enacted the provision for counsel fees — not simply to penalize litigants who deliberately advance arguments they know to be untenable but, more broadly, to encourage individuals injured by

36

---

118.   377 F.2d at 436 (emphasis in original).

119.   §204(b), 42 U.S.C. §2000a-3(b) (1976).

120.   Age Discrimination in Employment Act, P.L. 93-259, 88 Stat. 74, 29 U.S.C. §621 et seq. (1976); Fair Housing Act of 1968, P.L. 90-284, 82 Stat. 81, 42 U.S.C. §3601 et seq. (1976); Emergency School Aid Act of 1972, P.L. 92-318, 86 Stat. 354, 20 U.S.C. §1601 et seq. (1976); Rehabilitation Act of 1973, P.L. 93-112, 87 Stat. 355, 29 U.S.C. §701 et seq. (1976); Equal Educational Opportunity Act of 1976, P.L. 93-380, 88 Stat. 484, 20 U.S.C. §237 et seq. (1976).

racial discrimination to seek judicial relief under Title II.[121]

Thus, the highly useful concept of "private attorney general" was declared, one which permits private plaintiffs in civil rights actions to press their legitimate claims through skilled counsel without concern that such counsel will not be available to them because the fee cannot be paid. The Court later embraced the concept with respect to the subsequent enactment of the Fair Housing Act of 1968.[122] The concept has now been written into law by Congress with respect to all civil rights statutes, those enacted subsequent to 1964 as well as those passed during the Reconstruction era.[123] As a student in college, I remember hearing Thurgood Marshall, when he was chief counsel for the NAACP Legal Defense Fund and before I was hired by him at the Fund, say: "When prejudice comes up against pocketbook, prejudice will give way." Because of the development of the "private attorney general" concept resulting from the interpretation of the 1964 Civil Rights Act, we are closer today to having prejudice give way than we would have been if there had been no leadership, no movement, and no law following in its wake.

The third, and last of the Title II problems, relates to that portion of the statute which proscribes discrimination in "any motion picture house, theater, concert hall, sports arena, stadium, or other place of exhibition or entertainment. . . ."[124] Patricia Miller's suit here against Fun Fair Amusement Park[125] raised the question of the meaning of the phrase, "other place of exhibition or entertainment," and became a landmark in the expansion of that section of the Act to include facilities like Fun Fair whether or not they served food, a matter which had not been made clear in the legisla-

---

121. Newman v. Piggie Park Enterprises, Inc. 390 U.S. 400, 401-02 (1968).

122. *See* note 120 *supra;* Trafficante v. Metropolitan Life Insurance Co., 409 U.S. 205 (1972)(citing *Newman*). *See also* Albermarle Paper Co. v. Moody, 422 U.S. 405 (1975) (Title VII of 1964 Civil Rights Act) and Northcross v. Board of Education of Memphis City Schools, 412 U.S. 427 (1973) (Emergency School Aid Act).

123. The Civil Rights Attorney's Fees Awards Act of 1976, P.L. 94-559, §2, 90 Stat. 2641, 42 U.S.C. §1988 (Supp. 1980). The older civil rights statutes to which the Act applies are 42 U.S.C. §§ 1981-1983, 1985 and 1986 (1976).

124. §201(b)(3), 42 U.S.C. §2000a(b)(3) (1976).

125. Miller v. Amusement Enterprises Inc., 259 F. Supp. 523 (E.D. La. 1966), *dism. aff'd*, 391 F.2d 86 (5th Cir. 1967), *reversed on rehearing en banc*, 394 F.2d 342 (5th Cir. 1968).

tive history at the time of the Act's consideration.[126] But was it consistent with the ends the Act was seeking to accomplish—not to include all places where people go for recreation and amusement such as amusement parks, with the other places specifically mentioned? And should the failure to specifically mention them by some such phrase as, "and other places of recreation and amusement," or the like, mean that such places should not be covered? That was the question that I and Johnnie Jones confronted in that case. We argued successfully as it turned out (though the decision was made only after reargument to the *en banc* Court of Appeals for the Fifth Circuit in Houston in 1968) that whether or not such places served food, they ought to be covered by "the other place of exhibition or entertainment" language because they did provide entertainment; because they satisfied the test for "affecting commerce" in section 201(c) (3)[127] of the Act since the facilities which formed the basis for the park's operation moved in commerce; because it would have made no sense to exclude these places and their inclusion was certainly consistent with the spirit and sense of the law if not precisely in accord with its language. But you see, there was the possibility that the appellate court would accept the restrictive interpretation of the local district judge here, E. Gordon West, who had held that the only places covered by that phrase were places like those enumerated before it and amusement parks were not such places.[128] Thus even though the statute had been enacted, the legal problem of advocacy for full realization of its principles persisted and had we not persisted in advocacy, the rights that we now take for granted might not have been accorded or at least would have been delayed. Because of this expansive interpretation of the Act, it quickly became the rule rather than the exception that all places open to the public providing some form of recreation or amusement would be deemed open to blacks and other minorities, including bowling alleys,[129] skating rinks,[130] and bars[131] which the

---

126. The *en banc* Court of Appeals agreed that the history was "inconclusive," 394 F.2d at 349.

127. 42 U.S.C. §2000a(c)(3) (1976).

128. 259 F. Supp. at 525-26.

129. Fazzio Real Estate v. Adams, 396 F.2d 146 (5th Cir. 1968); United States v. All Star Triangle Bowl, 283 F. Supp. 300 (D.S.C. 1968); United States v. Galiney, 12 RACE REL. L. SUR. 999 (1967).

Fourth Circuit in the *Piggie Park* case had thought excluded because their principal business was not that of selling food.[132] The decision in *Miller*, by broadening the scope of the "other place of exhibition or entertainment" language, obviated the necessity of having to argue, on a case by case basis, questions of coverage of establishments based on the nature of their food service.[133]

Now let us look at some of the problems associated with Title VII of the Act which has become the focus of so much attention with respect to perhaps this nation's most pervasive problem, employment discrimination. The issue of increased and upgraded employment opportunity for Negroes was another critical part of the Birmingham movement. It had long been recognized that a crucial reason for the powerlessness of blacks in America — a heritage of the slave system — was the lack of access to the economic status associated with meaningful work. Thus part of the legislative response to the Birmingham protests was the provision outlawing what the Act calls "unlawful employment practice[s],"[134] defined as discrimination based on race, color, religion, sex, or national origin.

In the decade and a half during which the Act has been effective,[135] this Title has prompted more litigation — that is

39

---

130. Evans v. Seaman, 452 F.2d 749 (5th Cir. 1971); United States v. All Weather Roller Dome, 1 Race Rel. L. Sur. 190 (M.D. Tenn. 1969).

131. United States v. Fraley, 282 F. Supp. 948 (M.D.N.C. 1968); United States v. Vizena, 342 F. Supp. 553 (W.D. La. 1972); United States v. DeRosier, 473 F.2d 749 (5th Cir. 1973); United States v. DeYorio, 473 F.2d 1041 (5th Cir. 1973); United States v. Deetjen, 356 F. Supp. 688 (S.D. Fla. 1973); *cf.* Cuevas v. Sdrales, 344 F.2d 1019 (10th Cir. 1965).

132. 377 F.2d at 436.

133. By expansion of the "place of entertainment" language of section 201(b)(3) other facilities have now been subjected to the nondiscrimination requirements of Title II: *Rousseve v. Shape Spa for Health and Beauty, Inc.*, 516 F.2d 64 (5th Cir. 1975) (health spa); *United States v. Williams*, 376 F. Supp. 750 (M.D. Fla. 1974)(pool hall); *United States v. Slidell Football Assoc.*, 387 F. Supp. 474 (E.D. La. 1974) (youth football league); *United States v. Central Carolina Bank and Trust Co.*, 431 F.2d 972 (4th Cir. 1970) (golf course and golf shop); *Bonomo v. Louisiana Downs Inc.*, 337 So. 2d 553 (La. App. 1976) (racetrack); Scott v. Young, 421 F.2d 143 (4th Cir. 1970)(recreation area).

134. Civil Rights Act of 1964, §§ 703, 704, 42 U.S.C. §§2000e-2, 2000e-3 (1976).

135. Title VII did not go into effect until July 2, 1965. It has been twice amended: once to expand its coverage to educational institutions, state and local governmental agencies and federal employees (Equal Employment Opportunity Act of 1972, P.L. 92-261, 86 Stat. 103, March 24, 1972) and subsequently to amend the definition of sex discrimination to include pregnancy (Pregnancy Disability Amendment of 1978, P.L. 95-555 adding §701(k), Oct. 31, 1978). The latter amendment overturned

more problems — than any other. Many of the problems lawyers have had to grapple with have been procedural problems.[136] But beyond the many procedural problems, the proper resolution which of course has been essential to the effectiveness of the Act — and those problems continue[137] — are problems at the core of what meaning should be given to the concept of discrimination. Quite clearly, the most obvious meaning is that which the courts have labelled "disparate treatment," that is simply treating a member of a racial minority, a religious group, an ethnic group or a woman differently in a given circumstance because of that fact and none other.[138] It certainly was this clear and obvious kind of discrimination that all agree, because of its obviousness, was the kind that Congress had in mind when the Title was passed. But time has revealed to many in the nation who were not as acutely aware of it as those affected by it, that beyond sheer differences in treatment are some very real systemic problems resulting from the denial of equal opportunity for more than a century since the formal abolition of slavery. Thus, six years after the statute became effective in 1965, the Supreme Court in a watershed decision interpreting the Act, took cognizance of one facet of this deeply embedded discrimination: that there are a host of employment practices which as applied to the groups designed to be benefitted by the Act have the appearance of fairness or neutrality, but nevertheless result in discrimination in fact. This concept was stated in *Griggs v.*

40

---

the decision in *General Electric Co. v. Gilbert*, 429 U.S. 125 (1976).

136. The procedural questions included such things as the requirements for initiating proceedings under the Act, whether class suits could be brought, whether jury trial was required to receive back pay, etc. *See generally* Belton, *Title VII of the Civil Rights Act of 1964: A Decade of Private Enforcement and Judicial Developments*, 20 ST. LOUIS U.L.J. 225 (1976).

137. *E.g.*, problems of the timeliness of filing of discrimination charges. *See* Mohasco Corp. v. Silver, 100 S. Ct. 1308 (1980). *See also* Chappell v. Emco Machine Works Co., 601 F.2d 1295 (5th Cir. 1979); Leake v. University of Cincinnati, 605 F.2d 255 (6th Cir. 1979)(question of equitable tolling).

138. " 'Disparate treatment' . . . is the most easily understood type of discrimination. The employer simply treats some people less favorable than others because of their race, color, religion, sex or national origin. Proof of discriminatory motive is critical, although it can in some situations be inferred from the mere fact of differences in treatment . . . Undoubtedly disparate treatment was the most obvious evil Congress had in mind when it enacted Title VII." International Brotherhood of Teamsters v. United States, 431 U.S. 324, 335 n.15 (1977). For the order and allocation of the burden of proof of disparate treatment, *see McDonnell Douglas Corp. v. Green*, 411 U.S. 792 (1973).

Duke Power Co.[139] in 1971, a case involving the application of seemingly neutral testing requirements as follows:

> The Act proscribes not only overt discrimination but also practices that are fair in form, but discriminatory in operation. The touchstone is business necessity. If an employment practice which operates to exclude negroes cannot be shown to be related to job performance, the practice is prohibited.[140]

Certainly, the most intractable of the systemic problems associated with the passage of Title VII is that of how to overcome the present effects of long standing past discrimination. How does one, by analogy to the common race track example, assure equal opportunity, an opportunity that will permit equal or superior achievement, for those who have been traditionally excluded from jobs and promotions with those who have benefitted, certainly unfairly, from the exclusion and accordingly start the race toward the achievement line so much farther ahead? It is this problem, the problem of meaningful affirmative action, that today is causing the most difficult problems for leaders, lawyers, the judicial system, and the nation as a whole. There is no easy or painless solution; the problem is with us and will remain with us for a long time to come. Certainly the Supreme Court's decision in the *Bakke* case[141] dealing with the problem in the context of higher education admission is not totally satisfactory even though the Court did recognize the propriety of taking race into account as part of the decision-making process. The Court has fared somewhat better in the employment field covered by Title VII with its decisions in *Franks v. Bowman Company*,[142] and *United Steelworkers v. Weber*.[143] In the former case, the Court has endorsed some measure of relief against the continuing burden of existing seniority systems on those persons discriminated against since the effective date of the Act, but its later opinion in *International Brotherhood of Teamsters v. United States*[144] certainly left in place the effects of discrimination associated with these systems that occurred before

41

---

139. 401 U.S. 424 (1971).
140. *Id.* at 431.
141. Regents of the University of California v. Bakke, 438 U.S. 265 (1978).
142. 424 U.S. 747 (1976) (retroactive seniority relief).
143. 443 U.S. 193 (1979).
144. *See* note 138 *supra*.

1965 when the Title became effective. In the *Weber* case the Court did endorse the voluntary adoption of affirmative action programs by businesses, but certainly that is not a cure-all since many Title VII defendants might still be willing to court the risk that they will not be found in violation of the Act. And the problem persists in yet another area: newer legislation recently considered by the Supreme Court providing a set aside of 10% of public works contracts in the construction industry for award to minority businesses.[145] These are real and important problems for us today and their ultimate resolution will affect everyone in this audience and elsewhere far into the future. Yet, we must recognize that we have some means of effecting a proper solution precisely because the enactment of Title VII and the decisions interpreting it are the result of the events I have described.

The third of the Titles included in the 1964 Act with great impact is Title VI outlawing discrimination in "any program or activity receiving Federal financial assistance."[146] This provision, long sought during several terms in Congress by the late congressman Adam Clayton Powell, Jr., so insistently that it became known as the "Powell Amendment", was finally written into law as a consequence of the Birmingham movement. Its signal impact has been to give the executive arm of the federal government a role in enforcing nondiscrimination in a broad range of public and private institutions, including colleges and universities,[147] with the ultimate sanction

---

145. On July 2, 1980, the United States Supreme Court upheld the "minority business enterprise" provision of the Public Works Employment Act of 1977, P.L. 95-28, 91 STAT. 116 which provided for the set aside. Fullilove v. Klutznick, 100 S. Ct. 2758 (1980).

146. Civil Rights Act of 1964, §§601 et. seq., 42 U.S.C. §§2000d et. seq. (1976).

147. United States v. El Camino Community College, 454 F. Supp. 825 (C.D. Cal. 1978), (injunction issued requiring college's compliance with non-discriminatory employment practices); Uzzell v. Friday, 591 F.2d 997 (4th Cir. 1979) (state university policy requiring inclusion of two minority student representatives to serve on legislative branch, even if not elected by student body, prohibited as violation of civil rights under Title VI); Flanagan v. President and Directors of Georgetown College, 417 F. Supp. 377 (D.D.C. 1976) (University policy of providing 60% of financial aid to minority law students comprising 11% of student body prohibited by Title VI).

Title VI has been extended to prohibit discrimination against black children (Bossier Parish School Bd. v. Lemon, 370 F.2d 847 (5th Cir. 1967), *cert. denied*, 388 U.S. 911 (1967); Spanish-speaking children, (*Serna v. Portales Municipal Schools*, 351 F. Supp. 1279 (D.N. Mex. 1972), *aff'd* 499 F.2d 1147 (10th Cir. 1974); Chinese-American children (*Lau v. Nichols*, 414 U.S. 563 (1974)); and emotionally handicapped children (*Lora v. Board of Education of City of New York*, 456 F. Supp. 1211

being that of withholding government funds.[148]

But the Title has also prompted judicial decision-making on another question: that of whether private persons in addition to the government, may seek a remedy against facilities

---

(E.D. N.Y. 1978)). It has been used to challenge the discriminatory hiring practices of teacher and school personnel (*Otero v. Mesa County Valley School District*, 568 F.2d 1312 (10th Cir. 1977)); and to regulate the assignment of teachers to certain districts (*Caufield v. Bd. of Education of City of New York*, 583 F.2d 605 (2nd Cir. 1978)).

Title VI has been used to prohibit discriminatory membership standards for a rural recreation association (*Hawthorne v. Kenbridge Recreation Association*, 341 F. Supp. 1382 (E.D. Va. 1972)); redlining (*Laufman v. Oakley Bldg. and Loan Co.*, 408 F. Supp. 489 (S.D. Ohio 1976)); discriminatory loan practices of Small Business Association (*SCLC v. Connoily*, 331 F. Supp. 940 (E.D. Mich. 1971)); discriminatory hiring practices of state office distributing federal grant money (*United States v. Frazer*, 297 F. Supp. 319 (M.D. Ala. 1968)). It was the basis of a challenge to a proposed move of a major medical facility, which would conceivably adversely affect the black community, (NAACP v. Medical Center, Inc., 599 F.2d 1247 (3d Cir. 1979)).

At times, Title VI has been turned against HEW itself, as well as other branches of government: *Adams v. Califano*, 430 F. Supp. 811 (D.D.C. 1977) (HEW held in violation of Title VI for accepting school desegregation plans which fell below previous HEW standards); Adams v. Richardson, 480 F.2d 1159 (D.C. Cir. 1973) (HEW ordered to effect compliance of school boards with school desegregation plans); *Brown v. Weinberger*, 417 F. Supp. 1215 (D.D.C. 1976) (HEW violated Title VI by failing to initiate investigations of possible acts of discrimination, and by refusing to cut off funds to schools which have been found to be discriminatory); *Shannon v. Department of Housing and Urban Development*, 436 F.2d 809 (3rd Cir. 1970) (HUD violated Title VI by changing urban renewal plans without regard to discriminatory effect); *NAACP, Western Region v. Brennan*, 360 F. Supp. 1006 (D.D.C. 1973) (Department of Labor officials violated Title VI in discriminatory practices of federally funded employment services for farm laborers); *Thomas v. Housing Authority of City of Little Rock*, 282 F. Supp. 575 (E.D. Ark. 1967) (policy of evicting any family if a member of the family has an illegitimate child is violation of Title VI); *Garrett v. City of Hamtramck*, 357 F. Supp. 925 (E.D. Mich. 1973), *rev'd on other grounds* 503 F.2d 1236 (6th Cir. 1974), (Title VI violation where city discriminated in providing housing for black residents displaced by urban renewal).

Extensive discussion of the origin, purpose and role of Title VI and the utility of HEW guidelines in school desegregation cases was undertaken in *United States v. Jefferson County Board of Education*, 372 F.2d 836 (5th Cir. 1966) (per Judge Wisdom), *aff'd en banc* 380 F.2d 385 (5th Cir. 1967). A more recent extended judicial treatment of Title VI in the context of "affirmative action" occurred in *University of Calif. Regents v. Bakke*, 438 U.S. 265, 325 (1978) (opinion of Mr. Justice Brennan).

148.   Funds have been withheld where construction of public housing would perpetuate a racially segregated system of housing in the city (*Blackshear Residents' Organizations v. Housing Authority of City of Austin*, 347 F. Supp. 1138 (W.D. Tex. 1971), *Hicks v. Weaver*, 302 F. Supp. 619 (E.D. La. 1969)) where a state had failed to take affirmative steps to cure impact of its past policies of segregation in schools (*State of Georgia v. Mitchell*, 450 F.2d 1317 (D.C. Cir. 1971)) where state officials practiced segregation in operation of state's mental health system (*Marable v. Alabama Mental Health Board*, 297 F. Supp. 291 (M.D. Ala. 1969)) where a state failed to file an assurance agreement with HEW acknowledging responsibility for, and assuring a good faith effort toward, elimination of racial discrimination (*Gardner v. State of Alabama*, 385 F.2d 803 (5th Cir. 1967), *cert. denied*, 389 U.S. 1046 (1968)).

that accept federal funds. This issue was first broached in a case I argued before a panel of the Fifth Circuit Court of Appeals.[149] The case involved the public schools of Bossier Parish near Shreveport which because of the proximity of a military installation, educated the children of servicemen with federal money being paid the school system under the Federal Impact Program.[150] The court decided that though the statute didn't say so explicitly, nevertheless members of the class of persons designed to be benefitted — the black school children — had standing to bring an action in court to enforce their rights under Title VI.[151] I was gratified to see that case cited last year when a similar issue was decided by the United States Supreme Court involving Title IX of the Education Amendments of 1972,[152] which proscribes sex discrimination in educational programs receiving federal financial assistance. Because of the court's ruling that a woman who had been excluded from admission to the University of Chicago's medical program had an implied private right of action under Title IX,[153] it has become even clearer that individuals proceeding under Title VI can sue on their own behalf as the court not only cited *Bossier*[154] but also cited with approval several other decisions consistent with it.[155] Thus the *Cannon v. University*

44

---

149. Bossier Parish School Bd. v. Lemon, 370 F.2d 847 (5th Cir. 1967), *cert. denied*, 388 U.S. 911. Jesse Stone (note 176 *infra*) was co-counsel.

150. 20 U.S.C. §§631-645 (1976).

151. 370 F.2d at 852.

In the absence of a procedure through which the individual protected by Section 601's prohibition may assert their rights under it, violations of the law are cognizable by the courts. . . . The Bossier Parish School Board accepted federal financial assistance in November 1964, and thereby brought its school system within the class of programs subject to the section 601 prohibition against discrimination. The Negro school children, as beneficiaries of the Act, have standing to assert their section 601 rights. *Id.*

152. 20 U.S.C. §§1681 et. seq. (1978).

153. Cannon v. University of Chicago, 441 U.S. 677 (1979). *Cf.* Davis v. Passman, 442 U.S. 228 (1979) (implied right of action under 5th Amendment in sex discrimination case).

154. 441 U.S. at 696 n.20.

155. *Id.* at 696 n.21. In the following cases decided since *Bossier*, a private right of action was implied under the statute involved — Voting Rights Act of 1965, §5, *Allen v. State Board of Elections*, 393 U.S. 544 (1969); Urban Mass Transportation Act of 1964 §13(c), *Local 714, Amalgamated Transit Union v. Greater Portland Transit Dist.*, 589 F.2d 1 (1st Cir. 1978); Federal Aviation Act of 1958, §1007(a), *Bratton v. Shiffrin*, 585 F.2d 223 (7th Cir. 1978); NASA Act of 1958: *Lodge 1858, American Federation of Gov't Employees v. Webb*, 580 F.2d 496 (D.C. Cir. 1978); Rivers and Harbors Appropriation Act of 1906, *Riggle v. California*, 577 F.2d 579 (9th

of Chicago[156] decision not only clarifies this aspect of Title VI — which the court in the *Bakke* case assumed without deciding[157] — but also demonstrates what has been so often the case: that rights written into law as a consequence of blacks facing up to their problems as I have described, will be ex-

Cir. 1978); Rehabilitation Act of 1973, §503, *Clarke v. FELEC Services, Inc.*, 48 L.W. 2785 (D.C. Alaska 5/5/80); Rehabilitation Act of 1973, §504, *Davis v. Southeastern Comm. Coll.*, 574 F.2d 1158 (4th Cir. 1978), *cert. granted*, 439 U.S. 1065 (1979); *United Handicapped Federation v. Andre*, 558 F.2d 413 (8th Cir. 1977); *Kampmeier v. Nyquist*, 553 F.2d 296 (2nd Cir. 1977); *Lloyd v. Regional Transportation Authority*, 548 F.2d 1277 (7th Cir. 1977); *Camenisch v. University of Texas*, 48 L.W. 2769 (5th Cir. 4/28/80); *Chaplin v. Consolidated Edison Co. of N.Y., Inc.*, 48 L.W. 2541 (S.D.N.Y. 1/18/80); *Patton v. Dumpson*, 48 L.W. 2523 (S.D.N.Y. 1/23/80); Small Business Act, *SCLC v. Connolly*, 331 F. Supp. 940 (E.D. Mich. 1971); Social Security Act, *Like v. Carter*, 448 F.2d 798 (8th Cir. 1971); Warsaw Convention, Art. 28(1), *Benjamin v. British European Airways*, 572 F.2d 913 (2nd Cir. 1978), *cert. denied*, 439 U.S. 1114 (1979); Investment Advisors Act, *Abrahamson v. Fleschner*, 568 F.2d 862 (2nd Cir. 1977), *cert. denied*, 436 U.S. 913 (1978); Home Loan Bank Act, *Association of Data Processing Services Organizations v. Federal Home Loan Bank Board*, 568 F.2d 478 (6th Cir. 1977); Banking Act of 1933, §§16 and 21 (Glass-Steagull Act), *New York Stock Exchange v. Bloom*, 562 F.2d 736 (D.C. Cir. 1977), *cert. denied*, 435 U.S. 942 (1978); Labor-Management Relations Act of 1947, *Nedd v. United Mine Workers*, 556 F.2d 190 (3rd Cir. 1977), *cert. denied*, 434 U.S. 1013 (1978); 39 U.S.C. §3009 (Unsolicited mailing in re unfair trade), *Kipperman v. Academy Life Ins. Co.*, 554 F.2d 377 (9th Cir. 1977); Davis-Bacon Act §1, *McDaniel v. Univ. of Chgo.*, 548 F.2d 689 (7th Cir. 1977) *cert den.*, 434 U.S. 1003 (1978); Securities Exchange Act of 1934, §6, *Higher v. Dempsey Tegeler & Co.*, 534 F.2d 156 (9th Cir. 1976), *cert. denied*, 429 U.S. 896 (1976); Securities Exchange Act of 1934, §10b, *Healey v. Catalyst Recovery of Pa.*, 616 F.2d 641 (3rd Cir. 1980); Securities Exchange Act of 1934, §14(a), *J.I. Case Co. v. Borak*, 377 U.S. 426 (1964). *But see Touche Ross & Co. v. Redington*, 442 U.S. 560 (1979) (§17(a) of the Securities Exchange Act of 1934). Trust Indenture Act of 1939, *Zeffiro v. First Pa. Banking & Trust Co.*, 48 L.W. 2823 (3rd Cir. 5/29/80); Developmentally Disabled Assistance and Bill of Rights Act, 42 U.S.C. §6010, *Halderman v. Pennhurst State School and Hospital*, 612 F.2d 84 (3rd Cir. 1979); *Naughton v. Bevilacqua*, 458 F. Supp. 610 (D.R.I. 1978); Economic Stabilization Act, §210, *Bulzan v. Atlantic Richfield Co.*, 48 L.W. 2702, (U.S. Temp. Emer. C.A., 4/7/80); Securities Act of 1933, §17 (a), 15 U.S.C.A. §77g(a), *Daniel v. Int'l. Brotherhood of Teamsters*, 561 F.2d 1223 (7th Cir. 1977), *rev'd on other grounds*, 439 U.S. 551 (1979); Commodity Exchange Act, §4(b) (anti fraud provision): *Curran v. Merrill, Lynch, Pierce, Fenner & Smith*, 48 L.W. 2770 (6th Cir. 5/12/80); *Witzel v. Chartered Systems Corp. of New York, Ltd.*, 48 L.W. 2823 (D. Minn. 5/27/80); *Grayson v. Conticommodity Services, Inc.*, 48 L.W. 2807 (D.D.C. 5/23/80); *Navigator Group Funds v. Shearson Hayden Stone, Inc.*, 48 L.W. 2680 (S.D.N.Y. 3/20/80); *Alken v. Lerner*, 48 L.W. 2616 (D. N.J. 2/22/80); Title VI, *Shannon v. HUD*, 436 F.2d 809 (3rd Cir. 1970) [also using Title VIII]; *Eresti v. Stenner*, 458 F.2d 1115 (10th Cir. 1972); *Gautreaux v. Chicago Housing Authority*, 265 F. Supp. 582 (N.D. Ill. 1967); *Blackshear Residents Organization v. Housing Authority of City of Austin*, 347 F. Supp. 1138 (W.D. Texas 1972); *Hawthorne v. Kenbridge Recreation Association, Inc.*, 341 F. Supp. 1382 (E.D. Va. 1972); *Hicks v. Weaver*, 302 F. Supp. 619 (E.D. La. 1969).

156. *See* note 153 *supra*.
157. 438 U.S. at 284.

tended to benefit others in the society. Obviously, the ability of persons to proceed on their own under Title VI is significant for today and beyond.

Let me also mention another part of the 1964 Civil Rights Act which enacted an important procedural change regarding the relationship of courts in our federal system. You will recall that I said that during the Birmingham period, we adopted the tactic of removing the criminal cases resulting from the demonstrations from the state to the federal court for the purpose largely of buying time and helping the protests to continue even though we recognized that eventually the cases would be remanded and that once remanded, there was no possibility of having the decisions reviewed because the civil rights removal statute at that time did not provide for appeal. Another change in law occasioned by the Birmingham protests was Title IX of the 1964 Act,[158] which permitted appeal of orders remanding cases removed under the civil rights removal statute first enacted in 1866.[159]

Pursuant to this authority, the Supreme Court was given the opportunity to clarify the conditions under which such removal was appropriate through its decisions in the 1966 cases of *Georgia v. Rachel*[160] and *Greenwood v. Peacock*.[161] The

---

158.   § 901, 28 U.S.C. § 1447(d) (1976).

159.   *See* note 68 *supra*.

160.   384 U.S. 780 (1966) (Removal granted when federal law conferred a right to break state law requiring segregation of lunch counters. Prosecution itself was violation of defendants' civil rights.)

161.   384 U.S. 808 (1966) (Removal denied when defendants were charged with trespass as the result of civil rights demonstration. Distinguished from *Rachel* since no federal right conferred to break state trespass laws). *Peacock* has been followed in the great number of civil rights removal cases. *See, e.g.,* People of N.Y. v. Davis, 411 F.2d 750 (2nd Cir. 1969), *cert. denied* 396 U.S. 856 (1969) (violation of Fair Housing Act is not sufficient for removal, unless it has substituted a right for what under state law is a crime); Baines v. City of Danville, 357 F.2d 756 (4th Cir. 1966), *aff'd*, 384 U.S. 890, *reh. den.*, 385 U.S. 890 (1966) (since state injunction barring demonstrations was not unconstitutional on its face, and a factual hearing would be required to determine the presence of discrimination, removal was denied); State of North Carolina v. Hawkins, 365 F.2d 559, 562 (4th Cir. 1966) *cert. denied* 385 U.S. 949 (1966) (citing *Peacock* for proposition that no federal law confers immunity from state prosecution growing out of attempts to secure the right to vote); Commonwealth of Virginia v. Wallace, 357 F.2d 105 (4th Cir. 1966) *aff'd* 384 U.S. 891 (1966) (even though discrimination in jury selection constitutes state action and judgment tainted with such discrimination will be reserved on certiorari to state court, it is not removable in advance). The most recent Supreme Court removal decision is *Johnson v. Mississippi*, 421 U.S. 213 (1975) (state criminal prosecution for conspiracy and boycott is not sufficient for removal where there is no federal statutory right precluding the orderly

amendment, at the very least, has made available to litigants the opportunity for appellate review of remand orders should circumstances requiring removal arise again.

Finally, you must be wondering what happened in the contempt case. Its resolution confirms the fact that struggle, once begun, is a long term proposition and that not all problems are solved immediately nor satisfactorily and indeed cannot be solved through any single means. Notwithstanding the circumstances which mandated defiance of the injunction, the Supreme Court in 1967 upheld the convictions of King, Abernathy, Walker, Shuttlesworth, and the others resulting from the Good Friday and Easter Sunday marches[162] and they eventually served the five-day sentence imposed. But I think they would say, and that you and I would agree, that the penalty was small in comparison to the changes that resulted.

The last of the series of pivotal events that requires our attention because of their importance for us today, is the campaign for voting rights that occurred in the so-called "black belt" of Alabama in the early months of 1965. The critical nerve center of that campaign was Selma, Alabama, a small community in the South Central part of that state whose name will be forever associated with the problems of leadership encountered in the effort to correct the denial of the voting rights of black Americans as Birmingham has become associated with the effort I've already described. Once again, the pre-existing scene should be set.

Selma, and Dallas County of which it is the county seat, were communities like many in the area in which the black population was considerably larger than the white. In these counties, though blacks far outnumbered whites, they were totally subject, for the most part, to white control in every aspect of life. The major cause of this nearly complete subjection was the denial of the vote with minor exceptions, to the black majority by the white minority.

The first attempts at changing this situation occurred in 1963 through beginning efforts, as in Birmingham, of a local organization, the Dallas County Voters' League. A black busi-

47

---

process of state law).

162.   Walker v. City of Birmingham, 388 U.S. 307 (1967). An incisive criticism of the decision is in MAHONEY, *supra* note 32, at 273-99 (ch. 16). The decision, however, has met with approval and has been followed in other contexts. *See* MAHONEY, *supra* note 32, at 329-30.

nesswoman, Amelia Boynton,[163] whose son incidentally was the plaintiff in the first sit-in case to reach the United States Supreme Court,[164] which had upheld the right of Negroes to use interstate bus facilities and which was decided coincidentally, on the day that I joined the legal staff of the Legal Defense Fund, provided the dominant leadership of the Voters' League. The League's efforts were aided initially in 1963 by the Student Non-Violent Coordinating Committee formed out of the student sit-in movement in 1960[165] but these efforts were largely unsuccessful. The federal government had filed several suits against Selma and Dallas County officials under then existing voting rights legislation, but these suits, not suprisingly, were ineffective due to the inadequacy of the legislation.[166] My initial involvement in the leadership efforts of the Voters League and Student Non-violent Coordinating Committee (SNCC) was in the fall and early winter of 1963 when I was asked by another black Birmingham attorney, Peter Hall,[167] to assist in the defense of some SNCC members who had been charged with violating local law because of their activities in Selma. My first impression of Selma in that year confirmed for me how small an impact had been made on the situation there and that a great deal more was needed to remedy it.

A great deal more occurred at the beginning of 1965. In January, a massive campaign of protest demonstrations was launched with Selma as the focal point, by Dr. King's organization, SCLC, which had decided to join the SNCC Program and that of the Voters' League. Immediately, the campaign

---

163. See note 14 supra.

164. Boynton v. Virginia, 364 U.S. 454 (1960).

165. MAHONEY, supra note 32, at 34.

166. See United States v. J.P. Majors, 7 RACE REL. L. REP. 463 (S.D. Ala. 1962); United States v. Atkins, 210 F. Supp., 441 (S.D. Ala. 1962), rev'd, 323 F.2d 733 (5th Cir. 1963); United States v. Dallas County, 229 F. Supp. 1014 (S.D. Ala. 1964); United States v. McLeod, 229 F. Supp. 383 (S.D. Ala. 1964). Injunctions were granted in Majors and Atkins (on appeal) but there were of little value; in the other two cases, relief was denied.

167. Peter Hall, a distinguished looking man of chestnut brown complexion and mercurial temperant, was born in Birmingham, Alabama, August 21, 1912. He took his law degree at Chicago's DePaul University and had been practicing for many years in Birmingham by 1963. I worked closely—and exhaustively—with him during the Selma/black belt campaign often driving two hours each way over periods of several days between Birmingham and Selma. He is now a state court judge in Birmingham.

encountered the most severe repressive action. In addition to the now familiar pattern of arrests, there was outright violence, official and nonofficial. The symbol of these repressive measures was the Dallas County sheriff, Jim Clark. During the third week in January, I and other black attorneys from my office and from Birmingham, began filing several lawsuits designed to deal with the opposition measures taken. First, we removed criminal prosecutions to the federal district court in Mobile, Alabama,[168] as had been done in Birmingham, but now because of the provision of the 1964 Civil Rights Act permitting appeal from the denial of such removal petitions, we were in a better legal position to challenge the prosecutions at the appellate level. Selma and Dallas County officials had also obtained a state court injunction against SNCC in July 1964 and this case too, was removed to the federal district court in an attempt to dissolve the injunction.[169] In some of the arrest situations we succeeded in securing the release on federal habeas corpus of demonstrators to whom officials had refused bond. We also took the offensive as we had been unable to do in Birmingham, by challenging the arrests in federal court because they denied the right to vote.[170] This legal right, unlike the right of access to privately owned facilities in the Birmingham situation, was clear.[171] Consequently, we were able to achieve in Selma at an early point what we had not been able to achieve in Birmingham: a federal court injunction against Selma and Dallas County officials preventing their interference with peaceful assembly for the purpose of exercising the right to vote, encouraging others to exercise it and protesting its denial by harassment, threats and intimidation.[172] This injunction, in a reverse of the Birmingham situation, was the basis of a later successful contempt proceeding

49

---

168. Alabama v. Allen, 10 RACE REL. L. REP. 234 (S.D. Ala. 1965); Cooper v. Alabama, 353 F.2d 729 (5th Cir. 1965); Alabama v. Boynton, (C.A. No. 3385-64, S.D. Ala. 1965) (companion case to *Cooper*).

169. Dallas County v. SNCC, 10 RACE REL. L. REP. 234 (S.D. Ala. 1965). The injunction was dissolved April 16, 1965.

170. King v. Baker, C.A. No. 3572-65 (S.D. Ala. 1965). Another suit from these events successfully challenged segregated courtroom seating in the Dallas County courtroom, *Bevel v. Mallory*, 11 RACE REL. L. REP. 1422 (S.D. Ala. 1966). *Cf.* Johnson v. Virginia, 373 U.S. 61 (1963).

171. U.S. CONST. amend. XV.

172. Boynton v. Clark, 10 RACE REL. L. REP. 215 (S.D. Ala. 1965).

against Jim Clark.[173]

This brief recital of the number of actions that were filed points up other problems from the legal standpoint that existed in Selma that did not exist in Birmingham: the sheer volume of lawsuits that we seemed to be filing on almost a daily basis to try to cope with the repressive conduct. Compounding that problem was a matter of logistics which made one of the problems of Selma simply a matter of sheer physical as well as mental exhaustion. Unlike Birmingham where everything was localized, the events, the state courts and the federal courts, the Selma episodes required an enormous expenditure of physical effort in coordinating the movement of lawyers by automobile among Selma and the other communities in the black belt[174] where the events were occurring and where the state courts were located; Mobile, approximately 100 miles to the south where the federal court was located; Birmingham where the local attorneys were, and New York from which I and my associates were traveling incessantly by plane to all these places then driving at all hours to observe events, interview witnesses, consult with the clients, file papers and make court appearances.

The problems for the activist leadership despite the injunction we obtained, were similar to those that occurred previously in other places, including again the arrest of Dr. King and his incarceration for several days in Selma. But they went beyond that. There was an overlay, as I have said, of sheer violence! Before these events concluded persons would be murdered, including some whites who had left their homes elsewhere to join in the demonstrations.[175] Martin King,

50

---

173. Clark v. Boynton, 362 F.2d 992 (5th Cir. 1966), vacating and remanding, 10 RACE REL. L. REP. 472 (S.D. Ala. 1965) for clarification on question of civil versus criminal contempt. On remand, 12 RACE REL. L. REP. 620 (S.D. Ala. 1966), the court determined the contempt to be civil and levied a fine against Clark that was never paid.

174. Some of the communities were Perry County (Marion), Lowndes County (Hayneville), Marengo County (Demopolis), Greene County (Eutaw), Hale County and Wilcox County. Surely, unknown and unnoticed place names on America's map—and until 1965, unexciting as well.

175. Reverend James Reeb, a Boston minister, had his skull crushed from behind on March 9, 1965 as he was leaving Eddie Walker's cafe in Selma, a restaurant frequented by participants in the movement (at which I and my associates ate many times). New York Times, March 10, 1965, at 1, col. 8. Three defendants charged with the murder were acquitted. New York Times, Dec. 11, 1965, at 1, col. 4. Viola Liuzzo, a Detroit housewife, was shot and killed while riding in an automobile with a black

through talks I had with him and his associates during this period, I know felt the effects not only of the actual violence but the continually threatening air of violence.

The situation came to a head in what was probably the most dramatic episode in the history of those times. On Sunday, March 7, as I was flying from New York City to Shreveport, Louisiana for trial of a school desegregation case with Jesse Stone,[176] a march was attempted from the Edmund Pettus Bridge in Selma to the state capitol in Montgomery. The march was broken up by Jim Clark, his deputies, members of his so-called "posse," and Alabama state troopers wielding clubs, electric cattle prods, and using tear gas. Some persons who fell to the ground in the assault were trampled. Tear gas canninters were thrown as they were lying on the ground. Others were chased back across the bridge into Selma by the flying hooves of horses. I heard about these events as they were occurring when I landed at the Birmingham airport to make a connection with the plane to Shreveport when I called a friend who had listened to the reports of the occurrence on the radio.

Because of what happened on what came to be known as

51

man on U.S. Highway 80 between Selma and Montgomery the night of the completion of the Selma-Montgomery March, March 25, 1965 (*see* note 178 *infra.*). New York Times, March 26, 1965, at 1, col. 6. (A short time before the shooting, I had been driving on the same highway). A successful federal prosecution was brought (state prosecution resulted in a hung jury). New York Times, Dec. 4, at 1, col. 3. The conviction was upheld on appeal—*Wilkins v. United States,* 376 F.2d 552 (5th Cir. 1967), *cert. denied* 389 U.S. 964 (1967). Her children, however, are now suing the United States because of the alleged complicity of a paid government informer in her killing. New York Times, Feb. 17, 1980, at 16, col. 2.

Before either of these deaths, a young black man, Jimmy Lee Jackson, a native of Marion, Alabama, was killed by Alabama State Troopers in February while participating in a march in Marion. New York Times, Feb. 19, 1965 at 1, col. 2. A grand jury later refused to indict anyone. New York Times, Sept. 30, 1965, at 2, col. 2.

176. Jesse Stone was counsel with me in two school desegregation cases filed in the federal district court for the Western District of Louisiana. The cases involved, respectively, the public school systems of Bossier Parish (County) outside Shreveport (*Lemon v. Bossier Parish Board of Education,* 240 F. Supp. 709 (W.D. La. 1965) aff'd 370 F.2d 847 (5th Cir 1967)); and of Shreveport itself (*Jones v. Caddo Parish School Board,* 10 RACE REL. L. REP. 1569 (W.D. La. 1965)). *Lemon's* significance is discussed *supra* at 267. It was the Shreveport case to which I was traveling that Sunday to begin trial the next day.

Stone, a large gregarious man, was born in Gibsland, La. June 17, 1924. He earned his law degree from Southern University Law School in 1950 and practiced law in Shreveport. He later became dean of Southern University Law School for one year before leaving to become Assistant Superintendent of Education for the State of Louisiana in 1972. He has served as President of Southern University since 1974.

"Bloody Sunday," instead of flying back to New York after the Shreveport trial as I had originally planned, I joined a group of associates in Montgomery the following Tuesday to begin preparation for trial of a suit that we had filed the day following the episode, in the federal district court in Montgomery seeking injunctive restraint of those who had perpetrated the violence and an order requiring that the march which had been aborted be permitted. The record of that trial which was incorporated in the eventual findings of the federal district judge, Frank Johnson, included references to the pattern of brutality and mass arrests that had occurred in Selma including an instance involving the forced march of school children with cattle prods and night sticks into the countryside for several miles which resulted in the contempt suit against Jim Clark.[177] The injunction was issued the week following the initiation of the lawsuit[178] and on Monday night of that week, March 15, just before the trial concluded, President Johnson went on television to propose what became the Voting Rights Act of 1965.[179] In that speech he echoed the words of the theme song of the movement: "We shall overcome."

The Voting Rights Act was passed by Congress and was signed into law on August 6, 1965. The events of Selma and the black belt and particularly the breakup of the initial march from Selma had triggered such revulsion that for the first time in the nation's history an *effective* piece of legislation protecting voting rights was enacted. Its provisions which have subsequently been extended[180] required automatic registration of voters in areas which in accordance with its triggering formula had exhibited widespread denial of the right to vote.[181] There are also provisions for the use of federal regis-

---

177. *See* note 8 *supra*.

178. Williams v. Wallace, 240 F. Supp. 100, 104 (M.D. Ala. 1965). The forced march occurred on February 10, 1965.

179. P.L. 89-110, 79 Stat. 437, 42 U.S.C. § 1973 et seq. (1976).

180. The Voting Rights Act Amendments of 1970 (P.L. 91-285, 84 Stat. 314, 315) extended the Act for five years. The Voting Rights Act Amendments of 1975 (P.L. 94-73, 89 Stat 400-406) extended the Act for seven more years until 1982.

181. The triggering formula contained in Section 4 of the Act, provides for the suspension of literacy tests and similar devices (which had been used to thwart Negro voting) in states and political subdivisions of states in which fewer than 50% of the eligible voting age population were registered to vote in the previous Presidential election; determination of covered areas "shall not be reviewable in any court and shall be effective upon publication in the Federal Register." (§4(b), 42 U.S.C.

trars to supplant local voting officials[182] and for the first time stiff criminal penalties were enacted to encompass both state officials and private persons who would deny the right.[183] Other provisions required that any change in voting standards, practices or procedures different from those that existed before the Act was passed be approved either by the Attorney General of the United States or by a district court in the District of Columbia.[184] The basic provisions of the Act were upheld in *South Carolina v. Katzenbach*[185] and in a case that I argued before the Supreme Court in 1968, *Allen v. Virginia State Board of Elections*,[186] the approval provisions of the Act were also upheld[187] and the right of private plaintiffs to sue was declared[188] even though in the main, the Act con-

53

---

§1973b(b) (1976)). The bar on literacy tests was extended to the entire country by the 1970 amendments (which also, in advance of the 26th Amendment to the Constitution, lowered the voting age from twenty-one to eighteen, abolished durational residency requirements longer than thirty days and provided national standards for absentee voting).

182. §§6-9, 42 U.S.C. §§1973d - 1973 g (1976).

183. §§11, 12, 42 U.S.C. §§1973i, 1973j (1976).

184. §5, 42 U.S.C. §1973c (1976).

185. 383 U.S. 301 (1966).

186. 393 U.S. 544 (1969).

187. Section 5 (42 U.S.C. §1973c) requiring pre-clearance of any change in voting practice or procedure, has been given a broad interpretation, requiring pre-clearance of a new procedure for casting write-in votes (*Allen v. Virginia, State Board of Elections*, 393 U.S. 544 (1969)); change from district to at-large voting (*Id.*, although at-large voting, often resulting in racially disproportionate representation, is not unconstitutional per se, *City of Mobile v. Bolden*, 446 U.S. 55, 100 S. Ct. 1490 (1980)); change from elective to appointive office (*Allen*); change in requirements for independent candidacy (*Id.*); changes in polling places (*Perkins v. Matthews*, 400 U.S. 379 (1971)); changes in municipal boundaries through annexation of adjacent areas (*Id.*); and requirement that county employees take unpaid leave of absence when becoming candidates for political office (*Dougherty County, Va. Board of Educ. v. White*, 439 U.S. 32 (1978)). This section applies to all entities having power over any aspect of the electoral process (*United States v. Board of Commissioners of Sheffield*, 435 U.S. 110 (1978)). The burden of proof remains on the state to show that proposed changes will be enacted without discriminatory purpose or effect (*Georgia v. United States*, 411 U.S. 526 (1973)). And the "bailout" provision of the Act (§4(a), 42 U.S.C. §1973(b)) allowing a covered jurisdiction to escape Section 5's pre-clearance requirements by bringing a declaratory judgment action to establish that a "test or device" has not been used to deny the right to vote, is not available to a city which is part of a covered state (*City of Rome, Georgia v. United States*, 446 U.S. 156 (1980)).

The constitutionality of the suspension of all literacy tests has also been upheld, *Oregon v. Mitchell*, 400 U.S. 112 (1970). Even where literacy tests had been administered without discrimination they have been struck where it was found that unequal educational opportunities invalidated their nondiscriminatory administration (*Gaston County, N.C. v. United States*, 395 U.S. 285 (1969)).

188. 393 U.S. at 555. *See* text accompanying notes 149-156, *supra*.

templates government enforcement.

The results of the legislation are clearly evident today. We have seen the results in the number of black elected officials,[189] including a mayor in Birmingham, Alabama.[190] Black led governments are in place now in many places in the black belt where the demonstrations occurred. And in the presidential election of 1976 we saw the prediction come true that one day "the hands that picked cotton would pick a President."

None of this of course means that all problems have been resolved. We know that is not true. But we also know that the problems we face today are of a different order of magnitude than the problems of de facto leadership and legal action that I have discussed here. But, because these problems were faced at the time, at the places, and in the way that I have described, there is firmer, more solid ground for you and all of us to confront and seek solutions to today's problems of de facto leadership. The confrontation of these problems of a decade and a half ago in the streets, on the highways, in the courts, and in the congressional legislative corridors form a springboard for today's leaders to confront problems in the precinct and ward organizations, council chambers, state legislative halls, regulatory agencies, union halls, the banks and insurance companies, the classrooms and faculty lounges of colleges and universities, and in the corridors, suites, and board rooms of American industry which present the challenge of de facto leadership today. To describe that challenge is to paraphrase the poet's account of the exhortation of a mythical hero in his search for "a newer world": "To strive, to seek, to find and [never] to yield"[191] in the quest for justice, in the belief of its attainment, and most importantly, in the effort needed to achieve it.

54

---

189. As of July, 1979, there were 4,607 black elected officials in the United States. Of this number, there were 208 in the State of Alabama (including 3 state senators, 13 representatives and 12 mayors), 334 in Louisiana, and 327 in Mississippi. *Annual Roster of Black Elected Officials*, Joint Center for Political Studies, Wash., D.C.

190. Dr. Richard Arrington, Jr., son of a sharecropper, educator and former Dean of Miles College in Birmingham was elected in 1979. Arrington was born in Livingston, Ala., October 19, 1934. He graduated from Miles College in 1955, received an M.S. degree from the University of Detroit in 1957 and a Ph.D. from the University of Oklahoma in 1966. Prior to his election as mayor, he was a member of Birmingham's City Council.

191. A. TENNYSON, ULYSSES.

The Southern
Freedom Movement
in Perspective

ANNE BRADEN

Contents

NOTES FROM THE EDITORS

We are pleased to reintroduce to our readers with this issue, Anne Braden, author of the MR Press book, *The Wall Between*. which tells the incredible story of the witch-hunt that ensued when Anne and Carl Braden bought a house in a white section of Louisville and turned it over to Negro friends. The late Eleanor Roosevelt described the book as "a most remarkable story" by a woman of courage and extraordinary objectivity. Mrs. Braden is presently the editor of the *Southern Patriot,* official organ of the Southern Conference Educational Fund, and is also, along with her husband, a field secretary for that organization.

INTRODUCTION

In January of this year, one of the editors of MONTHLY REVIEW asked me what was happening in the Southern freedom movement. What, he asked, had it accomplished, what were its long-range objectives, where did it appear to be going?

This article is an attempt to deal with these questions.

It is not really an attempt to answer them. I have been active in the movement in the South for the past 17 years, but I don't know the answers to all these questions—and I'm not sure anyone else in the movement does either.

Fundamentally, I think, the Southern movement is now groping and searching. About a year ago it came to the end of an era, for one phase of the battle—the struggle for desegregation of public accommodations—was essentially won. The official victory came with passage of the 1964 Civil Rights Act, but the end was clearly in sight even earlier. This does not mean that there are not still today, in some parts of the South, lunch counters, restaurants, theaters, and other public accommodations that bar Negroes. There are certainly some and, in the rural areas and small towns, many. But in major cities throughout the region and even in smaller communities in many sections, major public facilities are now open.

Yet, despite this victory—to the surprise of some but as many had expected—life in the South has not really changed very much either for the Negro or for the white. Schools are still basically segregated, jobs are getting harder than ever to find, and if anything housing is becoming more segregated. "The South is getting more like the North every day, and that's not good," said one civil rights worker. He meant that segregation by law is passing, but segregation in fact is increasing.

Most of the major civil rights organizations are now concentrating their work in what is called the Black Belt—those 100 or more counties stretched across the Deep South, mostly rural, where Negroes are in the majority or near-majority. This is the area where oppression of the Negro has been most open and brutal, where he has traditionally been denied the vote as well as every dignity of citizenship. The battle

I

in these areas now is for the vote, and it is a crucial battle because the Black Belt holds great potential of political power.

This is the battle that produced the great upsurge around Selma, Alabama, this winter and spring. The events there were historic because they aroused the nation as nothing in the freedom movement had done before and brought the greatest outpouring of support for the Negro's fight against oppression that has yet been seen.

There will be more Selmas, because extreme racists are still in control in large sections of the Black Belt; and when they use terror to stop the Negro drive to freedom, there will be more crises. It is important that people in the rest of the country continue to respond as they did to Selma; in fact, it is important that some way be found to keep the concern of the nation active between the times that such campaigns boil to the front pages. For these areas are still very much like police states, and history seems to show that police states can be broken only if the people in them have help from the outside.

On the other hand, it should be remembered that even if the battle of all the Selmas is won, as it will be—even when the Negro wins the vote everywhere in the South and the violent elements are brought under control of the moderates—the question of making freedom real will still remain.

For what do you do after Sheriff Jim Clark stops clubbing people and the registrars agree to register them, and the police let them walk unmolested on the highways—yet Negroes still can't get a decent job in Selma? That is what has happened at the scenes of earlier violence in the South. And what do you do if white politicians who make moderate statements get elected to office instead of those who shout racist slogans, and even some Negroes get elected too—but the majority of Negroes still live in slums and have no hope of getting out? This too has happened at the centers of earlier campaigns against racism.

What about places like Nashville, where there has not been a demonstration in more than a year, where the restaurants and hotels are open to all comers—but where thousands of Negroes still live in ghettos and many of them in slums. What about places like Memphis where Negro voter registration is among the highest in the South, but where segregation in housing and schools is increasing all the time? Or places like Albany, Georgia, where Negroes aren't marching in the streets anymore, as they did when this town shook the world in 1962, but where unemployment among Negroes is worse than it has ever been?

Up until now, the struggle of the Negro in the South has been essentially a struggle for symbols. This was important, and it probably

58

2

had to come first, because with the symbol went human dignity. The cry that has filled the Southern countryside has been "Freedom Now!" Many who shouted it could not have told you exactly what they meant by it—not because they didn't know what they were struggling for, but because it was a concept too big to put into words. Freedom—an end to all that was wrong—an end to oppression—an end to second-class citizenship—an end to terror. Freedom—not only an end, but a beginning too—a new world where things are different, where people are different, the promised land, not in some next world, but *Now*. Freedom in the abstract, too big to articulate, but something a person feels the meaning of in his guts; and people, overcoming the fears of centuries, fought for it, and were willing to go to jail and die for it. And because it was too big to comprehend in specifics, it had to be looked for in symbols.

59

Even something like Alabama's giant march for the vote on U.S. Highway 80 had strong symbolic significance. The vote itself is more than a symbol; it is a very real weapon that people need. But when the demand of the people of Selma for the vote was met with violence, tear gas, and billy clubs their struggle became another symbolic one for the rest of the Southern movement, for the nation—and even to a certain extent for them. Here was racism in its most ugly and obvious and terrible form. Here was hatred and corruption and degeneration —all the fruits of racism—clear and plain to see. And when 30,000 people marched into Montgomery, it was a great victory—but it was a symbolic one, because for the Negro in the Alabama Black Belt life had not changed at all, not even his inability to register and vote.

Symbols are important, but there comes a time when they are not enough. No one can say for sure just when this time came in the Southern movement, but it started long before passage of the 1964 Civil Rights Act and it spread steadily after that: the cold hard realization that it was not only freedom in the abstract that was needed but freedom in the concrete. Symbols provide a rallying point, but they don't put bread in hungry mouths or make it any more pleasant to live in a house without running water. Symbols don't even help much when the school that was once the white school and then the showpiece token integrated school is fast becoming the resegregated school, as the white families flee to northern-type suburbs and Negroes stay locked in the city by gentlemen's agreements among those who control real estate—or in prescribed and limited suburbs of their own.

The rather obvious problems and frustrations have led some people, especially white liberals, to conclude that the answer lies in war-on-poverty programs. A newspaper columnist wrote at the height of the Selma demonstrations that white "moderates" in Alabama had

3

been hoping that the poverty program would absorb the interests and energies of Negro militants. But it obviously has not done so. More Negroes were willing to walk into police lines and possible death to demonstrate for an abstract freedom on the Selma-to-Montgomery highway than have been willing to involve themselves in meetings to plan anti-poverty programs in most places. This is not because they don't know that bread-and-butter matters are urgent; and it is not, as some might suggest, that they don't know enough to operate at the level of "constructive" programs. A partial reason is that anti-poverty program planners have not sought hard enough to involve Negroes (and in most of Alabama actually tried to keep them out). But there is more to it than that.

60

The fact of the matter is that the average Negro militant in the South knows instinctively that the kind of measures being proposed under the anti-poverty program are not big enough to touch his real problems. He knows, even if he does not put it into words, that his world is not really going to be changed by day nurseries for working mothers, training schools for high-school dropouts, and work with a neighborhood job corps at $1.25 an hour. These things are desirable and needed; but they are not on a scale big enough to deal with what is wrong. People know without saying it in words that the problems they face are giant ones, and since they see no giant answers in concrete terms, they turn once again to the gigantic symbols. These are valuable because through them people are mobilized and they learn their own strength. But where will we turn when these symbolic battles are all won, when there are no more symbolic worlds to conquer, and finally, irrevocably, we must come face to face with the hard need for real change?

It will be 10 years next December since the present phase of the Southern struggle against racism and for freedom had its beginning in Montgomery, Alabama, the cradle of the Old Confederacy. It is only 50 miles from Montgomery to Selma along U.S. Highway 80 where the marchers walked this spring, but it is a far distance in time from the Montgomery bus protest that started it all to the Selma demonstrations of 1965 when hundreds of thousands of people all over the country rallied behind the movement. Even if the battle has been for symbols and little that is fundamental has changed, it could never be said that little has happened. New ways have been tried, new frontiers assaulted. Heroes, known and unknown, have emerged, a social movement has developed that ranks with only a few others in top importance in our history, and the world has been shaken.

What I have written here is mainly for those who are concerned about these events in the South but have watched them from a distance or have been involved only for short periods of time. Thus, it is an attempt to put fast-moving events into their chronological order and to indicate the pattern that makes them intelligible. And it is an attempt to analyze, because most commentary on these developments has been by writers looking on from the outside, and many may wonder how the pattern looks from the inside.

In addition, I suppose this article is also a letter to myself. In writing a summary for the outsider looking on, I found I had to dig back and remember things I had forgotten, read things I had laid aside, think about questions I had pushed to the back of my mind to wait "until there's more time." This is the kind of thinking most of us who are active in the South rarely find time for. We tend to live from day to day, from crisis to crisis. It was good for me to have to think back and analyze. I would be glad if others in the movement, through reading what I have written, would be stimulated to do their own probing—even though I am sure many would come to conclusions and even questions that are different from mine.

No one could attempt such an analysis as this without serious misgivings. The Southern movement is big and diffuse and far-flung. No one person could possibly know about it all. Interpretation of history must always reflect the vantage point from which it is viewed, and some will disagree with mine. The fact that I am white instantly raises questions as to whether my views can have basic validity in regard to this particular movement. The fact that I am still living and breathing and taking part in the struggle instantly presents the possibility that I may change my opinions on almost any question within the next few years, or even the next few months.

On the other hand, it is perhaps just such hesitations as this that have limited the consideration of basic issues within the Southern movement. It is not only that we don't have time. It is also because in a world that is changing as fast as ours and in a movement as fluid as this one, we are reluctant to stake out any hard and fast theories and commit them to the seeming finality of the written word.

We need to take some chances, I think, on being wrong. We need to experiment a little more with ideas. We need to lift our eyes occasionally from the heat of today and look down a long road.

And before we can look forward with vision to where we are going, we need to look back and try to understand just where we have been.

61

1

THE EARLY SEEDS OF FREEDOM

To understand what has transpired in the South in the last decade, we have to realize that the freedom movement did not start in 1955. A new phase of it started then—but the Negro's drive against oppression reaches much further back.

Actually, it started on the day in 1619 when the first ship bringing slaves to the New World landed on the coast of Virginia. From then until the Emancipation Proclamation technically freed this country's slaves more than 200 years later, there was a series of slave revolts. Some were small, some were widespread; and serious scholars now agree that many revolts were never recorded anywhere. Meantime, thousands of slaves escaped to freedom on the Underground Railroad, the secret system by which slaves traveled to the North and to Canada, passed along in darkness from one hideout to another. Others lived to fight for their own freedom in the Civil War.

Thus, today, when people speak of the "new Negro," the concept is misleading. The phrase is used to describe a Negro who is standing up for his rights, implying that this type of Negro just emerged in mid-twentieth century. But obviously, from the beginning, American Negroes have had their militants and those who stood up and said "no," even if to say it meant death. The new thing that happened in the mid-twentieth century was that the Negroes who said "no" found a way to organize and to fight.

This didn't happen until almost 100 years after the formal end of slavery for a very simple reason: during much of this century real police-state tyranny gripped the South.

For a brief time, immediately after the Civil War, during the period known as Reconstruction, it appeared that there would be a shift of power in the South. The slave-owning landowners who had dominated the area were defeated; and under the protection of federal troops, new state governments were being established. The new leaders included freed slaves and—although school textbooks ignore this—at least some of the poor white people who had never benefited from slavery and had never supported it. It was a time of great promise; the new governments guaranteed the right to vote to all, gave the

South its first real free public education, initiated prison reform, government care for handicapped persons, and other social reforms. (There are now available a number of studies which refute the old myths about this period, the most recent of which is the excellent and simply written new book, *Freedom Bound* by Henrietta Buckmaster.) The new governments probably made some mistakes too, as most revolutionary governments do. But if they had had the chance to continue, it is likely they would have gone on to land reform and other basic changes that could have laid the foundation for an egalitarian society in the South.

They never got that chance. In 1877, white politicians in the North agreed to withdraw federal troops from the Southern states and to end any effort by the federal government to enforce the constitutional rights of the freed slaves. This shameful abdication, known as the Compromise of 1877, was precipitated by a disputed presidential election in 1876, in which Northern Republicans agreed to these concessions to get Southern votes for their candidates. But as several recent historians have pointed out, the issues went much deeper. Howard Zinn says that the Compromise "came out of the general conditions of the post-Civil War era, in which Northern politicians and businessmen needed Southern white support for peaceful national development along the lines they desired."

The Compromise of 1877 marks the beginning of the Southern police state that continued into the twentieth century and still exists in parts of the Deep South. Even before 1877, the Reconstruction governments and their supporters were under violent attack by mob and assassin in many places. As soon as the Federal troops left the South, the situation was hopeless. The old rulers began to reclaim power by terror. The Ku Klux Klan became a law unto itself—terrorizing, flogging, and murdering. Lynching became commonplace. The Negro was forced back onto the land of big plantation owners, no longer nominally a slave but living under conditions almost as intolerable.

The terror did not descend in full force all at once, for the white South, then as now, had its moderates, and they tried to soften the blows. Then in the early 1890's there was a brief movement toward unity of Negroes and poor whites under the Populist banner. (Historian C. Vann Woodward says that during this brief upheaval, "Negroes and native whites achieved a greater comity of mind and harmony of political purpose than ever before or since in the South.") This frightened Southern ruling forces so badly that moderate influences lost out entirely, and terrorists took complete control. The poor white Southerner had always been torn within himself—part of

63

7

him knowing that he should identify with the Negro who was also downtrodden, another part of him forever wanting to identify with the white man who had the power and wealth he longed for. Now under pressure of frightened people in power, this poor white man (in the mass, if not every individual) let himself be convinced that it was the Negro who was his enemy.

Thus as the nineteenth century closed, the Southern Negro stood alone. The rest of the country had deserted him, in the South the most extreme racists were in complete control, and all around the globe the white man still reigned supreme. (Vann Woodward points out that the white South got a "permission-to-hate" when the United States in this period plunged into "imperialisic adventures and aggressions against colored peoples in distant lands.") Between 1890 and 1905, the South enacted its fantastic network of segregation laws, and took Negroes by the thousands off the voting rolls. In some parts of the South, Negroes continued to hold office until 1900, but by the beginning of the twentieth century, the lights had gone out all over the region.

It should be noted, of course, that the South was never all of one piece. It is a large area and infinitely varied, both in terrain and sociology. Usually when we speak of "the South," we refer to the 17 states in the Southeastern part of the United States which, along with the District of Columbia, had laws requiring school segregation before the Supreme Court ruled them unconstitutional in 1954. This area includes extensive mountain and hilly lands, which have never had much in common with the cotton-growing flatlands. The area also includes the "border" states, those which did not secede from the United States to become a part of the Confederacy during the Civil War and where loyalties were divided.

The area that controlled the South, however, was the Black Belt—the vast farming lands, rich and flat, which reach across the South in a half-circle, from the eastern shore of Virginia down through the Carolinas, Georgia, Alabama, Mississippi, Louisiana, and into East Texas. White Southerners claim that this area is called the "Black Belt" because of its rich black soil, but the name also refers to the fact that the area has traditionally had more Negroes than whites. It was here that the greatest concentration of slavery developed, because it was here that slaves were useful. The landowners who have ruled the Black Belt—both before the Civil War and after the Compromise of 1877—have possessed power out of all proportion to their numbers because state legislatures were weighted in their favor —and still are to a high degree. Also, these same people have wielded

64

disproportionate power over the nation, because their representatives were elected to Congress where they came to dominate key committees.

Gradually, in this century the agrarian economy of the South began to give way to some industrialization, and some natural tensions developed between landowners and new industrialists, the Black Belt areas and the growing cities. In the beginning, however, this didn't change things much for the Negro. More recently, industrial leaders of the South have often become a moderating force because they want to keep peace, and oppressed people demanding freedom disturb the peace. But in the early part of this century, there was no mass movement demanding freedom. Industry was coming South looking for low wage scales, and it was an advantage to have a dual and divided labor force, colored and white. So institutionalized racism—as contrasted with the more formless variety in the rest of the country—continued to infect the entire Southern and border-state area, and the police state atmosphere, developed in the Black Belt, spread its poison throughout the region.

65

Something happens to people when they live in a police state. The will to resist never dies entirely, and every oppressed people must have had its unknown and unsung resisters. The Southern Negro of the early twentieth century obviously did too, and even today there are folk tales of the sharecroppers who shot the landlord to defend their families. But these people were soon mobbed—or in some rare instances escaped to the North and silence. For the most part, Southern Negroes—like people living under complete tyranny anywhere—accommodated and survived. Some were crushed, some found little ways to get even with the white man, some found ways to get around him, ways to say one thing and mean another, and some way to live. The white South built up its mythology that Negroes were happy with the way things were, and the white North built up its mythology that it was none of its business; and for years there was no organized resistance because none was possible.

By the late 1920's and the early 1930's, there were moderating forces because some Southern whites tried to curb the anti-Negro violence—for example, the white women's organization to oppose lynching, and various regional and local interracial committees. These helped to alleviate the worst terror, but it is doubtful that alone they ever would have conquered it, because their aim was not to change in a real way the social fabric. Seeds of real change were planted only when Southern Negroes began to organize themselves, and this happened only after influences from outside the South began to make themselves felt there—giving support to the theory that a police state cannot be broken without outside help.

9

One of these early influences was the NAACP—the National Association for the Advancement of Colored People. The NAACP did not originate in the South; it was organized mostly by Northerners under the leadership of Dr. W. E. B. DuBois in 1909, at a time when the Southern police state was at its worst. But during the First World War it began to work in the South—exposing atrocities to national view and challenging the worst inequities in the courts. One of its most important court battles from its early years was for the right of the Southern Negro to vote. Soon it was also establishing local chapters through the South, and a corps of Southern leadership was developing.

Today militant people tend to think of NAACP leaders as very conservative, slow-moving, and respectable. This is not always true even now in the South, and it certainly was not true in those early days. A man or woman had to be a person of courage and dedication to become identified with the NAACP, and only the brave qualified. Nor did they find any great rush of people ready to support them; the path of the early NAACP pioneer in Southern communities was a lonely one.

The battle at that time was not against segregation as such. It was primarily for the right to vote, and for equal justice in the courts. Before the days of the NAACP, a Southern Negro had virtually no chance in court at all—unless he was in the good graces of some white man who could "get him off"; and the idea of bringing to court a white man who had wronged a Negro was unheard of.

This situation improved when the NAACP became a factor, bringing its lawyers into Southern courts; just this possibility made prosecutors and police a bit more careful. Early NAACP leaders concentrated on the dangerous job of gathering facts in the myriad cases where Negroes were unjustly accused of crime. E. D. Nixon, the Montgomery, Alabama, pullman porter who later organized the bus protest there, was one who pioneered in this work—traveling the dark country roads to find witnesses who would testify, and risking his life every minute to do it. There were not many spectacular victories, but a consciousness spread through the Negro community that a person did not have to take what the white world handed him without protest and that somewhere—even if far away in New York—there was an organization that cared.

Other seeds of freedom were planted in the South by the general ferment of the 1930's and the organizations that sprang up in that ferment. The young Congress of Industrial Organizations (CIO) unions tried to organize in the South, and in some places, even if for a brief time, black and white workers came together. Organizations

66

of the unemployed also reached into the South, and Negroes found in them a weapon they could use. Crusades like the worldwide one around the Scottsboro case let it be known inside as well as outside the South that injustice could be stopped if enough people knew and protested. By 1938, so many people, both black and white, were in motion that a new coalition, the Southern Conference for Human Welfare (SCHW), drew 3000 people to a meeting in Birmingham and presented a challenge to Southern entrenched political power.

The SCHW was not a Negro freedom organization in the sense that we know such groups today; it was a coalition of Southern whites and Negroes, liberals and radicals, intellectuals and workers and union organizers, who were brought together by a belief that Franklin D. Roosevelt's New Deal offered hope for the poverty-stricken South. They also wanted to win popular support for Roosevelt's program at a time when it was being riddled by Southern Congressmen. But the SCHW played a part in the embryonic Negro movement of the South, because it fought against the poll tax and for fair employment practices and other civil rights measures; also many Negroes developed into leaders in the SCHW.

67

Another important seed was planted in 1941 when A. Philip Randolph, the Negro who had brought the nation's pullman porters into a militant union, organized for a giant March on Washington to demand a federal order against racial discrimination in employment. Randolph's union had some membership in the South, and support for the march grew there. The planned march was the first serious proposal that the Negro use mass direct action in his quest for justice. Even though it never actually took place, since President Roosevelt signed a Fair Employment order to head it off, the idea embedded itself in the minds of many people.

Yet another force which was impinging on the Southern police state, although many people don't want to admit it now, was the work of radical political groups, especially the Communist Party. In the nation as a whole, ideas were freer then than they are today, and no one was stopping Communists from speaking. In the South, they faced the danger of jails and mobs, but so did the CIO and NAACP organizers, and Communists were not considered any more outlaw in the South than these were. Furthermore, since the risks of organizing any protest in the Deep South were great, even as they are now, there was a need for very dedicated people. Dedication comes most often in people who have their eyes fixed beyond immediate suffering to a vision of a new world—and this many Communists of that day, both white and black, had. Thus they often faced dangers in the South that others would not. Often the CIO sent its Communist organizers into the South because they were the only ones who were willing to go and risk getting their heads beat in. This was before either the labor movement or any other institution trying to change America had let itself be divided by the notion that the test of a man is his anti-Communism rather than his devotion to the task at hand. Thus Communists moved and worked freely in the South, and their attack on the economic causes of Negro oppression opened new doors of thought for many people and contributed to the general ferment.

By the time the Second World War came, all these forces had poured in upon the South, cracking open the police state even if not changing the status quo; and leaders of a resistance movement among Southern Negroes were emerging. The war speeded up the process. The fact that it was a war against Hitler and supposedly against racism set many people in America to examining this country's own cancer of racism. Books were written, people were talking, ideas were circulating. Furthermore, people were traveling and coming in contact with new people, new conditions, new ideas. The Southern Negro found out for himself that there were places in the world quite different from the cotton patch where he grew up—and thousands went back home after the war, determined that they would not live the way their parents had.

Veterans had come back with these ideas after the First World War too, but were quickly crushed by a new wave of terror and a resurgent Ku Klux Klan. This threatened after the Second World War also, but many things were different this time. The ferment of the 1930's could not be undone; there were organizations now, new forces, in the white South as well as the black, that would not condone the Klan. Furthermore, the world was different now. The drive toward freedom and independence among the colored people of Africa and Asia was beginning to impinge on the consciousness of the white Western World, and sophisticated people felt it and saw the handwriting on the wall. The "image" of the United States in a world where whites are in the minority was beginning to be a factor. Thus, although a postwar revival of the Klan brought some tragic violence, there were also protests. More than 15,000 people, led by labor, veterans, and civil rights organizations, massed at the Lincoln Memorial in Washington in 1946 to call for Federal action; people turned out for protest meetings in North Carolina, Texas, Louisiana. The Klan was attacked by many Southern newspapers, by the CIO, and ministerial groups. The world of 1946 was not the world of 1919.

In 1944, the NAACP legal staff won an important victory when it got the white primary declared illegal. In the South until very recently the Democratic primary was the only election that mattered, since the Republican Party was of little consequence. As long as primaries were closed to Negroes, they were effectively denied a political voice. The 1944 court decision came in a Texas case, but it spurred demands for the vote everywhere; this too came to a head as the veterans came home. Many Southern officials empowered to register voters ignored the court order just as many do today, but the demands were rising.

In Birmingham in 1946, hundreds of Negro veterans marched to the courthouse to seek the right to vote. Similar marches occurred elsewhere. Simultaneously, there were reports of Negro passengers removing the white and colored signs on buses. A Negro just missed by 200 votes being elected to the Virginia legislature. Several hundred persons, Negro and white, appeared before a legislative committee in Virginia to demand an end to Jim Crow laws. In Birmingham, Negroes and some whites defied Police Commissioner Eugene "Bull" Connor (the same one who led assaults on Negro demonstrators 15 years later in 1963) to attend an integrated meeting, and some were arrested. Hundreds of persons, Negro and white, came to a meeting of the Southern Conference for Human Welfare in 1946 to call for an end to "all discrimination based on race, creed, and color," as well as to define such goals as "raising the per capita income, and the housing, health, educational and recreational opportunities of all Southerners. . . ." Chapters of the NAACP were mushrooming, as were chapters of the Southern Conference and also the Southern Negro Youth Congress, a more radical organization.

Thus, by the postwar period, the seeds of freedom were growing, providing the makings of a mass movement for Negro freedom. Why, then, was it almost 10 years later before it finally came? No one can answer that question for sure, but one reasonable theory is that the delay was related to the general atmosphere that pervaded the nation between 1945 and 1955.

As all Americans know, the period after the Second World War did not bring the progress many had expected, but a period of reaction. People who had felt power slipping from their hands during the ferment of the 1930's reached out to reclaim it, to capture and control what new forces they could, including the labor unions, and to destroy those they could not control. All organizations working for social change came under attack, and the world situation made it easy to brand them all subversive. Thus many organizations were destroyed and others divided, and many people were confused.

This all had its effect in the South, as elsewhere. The CIO, which had provided promise of uniting Negro and white in struggle,

69

announced several times that it would embark on a gigantic "Operation Dixie" organizing drive, but the drive never really came off. Nationally the CIO was fighting off the new anti-labor Taft-Hartley Act and was beset by divisions arising from the red scare. Organizations like the Southern Conference for Human Welfare and the Southern Negro Youth Congress which refused to go along with purges of those accused of "subversion" were weakened by attack. Others, like the NAACP, which did follow a purge policy, were weakened by resulting divisions. Every organization working for change was embattled and all were on the defensive. Thus the Southern Negro, while ready to revolt, had no framework in which he could act.

The lack of a framework does not stop a revolt that is ready to be born; if it is ready, it just creates its own form, and that eventually is what the Negro revolt did. Had there been on-going movements when the first embryonic stirrings swept over the South with the veterans returning from the war, it might have come sooner. It might also have been a different movement. A Negro revolt rising directly out of and related to the social movements of the 1930's and early 1940's might not have been so completely all-Negro as was the revolt that finally developed. It is also possible that for this very reason it would have been more equivocating on the issue of Negro freedom. A movement tied to the earlier ones might have attacked a broader area than the single issue of segregation and thus might have borne the germs of answers to some of the problems that are plaguing the civil rights movement now. On the other hand, without the single-minded attack on segregation, it is possible that this battle would never have been raised to the level where it now is. No one can ever know.

What we do know is that in the years following the war, the United States sank into a period of citizen-silence. What started as attacks on organizations working for social change became an attack on any individual who raised his voice on a subject of controversy. The attacks became institutionalized through the House Un-American Activities Committee, later the similar committee of Senator James Eastland of Mississippi, and most flamboyantly through the work of Senator Joe McCarthy. People even suspected of radical ideas or activities and some simply suspected of ideas that were "different" were fired from their jobs, driven from their home towns, and cast into the darkness of ostracism.

By the early 1950's, this madness had reached its height, and the great majority of American citizens, both white and black, had quit going to meetings, joining organizations, or signing petitions. They were devoting themselves to their own backyards, their own

70

private lives. Young people coming out of school were being careful not to become involved in anything more controversial than the Parent-Teacher Association (PTA); we were raising a generation of young people convinced that before it is all right to do something you must get approval from somewhere—from the government, from powers-that-be. An atmosphere developed in which anyone who dared to suggest that all was not perfect in the United States—that some people were hungry and ill-housed, and that millions lived as second-class citizens—was automatically suspected of disloyalty. Some polite agitation for civil rights continued, but it was always necessary to assure everyone that things were getting better all the time, and there were just a few little injustices that needed clearing up.

About this time, in 1954, the Supreme Court handed down its decision saying segregation in the nation's schools was illegal. Credit for this goes not to anything the current generation was doing to make itself felt, but to the ferment of a previous generation, to the superb arguments of the NAACP lawyers, and mostly (to the shame of America) to the force of world opinion in a largely non-white world. It was an historic event, however, and it could have been a turning point. But much of the promise of the decision was lost because, except for actions by a few individuals and groups, it was met in the South by utter silence.

71

Here and there Negroes applied for admission to the "white" schools in 1954 and 1955. They were rebuffed; and since there was no mass movement, the individuals who had acted often suffered reprisals. In the white South, no committees for compliance sprang up; a vacuum existed, and within a year the extreme segregationists (who had been stunned by the decision at first and weren't ready to act either) took the initiative and organized the opposition that caused the South so much grief before the decade ended. Later many people over the country asked why the "good white Southerners" weren't organizing in this period. The questioners forgot that this was a time when advocates of social change were not organizing anywhere in the United States. It was a time of social paralysis.

And then at the depth of it, at a time when fear had worn itself out and apathy and cynicism had almost taken its place, at a time when the democratic processes seemed dead and the country's vitality drained away—just at this moment, the most unlikely time in the world, and in the most unlikely place in the world, Montgomery, Alabama, the old capital of the Confederacy—an unassuming Negro woman sat down on a bus and started a new mass movement that would eventually shake the nation and the world and make the American people come alive again.

2

THE NEW ERA: 1955-56

The Montgomery bus protest was the beginning of a new era in the South, for it was here that Southern Negroes themselves joined forces and said "no" to oppression. Montgomery marked a qualitative change because it was a mass movement, and it was direct action— that is, action that involved each participant in a challenge to the status quo.

It started in early December, 1955, when Mrs. Rosa Parks, a Negro woman, refused to give up her seat on a city bus to a white man and, on orders of the bus driver, was arrested. In two days' time a call had gone out through the Negro community to stay off the buses—and Montgomery Negroes stayed off. For a year they walked, or organized their own jitney service. They continued despite the threat of jail, the bombing of their homes, and the threat and sometimes the fact of lost jobs. There were 50,000 Negroes in Montgomery and for a year they united, spurred on by a sense of purpose that gave hope to the old and inspired the young.

No one can say why it happened in Montgomery and at that time. There exists a tape recording of a discussion held six months earlier at Highlander Folk School in Tennessee, the conference center where Negro and white met during these years to talk about ways to change the South. At that discussion in the summer of 1955, there were several Negro participants from Montgomery. Each of them, including Mrs. Parks, said they feared that Montgomery Negroes would never "stick together." Even when Negro leaders issued the call to stay off the buses after Mrs. Parks' arrest, they did not know whether the people would respond. Some of them, as they reported later, were as surprised as city officials when they looked out their windows that morning and saw the buses rolling by—empty. Not one would have predicted that a year later the people would still be walking. Something had happened.

Certainly, there were in Montgomery many of the necessary ingredients for a mass protest movement. The grievances were real and deep. Montgomery is as Deep South as you can get: located in the heart of Alabama's old plantation country, it is Old South in

16

tradition and proud of being the first capital of the Confederate States of America during the Civil War, the "Cradle of the Confederacy." Negroes in Montgomery in 1955 were completely segregated, almost completely poverty-stricken, victims of frequent police brutality and constant insult, and, with the exception of a relatively few who persisted long enough, denied the vote.

City buses were a special point of irritation, not only because they were segregated, but because Negroes had no rights on them whatsoever and were often treated like animals by the drivers. The pre-protest system in Montgomery, as in many Southern cities at that time, required that Negroes fill the bus from the back while whites seated themselves from the front—and when the two met and there were not enough seats, Negroes were supposed to stand and let the whites sit. Actually, Mrs. Parks was arrested not for sitting in the front of the bus, but simply for refusing to move from her seat in what had been the Negro section after the front filled up and the driver ordered her to give her seat to a white man. Even in the early weeks of the protest, the demand of the Montgomery movement was not for integrated buses but simply for a change in this system to a first-come-first-served arrangement. It was only after this mild demand met with outraged and violent resistance that the protesters broadened their objectives and demanded complete integration of bus seating, which is what they finally won.

But the real demand of the bus protest was for human dignity. Before the protest, it was common practice, as the bus began to fill, for the driver to call out—as if shouting to a bunch of cattle—"All right, move back, niggers." The oppression which finally united the city's Negroes was not only the denial of seats to tired bodies but the denial of their very humanity.

Another necessary ingredient for the development of a mass movement that was present in Montgomery was a collection of some remarkable people.

First, there was Mrs. Parks herself. As Montgomery became famous, she was often painted as a naive, retiring, inexperienced little seamstress who just suddenly on that December day decided for the first time to resist segregation. The picture was not entirely accurate. She was a seamstress, and she was (and is) a retiring person who never especially relished the role of heroine. But she was neither naive nor inexperienced, and she had been fighting segregation a long time. Her first memory of resistance to oppression goes back to the 1930's when she can recall her husband and his friends gathering secretly in her living room in Montgomery to collect money for defense of the Scottsboro case. She herself had no part

73

in this; she was a young bride who felt her place was in the background. But years later she joined the NAACP and, she relates modestly, because there were so few people she was soon elected secretary of the Montgomery branch. For years thereafter she helped hold the branch together, patiently investigated cases of injustice, urged people to testify, walked the streets seeking memberships. Mrs. Parks often said that she had no thought on that day in 1955 of making a test case—that she was tired and when the driver shouted at her to move, something simply arose from deep in her being and said "No." But long years of patient struggle had prepared her for that moment.

Another of the remarkable people in Montgomery was E.D. Nixon, pullman porter, union organizer, NAACP leader. Mrs. Parks called him when she was jailed, and he began to spread the word that the time had come to stay off the buses. Working with him were a relatively small group of other Montgomery Negroes, especially an active group of women. All these people were veterans of long years of lonely struggle.

The other remarkable person in the picture, of course, was Dr. Martin Luther King, Jr., who was unknown before he emerged into prominence in the Montgomery movement. His emergence was almost an accident. He had recently come to Montgomery as a young minister, and Nixon and the others settled on him as the leader for the new Montgomery Improvement Association (MIA) partly because he was too new to have become involved in factional divisions.

Once he had assumed the presidency of MIA, however, there is no doubt that King injected a new dimension into the bus protest. With him as its spokesman, the campaign became not just a battle for a seat on a bus but a war against an entire system of segregation and degradation—and beyond that a struggle for a whole new world. He was a master of powerful oratory, and his words thundered first through Montgomery and then across the nation: "We are tired of being segregated and humiliated; we are tired of being kicked about by the brutal feet of oppression. . . . We are protesting for the birth of justice in the community. . . . We have a new sense of dignity and a new sense of destiny. . . . We will walk the streets of Montgomery until the walls of segregation are finally battered by the forces of justice. . . . And when the history books are written in future generations, the historians will have to pause and say, 'There lived a great people—a black people—who injected new meaning and dignity into the veins of civilization.' "

Negroes listened, they were aroused, and they followed him—first in Montgomery and then elsewhere. They followed because he

74

gave them a new sense of their worth and a new sense of power—
and because he said things they already knew but had not put into
words. This is perhaps King's greatest genius: that he sensed the
aspirations of masses of people and put them into words. Whether
the Montgomery bus protest would have lasted as long or reached
as far as it did without a spokesman like King is highly problematical.

Yet none of this really explains why the bus protest happened
when and where it did. The same unbearable conditions that existed
on the Montgomery buses also obtained in cities across the South,
and they had existed in Montgomery for a long time. As for the
leaders in Montgomery, as remarkable as they were, they had their
counterparts elsewhere. There were persistent, faithful, hard-working
women like Mrs. Parks in other NAACP branches through the
South; there were courageous and skillful organizers like E.D. Nixon
in other Southern communities. There may well have been other
potential Martin Luther Kings.

Thus it must be concluded that Montgomery happened because
the time had come when it was inevitable that Southern Negroes
would revolt in mass, that if it had not happened there it would
have happened somewhere else, and that a new force was moving
in the history of the country.

After a year, the Montgomery bus protest ended in victory and
the buses were integrated. The victory came technically after a court
decision nullifying the local bus segregation law, and those who be-
little mass direct action have said it was this decision and not a year
of walking that made the difference. Obviously, however, the court
decision would not have come when it did without the long walks of
50,000 Montgomery Negroes.

The Montgomery movement won something far bigger than a
change in bus policy. The participants won a new sense of dignity,
freedom, and power. They had discovered for themselves that masses
of people in motion can change the world around them. They would
never be the same again, and neither would the South. It was late
1956 when the Montgomery protest ended, and the ideas it generated
had already begun to spread over the South.

They did not catch fire overnight, however, and for most of the
remaining 1950's civil rights forces remained on the defensive. Extreme segregationists—acting through mobs, semi-respectable White
Citizens Councils, and often through state and local governments—
had grabbed the offensive within a year after the 1954 Supreme
Court school decision, and for most of the decade they held it. They
outlawed the NAACP in Alabama and hampered it in other states.
They purged thousands of Negro voters from the rolls in Louisiana,

75

enacted new laws to restrict voting rights in some states, murdered the Rev. George Lee, shot and injured Gus Courts, and slew nameless others who tried to mobilize registration drives in Mississippi. The 1957 Civil Rights Act, which was supposed to guarantee voting rights, had little effect. Meantime, state legislative or administrative committees, modeled after the House Un-American Activities Committee of the Congress, attacked all civil rights organizations as "subversive" in Arkansas, Louisiana, Florida, Mississippi, Virginia, and Georgia; and in Tennessee a legislative committee began an attack which finally (in 1961) forced the closing of Highlander Folk School, an oasis where white and Negro Southerners had met together for a generation.

76

The most effective offensive of Southern segregationists was their drive to thwart the Supreme Court ruling against school segregation. In the border states of Kentucky, West Virginia, Delaware, Maryland, Missouri, and in parts of Texas and Oklahoma, there was some compliance. But in the rest of the South, the decision met open defiance, closed schools, or devious circumvention. The federal government took a hands-off position that left enforcement of the decision to organizations like the NAACP and individual Negro students. Thus every autumn from 1954 through 1960 the front pages of the nation's newspapers were dominated by news of either violence or closed schools, or both. By the end of the decade the bright promise of the 1954 decision had all but melted away.

From the other side, the only assault on the schoolhouse doors came from repeated NAACP actions in the courts and from the handful of brave individuals—the young people, little children and parents—who walked through mobs to be the pioneers. From Autherine Lucy, who braved a mob to try to enter the University of Alabama in 1955, to the first-graders in New Orleans in 1960, there was an honorable procession of the courageous few. No one who lived through this period will ever forget the pictures of young Elizabeth Eckford, head held high, walking by the jeering ugly faces in Little Rock; or the words of the high school boy who listened to his mother beg him not to return to the dangerous scene and then replied simply: "As long as I can walk, Mother, I am going back." These and others like them were the heroes and heroines of the decade, but alone they could bring no real change; they could only keep the doors open.

The only counter-movement to the segregationist offensive was the effort of white moderates, beginning in the latter part of the decade, to stem the violence and save the South's public school system. This was a welcome development in the midst of chaos; but it was not an integration movement, nor a civil rights movement, nor a Negro freedom movement, and it should never be interpreted as any of these things. A local movement for moderation started, for example, after the night bombing of a newly integrated school in Nashville in 1957, and it restored law and order to that city. But it made no effort to increase the ranks of the 13 Negro children enrolled in desegregated schools in that supposedly enlightened city. Finally associations of white ministers in Southern cities began to make statements calling for an end of the terror that gripped the region, but a Negro minister and civil rights leader, the Rev. Samuel Williams, pinpointed their shortcomings by commenting that "When the white church finally spoke, it was too late and what it said wasn't Christian." He meant that almost invariably the ministers' statements called for law and order, without mentioning any moral issues involved in the deprival of equal rights to all men.

77

The movement of Southern moderates reached Southwide proportions under the leadership of Virginians after their state closed the schools in several communities with massive resistance laws in the fall of 1958. This left 13,000 young people without schools, in order to keep out 51 Negroes. Parents, teachers, businessmen, and many civic leaders organized a save-the-schools movement and made themselves heard. At the same time the schools in Little Rock, Arkansas, were also closed, and white people there began to organize to reopen them.

The tide actually turned in favor of the moderates in early 1959, when massive resistance collapsed in Virginia. Rural Prince Edward County abandoned public education after that for five long years, but in 1959 extreme racists lost their hold on the Virginia state government. "This is Appomattox; Richmond has fallen," wrote a Southern journalist, Harry Ashmore, as schools in Virginia reopened, desegregated.

In a way, he was right; this was the beginning of the end of power for those Southerners who said "Never" to any change. Some are still in power in Alabama and Mississippi and parts of other Deep South states, but after 1959 they were losing out. Little Rock too soon reopened its schools. In Georgia, the moderates began to organize *before* the schools closed. In Dallas, leading citizens planned the beginning of school desegregation before trouble could start. This pattern spread.

It should be clear, however, that the objectives of these moderate movements never went beyond controlling the mobs and allowing a handful of Negro youngsters into a few previously white schools.

Thus, there emerged in the South that phenomenon that for some reason none had foreseen a few years previously—tokenism. In late 1958, the Supreme Court handed down a decision that was little noticed at the time upholding the constitutionality of Alabama's so-called pupil-placement law. This law did not mention race but empowered school officials to assign pupils to certain schools according to a whole set of other criteria, including "psychological qualification." It became clear that this was a device by which tokenism could become institutionalized throughout the region; by the end of the decade fewer than one per cent of the South's Negro children were attending desegregated schools. Some indication of how completely the promise of 1954 had been debilitated came in 1961 when the peaceful entry of nine Negro high school students into four previously white schools in Atlanta—supposedly one of the South's enlightened cities—was considered a great victory. Compared with preceding years, it was, and few people remembered that desegregation had once been thought to mean an end to the dual school systems of the South.

Meantime, the forces that could bring real change were building up in Negro communities across the South, but usually they were still beneath the surface. At the end of the decade, the catalysts were still the individual heroes: the school children who pioneered, people like Amzie Morre and the Negro Catholic priest, Father John LaBauve, who quietly risked their lives to conduct voter registration classes in the Mississippi Delta, the lawyer who went to jail in North Carolina for defending his client before the voting registrar.

Beyond the individuals, new grass-roots organizations designed to seek full citizenship rights sprang up all over the South. In a few places, in the wake of Montgomery, these groups tried mass action. There were bus boycotts in Tallahassee, Florida, and in Rock Hill, South Carolina. In Birmingham, Alabama, known as the most rigidly segregated city of its size in North America and a city of terror for Negroes, the militant Negro minister, Fred Shuttles-worth, emerged as a leader and organized a mass movement. When Alabama outlawed the NAACP in 1956, he formed the Alabama Christian Movement for Human Rights to carry on in Birmingham. This group challenged segregation in the schools, parks, and public places, and in 1958 encouraged Negroes to "ride up front" on the buses. When the leaders were jailed, 3,000 Negroes massed in silent protest at the county courthouse.

In Tuskegee, Alabama, home of famed Tuskegee Institute, where there had long been a determined campaign for the right

78

to vote, Negroes took up the weapon of the boycott and withdrew their business from the town's stores when white leaders got the city's boundary lines redrawn to gerrymander the Negroes out. In 1959, on New Year's Day, Negroes in Virginia (and a few whites) marched 2,500 strong to the state capitol to protest massive resistance. In Burnsville, North Carolina, Negroes boycotted school rather than ride 40 miles on a bus to a segregated one. In Greenville, South Carolina, 600 Negroes marched in protest against segregation of airport facilities after Jackie Robinson was refused service there.

All these actions created tremors heard by those who wanted to hear, and a group of Negro ministers led by Martin Luther King, Fred Shuttlesworth, and Ralph Abernathy organized the Southern Christian Leadership Conference (SCLC) in 1957 in an effort to coordinate some of them and to stimulate more. For individuals who took part there was a new sense of strength. "It is a wonderful thing in the South to be able to walk the streets without fear . . . because you have discovered that you are an American citizen and you have taken a stand," said the Rev. David Brooks in 1957, describing his feelings after the Tallahassee bus boycott.

But for the most part, such actions were still on a small scale, involving relatively few people; much of the ferment was still hidden, and the 1950's ended without any other action that approached Montgomery in scope, size, and impact. It remained for a new generation in the South to pick up the weapon of mass direct action and carry it to a new level.

3

THE STUDENT REVOLT: 1960-61

It was the Negro student revolt of 1960 that turned the Southern civil rights movement into a Southwide mass movement.

The incident that triggered it was the now famous action of February 1, 1960, when four Negro college students in Greensboro, North Carolina, walked into a dime store, sat at a lunch counter, ordered coffee, were refused service—and continued to sit. From there the idea swept the South; by May there had been student demonstrations in at least 89 cities, including some in every Southern and border state. Hundreds sat at lunch counters; thousands marched in street demonstrations; hundreds went to jail. The Negro South was electrified, the white South was shocked—and the nation as a whole, still trapped in the silence, fear, and apathy of the 1950's, rubbed its eyes and realized that the democratic processes of protest, although rusty from disuse, were still available to those with the courage to use them.

Just as it is impossible to explain why the Montgomery bus protest started when and where it did, so there is no clearcut explanation for the timing and development of what became known as the sit-in movement. The sit-in technique was not new. It had been used since the early 1940's by the Congress of Racial Equality (CORE) in Northern cities. In the late 50's there were a few small CORE groups staging sit-ins around the edges of the South, in such border cities as Baltimore and St. Louis. In Oklahoma City in 1958, an NAACP youth group conducted a mass sit-in campaign that opened lunch counters there; this was widely publicized, but it did not spread.

Many people refused to believe that the sit-in movement growing from Greensboro was spontaneous, but it was, and nobody active in the civil rights movement would have predicted it. In fact, the constant lament among adult activists in that period was, "Where is the younger generation?"

The only explanation is that this generation, unbeknownst to

24

its elders, had simply—individually and collectively—had enough, and when somebody struck the right match at the right moment the social bomb went off. Some sociologists have theorized that it happened to this particular generation because they were just old enough to be aware of what the Supreme Court decision of 1954 should mean to them, and when after six years it had not meant anything, their frustrations broke into action. This was also a generation whose parents matured during the earlier ferment of the 1930's and the early 1940's. That generation never developed a full-blown revolt, but they raised their children in a different tradition. "My generation of parents," said one Negro leader in the mid-50's, "is not telling our children—as our parents told us—that they have to subject themselves to every whim of the white community." Also, some of the students who coalesced into a Southwide movement had been protesting as individuals for a long time. For example, John Lewis, later a leader of the new student movement, says that long before the sit-ins, he tried to integrate the library in his home town in Alabama. Virginius Thornton, another sit-in leader, had several years before organized Negro high school students to stay off a bus sent to take them to a segregated school.

81

When the students finally merged into a Southwide movement, they had no definite goals beyond the lunch counter, but everyone knew that this was only a symbol and the real objective was much larger. It is doubtful that any participant in the sit-in movement ever really thought the objective was a hamburger and a cup of coffee. "We want the world to know," said a mimeographed newsletter from a small college in North Carolina, "that we no longer accept the inferior position of second class citizenship. We are willing to go to jail, be ridiculed, spat upon and suffer physical violence to obtain first class citizenship." An Alabama student, arrested in a demonstration, told a reporter: "There are not enough jails to hold us. There are not enough roads for us to leave the state." When the students met in their first Southwide conference at Raleigh, North Carolina, on Easter weekend in 1960, one of them declared in a meeting: "This is the most significant gathering ever held in America since the Constitutional Convention." Students of history may feel that this was an exaggeration, but it was the way these students felt in 1960. They burned with a sense of mission and a sense of history.

It was partly because the breadth of their vision often seemed too big to put into words that this movement turned so much to song. Music became the movement's most effective means of communication; students learned old songs from the church and the labor movement, added their own words, and made up new songs.

25

Each jail cell produced its own verses. No other movement in our history, not even the early labor movement, has been such a singing movement as this one became.

An interesting aspect of the movement's music relates to Highlander Folk School, formerly in Monteagle, Tennessee, which the state of Tennessee was then in the process of destroying. It was from Highlander that the music of the Southern civil rights movement came. The song that later swept the nation, "We Shall Overcome," for example, was a Highlander song. It came originally from the Negro church, and was adapted by striking tobacco workers in South Carolina, who sang it on picket lines. Zilphia Horton, wife of Highlander director Myles Horton and a talented folk singer, learned it from the strikers in the early 1940's and brought it to Highlander, where she taught it to successive groups of visitors. One of these was Pete Seeger, the folk singer, and he began to sing it around the country. Guy Carawan, a young folk singer on the Highlander staff in 1960, taught it to the emerging student activists; they gave it new verses and soon it was the theme of demonstrations everywhere.

There is something symbolic about this development. By 1961, Tennessee had succeeded in closing Highlander and although it later opened a smaller center in Knoxville, its main building on the mountaintop at Monteagle was burned by vandals at night—as if someone wanted to erase its memory from the face of the earth. Yet by that time "We Shall Overcome" was on the lips of people across the nation and would four years later be quoted by a President addressing Congress. Here is some indication of the indestructible nature of the movement arising in the South and of the futility of the actions, even the worst actions, of those who were trying to hold back the dawn.

The defenders of the Old South were still at work in those early 1960's. Police were using tear gas to break up demonstrations. At some state colleges, teachers were fired and student demonstrators were expelled. Libel suits were filed against civil rights leaders (and against the *New York Times*) in Alabama. Many individuals were hurt by these attacks. Some became martyrs—like Clyde Kennard who was sent to jail for seven years on a trumped-up charge after he applied to enter a white college in Mississippi and later died of cancer when early symptoms were neglected in prison. But the movement as a whole pushed forward; in contrast to the 1950's when the segregationists held the initiative, it was now the civil rights forces that were on the offensive; and it was a time of victories.

Within six months after the sit-ins started, 28 cities had integrated their lunch counters; by the fall of 1960 the number had risen to almost 100, with protest movements active in at least 60 more. There were kneel-ins to integrate white churches, wade-ins at the swimming pools and beaches. By the spring of 1961, the sit-in movement finally reached Jackson, Mississippi—the first place where police dogs were used against demonstrators. More than 3,500 walked in a silent march to Nashville to protest the bombing of a civil rights attorney's home and forced a statement from the mayor on the City Hall steps supporting equal rights for all. Eight thousand gathered in mass meetings in Atlanta, and 2,000 students marched in the streets.

Years before, the Southern satiric writer Harry Golden made people laugh with his suggestion that since Southerners did not object to integration when people were standing up (as in supermarkets or on the street) desks should be taken out of schools and "vertical integration" initiated. No one thought then that it might ever happen, but sure enough—although not in schools—it began to happen after 1960; some lunch counters removed their stools and integrated. More often they integrated with everybody sitting down and many Southerners were startled to find the sky did not fall in at all; businessmen reported in surprised pleasure that their business went up instead of down. "I used to say this town was not ready for desegregation," said one Nashville white man, "but the sit-ins made it ready." A prominent white Southern attorney, Marion Wright, said: "Many people have said it takes time to change customs. They should look at the South now. In eight months' time we have completely altered the customs of our public eating facilities." It was a daily newspaper in North Carolina, and not a civil rights publication, that first in referring to the student sit-ins quoted Victor Hugo: "There is nothing so powerful in all the world as an idea whose time has come."

Permanent organizations coalesced around the student movements in some communities. One of the most remarkable was in Nashville, Tennessee, where entire student bodies participated, and where the first breakthrough on citywide integration of lunch counters occurred in May, 1960. The Nashville students developed a system of "group leadership" under the guidance of a young Negro minister, the Rev. James Lawson. Often they would meet all night until in the dawn hours they could reach unanimous "sense of the meeting" decisions. Because they were ready to go to jail and stay if necessary, they won the trust of the other students, so that when the time came for mass action the masses were there. Out of this Nashville group came many of the students who emerged as Southwide leaders later: the Rev. James Bevel, Diane Nash (later Mrs. James Bevel),

83

Bernard Lafayette, John Lewis, Marion Barry, Lester McKinnie, and others—and also the young ministers, C.T. Vivian and Kelly Miller Smith, who rose to leadership in the Southern Christian Leadership Conference.

Regionally, the lasting organization that came out of the sit-in movement, which probably changed the course of history in the South, was the Student Nonviolent Coordinating Committee (SNCC—pronounced SNICK). This organization was set up at the 1960 Easter conference in Raleigh, to which students from the various sit-in movements came. The Raleigh conference was called by SCLC when it became obvious that some sort of coordination of the sit-in movement was indicated. There were 142 Southern students present, with every Southern state and about 40 campuses represented. SCLC provided some speakers and workshop leaders; and the woman who was to become a kind of godmother, adviser, helper, and patron saint to SNCC, Miss Ella Baker, organized the conference as an SCLC staff member. But when the students gathered, they grabbed the reins for themselves, and it became apparent that they wanted their own independent organization. This became a position that they maintained with dogged determination, and under great counter-pressures.

Thus, with the development of mass movements around the sit-ins, the South now had four major civil rights organizations working to organize Southern Negroes: the NAACP, SCLC, CORE, and SNCC. These were in addition to the Southern Conference Educational Fund (SCEF) which had been working for many years to involve white people in the movement for equality.

The NAACP was the pioneer. Theoretically, the NAACP was a mass organization, with its basic support supposedly the $2-a-year membership. In practice it never really became that, and its work was usually carried on in each community by a select few. In the South, these few were an elite only in terms of courage, and they struggled against great odds to involve more people. But the principal thrusts of the organization were through the test cases in the courts, the demand for justice for an individual under attack, the fruitless but persistent push for national legislation, and the steady if largely unsuccessful effort to get Negroes registered to vote.

When direct action broke into the streets in 1960 and afterward, these methods looked very conservative to many people; and the NAACP, although still a devil in the eyes of segregationists, developed the reputation of being the most conservative of the civil rights groups.

In a region as large and varied as the South, it is risky to make generalizations, and in some communities it was the NAACP youth councils that led direct action campaigns. Southwide, however, after 1960, the conservative image of the NAACP became self-perpetuating and it tended to attract more conservative Negroes—those who wanted change but with as little fanfare as possible and who were not much concerned with involving many lower-income Negroes in the process. They concentrated on voter-registration campaigns and court action. Their preferred court action was in aggressive test cases battering down the legal walls of segregation, as in the repeated school cases. They were less interested in the defense of demonstrators who got arrested because they did not always approve of the demonstrations that brought on the arrests. But after SNCC began turning to the National Lawyers Guild for some of its legal work, and after SCLC began to set up its own legal defense foundation (the Gandhi Society), the NAACP Legal Defense and Educational Fund (a separate organization from the NAACP but its legal wing) took on the mass legal defense of both SNCC and SCLC demonstrators and became again the major legal arm of the Southern movement.

85

SCLC, as previously noted, was formed in 1957 under the leadership of Martin Luther King, Jr., and other Negro ministers. Its objective was to develop mass movements in Southern communities and make use of direct action; its channel of work was primarily the Negro church where much of the ferment of the period was brewing. It was not very successful at first in creating mass movements, but its ideas were circulating. One of the healthiest developments of the period was the seemingly spontaneous development of grass-roots social action organizations in Negro communities across the South. Many of these associated themselves with SCLC and some coordination developed.

SCLC's greatest weapon was King himself, for he had captured the imaginations of Negroes and could go into any Southern community, draw a crowd, and electrify it. The organization had no staff initially and depended on communication among the various militant minister-leaders. Then organizational foundations were laid by Dr. John Tilley and Miss Ella Baker, a former director of branches of the NAACP who had pioneered in organizing in the South. Later the Rev. Wyatt Tee Walker, a young Negro minister who had risen to leadership in the Virginia sit-in movement, came and applied both Madison Avenue techniques and a good bit of hard work to welding SCLC together. As civil rights action increased, the organization became more prominent and built a full-time staff.

Later it branched from direct action into voter registration, leadership training, and legislative action. But its main thrust remained mass direct action, and its greatest successes were mobilizations of entire communities in a way that attracted national attention.

CORE, like NAACP, was an old organization, but before 1960 a tiny one, concentrated almost entirely in the North. Its Southern work prior to the sit-ins was almost wholly in Nashville where it did a remarkably good job of encouraging Negroes to apply to the supposedly integrated schools; in South Carolina where it developed voter registration drives; in Miami where it began some direct action; and in the border city of St. Louis. After the Greensboro sit-ins, CORE grew rapidly. It knew more about sit-in techniques than any other organization, and had more calls for help than it could handle. It expanded its staff and sent organizers into the South. CORE chapters then sprang up in considerable numbers. These sought to lead mass movements, but the basic CORE organization was a relatively small group of well-trained individuals, dedicated to direct action. In the beginning CORE placed some stress on making its Southern groups interracial. Subsequently, it became less of a Southwide force and began to concentrate in the Deep South and in Negro communities, especially in voter registration in North Florida, parts of Mississippi, and Louisiana.

Another organization which is often mentioned nationally as a "major" civil rights group is the Urban League. Chapters of the Urban League have long existed in the South. When the segregationists were on the offensive in the 1950's the Urban League came under vicious attack along with all other groups identified with the Negro cause. However, among people in the movement, the Urban League was not thought of as a real civil rights organization. Its original purpose, as its name suggests, was to help rural Negroes adjust to urban life. Its specialized effort was to open up job opportunities to Negroes, mainly through quiet negotiations. Sometimes the Urban League worked in the background in cooperation with more public campaigns sponsored by more militant groups, but it was not in the main current of Southern revolt.

If there was any one single factor that shaped Southern history in the early 1960's, it was the unexpected turn that SNCC took. For SNCC attracted the young, the unencumbered, the daring, the image-breakers and the pioneers; and they became the catalysts as only the young can be. The important turning point came when SNCC looked away from the campus and into the community.

For its first year and a half, SNCC was exactly what its name implied—a coordinating committee. After the Raleigh conference

86

it set up a tiny cubbyhole office on Auburn Avenue in Atlanta and had one full-time, although rarely paid, employee. The center of SNCC was an actual coordinating committee with representatives from each Southern state, who met approximately once a month between April, 1960, and the summer of 1961.

By the spring of 1961, most Negro campuses were quiet. In some places, lunch counter victories had been won. In others, movements had been crushed by expulsions of students and firings of sympathetic faculty. Everywhere there was a realization that those who continued in the movement would have to take on bigger issues than lunch counters and that the next stages of struggle would be harder. "The glamorous stage is over," said one student at the SNCC conference in late 1960. "From now on, the need is for people willing to suffer."

87

The Rev. James Lawson was a main speaker and a key influence at that conference. Lawson was a pacifist who had been to India and studied Gandhi's methods. During the 1950's he worked in the South for the Fellowship of Reconciliation and traveled about the region seeking to bring small groups of whites and Negroes together to act. Later he decided that this kind of activity was not the key to social change, and turned instead to the organization of Negro mass movements for direct action—in which his efforts coincided with the rise of the student sit-in movement.

Lawson constantly urged the students to define deeper issues and long-range goals beyond the lunch counter; he advocated what he called "nonviolent revolution" to revamp the entire society. One tactic he advocated was filling the jails and refusing to make bond. This had been talked about from the beginning of the sit-ins but rarely practiced for long, as older Negro leaders and parents, feeling that it was not quite respectable for the college youngsters to be in jail, raised bail by the thousands of dollars and got them released. Lawson himself had reluctantly agreed to make bond after his arrest in the Nashville sit-ins when white faculty members at Vanderbilt University where he was a graduate student came to the jail with the bond money. "I left jail," he said at the time, "because the approach of the Divinity School faculty marked the first time the white community had come to the Negro's help in the sit-in. For me, it was symbolic."

Later, Lawson apparently felt a greater imperative had been sacrificed and at the 1960 fall SNCC conference he said in his speech:

We lost the finest hour of this movement when so many hundreds of us left the jails across the South. Instead of letting the adults scurry around getting bail, we should have insisted that they scurry about to end the system which had put us in jail. If history offers us such an opportunity again, let us be prepared to seize it.

History never has—not for the student movement as such. In the late winter of the school year 1960-1961, there were some efforts at a jail-instead-of-bail movement on Southern campuses, and at one point there were in various towns as many as 100 students serving sentences instead of appealing. But the student movement, as a campus uprising, had by then passed its peak, and still in the spring of 1965 no campus-based movement comparable to 1960 has yet appeared again in the South.

What happened by the spring of 1961 was that a group of students connected with SNCC emerged from the sit-in movement with the realization that efforts to change the South must, for them, be a serious adult commitment. There were only a handful of them, but within four years they were to become the core of a new army of young people who would not only invade the Deep South but the ghettos of the North and the poverty-stricken areas of Appalachia. By 1965 this army had grown to such proportions that the federal government devised a domestic peace corps (VISTA) and developed semi-official governmental groups such as the Appalachian Volunteers in obvious efforts to absorb the energies of youth looking for something meaningful to do with their lives. People in control of society would prefer that youthful energies go into efforts more easily controlled by the power structure and therefore not likely to challenge the present control.

It was February, 1961, when the first group of SNCC pioneers experimented with the concept of going beyond their own community to challenge segregation. Students were arrested at Rock Hill, South Carolina, for attempting to integrate lunch counters. They chose jail instead of bail and served out 30-day sentences. Meantime, four SNCC leaders from elsewhere went to Rock Hill, demonstrated, were arrested and joined the local students in jail, and then sent out a call to other students across the South to join them there. The four were part of the vanguard who would become full-time crusaders later—Charles Jones of Charlotte, North Carolina, Charles Sherrod of Richmond, Virginia, Diane Nash of Nashville, and Ruby Doris Smith of Atlanta. Their call for other students failed, but the idea of the traveling challenger of segregation and the technique of concentrating many people from many places at one point of challenge was to become important in the Southern movement later.

88

Meantime, in May, CORE launched its Freedom Ride—a pilgrimage of whites and Negroes riding Southward from Washington, D.C., bound for New Orleans, planning to integrate bus station facilities all along the way. The ride was relatively uneventful until it reached Alabama. Then a bus was burned in Anniston and the riders were attacked by mobs there and in Birmingham; and yet another phase of the Southern struggle was underway.

The original riders, many beaten and bloody, abandoned the ride at Birmingham, but the Nashville student group picked it up, rode a bus on to Montgomery where they were beaten by a mob; from there riders proceeded on to Jackson, Mississippi, where they were quietly and efficiently arrested. Throughout that summer Freedom Riders continued to roll South—all of them destined for the jails of Jackson and Mississippi's Parchman State Prison. By the end of August, more than 300 had come, three-fourths from the North, about half students, and over half of them white. Most got sentences that would amount to six months if fines were not paid, and most stayed in jail for 40 days, the deadline to appeal convictions.

89

The Freedom Rides were a good illustration of the symbolic nature of the Southern struggle. This was pointed up by a Southern journalist who commented on the difficulties he and other newspapermen had in trying to explain the Freedom Rides on a program recorded for overseas broadcast by the Voice of America. "We had to try to explain, among other things," he said, "how some of those white people who joined the mob that beat the Freedom Riders at the Montgomery Greyhound station rode on integrated city buses to get there. We were not at our most lucid best."

Other newspapermen pointed out in their reports that the Greyhound station in Montgomery had actually been integrated quietly several weeks before the Freedom Riders arrived—by a small group of Negroes who came without fanfare from another Alabama city.

Some Southern white liberals wrung their hands and wondered wistfully why the Freedom Riders had to be so flamboyant in their assault on the segregated waiting rooms.

"I'm no gradualist," one said. "I know somebody has to challenge these things. I don't say there shouldn't be an organized campaign to integrate the bus stations. But why all the advance publicity? That's what stirs people up. Most of the terminals in the South could be integrated if it were just done quietly."

He was probably right. Those white men the journalist found it hard to explain to people abroad—the ones who rode the integrated Montgomery buses to get to the Greyhound station and beat the

Freedom Riders—very likely did not consider it a life-and-death matter whether Negroes sat in the "white" waiting room of that station. But they had been aroused to rage by the advance newspaper stories saying the Freedom Riders were coming and their rage resulted from an instinctive knowledge that much more was at stake than seats in a bus station.

The Freedom Riders knew it too, and that, rather than any desire for publicity for its own sake, is why they had to do what they did with flamboyance and publicity and would not, if they could, settle for the quiet one-by-one integration of the South's bus stations. The bus station was the symbol, and the real stakes were much higher: equality, human dignity, a place in the sun. The mobs knew it, and the police in Jackson knew it, and the Freedom Riders knew it. And that is why they all responded as they did—those who felt threatened by the drive for equality reacting in fear and hatred, those identifying with the movement for freedom reacting with a willingness to risk their lives for seats in Southern bus stations.

Finally in the fall, the Interstate Commerce Commission ruled that all bus and train stations must integrate. Thus, although compliance was not immediately complete, the Freedom Riders won their specific objective.

In their broader symbolic significance, they did a good many other things too. They widened the Southern struggle into the national arena, for the first time giving Northerners something direct they could do in the South. They also brought encouragement to thousands of Southern Negroes, and the term Freedom Rider became legendary; even today many a Negro sharecropper in remote areas of the South refers to all civil rights workers as Freedom Riders. The rides also introduced and popularized a new concept which became proverbial in the movement: "Put your body into the struggle." That concept was one factor that helped propel those searching SNCC students from the campus into the community.

They were further propelled, although indirectly, by forces in the national power structure which the Freedom Riders unintentionally set in motion.

4

MOBILIZATION AT THE GRASS ROOTS: 1961-62

Early in that summer of 1961, a group of SNCC leaders went to Jackson, Mississippi, and began to organize support there for the Freedom Rides. They met with some success, and a Jackson student movement began.

More important, the experience crystallized a dream some key young leaders had developed over the previous year: if they were going to change the South, they could not remain just a student movement; they had to organize the communities.

Actually, the very existence of the student movement since 1960 helped stimulate action by all age groups. In West Tennessee, a militant voter-registration movement grew under the adult leadership of John McFerren; when sharecroppers who had registered to vote were evicted by their landlords, they attracted national support by setting up a "tent city" in which to live. In Hopewell, Virginia, and in other communities in that state, direct-action movements cut across age lines. In some communities older Negro leaders saw the student uprising as a threat, but others looked eagerly to it for help.

The other important thing that happened in that summer of 1961 was that powerful people, from the White House down, got very much worried about the "bad image" the disorders surrounding the Freedom Rides were creating for this nation abroad. They were eager to get the movement "out of the streets" and into other arenas. Also, the Kennedy administration was much interested in registering Southern Negroes to vote; Negro voter registration in the South was 1.3 million out of a potential 5 million. Whether the Kennedys were interested because of moral concern or the belief that registered Negroes would vote for Kennedys is not important. The important thing is that they were willing to do something about it. Attorney General Robert Kennedy pointed out that this was one area where the federal government had laws to use; both the 1957 and 1960 Civil Rights Acts were supposed to protect voting rights. He urged

the young people—and other civil rights organizations—to concentrate on a gigantic registration campaign in the South.

Simultaneously, and openly related to the Kennedy effort to
steer the movement into voter registration, civil rights groups were
approached by private foundations offering to give large amounts
of money for registration drives. To many in SNCC, this was the
opportunity they had been looking for—now there would be money,
they thought, so they could work full time. There were also rumors—
never confirmed officially—that young people working in voter
registration would get deferment from the military draft.

"We've been saying we want to give ourselves to the struggle,"
said one Negro student. "Now the way is open. The only question
is, are we willing to give our bodies to it?"

For some in SNCC it did not seem that simple, and the organization was almost torn apart by the resulting debate. Students
who had been deeply involved in direct action felt that voter
registration was a tame operation and a draining of their energies
into ineffective channels. Nashville students noted that Negroes there
had had the vote for a long time—but that nothing changed until
thousands marched in the streets. After their lunch counter victory,
they tried a registration drive but found students remarkably un-
interested.

The other group in SNCC—the pro-registration people—argued
that it was only through the vote that real changes could come.
"This is a matter of power," one of them said. "It doesn't matter
how many lunch counters you integrate—until you get political
power things don't change." Besides, these advocates argued, in the
Deep South areas—where terror awaited the Negro who tried to
register—voter registration would actually be direct action.

The argument was never really settled that summer, but SNCC
managed to hold together by dividing into two wings—the voter-
registration wing and the direct-action wing. This turned out to be
temporary, because as the work moved into the Deep South those
who had said that voter registration and direct action were one
and the same proved right—and the lines between the two blurred.
Meantime, the important thing was that the offer of financial support had propelled a group of dedicated young people into the Deep
South to organize. Jim Forman, the Mississippi-born Chicago teacher who came South to write and found that history pushed him into
the administrative job of executive secretary of SNCC, summed it
up this way later: "Sixteen cats in 1961 decided it would be good
if a small group devoted itself full time to the movement." And that
was the beginning.

92

The first venture of students into community organizing was abortive. It was in the late summer of 1961 in Monroe, North Carolina. This was not a SNCC project—but it involved some students who were already or would later be a part of SNCC.

Monroe is a small town in southwestern North Carolina where Robert Williams, a militant young Negro, was a leader. Williams had fallen into disfavor with national civil rights leaders when, after seeing two white men freed by the courts after vicious attacks on Negroes, he suggested that Negroes must protect themselves by "meeting violence with violence." This statement was widely publicized and upset many people, including some who made no claims to being advocates of nonviolence but said Williams should not have said such a thing publicly. This, along with other militant positions he had taken (such as embarrassing the United States by publicizing North Carolina injustice overseas) caused the more respectable civil rights organizations to tag him as "uncontrollable." Once he was cast into outer darkness by these groups he found it harder and harder to get even meager police protection. Thus, in 1961 when the Freedom Riders at least had some protection from federal marshals after a nationwide protest demanded it, pickets attacked by hoodlums at an all-white swimming pool in Monroe, were still ignored by local, state and federal agencies.

Some young Freedom Riders were disturbed by this and decided to go to Monroe and try to help. They also wanted to try their hand at community mobilization.

It didn't work. When they set up a picketing operation, they were attacked by white mobs. Police looked the other way, and several people almost got killed. Robert Williams and other Monroe Negroes, along with some of the students, were charged with kidnapping a white couple, and Williams fled Monroe to keep from being murdered. The kidnapping case was obviously a frame-up. Williams left the country, convinced that he would be killed if he stayed to face trial. The other four defendants received prison sentences ranging up to 20 years. A higher court reversed their convictions in early 1965 on grounds of racial discrimination in jury selection, but Monroe officials got new indictments against them in May.

Since 1961, thousands of words have been written about Monroe. Believers in nonviolence have used it to prove that violence does not work, and opponents of the nonviolent theory have used it to prove that nonviolence won't work. Actually it proves that a group of young people with admirable intentions but with little experience

93

and little planning run into problems when they rush into such a community.

Jim Forman, who was one of them and who later became one of the most skilled community organizers in the South, said immediately after the Monroe fiasco:

We were hoping a pattern could be set whereby teams of 10 or 12 young people could spend their summers in Southern rural communities, attempting to develop nonviolent movements for justice. . . . The movement has succeeded at the lunch counters in the cities. But what about the Negro in the small town who does not have the money to go to the lunch counter? We hoped to offer an answer to the economic problems of lower class Negroes.

94

This approach became a guideline as SNCC moved into Deep South communities, and the failure at Monroe no doubt became an ingredient of the more soundly organized campaigns later.

The first thing decided by those "16 cats" who determined to "put their bodies into the struggle" was that they would concentrate in Deep South rural areas. These sections still dominated the politics of the South. They were also the toughest areas, where people were the most oppressed.

They decided to concentrate first on, of all places, Mississippi— the state generally considered the worst. This was partly because that is where student organizers, following the Freedom Riders, had made some beginnings. It was also because the young New York school teacher, Bob Moses, was already laying groundwork there.

It may be significant that Moses developed his dream of grass roots political organization in Mississippi without regard to the overtures from foundations and the federal government in that summer of 1961. He first came South in the summer of 1960 and toured Mississippi to recruit students for the second SNCC conference. There he studied what he saw and began to think, and there he met Amzie Moore and began to dream about what might happen if Negroes could vote in that state where they were 42 percent of the population but where only 5 percent of voting-age Negroes were registered. Moses went back to New York that winter, but in the summer of 1961 returned to stay. Actually, he took virtually no part in the debate raging among SNCC people that summer; while the others were talking, he was quietly working in Mississippi: contacting people, finding places for civil rights workers to live, looking for meeting places.

This relates to the other important decision SNCC made at that time: that if people were going to organize an area they must move into it, and become a part of it. This they did—first that initial group, later many more—into small towns, country villages, onto back roads, first in Mississippi but soon also in Southwest Georgia, Black Belt Alabama and rural Arkansas. The money promised by big foundations didn't begin to come through until the following year because there were complications about channels for it. But the young people learned to live some way—seemingly on air and dedication. Often local families took them in, and they picked squash or chopped cotton for their keep. Many times they went hungry. One of the early student organizers in Mississippi made it a habit to eat just once a day—about 2 a.m. before he finally went to bed, because, he said, he didn't like to "go to bed hungry."

95

Under the impact of this operation, over the next year and a half a complete metamorphosis took place in SNCC. The early sit-in leaders were not, by and large, middle-class in origin, as some observers claimed; most well-to-do Southern Negroes sent their sons and daughters East to college or to the very few prestige Negro institutions in the South. But the early movement *was* middle-class in its aspirations. Many of the leaders came from rural cabins or city slum streets, but hard-working parents had saved to send them to college and they were on their way up. When they spoke of civil rights, they usually meant the right to get rich with the white man's son and move into the suburban split-level house. The symbol of that early sit-in movement—as widely depicted in photograph and cartoon—was a well-dressed young man, in suit and tie, seated in dignity at a lunch counter. Middle-class white Southerners, contrasting this picture with the white hoodlums who were dropping lighted cigarettes down the students' backs, breathed a sigh of relief and decided that perhaps Negroes, after all, were nice and respectable like themselves.

Three years later, at the 1963 SNCC spring conference, most of the organization's active workers showed up in overalls. The change in dress was no prank. The overalls had become the uniform of the youth movement. It was the students' way of saying that their identification was with the great majority of the South's Negroes who are desperately poor.

"I used to think the thing to do was work hard and get ahead," explained one student. "Now I know I can't be really free until all Negroes are free."

With the change in dress and identification came a change in goals too. All through SNCC there was less talk about lunch counters and more talk about the freedom to have a decent job and enough money to feed a family. The young organizers were reflecting the drives of the poor in the communities where they were working. They had walked the dirt roads of Mississippi, had seen the children hungry and the mothers cutting up the living room furniture for firewood; and integrated lunch counters came to seem less and less important.

There were also other influences prodding the movement beyond the lunch counter. Some were in SCLC. It too turned more toward the Deep South areas where the struggle promised to be sharpest. At the 1961 SCLC fall conference, the Rev. Jim Lawson spelled out his idea of "nonviolent revolution":

> It would be well to recognize that we are merely in the prelude to revolution, the beginning, not the end, not even the middle. . . . We have been receiving concessions, not real changes. . . . We must sweep away the tyranny of centuries, even institutions away. . . . While we recognize segregation as harmful to the whole nation and the South, we rarely blame this on the system and the structure of our institutions. . . . But if after over 300 years, segregation (slavery) is still a basic pattern rather than a peripheral custom, should we not question the "American way of life" which allows segregation so much structural support? . . . The economy of the South encourages segregation—with cheap labor, keeping certain groups of Negroes and whites pawns of the financial interests, using race hate to stop unions.

As a method of attack, Lawson proposed the formation of a "nonviolent army" of from 2,000 to 8,000 volunteers for "mass nonviolent action in the Deep South."

> Let us recruit people who will be willing to go at a given moment and stay in jail indefinitely. . . . The Freedom Rides were a start at this, but they involved too many people for a court test and too few for a jail-in. Imagine what would happen if in the next 12 months we had such an army ready. A campaign with such an army would cause world-wide crisis, on a scale unknown in the Western world except for actual war; not even a Berlin crisis could be used as an excuse for America to escape its cancer at home.

Lawson noted that young Americans give a year or more of their lives to service in a "violent army," and asked why they should not be willing to give similar time in a "nonviolent army" for a revolution at home.

The SCLC endorsed Lawson's proposals nominally in 1961, but only a few people made serious efforts to implement them and the army never materialized as he proposed it. However, something similar began to develop, without this name, in the various actions in Albany (Georgia), Birmingham, and Selma in 1965.

Another SCLC thrust beginning in 1961 was an effort to develop grass roots leadership through citizenship training. This was initiated among the unlettered people on the Sea Islands off the coast of South Carolina by Mrs. Septima Clark. Because she refused to resign from the NAACP, Mrs. Clark lost her job as public school teacher and became director of education at Highlander Folk School from which she extended the citizenship education program to other parts of the South. After Highlander closed, SCLC took over the program.

Under this program, people with leadership potential were trained to be teachers of others in their home communities. They learned techniques of teaching the unlettered to read and write. They also learned to teach the rudiments of government and the democratic process. What resulted was a literacy program, but unlike some approaches, this was literacy with a purpose. It was always clear to everyone that the basic objective was to encourage Negroes to vote and to take control of their government. Mrs. Dorothy Cotton, one of the program leaders, has noted that people who have a reason to learn do so very quickly; thousands of people learned to read and write in the citizenship classes.

97

The Rev. Andrew Young, another SCLC leader, said the ultimate purpose of the program was to make the Southern movement a true mass movement. "It must be that," he said in a report to an SCLC convention, "not only in numbers but because it is a movement of the common man. It is the grass-roots people who can bring change."

He maintains that there is great hidden talent in those grass roots. "You have to know the Negroes in the South to understand it," he said. "You meet a man who never went beyond the second grade and he's spent all his life in a cotton patch. But you talk to him and you realize that he's got a Ph.D. mind."

That was the job of the citizenship program, Young said— "to comb the South for those Ph.D. minds that have been wasted in the cotton patches."

Despite these various thrusts from civil rights groups, there was no immediate response from the silent masses of Southern Negroes. SNCC organizers going into the rural Black Belt communities at first found local Negroes crossing the street to avoid them. The young organizers were no "outside agitators" either; sometimes they were Negroes from nearby counties. But they were identified with the movement—they were "freedom riders," as they were indiscriminately called. So they were dangerous. To local Negroes, association with movement people meant likely loss of job and possible death. SNCC organizers in Mississippi once escaped through a back window of their Greenwood office as a lynch mob approached on the other side. In Southwest Georgia, a woman who taught SCLC citizenship schools and took in SNCC workers had shots fired into her home. The same thing happened in Delta homes. In Amite County in Southwest Mississippi, Herbert Lee, a farmer who worked with Bob Moses, was shot and killed in 1961—and in 1964 a man who witnessed his murder, Louis Allen, was also killed. And so it went.

There were reasons other than fear for the lack of response. As one SNCC worker in Southwest Georgia put it: "People have such a struggle just to live. When you work in the cotton fields all day and come home to eat nothing but pork and beans—and get ready for another day—it's hard to even think about registering."

But gradually, despite the danger and the seeming hopelessness of their lives, people took a stand. Some were young—like 16-year-old Brenda Travis who led student sit-ins in McComb, Mississippi, and went to reform school for it; some were old like Mrs. Annie Raines, 68, of Lee County, Georgia, a practical nurse who had delivered 1,000 babies in her community, both white and black, and serenely watched her former patients turn on her as she exchanged paternalism for democracy and joined the movement. Each in his or her own way, made some inner decision—like that of Brenda Travis who describes her feelings when she decided to join the NAACP; how she set out walking to the home of the local president and wouldn't let herself stop, saying inwardly, "I'm going to rule myself; I'm not going to be afraid."

Sometimes the new leaders emerged under dramatic circumstances, from what had seemed to be a paralyzed Negro community. For example, the first mass breakthrough in Mississippi came in the spring of 1963 in Greenwood, after the arrest of one young Negro SNCC worker, the near-fatal shooting of another, and a decision by county officials to cut off the surplus-food program, on which many Negroes depend for survival in the winter. Until then, SNCC had been unable to reach many people. All of a sudden now, they began to come in from the countryside; hundreds marched to the courthouse to try to register. It was the movement's first mass confrontation in a rural area of the Deep South. One factor in the breakthrough was that SNCC was able to organize campaigns over the country to send in food and clothing quickly after the government food was cut off. Thus Mississippi Negroes knew that they were not alone, not totally dependent on the toleration of local white men. Again the police state could not be broken entirely from within.

In contrast to this dramatic situation, sometimes new movements developed very quietly. For example, in Perry County, Alabama, where Marion is located, when civil rights organizers came in 1964 they found a solid organization that had been working for several years. These people had heard what was going on elsewhere and had caught the spirit.

Thus there spread over the Deep South a new layer of leadership. Most had not been the traditional "Negro leaders" in their areas. A few were middle-class, but more often they were poor, for dangers were great and only those with little to lose were attracted. Even when they were ministers, which might sound professional and middle-class elsewhere, they were often men who preached for virtually nothing on Sundays and during the week worked wherever they could in order to live.

One important pattern developed as the student movement sent full-time organizers into communities: wherever they went, and no matter how much they talked about voter registration, direct action spread in their wake. That was not, except perhaps in isolated cases, because the students were seeking voter registrants with one hand and organizing sit-ins with the other. Usually the direct action was spontaneous. The very presence of young organizers aroused some people in the community, usually first the young people. Once aroused, they were often remarkably disinterested in the vote. It was the familiar pattern: what was wrong seemed too big to tackle any other way, so they assaulted symbols. And they often risked their lives and certainly their immediate freedom to sit at lunch counters where they had no real desire to eat, because this was visible, this was oppression, this was something the individual could reach. This pattern developed, for example, in McComb, Mississippi, where SNCC workers first concentrated when they entered Mississippi. They went to register voters, but Brenda Travis and others walked downtown not to the registration office (they were too young anyway and their elders weren't going) but to sit in at a drugstore.

The first mass movement that followed the student move into the communities was in Albany, Georgia, and it was sparked by assaults on lunch counters and bus and train stations. SNCC organizers moved into Albany, a town of 58,000 population, 40 percent Negro, in Southwest Georgia, in the fall of 1961; they planned to make the city a base for work on voter registration throughout the rural Black Belt counties surrounding it. A group of young people were arrested for trying to use the white-only bus and train waiting rooms. There were protest marches, more arrests; Martin Luther King, Jr., was invited to come in and speak and help; he got ar-

99

rested and because of his national news value the campaign was soon on front pages over the nation. Albany became a concentration point for both SNCC and SCLC staff workers; arrests soared to over 1,100.

There were three phases to the Albany direct action drive: first, the actions of late 1961; second, an uneasy truce through the late winter and spring; and finally, another big flare-up of mass marches and mass jail-ins in the summer of 1962.

Albany was an important peak in the Southern civil rights drive because it was the first time since Montgomery that an entire Negro community had mobilized. The movement cut across all age and class lines. Even the local police chief told the city's white people that they must face the fact that the Albany Movement (as the civil rights coalition was called) represented the entire Negro community.

Southern Negro leaders said the Albany Movement was an advance over the Montgomery movement of six years before because, whereas Montgomery had been a mass withdrawal (in that Negroes stayed off the buses), Albany was an aggressive movement in which Negroes used mass marches, demonstrations, etc., to take the offensive against segregation. Furthermore, whereas Montgomery had focused on a single indignity, Albany was an assault on the total pattern of segregation.

But by the fall of 1962, direct action in Albany died away, with no clear-cut victory. The movement's main leverage was the power of masses of people staying in jail, and as one SCLC staff member later said, it just ran out of people to go to jail. Jail-staying was still a new concept in the movement, and for adults it means probable loss of jobs and income and a complete change in one's economic and personal situation, perhaps for a lifetime. Short of a truly revolutionary situation, there will always be a limit on the number of people willing to go that far. The Albany Movement did not end in that fall of 1962, but it began to channel its energies into voter registration, and it was no longer a point of national focus.

Significantly, the registration drives burgeoned after the direct action campaign as they have often done in such circumstances; people who get out in the streets and become directly involved in attacks on the deplorable conditions of their lives begin to sense a power, and they begin to grasp for other weapons, one of which is the vote. This laid the basis for future political action in Albany, and Negroes began to run for office there. But the over-riding fact to many people at the time was that after all the suffering, jails, and physical brutality against Movement people, the direct action

100

campaign ended and not one thing in Albany was desegregated except the bus station, which opened up after the Interstate Commerce Commission order.

Key leaders in Albany, however, firmly maintained then that Albany was not a failure—and they still take that position. To understand this point of view, it is necessary to realize that one of the first purposes of recent action in the South has been to spark change within the Negro himself. This has nothing in common with the so-called "improvement" plans of white liberals who suggest that Negroes should get educated and otherwise overcome the disabilities imposed by segregation before they demand an end to segregation. Rather it is a recognition on the part of emancipated Negroes that there are many Negroes, especially in the Deep South, who have never realized that it is possible to say "no" to oppression, a recognition that oppression creates an inner degradation and that its victims unconsciously accept the proposition that there is no way out.

101

Negro leaders of the Albany Movement maintained that the campaigns there in 1961 and 1962 forever broke those inner chains. Never again, they held, would Negroes in Albany bow down before an oppressor. The Rev. Wyatt Tee Walker, then aide to Martin Luther King, said the direct action movement was doing what the Emancipation Proclamation of 1863 did not—"freeing the Negro's soul." It was the difference, Walker said, between having something done for you and finding you can do it yourself. Jim Forman, by then executive secretary of SNCC, put it another way. Describing Albany in the fall of 1962, he said: "Victory has been won when people recognize the power they have in their own hands when they are organized."

By 1965, there was again great restlessness and frustration in the Albany Negro community. By then, ironically, the basic demands of the 1961-1962 movement had been won. Public accommodations desegregated in response to the 1964 Civil Rights Act—which the Albany Movement certainly had a part in achieving. The schools desegregated—in a token fashion, of course—in response to a court order which would never have been obeyed without the challenge of the Albany mass movement two years before. The Negroes of Albany finally got what they had demonstrated for in 1961-1962, although late. Whether what they were demonstrating for was all they really wanted is an entirely different question.

Meantime, the national spotlight moved away from Albany late in 1962. All through this period there was never any real quiet in the South; there were repeated upsurges in widely scattered communities: student demonstrations in Talladega, Alabama, finally broken by court injunction; a student drive in Baton Rouge, Louisiana, broken by expulsions from a Negro college and mass arrests; sit-ins in Huntsville, Alabama, by all ages including mothers with children; sleep-ins in Nashville hotel lobbies; picketing at Edenton in North Carolina's Black Belt; new demonstrations in Tallahassee, Florida; and then the next national focus of the Southern movement in the Birmingham demonstrations in the spring of 1963.

Birmingham was essentially an SCLC operation. The foundation had been laid by Rev. Fred L. Shuttlesworth and his Alabama Christian Movement for Human Rights. Shuttlesworth had built a mass movement involving hundreds and, at some crucial points, thousands; contrary to some distorted reports these were poor Negroes, not middle class and professional people, most of whom stayed aloof from the movement until it grew to national proportions. For more than a year, Shuttlesworth and other Birmingham leaders urged Martin Luther King and SCLC to come into Birmingham and turn a national spotlight on that city. Birmingham was known as the most rigidly segregated city in the world outside of Johannesburg, South Africa. Furthermore its police had a reputation for brutality. Shuttlesworth was convinced that Birmingham would never change without massive pressure from the outside, as well as from the inside. Furthermore, he was convinced that once the pattern of segregation cracked in Birmingham the beginning of the end was near for the entire South.

Never did an analysis prove more surely a prophecy. Birmingham was a turning point in the Southern struggle; it eventually changed the face of the South and awakened the nation. This does not mean that everything is perfect in Birmingham today. But the movement eventually got what it asked for there too. Whether it asked for all it really wanted is, as with Albany, another question.

The immediate objectives of the Birmingham campaign were a beginning on desegregation of public accommodations and a beginning on opening up job opportunities. As at Albany, thousands joined the movement and went to jail. Birmingham did not run out of people to go to jail before the nation was fully aroused. This was partly because the children of Birmingham became involved. That got SCLC and King much criticism, but usually the critics were white people who had never known, or conservative Negro adults who had forgotten, what it is like to be a Negro child—how early he knows that he is in a prison without bars and what it does to his personality *not* to protest. An eloquent defense of the involvement of children was published by a Negro newspaper at the time. The reporter described a six-year-old Negro boy in Birmingham, what

102

his life was like, and his inability to do anything about it. Then, the writer noted, the movement came and he could do something about it and King came and the world knew. "They said Martin Luther King was using that little boy," the report concluded. "The truth is that he was using Martin Luther King."

One thing that helped make the Birmingham campaign different from Albany was the nature of the opposition. In Albany the police chief worked hard to maintain a humane image, convincing many people that he was only doing what was necessary to maintain law and order. He maintained law and order all right, but as historian Howard Zinn noted in a major report, he did it by arresting every man, woman, and child who disagreed with him and by running the town with "the quiet efficiency of a police state." In Birmingham, the police commissioner was still Bull Connor who had been breaking up integrated meetings since the 1930's. He brought out the police dogs, clubs, and fire hoses. The nation and the world were shocked—and moved to action.

103

"We drew the poison of the Birmingham police yesterday," said Shuttlesworth, obviously triumphant, on the day after he himself was almost killed on a Birmingham street. People who don't understand the direct action movement interpret that remark to mean that this movement wants to provoke violence, but this is not the point. What it wants to do is to draw to the surface the underlying violence that strikes in darkness, to bring it out where the world can see. For decades Birmingham police had been invading Negro homes, brutalizing Negroes, and sometimes killing them—all under cover of darkness, unknown to the world. Only when they began to do it openly was there hope of change.

Another thing that made Birmingham a turning point was one of those unexplainable phenomena—as with Rosa Parks' action and the Greensboro sit-in. In a way that defies a completely rational explanation, sparks flew from the Birmingham demonstrations that ignited the South. No state remained untouched. In a single month, there was mass direct action in at least 30 cities. Some surveys placed the figure at 100 communities for that entire hot summer of 1963. For the first time, mass direct action against segregation was spreading into the North too.

In the South, the period was comparable to those early months of the 1960 sit-ins—when demonstrations leaped from city to city and the whole South seemed on fire. But there were important differences from 1960. Whereas then it had been mostly students, now the movement cut across age lines. And whereas then the demand had been lunch counters, it was now what came to be called an "open city"—that is, desegregation of all public accommodations. There was more talk too of jobs without discrimination.

The 1960 sit-in movement reached sufficient proportions to force both major parties to put the strongest civil rights planks ever into their platforms. The 1963 upsurge awakened the nation to the fact that it had to face some major changes. The young people in the Southern movement had long called their work a "revolution." Now this word found its way into the most respectable publications in the country. President John Kennedy, who earlier in 1963 told Negro leaders he would not propose any new civil rights legislation that year, sent to Congress the strongest civil rights bill yet proposed in this country—including a ban on segregation in public accommodations.

104

The great accomplishment of the summer of 1963 was that by the end of it the struggle for desegregation of public accommodations was essentially won. Some people don't mark up the victory until the following summer when the new civil rights bill was finally passed by Congress. But this was simply a writing into law of a victory that was already a fact. In the wake of the 1963 demonstrations, at least 79 cities instituted some desegregation. Later some people expressed amazement at the widespread compliance with the 1964 law, even in the Deep South. This too reflected the effect of the demonstrations that had gone before. As that white man in Nashville had said in 1960: "This town was not ready for desegregation before, but the sit-ins made it ready." There was also compliance in 1964 from some cities where there had been no demonstrations, as officials sought to avoid turmoil; but the most complete desegregation—with fewer evasive tactics like exorbitant prices to Negroes or conversion to private clubs—was in those communities where there was an active freedom movement. The struggle to open public accommodations was won in the streets, including the biggest street demonstration of them all in Washington in August, 1963, which insured that the victory would be written into law.

Much of the ferment of the nation came to a focus in that giant March on Washington which united 250,000 people from across the country. It was an historic outpouring on the part of many, many determined people, and it said once and for all that this nation could not ignore its oppression of the Negro.

Yet all was not well for the freedom movement on that day when thousands marched in Washington. The storms beneath the surface came into view when it became known that some of the more conservative leaders of the march had threatened to withdraw unless John Lewis, chairman of SNCC, altered his speech.

Lewis agreed to do so in the interest of unity, but even in altered form his speech was the most militant heard that day.

In the original draft, Lewis wrote:

In good conscience, we cannot support the administration's civil rights bill, for it is too little and too late. There's not one thing in the bill that will protect people from police brutality. . . . What in the bill will protect the homeless and starving people of this nation? What is there in this bill to insure the equality of a maid who earns $5 a week in the home of a family whose income is $100,000 a year?

In the toned-down version, Lewis said SNCC supported the bill but with "great reservations" and went on to spell out, pretty much unchanged, what they were.

105

He cut the sentence that read: "We cannot depend on any political party, for both the Democrats and the Republicans have betrayed the basic principles of the Declaration of Independence." But he left in this one which also frightened many people: "The party of Kennedy is also the party of Eastland. The party of Javits is also the party of Goldwater. *Where is our party?*"

The problem was that the Lewis speech attacked the federal government and the Kennedy administration and thus violated the unannounced but generally accepted "line" of the march. Early in the summer when pressure for a march on Washington began building up, the Kennedy administration was very cool to the idea. Then administration leaders apparently decided "if you can't beat 'em, join 'em," and rolled out the Washington red carpet for the marchers. The top march leadership responded by making the demonstration pro-civil rights and anti-segregation but not anti-Kennedy—and many of them sincerely felt that this was the way to get something done.

Lewis, on the other hand, who had been constantly on the front lines in the South reflected the thinking of people there. Despite the public accommodations victories in some parts of the South, this had been a time of serious failures too. A direct action campaign in Jackson, Mississippi, completely fizzled. So did one— although it took longer—in Danville, Virginia, where special deputies beat demonstrators brutally. It was also a time of widespread violence—from the murder of Medgar Evers in Mississippi in June until the church bombing (in September after the Washington march) that killed four Negro girls in Birmingham. In between there were a multitude of incidents—many never widely reported because they involved little known places and unknown people: church burnings in rural areas; mass arrests of demonstrators in

49

Americus, Georgia, where four student leaders were jailed on charges of insurrection; cruel beatings of civil rights workers in many places, sometimes by hoodlums, but often by police. Jim Forman, wherever he had access to a public forum, said over and over, "The Number 1 problem in the South is police brutality," but few people seemed to hear.

More and more, people working in Deep South areas were asking why the federal government could not or would not do something to stop these things. The question had been building up for a long time. In the early days of the new movement in the South, nobody really expected the federal government to do much. Traditionally Southern Negroes have looked on FBI agents with suspicion because whatever they told them seemed to get back to hostile local officials. Dwight Eisenhower was President when the new upsurge started in the mid-50's, and although he did send troops to Little Rock when the situation there reached chaos, he never claimed to be for desegregation in princple—refusing consistently to say more than that he would support law and order.

With the Kennedy administration, however, the expectations were different. John Kennedy ran on a strong civil rights platform. And it was Attorney General Robert F. Kennedy who a few months after he took office urged civil rights forces to concentrate on voter registration and promised them full support.

At first things did seem different. Now civil rights workers in the Deep South could call the Justice Department in Washington collect, and charges would be accepted. They could call federal officials at home in the middle of the night and get a polite response. All this made people feel better; no longer did Negroes and their white co-workers in hostile Southern communities feel so completely alone.

Gradually, however, the spell began to wear off. Somehow it became less and less enchanting to have one's collect calls accepted when the voice on the other end was always explaining why Washington couldn't do anything. Victims of police brutality filed affidavit after affidavit with the FBI—and nothing ever happened. FBI agents stood on the streets taking notes within a few feet of officers poking demonstrators with cattle prods—and nothing ever happened.

The explanation given by the FBI was that they were a factfinding agency. The explanation given by the Justice Department was that they were hamstrung by the doctrine of federal-state separation of powers, that local law enforcement was the domain of local officials. Highly respected constitutional authorities chal-

106

lenged this position, declaring that the Civil War of 100 years ago had supposedly established the proposition that the federal government has not only the right but the responsibility to protect its citizens. They pointed to specific statutes passed after the Civil War which they claimed the Justice Department could use to arrest both police and private citizens who violate the constitutional rights of others. To the average civil rights worker under a policeman's club, even if he knew no constitutional law, it just made no sense that the most powerful nation on earth could not protect the lives of its own citizens.

Then in the summer of 1963, just before the March on Washington, nine leaders of the Albany Movement were indicted—not by the state government but by the federal government. The case grew technically out of a grand jury investigation of a white grocer's complaint that the Movement had tried to put him out of business because of his vote on a federal jury in another case, involving the shooting of a Negro by a sheriff. The nine Movement leaders were charged with either conspiracy to injure a juror or perjury. Negroes in Albany were stunned. During the height of the Albany struggle, many affidavits had been filed with federal authorities detailing violations of Negro rights, and nothing was done. One of those now indicted was Slater King, who had helped organize the Albany Movement. In 1962, his wife was kicked by a deputy sheriff and soon thereafter lost her unborn child. Nothing was done about that either.

Later, civil rights attorney William Kunstler described the Albany case as a "bone thrown to the segregationists by the Kennedy administration." There is absolutely no way to explain it except as an effort of the Kennedys to carry water on both shoulders, and appease Georgia's segregationists while courting the civil rights movement.

"I want to know—which side is the federal government on?" asked John Lewis in his original Washington speech. He cut that sentence out of the delivered version, but people throughout the movement continued to ask the question. Organizationally, SNCC came to personify the most sceptical approach to the national administration, but the question was not confined to SNCC. The urgency of it was in direct proportion to the closeness of any person to the struggle in the Deep South, regardless of his organizational affiliation. "I've come to the conclusion," said an SCLC staff member, "that the only time the government is going to do anything is when there's about to be a riot and they have to."

Howard Zinn maintains that the problem is that the Compro-

107

mise of 1877 under which the federal government agreed to keep hands off the relationship of the Southern power structure to the Negro citizenry is still in effect—and that no President since then has had the courage to repudiate it. Zinn wrote that in 1964, and nothing that has happened since alters this judgment—despite President Johnson's "We Shall Overcome" speech in which he proposed new voting rights legislation. It was only a few weeks later that peaceful civil rights marchers in the Alabama Black Belt were being tear-gassed and arrested, and FBI agents were still taking notes.

Thus, over the past few years, the realization grew that the federal government is not in itself a savior. More and more people in the movement faced the fact that freedom cannot be handed down from above and decided that democracy, if it is to be real, must begin at the bottom. It was in Mississippi that this approach most clearly guided the direction of the movement.

Since 1961, the movement in Mississippi has been developing along different lines from anywhere else in the South. To understand this, we have to go back to the time when those first students went to Mississippi in the wake of the Freedom Rides.

These students, all Negro and college products, were as unprepared as white liberal intellectuals might have been for the deprivation of most Mississippi Negroes. Some had gone to Mississippi convinced that Negroes there were sitting on their doorsteps waiting for the young to lead them to a new society. When they found that centuries of oppression had crushed the spirit of revolt, some were disillusioned. Then they began to grope toward a theory that they must produce some inner revolutions before there could be an outer one.

"The young people here have never had a chance to hear about freedom—they don't know their own worth. We need our own school system," said one young worker.

"All they do is hang around in joints. How could they feel they are worth anything?" another asked. "Music dinning in their ears all the time—I believe it is a plot of the segregationists. We need community centers where people can go."

"My God," reacted one veteran of the civil rights struggle when she heard these comments, "they are all going to become social workers."

That didn't happen, but as most of the world knows, the Mississippi movement did go on to organize its own freedom schools, community centers, and cultural program. In the process, many Mississippi Negroes did indeed get new images of themselves—and many of those students, the ones who stayed, learned also. They

108

found they didn't have all the answers after all and that the un-educated sharecropper could teach them a number of things. The movement never became "social work" because its purpose remained to change society. But the effort to change people so they could change the world around them also changed the movement. It be-came less flamboyant. Direct action was minimized—not because the young organizers didn't believe in it, but because they thought it would be significant only when local people were ready to lead it themselves. The students had studied the effects of the Freedom Rides, which had been an important ground-breaking operation, but which had left life for Mississippi Negroes not much changed.

From the beginning the political side of the movement was emphasized in Mississippi too. Finding the official voting rolls closed tight, the movement began to set up its own polling places, make its own ballots, and run its own candidates in what became known as "freedom elections." In the first such campaign, Aaron Henry, who pioneered for years as state NAACP president ran for Governor, and the Rev. Ed King, an emancipated white Mississippian, for Lieutenant Governor. More than 85,000 Negroes voted, out of a potential 430,000—not bad for a start. The purpose was to show that Mississippi Negroes would vote if they could and to inject some real issues into Mississippi politics. The next step was in-evitable: that the disfranchised would set up their own registration system.

Thus was born the Freedom Democratic Party (FDP) which "registered" its own voters and was open to all, but in fact was almost entirely Negro. The FDP ran three candidates for Congress and one for the Senate in 1964. It organized at the precinct level, and held its own county, district, and state conventions. A sense of the political gripped people who had never been close to such things before. "Until a year ago, I never heard the word 'precinct,'" said one Jackson woman. "Now they can't call a meeting that I won't be there."

It was to assist the FDP, the freedom schools, and the com-munity centers, that hundreds of young volunteers, 85 percent of them white, went into Mississippi in the much-publicized Summer Project of 1964. The civil rights groups in the state had united to form the Council of Federated Organizations (COFO). Mississippi Negro leaders made it clear to volunteers that they were not being called upon to try to be heroes. Bob Moses, the young man whose quiet courage and careful sense of organization had given form to the Mississippi movement, told them: "You are not freedom riders. The idea is to stay out of jail if you can. Your job is to strengthen

109

local people. If each of you can leave behind you three people who are stronger and more skilled than when you came, that will be 3,000 more people we'll have to work with next year."

There was also the secondary purpose of the Summer Project which its leaders frankly stated—to involve a callous and deaf nation in Mississippi. It is stark testimony to the inherent racism of the United States that not until white people worked in the Mississippi movement did the nation look and care. Tragedy soon brought this point home. When Andrew Goodman and Michael Schwerner, both white and Northern, were killed with James Chaney, Negro and a Mississippian, everyone knew that if it had been only Chaney, few would have heard about it. Bob Moses repeatedly told the press in early 1964 that five Negroes were murdered in racial incidents in Mississippi in the preceding six months, and few took notice. But the Schwerner-Goodman-Chaney murder aroused the nation, and their martyrdom worked to save the lives of others.

The Summer Project didn't register many voters, because the state wouldn't allow it, but more than 55,000 Negroes registered in the FDP, 3,000 enrolled in freedom schools, and 40 community center programs were begun. Not all of these continued, but some did and everywhere seeds were planted. Most of all, the Summer Project left behind new rays of hope in Mississippi.

It did something profound to the people who came from the outside too. The Mississippi movement was not callously using them as cannon fodder. Those who came knew they were risking their lives and wanted to do it. For some it was the beginning of a lifetime of commitment; for almost all it was an experience that would forever make their lives more meaningful. SNCC, which conceived the project, sensed something most of the nation did not previously seem to know—that a sizable number of young Americans yearn for something meaningful to which they can relate their lives. The Summer Project was designed to harness that yearning to the needs of the Mississippi freedom movement. One result was that various groups planned summer projects for young people in 1965, both North and South.

The Mississippi movement has released creative energies in the lives of many people—both Mississippians and outsiders. People of many professions have come: teachers to work in the freedom schools, actors to the Free Southern Theater, doctors and nurses through the Medical Committee for Human Rights, lawyers mobilized first by the National Lawyers Guild and later by other groups. Ministers have come by the hundreds, sponsored by the National Council of Churches and various separate denominations. As an

110

organization, the white church in the South still vacillates on implementation of human rights (although many individuals within it have been heroic), but nationally the church finally responded to the challenge from the South. This has added great strength to the Southern freedom movement, but the benefit flows both ways: many a minister and rabbi have found in the movement a meaningful ministry and a significant channel for their religious beliefs—as the doctors, lawyers, teachers, and others have found a way out of the sham that dominates their fields of work in so much of America.

All this has happened in the movement throughout the Deep South, but the mass release of talent started in Mississippi. From a jail cell in McComb, in his early days in Mississippi, Bob Moses wrote to a friend about the "tremor" that was beginning in Mississippi— "a tremor in the middle of an iceberg—from a stone that the builders rejected." By 1964, it seemed that in the midst of an America grown sick with its own corruption and futility the stones that the builder had rejected were forming in Mississippi an embryo of a new society, one that was vital and young and challenging and that called forth the heroic and creative in those who dared to respond.

111

In a sense, this was happening because the Mississippi movement was withdrawing from the existing society. That essentially was what the freedom schools, the community centers, and the FDP represented—withdrawal from the white world and a setting up of new social, cultural, and political institutions.

Many movement people worried about this withdrawal. Was it not necessary, they asked, to come forth and confront the evil state? How long would people support the movement if it could not begin to crack the racist power?

In late August, 1964, there finally was a confrontation by the Mississippi movement—but not in Mississippi. It was at Atlantic City as the Freedom Democratic Party demanded that its delegates be seated at the Democratic National Convention instead of the regular Democrats from Mississippi. The confrontation shook not only Mississippi but an entire startled nation—a nation that had become used to thinking one could only go to the top through channels and that you can't fight City Hall, much less the Democratic National Committee.

The Johnson administration was shocked and frightened, for here for the first time in many years was a force in American politics that could be neither predicted nor controlled. Johnson wanted to mute the racial issue in the hope of avoiding showdowns that make elections hard to win. To Freedom Democrats from

55

Mississippi, racism was a cancer and not an issue to be muted. They refused to compromise in their demands for seats—winning for themselves and for SNCC which supported them the fury of the Johnson administration and some more moderate civil rights leaders.

But they also won something else. They won a place in history as the first truly grass roots political movement this country has known in a long, long time. To the sophisticated it seemed almost a miracle because they had no big money behind them, no political power, and in the beginning not even the big names of the civil rights movement. Yet here were Negro sharecroppers from Mississippi, some of the poorest people in the nation, speaking to the country and making themselves heard. Support groups sprang up all over—and by the time the FDP challenged the right of regular Mississippi Congressmen to sit in the House of Representatives in January, 1965, they had more than one third of the nation's Congressmen voting with them. Little people in many parts of the country began to feel that if the sharecroppers of Mississippi could make their voices heard, then maybe they could too—and a new possibility of meaningful grass roots politics seemed to be opening up. "We have decided in Mississippi," said Mrs. Victoria Gray, an FDP congressional candidate, to supporters from all over the nation, "that it is time for people to quit reacting to power and start making power react to us."

There is no myth about the grass roots nature of the FDP, and its development is probably the single most important thing that has happened in the modern freedom movement to date. Here it is being proved that even in our complex society, which some have said must turn men into machine cogs and machines into men, little people can organize themselves politically to take control of their own destiny—in other words, that democracy can work.

The first major confrontation on the voting issue within the South, however, came not in Mississippi but in Alabama. SNCC started working on registration in Selma late in 1962. All efforts met stony resistance, despite federal suits. Meantime, the Rev. James Bevel and his wife, Diane, formerly identified with SNCC but now of SCLC, had taken up the Rev. James Lawson's idea of a non-violent army and had moved to Alabama to implement it. The army did not develop in this form, but the Bevels and other SCLC staff began to concentrate in the Black Belt. In January, 1965, SCLC moved into the area in force—in a conscious effort to dramatize the continued denial of voting rights in the Deep South. Sheriff Jim Clark of Dallas County made it easy for them, as had Bull Connor in Birmingham, and once again the evil of racism was brought into the light of day. The result was the greatest upsurge of national support for Negro freedom that has yet been seen.

One by-product of the Alabama campaign was that long-simmering divisions between SNCC and SCLC began to get written about in the newspapers. There were vicious press attacks on SNCC, probably inspired by powerful forces starting with the White House and unfortunately possessed of some allies within the civil rights movement. These forces decided after the FDP challenge that SNCC was a threat to the political status quo and must be destroyed as uncontrollable.

Most of what has been written about the SNCC-SCLC divisions is distortion. For example, SCLC has been depicted as moderate and nonviolent, SNCC as wild and violent. This is falsification. Both SCLC and SNCC continue, as organizations, to espouse non-violent direct action as a means of social struggle; on the staffs of each of them are people with widely varied attitudes toward non-violence as a matter of personal philosophy and individual practice. Again, SCLC has been painted as responsible and more given to the long hard pull than to demonstrations, SNCC as a group of wild youngsters interested only in demonstrations for demonstrations' sake and not about "to pitch into the hard work of actually registering voters," as one columnist put it. This too is distortion. Many SNCC people did object, once demonstrations started, when Martin Luther King turned the march back as it approached the police line. But it was SCLC, not SNCC, that started mass demonstrations in Selma in 1965, and it was SNCC people who had been walking country roads for months, doing the tedious job of seeking out potential voters.

Despite these distortions, there are some real differences between SNCC and SCLC. The one basic dispute involves theories on the nature of social change. SNCC has held as a cardinal principle that the job of its staff is to help develop local people to be their own leaders. It has always resisted anything like a "great leader" idea. In SNCC's early years, it rotated the chairmanship at each meeting to avoid any one person becoming the personification of the organization. In late 1964, after Bob Moses rose to national fame as leader of the Mississippi movement, he left the state, changed his name and took up residence elsewhere to begin organizing anew. He told friends that the people of Mississippi must lead themselves and that with the image he had acquired he could only cripple them if he stayed.

This rejection of the great-leader idea reflects a disillusionment among the young with leaders of the past. It also reflects a conviction

113

57

that the only significant social action is what people do for themselves.

Within SCLC too there are people who try hard to develop local leadership. Nevertheless, emphasis on a single leader is inherent in the SCLC operation since it was built originally around King's person and personality. A fact of life is that King's name and presence galvanize a Negro community in the South. This may not be a healthy situation; it has certainly sometimes been a debilitating one, for many a movement has languished and died waiting hopefully for King to come lead it, and sometimes when he comes and then departs, a vacuum is left behind. But people who wait for King's presence want him because he attracts national attention and also because he inspires the people, as anyone knows who has sat in a Southern mass meeting while he speaks. King and SCLC did bring the Alabama Black belt into the national and international spotlight, something that SNCC, for all its hard work, was not able to do. Obviously, despite their difference, the two groups can in many ways effectively complement each other—and the forces which have tried to divide them undoubtedly know this. As of the spring of 1965, top leadership of both SNCC and SCLC were trying to minimize their differences publicly. No matter how much they might grumble privately about King, SNCC leaders were unhappy about students who spent a few days in Alabama and went home to make speeches, purportedly representing SNCC and attacking SCLC. Likewise, while King and other SCLC leaders might shake their heads privately over the tactics of SNCC, King apologized to John Lewis because a minister, purportedly speaking for SCLC, had publicly attacked SNCC. Both organizations know that a major split in the Southern movement could benefit no one but the racists.

For in the spring of 1965, the Southern freedom movement finds itself in the strongest position it has ever known. It has come a long way since those first SNCC organizers looked with coolness on the suggestion that they register Negroes to vote. The movement has turned political in a big way. This trend really started in earnest back in mid-1963, about the time it became apparent that the public accommodations battle would be won. But the political turn reflected more than that; there has been a qualitative change in the voter registration campaigns since 1961: then they were essentially the campaigns of the national administration into which civil rights workers were being drawn; by 1963 the campaigns were the movement's own. The change came with the realization that the Southern Negro could not depend on the federal government to establish his freedom for him.

114

58

The change also reflected a growing awareness within the Southern movement of the places in the world where colored people were taking over the reins of government. Interest in Africa, in particular, has been mounting. In the new African states, Southern Negroes for the first time saw black men not depending on concessions from the white man, but actually taking power. "Power" became a word that was used more and more in the daily conversation of civil rights workers.

More Negroes were running for office than ever before, and some got elected. The end of the county unit system in Georgia (which gave disproportionate political power to rural areas) and the reapportionment of state legislatures was giving more strength to urban areas where many Negroes were already registered. In the fall of 1963 SNCC leader Julian Bond said: "Which is more important, integrating a lunch counter or having four or five Negroes on the City Council where you can change all the laws?"

"Besides," he commented, "I agree with Dick Gregory that some of these Dixie towns aren't worth integrating."

In May, 1965, Bond himself won the Democratic nomination for state legislator in Georgia and is expected to win the general election. This will make him, at 25, one of the first leaders of the sit-in movement to win political office.

In 1965 in Selma, the Rev. James Bevel was saying: "We are no longer fighting for a seat at the lunch counter. . . . We are fighting for seats in the legislature."

The transition from the lunch counter was complete. Yet the road ahead was not clear. Some in the movement felt the vote drive was the real key. "Now we are going after where it's at—that's why they're so mad," said one SNCC staffer after the Selma drive. The active freedom movement was now concentrated in the Deep South— really in a few states, Alabama, Georgia, Mississippi, parts of Louisiana, and Arkansas, and mainly in the rural areas. Those who think this is "where it's at" maintain that once Negroes win the vote in the Black Belt repercussions will spread out through the state legislatures, the rest of the Southern states, the Congress and the nation, and that a general growth in democracy will follow. There seems some validity to this theory.

Yet many are not sure. The growing protest movement against discrimination in the North has had a profound effect in the Southern movement. Until a few years ago, there was a widespread naivete about the North among Southern Negroes and white Southern civil rights activists; many believed that it was only in the South that racism, discrimination, and segregation were major problems.

115

The growth of the Northern movement shattered these illusions, and it is impossible not to notice that in the North there are no barriers to keep Negroes from voting.

There are no barriers either in most parts of the upper South— nor in many cities even in the Deep South. Yet nowhere can it be said that basic problems have been solved. Many in the movement have become convinced that the vote is not the only key to a new society. Howard Zinn whose writings and teachings have influenced much of the student generation in the South put it bluntly in a speech to SNCC in 1963.

What do you tell people when you ask them to register and vote? Do you tell them, "I want you to register because that's really all that's missing. We have a beautiful working democratic mechanism here. The only problem is that you are left out of it." Well, I don't think this is an honest statement. I think it is truer to say, "If you register and if you vote, you will then have as much power as the rest of us, which is very little."

If freedom is more than a hamburger, the Rev. C.T. Vivian of SCLC once said, it is also more than a ballot.

But what, many people are wondering, and how do you get there?

116

5

BLACK AND WHITE TOGETHER?

The Southern civil rights movement has never been all-Negro, nor basically anti-white although sometimes it has come close to being both.

On the other hand, neither has it ever been more than tokenly integrated from the white side.

White opposition to racism, like Negro resistance to oppression, has deep roots in Southern history. The nation's first anti-slavery societies were formed in the East Tennessee mountains, and it was a white man from that area who went to New England and sold William Lloyd Garrison on the idea.

During the Civil War, many white Southerners fought with the Union. Tennessee, for example, had more Union volunteers than any other state. There are Southern counties which flew the Union flag throughout the war. These were in the hill country—as opposed to the flat rich lands with big plantations. It was people from these areas who joined with freed slaves in the Reconstruction governments. They were also the people who united briefly with Negroes in the abortive Populist movement.

By the time of the national ferment of the 1930's, with growing industrialization, there was a new white working class in the cities. Some of these people united, if but temporarily, with Negroes in early CIO efforts. There were also joint Negro-white tenant farmer unions. And, among middle classes and intellectuals, there was considerable activity against racial oppression. Later, in the Southern Conference for Human Welfare, white and Negro united in the beginnings of a real mass movement for change.

By the time the Negro upsurge started in Montgomery in 1955, however, there were very few white people working for civil rights in the South—just as, in the general paralysis of McCarthyism, there were very few people of any color anywhere in America doing anything about social problems. But two Southwide organizations did exist which were concerned with race relations and especially the white Southerner. These were the Southern Regional Council (SRC) and the Southern Conference Educational Fund (SCEF).

SRC was organized in 1944; it grew partly out of an earlier interracial commission which dated back to the early 1920's. Its purpose was to establish a dialogue between white and Negro and to work for Southern progress. At first it accepted the proposition that progress would have to come within the framework of segregation, but many individuals in SRC felt differently, and in 1953 it adopted a position opposing segregation. Generally SRC worked through influential people. After the 1954 Supreme Court decision, it obtained a foundation grant to establish human relations councils in Southern states and began to bring more people into dialogue across racial lines.

One thing that affected SRC's history was the fact that it was established in 1944 at least in part to be an alternative force to the Southern Conference for Human Welfare (SCHW), which was then growing rapidly. In recent years, criticisms of SCHW from the Center and Right have been over-simplified to charges that it included Communists. At the time SCHW was active, however, "Communist" was not the scare word it became later; there were Communists in many organizations—so the points of real difference among people and organizations were much clearer. Basically the difference between SCHW and SRC boiled down to age-old arguments between radical do-it-now approaches and moderate go-slow-but-steady ways. Some of the people who organized SRC felt that SCHW was trying to move too fast, and would make things worse instead of better. SCHW people felt that SRC was too oriented toward getting things done through manipulation of the power structure, whereas SCHW was committed to "organizing people, any people, not necessarily so-called important people." SCHW supporters felt it was a matter of democracy versus rule by an elite.

In the late 1940's, SCHW went out of existence. This was partly because of attacks from such groups as the House Un-American Activities Committee (HUAC), partly because it over-expanded too quickly and as a result ran into financial difficulties, partly because many of its active members threw themselves into supporting Henry Wallace for President in 1948 and were never, after that failure, able to regroup as a non-political organization. Also, the postwar period was simply not a time for a radical organization, and SCHW was radical.

SCEF was a child of SCHW—having been set up as its educational wing in 1946—and it survived. When SCHW died, Jim Dombrowski, Aubrey Williams, and a few other militant Southerners, white and Negro, decided to continue SCEF. SCHW had pursued a broad program to change the economic and political face of the

118

South—support for the labor movement, New Deal programs, etc. Those who continued SCEF decided that the great need at that moment was for a militant organization to unite Negro and white Southerner to oppose segregation. As one of them said later: "We knew there were still many other issues, but we felt that if we could end segregation, we could solve the others." The NAACP was struggling to organize Negroes. SCEF founders saw their main job as reaching white Southerners, finding those ready to speak, letting them know they were not alone, and telling the hesitant that now was the time to take a stand. A small interracial board committed to this ideal was pulled together. Between 1946 and the beginning of the Montgomery bus protest in 1955, SCEF did indeed, even in this unlikely period, encourage many white Southerners to speak against segregation. It maintained the old SCHW perspective of deeming the unknown housewife to be as important as the city official, but gave up any hope of creating a true mass movement at that time.

119

Immediately after the 1954 Supreme Court decision, SCEF began a series of community conferences over the South for compliance with the decision—the purpose being to bring together Negro and white to implement school desegregation. But by that time, Senator James Eastland of Mississippi had taken the Senate Internal Security Subcommittee to New Orleans for a circus-like investigation of SCEF and had solemnly labelled it a Communist organization, so its effectiveness was crippled. SCEF went ahead with its planned compliance conferences and two were actually held—in Richmond, Virginia, and Houston, Texas. They were well attended and helpful, but SCEF alone was not strong enough to buck the winds rising from the other side. A Southwide compliance conference was scheduled for the fall of 1956 in Atlanta, but by then the White Citizens Councils were firmly in control in the South, and liberals in Atlanta urged SCEF to cancel the conference. SCEF agreed—in the later opinion of some of its leaders, wrongly. That ended any large-scale effort launched by an interracial group to initiate desegregation. By that time, the Montgomery movement had signaled the beginning of a new era—when Negroes took the initiative and demanded freedom for themselves. There was no longer a possibility, for this period, of a truly interracial initiative toward change. After 1955, the role of whites could be only supportive.

Throughout the latter part of the decade both SRC and SCEF, each in its own way, tried to build that support. SRC, through its human relations councils, widened the circle of those who wanted to work quietly and meet in interracial settings, those who wanted to maintain their community niches, yet help the freedom movement. SCEF, by and large, sought those who wanted to take a more militant stand, the individual who would join a picket line or in some way identify publicly with the movement—and if necessary cut himself off from old relationships to do it.

Both of these approaches should be distinguished from the role of what came to be known as Southern "moderates." Moderates are people, usually powerful community leaders, who decide that change is inevitable and that they must help their communities adjust in order to avoid turmoil. As one of their spokesmen said in Birmingham in 1963, "Civil unrest is bad for business." Such people sparked save-the-schools movements, formed biracial committees, and tried to promote compromise with the freedom movement. They have often been a positive influence in the South, for they have brought under control the violent racist elements. But they tend to be more interested in peace than in justice and so are not in themselves a force for social change.

In life, such delineations of people tend to blur. Both SRC and SCEF have supported save-the-schools committees, and sometimes the same person who joins them will join the local human relations council, and later even a picket line. But although individuals can pass from one grouping to another, these different approaches are separate and distinct.

To make clear the function of interracial groups in the South, it is necessary also to note additional roles that both SCEF and SRC have played.

In addition to trying to involve whites in action, SCEF tended to become a Southern civil liberties organization. Circumstances forced it into this position because it was itself under heavy attack from groups like HUAC, Senator Eastland's committee, and similar state committees. SCEF leaders did not choose to placate such groups by parroting anti-Communist slogans; they felt that as long as Communism was used as a scare word to attack social movements and close doors to discussion, the Southern movement would be crippled, divided, and surrounded by a multitude of dead-end streets. History in the mid-60's is confirming this theory, for as the freedom movement moves beyond the narrow lunch counter concept, attacks by label and smear intensify. Fortunately, in the early 1960's, other Southern-based groups, SNCC and SCLC, also began supporting the idea of the indivisibility of civil rights and civil liberties. NAACP and CORE never have, and although they too have been labelled "red" by segregationists, some people in them refuse to associate with groups like SCEF and a few have even joined the attacks. The

120

reasoning of most of these people is that only if the civil rights movement can defeat the red label can it survive, and to this end it must avoid association with those most often called red. Those who take the civil libertarian approach, on the other hand, argue that the only sound way for the movement to avoid being destroyed by such labels is to put an end to the general atmosphere of witch hunt and thus make it impossible for irrational labels to be used as effective weapons by the segregationists.

Another role that SCEF has played is one of giving support to pioneering movements before they become big enough to attract wide attention. For example, it was SCEF that first mobilized support for besieged voter registration efforts in West Tennessee and sent the first tents there. This pioneering role was possible because SCEF, as an organization under constant attack, was necessarily small—and so was flexible and unencumbered by bureaucracy.

Additional roles played by SRC in this period included a superb program of research which made factual information about the South available in readily usable form.

In the early 1960's, SRC took on another role, when it became a channel for foundation funds that were pouring into the South. As a tax-exempt organization, SRC had always received foundation grants for its own work, and as civil rights activity mushroomed it also channeled funds to other groups. For example, money given by foundations for voter registration were funneled to various organizations through the Voter Education Project (VEP), an arm of SRC.

One of the several dangers of having movements for social change financed by large foundations is that it tends to concentrate power in a few hands. SRC, as a channel for tax-exempt funds, tended to become a self-appointed agency to try to decide which organizations and people were "acceptable" for work in the South. This concentration of power would be dangerous to democracy even if veritable saints were administering it.

But in their role of keeping the white South from being entirely silent in the last decade, SRC and SCEF both did valuable jobs. Additionally there were many incidents of individual heroism—a lone minister, a lone mother, a lone white high school student, who took stands, often without any advance encouragement from any organization. Many of them paid heavily for their witness, and many had to leave the South. But they, along with what organized effort existed, helped keep alive hope for a day when Negro and white would join forces on a large scale. New hope finally came with the student movement of the 1960's.

In the beginning the sit-in movement was almost entirely Negro;

121

only a dozen Southern white students showed up at the 1960 SNCC conference. It was SCEF which determined to take the challenge of the movement to the white campuses. In 1961, it set up a white student project by giving SNCC an annual grant to employ full-time staff to try to reach Southern white students. Bob Zellner, a young white Alabaman, was the first full-time worker. Both he and those who came later found it hard to force themselves back to the white campuses; after the vital world of the Negro freedom movement, it is difficult to return to the seemingly dead and corrupt world of uninvolved white society. But they kept doing it anyway, and they influenced by example too, and new ferment spread. By 1964 there was actually more direct action against segregation on predominantly white campuses of the South than on Negro campuses. A strange silence had fallen over the Negro colleges, as SNCC became community-oriented. In the fall of 1964, SNCC began to re-establish contact on Negro campuses, but its orientation was toward pulling students into community involvement.

By that time, white students had set up their own organization, the Southern Student Organizing Committee (SSOC). Some older persons deplored the dual student set-up, but it reflected realities. SSOC people felt like step-children around SNCC—partly because they were white but also because they were still campus-centered, whereas SNCC had left the campus for the "real world." In the fall of 1964, some SNCC leaders encouraged SSOC to organize on Negro campuses also. Negroes came into the leadership of SSOC, and an informal division-of-labor seemed to be shaping up: SSOC was a campus-based organization concerned with what students could do as students about social problems; and SNCC was a body of young community organizers, students only in the sense that they were just out of school or had left temporarily to work in the movement.

The important thing about SSOC is that here is a really sizable movement of Southern whites actively working against segregation. Their conferences have been drawing 150 delegates from more than 40 campuses—and these usually represent scores back home. They are doing such things as touring their states on weekends to recruit more Negro high school students to come to their colleges. They are also, along with Negro students, addressing themselves to such issues as academic freedom, abolition of capital punishment, world peace, and poverty.

One basic thing has been wrong with all the organizations working to move white Southerners—SRC, SCEF, and SSOC. They have touched only the intellectual and professional people, only the middle class. No one in the civil rights movement has been talking to the

122

poor white man, the working class white man, urban or rural. What labor movement exists in the South has stayed aloof from the freedom struggle; sometimes its leaders have been privately sympathetic, and have talked to their members, especially on the folly of closing the schools, but this has been about the limit of involvement. Generally, Southern middle-class liberal whites have assumed that white people at the lower economic levels are the most race-prejudiced group—and many Negroes assume it too. There has been much evidence to back up these assumptions—the mobs, the Klan terror, some local unions actually run by the Klan.

Despite all this, the thought has persisted among white Southerners active for civil rights that unless they could break out beyond their own circle, there was no hope of real change. "We're just talking to ourselves," one active person lamented.

123

With the future effects of automation now looming, this concern becomes more acute. As unemployment rises, is there any possibility of uniting Negro and white to seek a decent living for all— or must there be a fight between white and black for the few jobs that will still exist? If economic conditions worsen, somebody is going to organize impoverished Southern whites. The American labor movement has not. If the civil rights movement doesn't, who will? The potential mass base for a truly organized fascist movement has been obvious for a long time.

An interesting development that came with the formation of SSOC was that some of this new generation of Southern white students began to tackle this problem. "Our job is not to organize the downtrodden Negroes of Mississippi," said Sam Shirah, white Alabama student who conducted the SNCC-SCEF white student project in 1964. "Our job is to organize the downtrodden white people." He continued:

What about white slums? What about the white unemployed and those working for starvation wages? Our orientation has been wrong—the idea of bringing whites into the movement as it exists. Rather we should bring the movement into the white community of this nation. . . . I want to say that not only are some of my best friends Negro but some of my best friends are white. I want to ask, where is the forgotten white man in his poverty, and where is the movement that is attempting to handle his frustration, . . . to move into the white community and say that the goals of the white man are the same as those of the Negro? Where is the movement that will say to us whites that we are slaves to fear, to hate, to guilt, to an inferiority complex that the Negro has overcome and therefore we must catch up? This is our job.

67

Such talk spread through the movement, and many people were talking about this "poor Southern white man," but nobody really knew what he was thinking. Beginning in the summer of 1964, a group of Southern students began a pilot project in Mississippi—of all places—to find this white Southerner in the flesh. It was slow going: they learned more about how not to proceed than they accomplished. But it was a beginning. The most important thing they found out was that it was not so much anti-Negro prejudice that would keep the poor white man away from the freedom movement as the fact that he was living in a police state.

"We found that we could canvass successfully in the white community for the Freedom Democratic Party, even in integrated teams," said a report from the summer pilot project in Biloxi, Mississippi. "The reaction of the people was not generally hostile but rather neutral. . . . It is quite a shock to realize that these were the same people who attacked Negroes with chains at the beach wade-in of 1960. . . . Groups are more immoral than individuals."

Later teams of young people attempting to organize white day laborers in Mississippi farm country initially met enthusiastic response and a desire to work with Negro farmers. "If these people were prejudiced, they hid it well," said Bruce Maxwell, one of the students.

The entire situation changed and this particular effort failed when the landlords of the white farmers ordered the students away and pressure started from the sheriff's office. The white farmers then also asked the students to leave. Their fear was stronger than their need.

In the face of this reaction, some students have become discouraged. Others are convinced they must keep on.

"We must find a way to face the problem of fear of the poor white people," Maxwell wrote. "Retreat to the Negro community is destructive to our courage and to theirs. We must stay. Negro organizers encountered the same fears when they first went into the Negro communities. But they stayed and they overcame, and that is what we must do."

Some people feel that such efforts may go easier in places other than Mississippi, but this is problematical. Elsewhere pressures may be more subtle, but nowhere in the South do people in control want the poor Negro and the poor white to join forces. Much of Southern history has been a record of efforts to keep this from happening.

An attempt to build such unity is just beginning in the Southern Appalachian region. There several civil rights groups (SCEF, SCLC, SNCC, Highlander, and SSOC) are sponsoring the Appalachian Economic and Political Action Conference (AEPAC). This will try

124

to stimulate community-union organization of white and Negro unemployed and underemployed to demand permanent unemployment compensation of at least $60 a week, better medical and educational facilities, a voice in local politics, etc. This could have wide repercussions since nine Southern states have large Appalachian areas: Virginia, North Carolina, South Carolina, Georgia, Alabama, Tennessee, Kentucky, West Virginia, and Maryland. All but the last three also have Black Belt areas where the civil rights movement is concentrating. The significance of simultaneous organization in the Black Belt and Appalachian areas for future politics in these states is obvious.

No one knows whether it will work—this effort to unite the poor, regardless of color. All odds seem to be against it. It was tried during Reconstruction and failed; it was tried during the Populist movement and failed. W.J. Cash, writing his classic *Mind of the South* in the late 1930's, noted that in both of these instances, when the chips were down, the poor Southern white fled back to the false glory of his white skin rather than unite with his black brother. Cash predicted dismally that this would happen again with the then embryonic Negro-white unity of the early CIO. And of course later it did. Why, one might ask, should it be different in the 1960's?

There are some possible reasons. If automation brings the profound changes in the economy that are predicted, the economic needs of the white man may for the first time be greater than his need to feel superior to the Negro. Another difference today is the image that the benighted white man sees when he looks at the Negro. Before, he saw a slave or a servant. Today he sees a man standing straight and tall, marching on Washington 250,000-strong, marching on Montgomery 30,000-strong, welded into a movement with strength to shake the nation. The downtrodden white man may see that he too needs that strength. Support for this theory came in 1964 when a committee of unemployed white miners from Kentucky went to Washington to lobby for attention to their needs. They were inspired to go by the 1963 civil rights March on Washington; and they headed straight for the Washington SNCC office for help in finding their way around official Washington.

These trends offer hope, provided vision is combined with hard work. Meantime, the comparative handful of white Southerners who have in the past 10 years stood up to be counted have kept the door open.

White people from other parts of the country have helped too. It was in 1962 that SNCC brought the first white students from the

125

North to live and work in the South. Charles Sherrod took them to the rural areas of Southwest Georgia to work alongside Negro students, and everybody thought he was attempting the impossible. "We've been singing long enough about 'Black and White Together,'" one student said. "We have to practice it, live it, and as we do we make real a certain kind of dream."

The terror in Southwest Georgia was no greater than in Mississippi, where at that time virtually no whites were working, and soon more white students began to come South. By 1964 it was a national movement.

And there were the white martyrs: William Moore, who attempted his own freedom walk through Alabama in 1962; Andrew Goodman and Michael Schwerner in Mississippi in 1964; the Rev. James Reeb and Mrs. Viola Liuzzo in Alabama in 1965.

One wonders how many white Americans realize how much they owe these people—and some others who have given up their lives in little pieces in the committed drudgery of the Southern front lines? As Southern racism has become more overt in the face of the growing Negro movement, it is little short of a miracle that the movement has not become completely anti-white. If there remains any hope that this country can some day transcend color lines it exists because of the blood, sweat, and sacrifice of these people who died or offered their lives. And at best all they bought is time.

The attitudes towards whites among Southern Negroes in the movement would require a study in itself. Organized black nationalist movements were not important in the South until about two years ago. Since then, they have grown. They are still not the mainstream of Southern protest, but many more Negroes agree with their tenets than actually join them.

One important thing to remember is that the Southern movement is not—except in the minds of a few people—an integration movement. For a time many white people thought it was. The changing semantics of the movement are revealing. In the 1930's and early 1940's, when people spoke of Negro oppression and what to do about it, favorite words were "justice" and "equal rights." The term "civil rights" came into use during the 1940's. Then, more people realized that there could be no equality within segregation and the term "desegregation" became popular. Later, some people who looked farther down the road, talked about "integration." They said desegregation meant the breaking down of legal barriers, whereas integration meant a positive acceptance of people by each other. The word scared timid white liberals, but others pointed out that it meant "to make whole." The term finally gained

126

general usage and the movement was often called "the integration movement." But in the past three years (simultaneously, perhaps not incidentally, with the growing awareness of the new Africa in the Southern movement) the popular term has become "freedom movement," and this much more clearly expresses what the Negro is struggling for in the South.

"I don't think I'd ever walk down to the next block again to stand in line and try to integrate a white theater or a restaurant," said one militant young leader in Mississippi in late 1964. He had stood in many such lines in previous years.

What changed him? One thing was that the battle over the theater and restaurant was by then won in so many places, and he and thousands like him put into words what they had always known: that even if they had the money to go to these places, which most of them didn't, they really had very little desire to go. They certainly had no desire to be near white people because they were white, and many had a definite desire not to be. What they wanted to be in was a new world, a new society—and they had attacked the segregated public places not so much to get into them as because they seemed to stand as barriers between them and that new world. It was a Southern variation of the widely articulated feeling among Negro intellectuals that they do not care to be integrated into a rotten society.

The other thing that had happened to that young man in Mississippi was that as the movement intensified it led the Southern racist to bare the teeth of his viciousness. The older paternalism in the South took many and subtle forms and had convinced even militant Negroes of a potential decency in the white population that didn't come through very well when the chips were down.

"I used to think we could reach the conscience of the good white people," that young man in Mississippi said. "That was when I still thought there were some good white people."

And yet the dream of unity persists, buried deep beneath the frustrations, even when everything in the outside world denies it. A reporter, interviewing this same young man, referred in passing to his previous discussion of political action as "a program to elect Negroes to office."

"I didn't say elect Negroes to office," he interrupted. "I said elect good people to office."

"But you said earlier that there aren't any good white people," the reporter reminded him.

He looked startled and said almost wistfully, "But there *must* be some good ones somewhere."

127

There is real truth in the observation of the Southern historian, James McBride Dabbs, that "through the processes of history we have been made one people, and . . . it is disastrous to talk and act as if we were two."

Underneath, this is true, but the twin evils of oppression and paternalism run too deep for this unity to surface now. Before there can be any real integration, there must be victory for the Negro's freedom movement. Jim Forman, referring to Albany, Georgia, but in phrases that could apply all over the South, calls it the "breach before healing."

And if integration does come in the South, it is doubtful that it will grow out of any of the situations where token desegregation of Negroes has taken place. There is more chance of it in situations of "reverse integration," where a few whites have entered the Negro world (formerly Negro colleges that have desegregated or predominantly Negro neighborhoods where a few white people live) because Negroes are more likely to extend acceptance to the token whites among them than whites do to token Negroes. But even this has its shortcomings. Negro communities too take on all the values of the larger society, and this society inherently divides people along racial lines.

The greatest hope for real integration is for an expansion of the freedom movement itself until its spirit pervades wider and wider sections of the population. This movement is something like an embryo of a new society already growing within the old. It is a fact that the nearest thing to real integration today has taken place within the freedom movement.

This does not mean that all is sweetness and light in Negro-white relationships inside the movement. There are many tensions. Whites in the movement have made many mistakes. Most Negroes have ambivalent feelings about having them there even if they made absolutely no mistakes. Many Negroes who believe in principle that it should be "black and white together" feel that they have been deprived of everything else in America and that the freedom movement at least should be theirs. Yet there is something healthy about the way these problems are being met within the movement, because they are out in the open. The most perceptive people, both Negro and white, realize that they will not really be resolved in their generation, and probably not in the lifetimes of their children, but they continue to try. And sometimes in the heat of battle, under pressure of great sacrifice and great commitment, true human relationships between individuals do develop, even if temporarily. It is a start. It is enough to prove it can be done. It has created a new

128

kind of brotherhood that no one quite defines but that everyone in the movement knows exists, a brotherhood that one belongs to without joining any particular organization, without paying any dues, without signing any pledge, but which one knows one is a part of without wasting time talking about it, and whose other members one can always recognize across barriers of race, geography, and age.

Regardless of court orders, regardless of the mass marches, regardless of token desegregation, wherever you go in the Southern and border states there are still two worlds—a white world and a Negro world—as there probably are also in most places in the North. But for those who have found this invisible brotherhood of the committed there is what some have called a "world in-between." It exists nowhere in geography, but its existence is nonetheless real. To live in it demands a certain price of both Negro and white, but those who really want to can find it and can live in it—not just for a summer, not just for a few months, but for a lifetime if they wish.

129

6

NONVIOLENCE: PACIFIER OR POWER?

There has been a great deal written and spoken, pro and con, about nonviolence and violence in the Southern movement. Much of it has been nonsense.

Sometimes the advocates of the differing points of view seem to be speaking different languages, and neither comprehends what the other is saying. Consequently, the dispute takes place in a distorted context.

Criticism of nonviolence found its first nationally heard Southern spokesman in Robert Williams of Monroe, North Carolina. Williams served in the Marine Corps during the Korean War and came home determined to do something about the plight of Monroe Negroes. He became president of the local NAACP chapter and built it into a thriving organization. The Ku Klux Klan intensified activity and rode through the Negro section of Monroe shooting indiscriminately. Whereupon Williams and other Negroes armed themselves and got a charter from the National Rifle Association, which Williams knew about through his Marine connections. One night when the Klan shot into the community, Negroes shot back, and after that, Williams claims, Klan attacks declined.

There was virtually no press notice of this gunfire exchange.

Meantime, the "kissing case" arose—the case of two young Negro boys who were kissed by a little white girl and found themselves jailed. Williams had been a public relations officer in the Marine Corps and knew how to get news to the outside world. He organized a world-wide campaign of protest, which freed the Negro boys. That made Williams himself national news and so the world was watching when in 1959, in a state of fury and frustration over dismissal of charges against two white men who had attacked Negro women, he told reporters: "The demonstration today shows that the Negro in the South cannot expect justice in the courts. He must convict his attackers on the spot. He must meet violence with violence, lynching with lynching."

The important thing about the Robert Williams story is not

that Williams was so unique but that he was rather typical of his generation. Many young Negroes went home to organize after the Second World War and the Korean War, and many did. Williams may have been unusually capable, but others were too. Certainly the arming of Negro communities was neither new nor unusual. Most Negro homes in the South have guns in them (as do most white homes, especially in rural areas) and they have been used to scare off racist attacks. What really made Williams different was his knowledge of how to use publicity as a weapon for justice. He used this knowledge with a high degree of skill and astuteness in the kissing case, and that is why the world knew about him when he made his statement about violence.

After that, he became a symbol—of the Negro striking back. This frightened many white people, and they frightened many Negroes, who denounced Williams publicly and said privately that what he had said was right but that his mistake had been to say it. In the resulting emotion, rational discussion of Williams' position was virtually impossible.

131

What he said, when analyzed, was simply that people should defend themselves when attacked. Williams stated specifically that he did not advocate aggressive violence—that is, Negroes attacking white people. Since Williams first became news, other people and groups have advocated similar policies. A few have called for retaliatory violence—that is, a murder of a white man to pay for the murder of a Negro, or burning of a white church to repay the burning of a Negro church. But no one, at least publicly, has called for mass armed uprising, and most people who consider themselves opposed to nonviolence simply call for self-defense. This means a man prepared to defend his home and family with a shotgun if necessary, and, as Williams refined it, a community organized to defend itself collectively. It was Williams' stated belief that such community organization would actually decrease the amount of violence because, he said, if the racists knew a community was armed they would not attack. This is a deterrent theory on the community level.

None of these positions is compatible with a completely pacifist philosophy, but the self-defense aspect is completely compatible with traditional practice in America. Self-defense has always been acceptable in this country, both legally and in the court of public opinion. And the deterrent theory is, of course, the officially proclaimed basis of United States policy in international affairs. Therefore it is impossible not to conclude that there was a great deal of hypocrisy in the condemnation that descended on Robert Williams.

75

As for retaliatory violence, this is beyond the limits of legality, but it is strange that so few people have noted how remarkable it is, in the face of continued violence against Negroes in the South, that there have been so few instances of it. In the words of John Lewis (himself an advocate of nonviolence): "We are in the midst of a revolution. If it were going on somewhere else in the world, people wouldn't even expect it to be nonviolent."

Unfortunately, critics of the self-defense school have tended simply to condemn and not to discuss. The net result in the case of Williams was that he was made an outcast by powerful civil rights groups; local, state, and federal officials knew this, and consequently Monroe Negroes were denied even meager police protection. This reinforced their belief that they must depend on their own resources for self-defense. That was a vicious circle if there ever was one.

On the other hand, if there has been much misunderstanding of the self-defense position, there has likewise been among its advocates much misunderstanding of what the nonviolent direct-action movement is about. One paradox is that a chief target of attack for many advocates of self-defense is Martin Luther King, Jr., although King is one of the few of Williams's critics who was willing to engage in a rational discussion of the matter, instead of simply condemning blindly. One of the most enlightening discussions in print on the issue appeared in 1959 in the magazine *Liberation,* an exchange between Williams and King. They disagreed, of course, but there is an integrity about the discussion because both seem to say what they mean.

Among the popular misconceptions held by critics of nonviolence have been the beliefs that this is an attempt to "disarm Southern Negroes" so that they have no way to defend themselves, that it means submission in the face of racism (the picture of Negroes praying instead of resisting, for example), and that nonviolence as a philosophy is "draining the militance out of Southern Negroes."

Leaving aside any philosophic arguments, these ideas simply do not square with the facts in the Southern struggle over the last decade. As for "disarming" Negroes, there are a very few individuals in the movement who maintain a position of complete pacifism and refuse to keep arms in their homes. But the organized nonviolent movement has not said to any individual that he must remove the gun from his house. The position of the movement is that this is an individual question. What the movement does say is that in actions of organized social struggle, participants must adhere to nonviolence—

132

that is, when marching to the courthouse, for example, you leave your weapons, if any, at home.

As for draining away militance, the record in the South shows the exact opposite. Nonviolent direct action did not arise in the South as a counter to violence among Negroes; rather it arose, in Montgomery and elsewhere, as a counter to court and legislative action. It arose among people who decided that these methods were too slow. So they put their bodies into the streets, and on to lunch counter stools, into voting lines. Thus, nonviolence as it developed in the South was a weapon—a weapon of action, which the people picked up and with which they moved against the status quo. Follow the stories of many of the new Negro leaders and it is clear that nonviolence came into their lives as the weapon they had long been looking for. "I always knew I had to do something about the system and that there must be some way," says John Lewis, who grew up in Troy, Alabama. "In nonviolent direct action, I found a way."

133

The history of the South since 1955 is a story of community after community that has been stirred to action by nonviolence. Where nonviolent direct action took place, change in some form followed. The change may be limited in scope, if the original demands were limited, but the change that came was real. Negroes hold their heads high and demand respect; if public places are open, they use them occasionally even if not steadily. In contrast, in communities where change has been decreed by court order or by some bi-racial committee appointed by officials, the picture is different. Public places may be open in theory, but they are likely to be little used, and there is much less independence among the Negro population. Nonviolent direct action has provided a method by which each individual can become a part of the struggle and thus be emancipated from within as he seeks emancipation without.

One of the most unfair criticisms that is sometimes made of Martin Luther King, Jr., is that he destroys militance in the Negro communities. Again the opposite is true. There are grounds on which King and his work can be criticized, but this is not one of them. When he goes into a Southern community, people are aroused—not quieted down. People come to the mass meeting who sat home before. After hearing him, they walk into the street and risk danger and death to challenge the system. If anything, negative effects of King's leadership cut entirely the other way, because the problem in the South has not been King coming into a community and draining the militance away but communities sitting months or years and letting their militance fritter away while they wait hopefully for King to come and lead them. This has happened in too many places.

Whether King can be blamed for it is questionable. It is more likely the fault of local leadership and the traditional dependence on leadership that has too long pervaded society generally.

Critics of nonviolence have sometimes used the word "nonresistance" interchangeably with "nonviolence." Among Southern militants, the phrase is "nonviolent action" or "nonviolent direct action." To them, nonviolence has not been non-resistance; it has been the essence of resistance. Even those pictures of masses of people praying have been misinterpreted in some quarters. They are praying all right, but when hundreds of people kneel to pray in the middle of a highway in Alabama this is not prayer in the traditional sense of leaving the problem to a divine power. Not that the prayers are not sincere with many of the participants; many would tell you quickly that prayer is the source of their own strength. But with their appeal to a divine power they are merging the commitment of their bodies. And their prayer becomes a virtual roadblock, figuratively as well as literally, in the way of the racists. Prayer too, in this instance, is resistance.

Nonviolent direct action, as it has been used in the South, essentially means resistance to segregation and racism. First this resistance operates on the individual level. It is power that an individual generates from within (or according to the belief of some participants, with the help of a divine power) which enables him to stand up and say "no" to oppression. The Rev. James Lawson tells the story of a student, Paul Laprad: "He was hauled off a lunch counter stool by a group of white men, beaten, kicked, and clobbered over the head. As his assailants left, he stood up, brushed himself off and returned to the lunch counter stool." This, Lawson says, is nonviolence. Or there was Miss Annelle Ponder, described by Howard Zinn after an arrest in Mississippi. She was brutally beaten and when her friends came to get her they found her with a face so swollen that she could hardly talk. But she looked up at her friends and said one word: "Freedom." This, too, was nonviolence.

Such resistance by one individual may or may not be effective in changing a community. Sometimes it can be (the case of Rosa Parks is the prototype), but at the very least, in the thinking of advocates of nonviolence, it regenerates the individual. He becomes a resister instead of a submissive victim, gains new inner dignity, and becomes a whole human being.

But when such tactics of resistance are used by great numbers of people at the same time they take on an additional dimension. They become a very conscious weapon of social struggle, of defying tyranny and taking the offensive against it. They are a form of

134

attack on unjust conditions, in which the attackers use every means at their disposal—their voices, their feet, their bodies, and the mass weight of their very numbers—every means except physical violence, to destroy the system that they oppose.

In their most refined form, these tactics on an organized scale amount to what nonviolent actionists call "social dislocation." This means that by your nonviolent actions you so dislocate a community, a state, or the nation (or the world?) that it can no longer operate and therefore must grant your demands. The Southern movement since 1955 has been a series of minor "social dislocations." The bus protest in Montgomery, for example, dislocated that city so much that it was finally simpler for those in control to let the buses be desegregated than to fight it any longer. The student sit-ins "dislocated" the South enough so that segregated lunch counters no longer seemed important enough to preserve. The Southern movement as a whole has "dislocated" the nation sufficiently to make great numbers of people conclude that some changes must be made.

It can be seen, however, that all of these things are still merely toying with the method of social dislocation as it is presented by its most convinced advocates. The Southern movement has talked about "Freedom Now," but it has never really tried to throw a community or the region into nonviolent turmoil and keep it there until all the demands for Freedom were truly granted *Now*. It has extracted concession after concession from those in power—but never has it tried to continue the dislocation until the very seat of power was shifted. As Jim Lawson said, the movement thus far has sought mainly "concessions from the system, not to transform the system." People who talk seriously about "nonviolent revolution" believe that the Southern movement has hardly yet touched the techniques of nonviolent direct action.

There is yet another dimension to nonviolence that is also often misunderstood. This is the concept of love—or love of one's enemies. Most people in the Southern movement make no claim to loving their enemies. They say frankly that they see nonviolence merely as a tactic that sometimes works well, and when it quits working well they will turn to something else. But there are the minority (and they have often been in leadership) who see nonviolence as a "way of life," as they put it. With those who take this position, the concept of love has meaning.

It is not, however, affection for the individual one is fighting. Rather, it is an attempt to understand his corruption and the source of it and to see the evil as something that has made him its victim too. Even more basically, it is a way of looking at one's op-

135

ponent which holds out the possibility of ultimate reconciliation—not, it should be emphasized, through compromise but through transformation. Theoretically this possibility exists with every human being, and there have been instances in which jailers, sheriffs, and hoodlums who have been brutal to civil rights demonstrators have shown signs of change through association with their victims. These cases of individual transformation are rare, however, and there are few people in the Southern movement who really think there can be enough such private conversions to make a social change.

The more general belief is in a process of social transformation—that is, that in destroying the evil society by nonviolent direct action the protesters will build a new society in which decent human relationships are possible. Someone once asked Rev. Fred Shuttlesworth, one of the most uncompromising leaders in the Southern movement, what he was working for in Birmingham. He thought a few minutes and replied: "For the day when the man who beat me and my family with chains at Phillips High School can sit down with us as a friend." It is unlikely that Shuttlesworth expects ever to sit down with that particular man. But he has a vision of a society in which people like that man and people like himself can sit down together. It is this kind of vision that fires the imagination of some Negroes in the movement when there is talk of the possibility of an alliance of poor white and Negro—even though they have seen at first hand no evidence that it can work. They have a vision of the kind of world they are working for. This is what is meant when they talk about the "beloved community."

Some people unfamiliar with the Southern movement are repulsed by that phrase. They think it sounds sticky, sentimental, and hollow. But it doesn't at all on the lips of the right people. Not on the lips of C.T. Vivian or John Lewis, for example, both of whom use it often. When someone has walked into countless mobs and been beaten and jailed again and again, each time only to return from a sickbed to the struggle, when he has lived like that for a vision of a new kind of world, it does not sound sticky at all to hear him describe what he is working for as "the beloved community."

Or some people put it in economic terms without even identifying them as that. "I don't want to be like the white man, because what he got he stole from me," said Mrs. Fannie Lou Hamer, Mississippi Delta leader in one of her first speeches outside Mississippi. "What I want is a world where what I got, there won't nobody have to steal from me because there'll be enough for everybody."

The sense of fighting for a new kind of world where there can be a new kind of relationship grips thousands in the Southern move-

136

ment who would not describe themselves as "loving their enemies." Thus one of the ultimate values of the nonviolent philosophy has influenced masses in the movement, beyond its conscious advocates. Bitter hatred of the white world is certainly prevalent among Southern Negroes, but it is less prevalent among those in the movement, and this is not because anybody has drained away their militancy, which they obviously possess in abundance, and not usually because they have any conscious feeling of loving their enemies. Rather it is because they have been fired by a vision of a different world and have little time or energy left for hating. Hatred has not been eliminated, but it is no longer the dominant passion of their lives. There is a school of thought that holds that hatred must be encouraged in oppressed people to give them the will and the drive to resist. In this movement, it has been shown that a positive vision can also supply that drive.

137

There are weaknesses in the nonviolent movement too, however. Although it came onto the Southern scene as a positive weapon, powerful people in America and their press did not understand it that way. They got the idea, many of them, that this was a nice sweet movement that was going to keep peace in the South, and they began to sing its praises and to heap adulation on its leaders. There has been the persistent danger that nonviolent leaders would themselves become bewitched by this nice, peaceful image of themselves and, unconsciously, try to conform to it. If that happens, nonviolence will indeed become what those who have caricatured it say it is: a movement to keep people quiet and debilitate them. Its critics to the contrary, that has not happened yet. Regardless of what his critics say, this softening-up process has not yet happened to Martin Luther King, Jr. It could happen someday. The pressures on him to become a control, a harness on a mass movement are almost irresistibly powerful; sometimes it seems he will have to be almost superhuman not to give in, but so far the movement King leads in the South is attacking, not pulling back.

One key to keeping it that way is for the nonviolent movement to keep concentrating on its power as an aggressive technique and not let itself be diverted into the role of counterforce to any violent outbursts. For example, it would be most regrettable for the future of nonviolence if this movement let itself be pushed into preaching nonviolence to such groups as the "deacons of defense" in Louisiana which received publicity this spring. The deacons are an armed community guard of the type Robert Williams advocated, which was set up to counter unbridled Klan terror in rural Louisiana.

As long as violence by racists persists, groups like this are going to appear. People who feel that their existence increases the danger of open armed conflict between white and black can best spend their energies insisting that local, state, and federal law enforcement agencies act to stop anti-Negro violence. It is not the role of the organized nonviolent movement, if it wants to stay a militant aggressive force, to attempt to cope with this situation by urging the Negroes to disarm. Rather let the people who believe in law and order, whether pacifist or not, insist that racists in the area be disarmed; and let the nonviolent movement continue to carry out aggressive attacks on the status quo and continue to prove that its weapons are more creative than guns.

138

Another key to whether the nonviolent movement continues to be aggressive lies in whether it broadens its battle to attack effectively what is wrong with economic and political structures. Sometimes, nonviolent leaders have been frightened by the effects of their own movement—when it seemed that masses of people set in motion could not always be counted on to remain nonviolent. An example of this was the night in Birmingham in 1963 when, in the wake of bombings of Negro homes, Negroes fought police with bottles. The people who threw bottles were not the same people who had defied fire hoses and police dogs to demonstrate. They were the very poor and disinherited (those who demonstrated were mostly poor too, but these others were the ones who had lost all hope), and they were striking out at the most visible sign of their oppression—the police. Some people saw their spontaneous outburst as potential revolution. It was not that, because they were not organized and had no program. They had not stayed away from the organized freedom movement because it was nonviolent, but because they saw no answers to their problems there. Their attitudes have been echoed in many a community where Negroes living in the worst slums have watched the sit-in movement and said, "Who cares? What I want is a job."

The nonviolent movement does not have to turn violent to win the allegiance of those who threw bottles at Birmingham and elsewhere, but it does have to develop a program radical enough to speak to their needs. Some people in the movement see this. Whether the movement as presently constituted will rise to this challenge remains to be seen.

But to make the question of nonviolence versus violence the starting point for a discussion of the current South, as many do, is to begin at the wrong point. The first question now is whether the freedom movement will be on the offensive or the defensive. There probably cannot be any large social movement without some violence occurring, but it is difficult to see what possibility for an offensive violence offers the movement. The very terminology of critics of nonviolence is otherwise. They talk about self-defense. Self-defense among Southern Negroes is not new. Guns in the homes of Southern Negroes have been the rule, not the exception. Even retaliatory violence is not new. Dr. Herman Long, president of Talladega College in Alabama, recalls that when he was a small boy in Birmingham right after the First World War there was a time of great anti-Negro terror and Birmingham Negroes formed an organization to strike back. They vowed that for each Negro killed, they would kill a white man. For a time they did. This may have discouraged some of the terror, but it didn't free the Birmingham Negro or change his life much. The movement for freedom did not start until Birmingham Negroes moved onto the streets in mass in an offensive against the status quo. They did that with the weapon of nonviolence.

139

It is difficult to see what comparable mass weapons for offense violence can offer the Southern movement unless someone is ready to propose the mounting of a true armed uprising, and no one has really suggested that.

In the fall of 1964, there was a reign of terror against Negroes in McComb, Mississippi—houses being bombed and freedom workers arrested on the slightest pretext. One night some Negroes became angry and began throwing bottles, but the terror went on and more people were arrested. There was discussion throughout the movement in Mississippi as to what could be done.

The question in this situation, as one nonviolent leader pointed out, was not so much whether the movement should be violent or nonviolent but how it could get on the offensive.

"A few bottles thrown one night—that's not an offensive," he said. "The movement there is completely on the defensive. It is not doing anything. They are just picking our people off. We've got mass arrests, but no mass movement."

This man said he thought nonviolence had an aggressive answer for that situation and similar ones. "I'd like to see Negroes there organize and say to the community: 'Look we have had enough—enough bombings, enough terror. We will not take it anymore. We will not strike back with violence. But we will paralyze your city. We will stay home from our jobs, we will block the highways into the city with our bodies, we will lie down on your streets. Nothing will move in this city.' "

And then, the man said, they should do it. He pointed out that it would not take all the Negroes in the community to make this kind of action effective. The more the better, but even a minority can cause a lot of "social dislocation."

That kind of action calls for much organization and commitment. But so does an armed uprising. The kind of nonviolent revolutionary action described here has been talked about often in the
South; it has never really been tried. Whether the nonviolent movement in its present form is ready to try remains a question. But
until it is tried, the question remains as to whether it makes sense,
even in desperation, to talk about violent revolution.

To many watching and participating in the Southern movement—and contemplating a world which has brought itself to the
brink of destruction by violence—it seems insane to scorn a course
of action which may offer a way to achieve social change without
death and destruction, especially when the varied possibilities of this
method have only begun to be tried.

140

7

THE UNANSWERED QUESTIONS

A Marxist making his first visit South a few years ago sat in on a meeting of young civil rights workers. Later he said:

I've been in many meetings but I never saw people quite like these. No heroics, nobody talking to hear his own voice, people listening to each other, willing to sit long hours until a problem is solved. We've read about how revolutions in other countries make a new kind of person out of those who take part in them. I always wondered if it was true. Now I know it is.

A Christian minister who worked in Albany, Georgia, during the movement there tells this story:

It was hot and stifling; they were crowding people into jail cells like animals. There were 30 women in one tiny cell, and all day they had nothing to eat or drink. Finally in the evening, a jail trusty slipped them a single glass of water. Nobody grabbed it, nobody gulped. Slowly they passed it among them and each woman took a sip. I've been in many churches where they held something they called the communion service, and it didn't mean a thing. To me, there in that jail cell, was the Holy Communion.

What the Marxist and the minister were commenting on, each in his own terms, describes the first and foremost accomplishment of the Southern freedom movement to date: it has created new people. Not all are saints, by any means, but they have been able to achieve a human level that is far beyond the norm in the society of the United States today.

The second solid accomplishment of the movement is that it has created a powerful social force, one of the few great mass movements in the nation's history. It has pulled great numbers of people together, made them a cohesive force, and shaken the country.

And the third accomplishment is that the movement has achieved virtually all of the specific goals it has thus far set for itself: It desegregated the buses; it opened the lunch counters; it eliminated all-white waiting rooms; it desegregated the restaurants, theaters, hotels, and other public accommodations; and now it is winning the vote. Not all of these battles have been won everywhere, but in the main they have been achieved. This is something people who criticize the movement and stress its shortcomings forget. It has gotten everything it asked for so far. Maybe it has just not asked for enough.

When the thousands of freedom marchers entered into Montgomery on March 25, 1965, and walked through the streets where Montgomery Negroes live and then down Dexter Avenue to the state capitol of Alabama, suddenly there was dramatized all that is right and all that is wrong with the freedom movement.

Here where direct action was first practiced almost 10 years ago was the largest demonstration yet seen in the South for Negro freedom. Montgomery Negroes walked alone in 1955, but now on the same streets walked thousands from every corner of the nation, black and white, Protestant, Catholic, Jew, and atheist, young and old. This was a movement that people were willing to travel thousands of miles and to die for if necessary. It was a movement they were willing to spend long hours in unsung drudgery for. It was a movement that seemed to harness all that was best in America, and it was powerful.

Yet, as they walked through the streets of Montgomery, the marchers passed mute testimony to the oppression the civil rights movement has not yet touched; for most of Montgomery's Negro population live in poverty, and many of the Negroes who came out to watch the march that day (and some to join it) came from dilapidated and primitive homes in the back alleys and the dirt streets.

It is not that nothing has been accomplished in Montgomery since 1955. The restaurants are open, hotels are open, the Greyhound bus station has only one waiting room, token desegregation has started in the schools—all things that 10 years ago many people white and black would have said were impossible in Montgomery.

But none of this alters the fact that the movement has not yet touched the things most Negroes need most: a decent place to live and the income to live adequately.

A Montgomery Negro leader, describing conditions there just a few months before the giant march, noted that if a Negro father was earning $40 a week he was doing well. Jobs for Negroes above the menial level are virtually non-existent. Most working women are in domestic service, making $16 to $18 a week.

And these conditions, in varying degrees, are what prevail in Negro communities across the South—and in much of the rest of the country.

This does not mean the freedom movement has failed. It only means its work has just begun.

Now the question is how can it go on from here, how can the powerful momentum it has built be directed to solving some of the basic problems that plague society?

This is a question which alert civil rights activists are well aware of. For several years it has been the subject of discussion anywhere people in the movement meet.

"Of what advantage is it to the Negro," asked Martin Luther King, Jr. in his address to the 1964 SCLC convention, "to establish that he can be served in integrated restaurants or accommodated in integrated hotels if he is bound to the kind of financial servitude which will not allow him to take a vacation or even take his wife out to dinner? . . . What will it profit him to be able to send his children to an integrated school if the family income is insufficient to buy them school clothes?

"What is at stake," Jim Forman told a meeting in the Alabama Black Belt early in 1965, "is political power. But it's more than political. It's economic exploitation. You make $18 a week and the white man makes $65 a week. So now we have to demonstrate, but we also have to organize. Like the Mississippi Freedom Democratic Party. . . . You've got to hold these meetings where you can talk about economics and politics as well as your spiritual well-being."

The problems the freedom movement is up against are essentially the same problems that confront the whole society—only more so. The movement leaders know that too. It was King who also noted that although a greater percentage of Negroes than whites live in poverty, 78 percent of the nation's poverty-stricken families are white (by the government's measuring rod of an under-$3,000-a-year income, which is unrealistically low).

Many people in the freedom movement also realize that programs like President Johnson's "war on poverty" are in the category of going to fight an enemy army with a pea-shooter. The new government programs may get a few jobless young men off the streets temporarily and into a Job Corps; they may do something toward providing pre-school training in slum areas, etc. But they are not going to change the basic conditions of men's lives. And as a matter of fact, unless people organize independently to exercise control over these programs and make them their own, these federal efforts are likely to become channels through which existing corrupt political structures can keep control of the very people who are supposed to benefit from them.

Something more basic is needed, and many active people sense

143

that too. SNCC workers at a 1963 conference heard one of the strategists of the nonviolent movement, Bayard Rustin, say: "When we asked for the right to ride the buses in dignity in Montgomery, we could—with a certain amount of social dislocation—get what we asked, because the seats were available. When we asked for the right to eat in a restaurant we could get that too, because there was room in the restaurant. But with jobs it's different. We are not going to get that which does not exist, and the jobs do not exist."

But despite such discussions—and there have been many of them—no one has yet found a way to bring to bear on these problems the tremendous power of the freedom movement.

144

In the absence of a program big enough to meet the needs that many sense, there are some obvious pitfalls that a social movement encounters. In the July, 1962, issue of *Harper's Magazine,* John Fischer, its editor, wrote a much-discussed article on what he called the need for a "first-class citizens' council" among Negroes. He said that the civil rights battle was virtually won (in 1962, he said this, no less) and that there was need for Negro leaders to recognize the great educational and cultural lag among masses of Negroes and do something about them. Although Fischer disclaimed such notions, the article definitely smacked of the idea that the Negro must "raise" himself to a certain level in order to "earn" the right to freedom. Civil rights leaders were infuriated and said so in numerous forums. Yet over the past three years, a rather curious thing has happened: the civil rights movement in some places is coming very close to doing what Fischer advocated. Tutorial programs in the slums, day nurseries for working mothers, youth programs designed to combat juvenile delinquency are very much "the thing" now both South and North. Often they are sponsored by civil rights groups; or people formerly active in civil rights work have drifted into them.

In the absence of any real change in society, such programs may be needed, but unless they are tied to an organized effort through which people can move to take control of their own destiny their value even to the individual affected is doubtful. For example, the freedom schools in Mississippi opened new horizons for many people because through them people found their way to the Freedom Democratic Party; this gave them a political voice in a movement that was trying to change the society that had thwarted them. A tutorial project in a slum, unrelated to any freedom movement, may be just a dead end, even for its participants. One of the most significant sociological facts that has come to light in the freedom movement is that wherever a direct action project has gripped an entire community (from Montgomery to Birmingham) both juvenile delinquency and crime in the Negro community have fallen to virtually zero. People fighting for basic changes in their lives have a reason to live and a reason to learn. Can these drives ever be created artificially?

The Urban League is proposing gigantic government-sponsored development programs in Negro communities. But can such programs be truly meaningful when they are built from the top down? Those administering the present anti-poverty program claim they are trying to tackle this problem by involving "poor people themselves" in the planning at every level. But will this work when the impetus still comes from the top? Most of the development programs now being projected for Negro communities (and poor white ones) South as well as North are tied to the present power structure either through the federal government or through private foundations which are an integral part of that structure. Can any such program—or any person, no matter how well intentioned, working for that structure—really encourage people to organize to take control of their own destiny? And short of that kind of organization, can people ever win freedom and dignity, or even bread?

It is easy for socialists to resolve this dilemma by simply saying that the answer obviously is socialism, and maybe it is. But to say just that is not enough either. People who advocate socialism need to come up with some specific answers to specific problems the freedom movement faces.

For example, what does socialism suggest as an answer for the Negroes in the Mississippi Delta? In addition to terror from the white man, they face a situation in which agricultural machines do the work now and their manpower is no longer needed; yet if they move to the cities—North, South, East, or West—they are not needed there either. And what about the people in the cities? Nobody likes slums, but nobody likes urban renewal either, for it tears down the slums and puts the people out—and where can they go that is any better? What would a socialist system do in this situation? What would a socialist system do about the growing ghettos of the South—as white people flee to the suburbs and Negroes stay confined in the inner city (as in the North) and the schools resegregate?

Socialists somewhere are probably discussing these questions, but such discussion seldom penetrates civil rights circles. In its 1963 summer issue, *Studies on the Left* published an article entitled "Socialism: The Forbidden Word," by Staughton Lynd, one of the most profound thinkers who is writing about the movement. His

145

thesis was that the years of McCarthyism had so stifled discussion in this country that most people feared to talk about socialism or had never heard enough about it to be able to talk about it intelligently. He said that not only the civil rights movement but other social movements were reaching a dead end because of this lack. He proposed that the concepts of socialism be dusted off for normal conversation and given an airing again.

146

Today the word "socialism" is not quite so forbidden, and one often hears it on the lips of some active young people in the freedom movement. But the years when it was forbidden took their toll. Many who claim they want socialism cannot really define it. They are disgusted with the way things are, they are against the "establishment" that exists—and socialism, somewhat mysterious and still somewhat forbidden fruit, seems like a good thing to be for. This is still not a program, and not the kind of concept that a sustained movement can be built around.

Furthermore, as a result of the years when discussion of socialism was considered almost treason, many intelligent people (including many in the freedom movement) are sincerely convinced that socialist answers cannot be applied without imposition of a new kind of slavery. Those who believe otherwise and advocate socialism need to initiate discussion and debate as to how exactly they propose to establish a socialist system.

One of the healthiest things about the Southern movement, especially the student part of it, is the way in which it has encouraged grass roots leadership and independent thinking on the part of people in the various localities. SNCC organizers, for example, make almost a fetish of their determination not to impose their ideas on a community. Because of fear that the "intellectuals" will control those without formal education, there was even recently a proposal that no one with more than an eighth-grade education be allowed on the SNCC governing body. This didn't pass, but it indicates the mood. With this kind of atmosphere it is utterly unthinkable that any socialist with complete blueprints for the new world could impose his ideas full-blown on the Southern movement.

But what could happen is that more socialist ideas could get into the general atmosphere, more socialist answers to specific problems of the South into discussions large and small. This would surely be all to the good, for it would stimulate discussion of the basic nature of our social order and what needs to be done about it. As and when various ideas on that question permeate the movement, people will take hold of them, refine them, adapt them, make them suit their needs. What finally emerges might very well be something new and different from the precise answers of traditional socialism—and it could be better.

No one need think it is going to be smooth sailing to open up free discussion of ideas like socialism. There are many pressures to encourage continued silence. One must look at the last 20 years whole: the anti-Communist hysteria of the postwar period, the investigations, the jailings, the lists, and the restrictive laws were all part of a pattern created by people who do not want things to change and do not want control of society to slip out of their own hands. It was for this that they silenced the country. The Negro revolt, starting in 1955, broke through this silence simply because the craving for freedom could not be stilled. The forces that want to maintain the status quo could not stop this revolt, so they moved to contain it; they have tried to dilute it, divert it, satisfy it with concessions before it forced an overhaul of the entire society.

When he was the Attorney General, Robert Kennedy said a revealing thing during mass demonstrations against segregation in 1963. He said that racial problems in the South were easier to solve than those in the North because the demands were simpler—open public accommodations, etc.—and that these things could be granted and a "valve released." The day when it was that simple has now passed, and the same forces that created a witch hunt 20 years ago can be expected to revive it now—and indeed they are doing so. They cannot undo the last 10 years, they cannot destroy the freedom movement, but they can try to divide it and they are trying. The new attacks on SNCC and the Freedom Democratic Party are part of this. The silence of some supposed liberals in the face of plans by the House Un-American Activities Committee to investigate the Ku Klux Klan along with what they call "extremism" in the civil rights movement (the "plague on both your houses" approach) is another manifestation.

All of this is to be expected. As Jim Forman says, "We are trying to take their power away from them; you expect to be hit in the head." The question is whether enough people will see through the subtle atmosphere of fear created by the banning of words and concepts like socialism, will see the need to break through the fetters this time and bring such concepts out into the open sunlight so that all ideas can be examined, will see the need to look for the causes as well as the effects of second-class citizenship, will see that when you set up forbidden areas of thought you choke off all creative thought and thus surround your movement with a maze of dead-end streets.

There are also internal pressures in the movement that discourage serious consideration of ideas like socialism. The most ac-

147

tive and militant people in the South, especially the young people, tend to shy away from big concepts and what they may consider proposals for final answers.

The most committed young people who go into social action today tend to prefer projects where they work closely with a relatively small number of people. They like to teach in a Southern freedom school, or organize councils of the unemployed in a Northern slum. Their object, they will tell you, is to find and develop local leaders, to help these people find themselves and organize to establish their own control over the decisions that affect their lives.

When Howard Zinn told the 1963 SNCC conference that they must face the fact that even the ballot would not give people much power, the solution he offered was to build up what he called "centers of power outside the official political mechanism" able to exert pressure on the social structure, and that is exactly what SNCC has been busy doing. All of this makes for a very healthy grass roots movement. But if you ask the people who are busy building these "pockets of power," as some SNCC people call them, what their ultimate goal is—just what "decisions that affect their lives" the people they are organizing are eventually going to be called on to make—many of them would rather not talk about it.

Partly this results from the organizers' fear that they will try to force their opinions on the people they are working with. It also reflects their rejection of most of the established social reform movements in the country. Young activists who take this position (and there are great numbers of them) tend to have no use for what they call "coalition politics."

The proponents of "coalition politics" within the civil rights movement favor an alliance among the civil rights organizations, labor movement, church and so-called liberal forces to bring economic changes in the country. Bayard Rustin advocates something like this—and some young people who say that contact with Rustin or his ideas was the first radical influence in their lives now consider him a conservative force. SCLC tends to lean in the coalition direction—although some younger people on the SCLC staff reject it, as do many more among SNCC workers. In the view of these people, the groups with which the proposed "coalition" is suggested are themselves a part of the corrupt system and cannot therefore be allies for the building of something new. These young people prefer to start from scratch, with grass roots people who can shape their own forms for political and social change.

Yet many of them, after rejecting the possibility of an alliance with existing groups to work toward broad social goals, go on to reject

148

establishing any broad goals of their own. So their refusal to give serious consideration to answers such as socialism reflects also a basic distrust of big solutions. Perhaps they acquired an unconscious sense of caution by hearing tales of an older generation of radicals who staked their lives on a belief in the perfectibility of man under socialism and then were cruelly disillusioned when perfection did not come. Or perhaps they reflect the mood of a generation that has been told so long about how complex is the world they live in that they no longer want to look at it all in a piece. We have here the paradox of a strange sort of cynicism in some of the most idealistic people one can imagine. They seem to feel, although many don't articulate it, that there probably are no big answers to society's problems, and that one must accept this, that the most an individual can do is build something creative and democratic in the corner that he can see and be a part of. This is not the thinking of everyone in the active Southern movement, but it is more prevalent than many people suppose; and it is, to one degree or another, the thinking of most of the people who are working the hardest and sacrificing the most.

149

One can admire their commitment, one can agree that the building of "pockets of power" is tremendously important. But is it ultimately enough? You can talk about new values and a new society, but some day don't you have to spell out the shape of it?

Is it possible that the moral fire of the freedom movement can yet be merged with a clear vision of a new social order for the nation? Is it possible that the great dream of human dignity can yet be tied to some hard and real understanding of economic systems and what they do to men? Is it possible that the passion of the freedom movement for the development of the individual can yet be combined with an overall plan that can hold a hope of freedom for all people? Is it possible that the determination of the young people to place power on a base of grass roots democracy can be achieved along with a rational economic order? Is it possible that enough people can glimpse such visions to mount a great crusade for them?

It may well be, to paraphrase the poet, that all of this is "not so wild a dream as those who profit by postponing it pretend."

KENNETH B. CLARK

The Civil Rights Movement: Momentum and Organization

The History of the Civil Rights Movement

THE AMERICAN civil rights movement in its most important sense is as old as the introduction of human slavery in the New World. From the beginning, the essential conflict of the civil rights movement was inherent in the contradiction between the practical economic and status advantages associated with slavery and racial oppression, and the Judao-Christian ideals of love and brotherhood and their translation into the democratic ideology of equality and justice. The presence of African slaves visibly different in culture and color of skin intensified this conflict which demanded resolution.

One could read the early history of America as an attempt to resolve this conflict by combining both, that is, by continuing slavery while making grudging concessions to religious and democratic ideology. The decision to convert some of the African slaves to Christianity and to teach some to read could be interpreted as the first "victory" of the civil rights movement, but at the same time it paradoxically intensified the conflict. It would have been more consistent logically to leave the African slave heathen and ignorant if he were to be kept in slavery. Yet the economic demands of slavery required that the slaves be skilled, adaptable, and efficient. The fact that such skill could be developed was evidence of the humanity of the African and the beginning of the end of human slavery in a society committed to social and political democracy. The dynamics of the contemporary civil rights movement continues to reflect this same struggle between the desire to deny the Negro full and unqualified status as a human being and the unquestioned evidence that such denial cannot be based upon fact.

Signs of a civil rights renaissance in the North emerged in the

1940's when Negro resentment mounted against segregation in the armed services and discrimination in employment. A new period of overt and sustained protest had begun. In 1941, A. Philip Randolph threatened a march on Washington to force President Roosevelt to issue the first executive order compelling fair employment of Negroes. Testimony to the depth of the ambivalence of the American nation on civil rights was the fact that Roosevelt, himself generally considered one of the most liberal and far-seeing Presidents in American history, only reluctantly issued this order. His noted charm was brought into play in an attempt to persuade Randolph to compromise his demands. He appealed to Randolph's patriotism and his unwillingness to embarrass the nation at a time of dire emergency; only when all of these appeals failed did he accede to Randolph's demand. This conflict between Roosevelt and Randolph marked the beginning of a new militance and assertiveness on the part of the Northern Negro. It has been sustained ever since.

Since World War II, the Negro had succeeded in eliminating segregation in the armed forces, and, unsatisfied with less in peace than he had won in war, he gained a series of victories in the federal courts, culminating in the historic May 17, 1954 *Brown vs. Board of Education* decision of the United States Supreme Court. He developed and refined techniques for nonviolent direct-action boycotts in the South, resulting in the elimination of the more flagrant forms and symbols of racial segregation. The massive legislative commitment to racial reform, codified by the passage of the 1964 and 1965 Civil Rights Acts, had begun. The American press justified and validated the claims of its freedom and responsibility in its generally objective recording of racial injustices, while television brought into American living rooms the stark mob faces of primitive race hatred. The importance of television must eventually be evaluated by historians, but to this observer it appears to have played a most crucial role in intensifying the commitment of both Negroes and whites and increasing the momentum of the civil rights movement.

International politics also played a strong role in the struggle for justice. With the overthrow of colonial domination in the postwar decade, white Europeans and Americans could no longer sustain their political dominance over the nonwhite peoples of Asia and Africa. The increasing dignity associated with the independence of these colored peoples provided a new source of strength for the American Negro. And one should not underestimate the role of the

Communist ideology as an aggressive world adversary of the American and Western concept of democracy. American Communists had never been successful in exploiting the grievances of the American Negro and attracting any significant numbers of Negroes to the Communist cause—probably because their dogmatic inability to understand the subtle but important psychological aspects of the Negro's aspirations and struggles had led them to advocate *segregation* under the guise of self-determination in the Black Belt. Nevertheless, the competitive struggle between world Communism and the American concept of democracy demanded an American response to this embarrassing and easily exploited violation of democratic ideals. America risked standing before the world as a hypocrite or resting its claims for leadership on might alone, subordinating any democratic ideological basis of appeal. The international struggle for the first time clearly placed racists on the defensive, in grave danger of being classed as subversives in their threat to America's ideological power.

153

One could define the civil rights movement in terms of organized and sustained activity directed toward the attainment of specific racial goals or the alleviation or elimination of certain racial problems. Such a definition, with its emphasis upon organization as the basis for changes in the status of Negroes in America, would suggest that the civil rights movement was synonymous with civil rights organizations. But this definition would obscure the important fact that the civil rights movement had its own historic and impersonal momentum, responsive to deep and powerful economic and international events and political and ideological forces beyond the control of individuals, agencies, or perhaps even individual governments. In fact, the uncontrollable power and momentum of the civil rights movement impelled it to create the necessary machinery, organizations, and leaders.[1]

The History and Character of the Civil Rights Organizations

There is an understandable tendency to think of the civil rights movement, organizations, and leaders as if they were interchangeable or as if they were only parts of the same historic and social phenomenon. But, while there are similarities and overlaps among them, they are not identical, and their important historical and contemporary dynamic differences need clarification if one is to understand the present nature and force of the civil rights movement, or if one is to assess accurately the role and power of the various civil rights organizations and the actual extent of personal decision-making power held by their recognized leaders. Confusion on these questions can lead only to dangerous miscalculations. Specifically, political and governmental leaders may make demands upon civil rights leaders, demands which they genuinely believe can be fulfilled in the normal course of social bargaining and negotiation. The parties to these discussions may enter into such agreements in good faith only to find themselves unable to fulfill them. Those who view the civil rights movement in terms of the model of the American labor movement, with elected labor leaders holding responsibility for negotiating and bargaining for a disciplined rank and file, misjudge the nature of the movement. One obvious difference is that civil rights leaders have not been elected by any substantial number of Negroes. Either they are essentially hired executives, holding their office at the pleasure of a board of directors, or else they emerge as leaders by charismatic power, later creating an organization which, in effect, they control. Whitney Young is an example of the one, Martin Luther King of the other. So far, no machinery exists to enable the masses of Negroes to select a leader, but, if an individual strikes a responsive chord in the masses of Negroes, they will identify with him and "choose" him. So, too, an organizational leader may be accepted as spokesman by default, by the mere fact that he has been able to avoid overt repudiation.

One cannot understand the nature and the problems of contemporary civil rights organizations without understanding some of their individual histories. The *National Association for the Advancement of Colored People* and the *Urban League*, the two oldest, were founded in the first decade of this century in 1909 and 1910 respectively.

The National Association for the Advancement of Colored People

The NAACP emerged from the Niagara Movement of W. E. B. Du Bois and other Negro and white liberals during that period when Negroes were moving North.

A meeting of some of the members of the Niagara Movement was held in 1908, and it was agreed that a call should be issued by whites and Negroes for a conference on the centennial of the birth of Abraham Lincoln to discuss the status of the Negro in the United

States. Oswald Garrison Villard wrote the Call for the Conference which was held in New York City on February 12 and 13, 1909. It read in part:

In many states today Lincoln would find justice enforced, if at all, by judges elected by one element in a community to pass upon the liberties and lives of another. He would see the black men and women, for whose freedom a hundred thousand of soldiers gave their lives, set apart in trains, in which they pay first-class fares for third class service, and segregated in railway stations and in places of entertainment; he would observe that State after State declines to do its elementary duty in preparing the Negro through education for the best exercise of citizenship. . . . Added to this, the spread of lawless attacks upon the Negro, North, South, and West—even in Springfield made famous by Lincoln—often accompanied by revolting brutalities, sparing neither sex nor age nor youth, could but shock the author of the sentiment that "government of the people, by the people, for the people, shall not perish from the earth." . . . Silence under these conditions means tacit approval. The indifference of the North is already responsible for more than one assault upon democracy, and every such attack reacts as unfavorably upon the whites as upon the blacks. Discrimination once permitted cannot be bridled; recent history in the South shows that in forging chains for the Negroes the white voters are forging chains for themselves. "A house divided against itself cannot stand;" this government cannot exist half-slave and half-free any better today than it could in 1861. . . . Hence we call upon all the believers in democracy to join in a national conference for the discussion of present evils, the voicing of protests, and the renewal of the struggle for civil and political liberty.[2]

155

The Call clearly indicates that, at its founding, the NAACP sensed that the status of the Negro in the North would not be significantly better than his status in the South. The founding of the NAACP anticipated the race riots of 1917, following the clues of the New York City riot of 1900. It was an attempt by the more perceptive and sensitive Negroes and whites to recapture the fervor, the purpose, and the concern of the pre-Civil War abolitionists.

The NAACP, from its beginning, took a more direct and militant stance, in spite of the fact that its founders and its Board of Directors were always interracial. The top staff tended to address itself to legislation and litigation. It pioneered in the use of direct action demonstrations. The more militant approach of the NAACP reflected, among other things, the role of W. E. B. Du Bois, paradoxically both a detached scholar and poet and an intense actionist. The direction and approach of the NAACP, to the extent that they can be attributed to a single person, were determined by his power and personality. In the tradition of a nineteenth-century New England aristocratic poet-actionist-crusader, Du Bois was a dignified intellectual, Harvard-educated, detached, aloof, and cold, but also intensely concerned and committed to the attainment of unqualified justice and equality for Negroes. He may well have been the most important figure in the American civil rights movement in the twentieth century. His importance lies not only in his role in setting the direction and the methods of the NAACP, but in his capacity to understand and predict the larger dimensions of the American racial problem. Like Frederick Douglass, he was a prophet and leader of the movement, but, unlike Douglass, he was a founder and leader of an organization within the movement, capable of articulating the purposes of that organization. Du Bois the scholar gave Du Bois the leader of the NAACP a deeper human understanding, and to the NAACP he gave a significance which a mere organization could not have had without him. Yet his temperament, facing the contradictions and the turmoil necessary to organizational struggle, determined that his role in the organization itself would be limited. One could speculate that the ardor, the intensity, the militance of Du Bois, his inability to tolerate anything other than acceptance of his complete humanity were viewed as a handicap to those willing to make the "necessary" compromises for the survival of the institution. He was a proud and uncompromising man.

The essence of the controversy between Du Bois and Booker T. Washington was that Washington could accommodate and adjust, while Du Bois could not. If the NAACP had been run by Washington, it would have been pragmatic and practical, but not militant or crusading. The clash between Washington and Du Bois was a clash of temperament and principle. Washington was willing to accept qualifications of his humanity; Du Bois was not. Du Bois' dignity and his inability to settle for anything less than total human acceptance set the tone for the approach, methods, and early militant stance of the NAACP.

The Du Bois-Washington controversy could be illustrated by their conflicting views on education for Negroes. Washington's support for a special kind of education "appropriate" to the caste status of the Negro—vocational education, the acceptance of separation (in a sense the acceptance of segregation itself)—was consistent with his pragmatic accommodation. Du Bois' insistence on academic education, his belief that, if the Negro were to progress in America, he would need to assume the same stance as whites, his belief that one could not make judgments about a person's role in

156

terms of his color, his slogan of the "talented tenth," all were consistent with his refusal to allow color to qualify the rights of persons. He took seriously the American ideology. Washington was the realist, the moderate, yet he never founded a civil rights organization, but operated from the institutional base of Tuskegee Institute. He had gained acceptance from the white power controllers without an "organization." It is indeed doubtful that he could have mobilized a civil rights agency. It may be that his power and his usefulness to the equally pragmatic white political and economic structure would have been curtailed by even the semblance of a functioning civil rights organization. That Washington was not a particularly significant influence in the movement during its earliest stages may be due to the fact that his domain by this time was clearly the Southern Negro. The civil rights movement was then becoming Northern-oriented. One could speculate that the doctrine of accommodation preached by Washington and reinforced by white power effectively curtailed the growth of a Negro civil rights movement in the South until the mid-twentieth century.

157

The National Urban League

The Urban League was founded a year later than the NAACP, in 1910, for the specific purpose of easing the transition of the Southern rural Negro into an urban way of life. It stated clearly that its role was to help these people, who were essentially rural agrarian serf-peasants, adjust to Northern city life. Until the termination of Lester Granger's tenure as director in September 1961, the League announced in its fund-raising appeals and to both business and government that it was essentially a social service agency with a staff of social workers. Its implicit assumption was that the problems of the Negro were primarily those of adjustment and that their need was for training and help. The League summoned whites to demonstrate their good will, relying upon negotiation and persuasion to show white business leaders that it was in their "enlightened self interest," to use Lester Granger's term, to ease the movement of Negroes into middle-class status. The Urban League played down the more primitive and irrational components of racial hostility, depending on the conviction that white leadership, particularly in the North, could be dealt with in terms of rational economic appeals. The League courted the white community through its national and local boards, considering itself an effective bridge between the Negro community and the white decision-makers; to this end, it recruited a staff skilled not only in social work but also in negotiation procedure and style. During the early 1950's, one member of the top national staff of the Urban League described the role of the League as "the State Department of race relations," in contrast to the NAACP, which was characterized as "the War Department." This was more than an analogy; the style of speech and dress and manner of the League tended to be a stereotype of the style of the staff of the American State Department.

NAACP and Urban League: Democratic, Nonpartisan, Conservative

These two civil rights organizations, the NAACP and the Urban League, had in common their Northern base and their interracial character. They also shared a basic assumption that major changes in the status of the Negro could be obtained within the framework of the American democratic system. They sought to manipulate the machinery of government and to influence other institutions. The Urban League's primary emphasis was placed upon the economic, industrial, and social-service clusters of power, while the NAACP's primary interest was in political and legal power, with a major emphasis upon propaganda which sought to reach the conscience of the American people, both white and Negro. The League's appeal was to self-interest—employ Negroes, or you will spawn large numbers of dependent people. The NAACP's appeal was to public and judicial conscience; their argument was that America is intended to be a democratic nation with justice for all.

From the very beginning, both organizations were politically nonpartisan and therefore in some measure effective in flexibility of appeal and action. They could not afford identification with a particular political group, for they faced an always imminent prospect of political changes in government and the possibility of retaliation. Their decision, on its face, seemed quite wise; but it limited the extent to which the civil rights organizations could, in any meaningful sense, be politically or socially revolutionary. They could not or did not identify with labor, and their sense of alienation was stimulated by the political immaturity of the American labor movement itself. The rank-and-file members of organized labor, if not its leaders, were contaminated by racism; thus, the civil rights organizations and American labor could not form a political coalition or develop a significant labor party. It would, however, be inaccurate to say these civil rights groups ever "sought" an alliance with a political labor movement. The mere fact that civil rights organizations were necessary made a civil rights-labor coalition impossible since one of the major sources of racial exclusion has been and remains the organized American labor movement.

The civil rights organizations were never revolutionary. Their assumptions and strategy and tactics were essentially conservative, in that they did not seek to change and certainly made no attempt to overthrow the basic political and economic structure. The social changes they sought were limited to the inclusion of the Negro in the existing society; the Negro wanted his own status raised to that of other American citizens. The NAACP and Urban League staked their strategies on a belief in the resilience, flexibility, and eventual inclusiveness of the American democratic system—in an ultimate sense, perhaps in a pathetic sense, upon acceptance and identification with the articulated American concept of democracy. They took literally the ideology and promises of the system and shared unquestioningly American democratic optimism. They believed in the words of Jefferson, the Declaration of Independence, the Constitution, and the Bill of Rights and asked only that these rights—and nothing less—be extended to Negroes. This was their main source of power. They could be considered revolutionary only if one tortures the meaning of the term to imply a demand to include other human beings in a system which promises fulfillment to others.

159

To call such modest requests disruptive or radical or extremist is to misunderstand and misjudge the logic of the original American revolution, and reflects the sickness of racism. In effect, a Marxist could justifiably accuse the civil rights movement from its beginning to the present, as well as the American labor movement, of being unrealistic and superficial in its belief that fundamental change for oppressed peoples was possible under a system within which the oppression occurred and was sustained.

The purpose of the civil rights movement has always been to counteract and destroy the lie that the Negro is subhuman, a lie that no one ever really believed, yet one that was reinforced by those with power. The fact that the Negro *is* human made him susceptible to and influenced by the same forces that influence other human beings in his society. Although the Negro's indoctrination in democracy was contaminated by the obvious reality of his rejection and exclusion by that democracy, he did not, astonishingly, respond by rejection of democracy itself. He seemed to show a sophisticated wisdom in understanding that the ideal of democracy itself was not to blame merely because democracy, as practiced, had not, for the Negro, advanced beyond verbal commitments. He sought a continuation of a revolution that had already begun. He desired only to join it and share its benefits.

Probably even more important is the compelling reality that the civil rights organizations could not have afforded to behave in a revolutionary manner. Even if a racial revolution were psychologically possible, it was not statistically possible. Negro slaves in the United States, unlike Negro slaves in the Caribbean or South America, remained a numerical minority. Attempts at rebellion during and after the period of slavery were ruthlessly suppressed and tended to introduce not the alleviation of oppression but a new period of intensified cruelty. The stark fact is that the Negro in the United States was never in a position to entertain seriously any notions of major disruption or changes in the existing economic or political system. If his condition were to improve, it would have to improve within the framework of the existing realities, realities which he could not modify in a fundamental way because he lacked the necessary power.

It may be that the strategies and techniques of the civil rights organizations could have been only more systematic and organizational forms of the very kinds of accommodations that individual Negroes were required to make in the face of the superior power of the white system. As the material economic, political, and military power of the United States increased during the twentieth century, the validity of this strategy of assertive accommodation on the part of the civil rights organizations became even more justifiable, practical, and realistic. It is important, however, to understand that these accommodations were never acquiescence in or acceptance of injustice, but rather tactical maneuvers, strategic retreats, or temporary delays, and the effective timing of demands for specific changes.

NAACP and Urban League: Leadership and Strategy

What were the effects of this strategy? There is no question that the rationale and techniques of the NAACP led to notable successes in the field of legislation and litigation. Civil rights victories in the federal courts, including equalization of salaries for teachers, the Gaines, Sweatt, and McLaurin cases, the restrictive covenant cases, and, finally, the *Brown vs. Board of Education* school-desegregation decision of 1954, are examples of the extent to which the NAACP has removed almost every legal support for racial segregation in all aspects of American life. Probably the only exception to this is the remaining laws dealing with intermarriage, and these laws may soon be declared unconstitutional.

The techniques, methods, and organizational structure of the NAACP in 1965 are essentially the same as they were in the 1920's. If one were to examine the NAACP today and compare it with the NAACP twenty or thirty years ago, the only significant difference one would find is an increase in the number of staff, particularly in the Legal Defense and Education Fund, Inc., staff.

161

This important legal arm of the NAACP has been officially separated as an independent corporation from the rest of the NAACP since 1939. But by the early 1950's this technical separation had increased in fact. The Legal Defense and Education Fund, Inc., has its own offices, budget, fund-raising program, and Board of Directors and staff. While there has remained a close working relationship with the NAACP itself, this increasing independence of the Legal Defense and Education Fund has made it possible for it to work closely and provide legal services to the newer more activist civil rights organizations such as CORE and SNCC.

The NAACP itself has added some staff for specialized work in such problem areas as labor and housing. The newer and more direct-actionist civil rights groups have forced the NAACP to initiate more concrete measures, but there is reason to believe that this advance was reluctant and that, left to its own devices, the NAACP would have continued to put its major emphasis on its traditional concerns. Ironically, ten, fifteen, or twenty years ago, such concerns seemed to be extreme militance. Today, in the view of the development of more activist civil rights groups, such as the Congress of Racial Equality (CORE), the Southern Christian Leadership Conference (SCLC), and the Student Nonviolent Coordinating Committee (SNCC), the NAACP is seen as a rather moderate, even conservative, organization.

As leaders of the NAACP, Walter White and, later, Roy Wilkins continued the tradition of Du Bois, but they stopped short where he had only begun. There is every reason to believe that Du Bois would have taken the NAACP to the front lines where CORE,

SCLC, and SNCC are now. Walter White developed the method of personal contact and friendship with top public officials, and during his administration an effective NAACP lobby was begun and the legal staff strengthened. Nevertheless this program and his predilection for a "first name" approach to power figures necessarily supplanted direct-action confrontation. It approached the methods of the Urban League and transformed the Du Bois style of militance into one of personal diplomacy. On the death of Walter White in 1955, Roy Wilkins became executive director of the NAACP, after serving as editor of *The Crisis,* the NAACP's official journal. His approach differs little from Walter White's, in spite of the counter pressure of the more militant groups and more activist and impatient forces within the Board and staff of the NAACP. His style, manner, background, and personality are not consistent with a mass appeal. He seems more comfortable in rational discussions with key decision-makers in economic and governmental centers of power than before a mass meeting of his "followers." Wilkins is the personification of responsible, statesmanlike leadership. He jealously guards his belief in the rational and intellectual approach to significant social change and refuses to be pushed even temporarily into the stance of the fiery leader. The value of this approach is clear; its dangers are more obscure but nonetheless real. Its chief danger is that a primary and understandable concern of civil rights leaders for a posture of respectability might make them more vulnerable to the shrewd, psychological exploitation of skillful political leaders. The power of civil rights leaders could probably be more effectively controlled by affability than by racial brutality.

The NAACP either was not able or did not desire to modify its program in response to new demands. It believed it should continue its important work by using those techniques it had already perfected. It may, of course, have been impossible for an old-line organization to alter its course dramatically, and thus it may have been inevitable that new programs would have to stem from the apparently more militant, assertive, and aggressive civil rights organizations.

The Urban League, contrary to popular opinion, has by no means been so visibly successful as the NAACP in attaining its stated goals. Certainly its desire and efforts to aid the smooth adjustment of the Southern Negro who moved to Northern cities, while quite laudable, have not prevented the massive pathology which dominates the expanding ghettos of such cities as New York,

162

Chicago, Philadelphia, Detroit, and Cleveland. The fascinating paradox is that the very areas in which the Urban League program has been most active—the blight of segregated housing, segregated and inferior education, and persistent and pernicious discrimination in employment—have been those areas in which the virulence of racism has increased in the North. Obviously, one cannot blame the program and activities of the Urban League for this blight. It remains a fact, however, that the approach used by the Urban League has not effectively stemmed the tide nor obscured the symptoms of Northern racism. The goals of the NAACP, resting on the vision and courage of the federal courts, were far more concrete and limited and hence more easily achieved. The ghettos of Northern cities and the forces which perpetuate such ghettos are clearly beyond the scope of an agency such as the Urban League or indeed any private agency. In response to this, there are indications that the League's present leadership is moving closer to direct involvement with governmental power.

163

It is clear also that the victories of the NAACP in the federal courts, the victories of all the combined forces of the civil rights organizations, leading to the Civil Rights Act of 1964 and the voting rights act of 1965 do not appear to be relevant to the peculiar cancerous growth of racism in American ghettos now spreading from the North back to more "liberal" Southern cities like Atlanta and New Orleans. The difficult truth civil rights agencies must eventually face is that so far no technique has been developed which seems relevant to this problem which now has emerged as the key civil rights issue. Protest demonstrations, litigation, and legislation do not seem to be specific remedies for this pattern of social pathology.

Within recent years, under the guidance of its new executive director, Whitney Young, the Urban League has indicated its awareness of the complexities of the present civil rights problem. The Urban League has joined with more "militant" civil rights groups, associating itself with mass protest movements, acknowledging that a social-service approach is not adequate to deal with the more flagrant predicaments of Negroes in the North and South. It has joined in demands for effective legislation. Whitney Young, probably by force of his personality, his background as an academician and administrative social worker, and his diplomatic skill, has managed to combine the traditional approach with a more dramatic and seemingly more militant stance without major disruption to the Urban League. He has not alienated white supporters; indeed, he has convinced them to increase their contributions. He has demonstrated beyond question that a more assertive insistence upon the inclusion of Negroes in the main stream of American life (his "fair share" hiring plan) and the willingness of the Urban League to identify itself with more "militant" direct-action dramatization of the plight of the Negro have not been at a financial sacrifice. Whitney Young demonstrated in the Urban League a degree of flexibility not yet so clearly apparent in the NAACP.

The Congress of Racial Equality

The Congress of Racial Equality (CORE), like the Urban League and NAACP, began in the North. It was founded in Chicago in 1942 and became a national organization in 1943. From its inception it emphasized direct action and the dramatization of special forms of racial segregation. The founders of CORE were associated in some of their activities with a pacifist-oriented group, the Fellowship of Reconciliation, and the organization was interracial. In the initial stages of CORE, the evolution of a civil rights organization with a larger political commitment seemed possible. The pacifist aura and direct-action orientation of early CORE founders and members suggested a significant divergence from the politically nonpartisan policies and programs of the NAACP and the Urban League. In fact, one of the rationales for the founding of CORE was that it felt that legalism alone could not win the war against segregation.[3]

It is significant that CORE did not become a major civil rights organization until the civil rights movement reached a crescendo after the Brown decision of 1954. Before that, CORE seemed to be a rather constricted, dedicated, almost cult-like group of racial protesters who addressed themselves to fairly specific forms of racial abuse which could be dramatized by their particular method of direct action and personal protest. In 1943, they sat-in at a segregated Chicago restaurant, successfully desegregating it; in 1947 they cosponsored with the Fellowship of Reconciliation a two-week freedom-ride to test discrimination in buses engaged in interstate travel; and through nonviolent stand-ins, they successfully desegregated the Palisades Amusement Park's pool in 1947-48.[4] These techniques could be viewed as the harbingers of the more extensive use of direct action, nonviolent techniques, which, since the Montgomery bus boycott, have become almost the symbol of the civil rights protest movement. Whether or not Martin Luther King, Jr., was aware of his debt to the CORE precedent, CORE set the pattern for Montgomery. The sit-in technique was initially CORE's, and CORE was also the first civil rights organization to rely upon nonviolent political pacifism.

James Farmer, executive director of CORE, was formerly a Methodist minister. He combines the appearance of personal calm and tolerant objectivity with a surprising forthrightness and fervent commitment. He makes no diplomatic accommodation to power figures, but demands uncompromising equality. In CORE's loose confederation of militant and seemingly undisciplined local chapters under a permissive national board, Farmer is a stabilizing influence, a convergence point; he holds power by virtue of his personal example of commitment. But while he is a symbol of the integrity of CORE and is generally accepted as such by the public and by CORE members, so far he does not seem able to control the activities of some of the more zealous and activistic CORE chapters.

165

When local CORE groups in Brooklyn threatened to use a dramatic, but seemingly ineffective tactic—the abortive stall-in to keep people from getting to the New York World's Fair in April of 1964 —Farmer was forced to intervene in an unaccustomed show of discipline to save the national organization. He allowed himself to be arrested at the Fair partly to demonstrate his own commitment to the cause but also to divert the spotlight from his unruly locals. Yet, whatever the anarchism of these locals and the inadvisability of demonstrations not directly related to concrete grievances, there is something to be said for the observation that, when multitudes are inconvenienced or threatened with discomfort, the very random quality of the action reflects the desperation of the demonstrators and has some impact, even if only irritation, upon the white majority. To the Negro, white irritation and anger is at least a *response*. And where chaos threatens, more responsible leaders of society intervene. The danger of disruptive demonstration, of course, is that the intervention may be repressive and the repressiveness may seem justifiable in the name of public order. But thus far CORE has not demonstrated that its tactics and methods are relevant to the problems and the pervasive pathology of the Negro in urban ghettos.

KENNETH B. CLARK

The Southern Christian Leadership Conference

The Southern Christian Leadership Conference, which Martin
Luther King, Jr., heads, has the distinction of being the first civil
rights organization to start in the South. It began in Atlanta in 1957,
primarily as an expression of the commitment of nearly one hundred
men throughout the South to the idea of a Southern movement to
implement through nonviolent means the Supreme Court's decision
against bus segregation. This commitment was made concrete
by formation of a permanent organization, the SCLC, and Martin
Luther King, Jr., was elected its president.

In order to understand SCLC and King, one must understand
that this movement would probably not have existed at all were it
not for the 1954 Supreme Court school-desegregation decision
which provided a tremendous boost to the morale of Negroes by its
clear affirmation that color is irrelevant to the rights of American
citizens. Until this time, the Southern Negro generally had accommodated himself to the separation of the black from the white society. In spite of the fact that Southern rural Negroes in Clarendon
County, South Carolina, were the original plaintiffs in the school-
desegregation cases, one could speculate that if the United States
Supreme Court had ruled against them, the Southern Negro would
probably have retreated into stagnation or inner rebellion or protest by indirection. The leadership of King came immediately, however, as a consequence of a Negro woman's refusal, in 1955, to make
the kinds of adjustments to racial humiliation that Negro women
had been making in the South throughout the twentieth century.
Rosa Parks' defiance was publicized in *The Montgomery Advertiser*, which also revealed the fact that Negroes were organizing.
Ironically, the chief boost to the boycott came from the white press.
Scores of Negroes, who would not have known about the boycott,
learned of it in the Montgomery newspaper and offered help to
King and other ministers.

The bus boycott catapulted King first into local leadership as
head of the Montgomery Improvement Association, formed for the
purpose of coordinating the bus boycott, and then by virtue of the
drama and success of that boycott into national leadership. He had
responded to forces beyond his control, forces let loose by the early
work of the NAACP in clearing away the legal support for segregation, by the urbanization and industrialization of society, and by the
pressures of America's role in a predominantly nonwhite world.

Here was a man who, by virtue of his personality and his role as minister, did not excite an overt competitive reaction from others. He could and did provide the symbol of unified protest and defiance. As a minister trained not only in theology, but in philosophy and history as well, sensitive and jealous of his understanding of world events and world history, King could develop and articulate a philosophical rationale for the movement, an ideology to support his strategy. Associating his role in Montgomery with the Gandhian philosophy of passive resistance and nonviolence, he emphasized another dimension of the civil rights movement in America, systematically articulating and developing the form of racial protest first used by CORE more than ten years before. The question has been raised whether or not this philosophy and the commitment to love one's oppressor is relevant to the effectiveness of the method itself. What happened in Montgomery was not a consequence of King's philosophy. The Montgomery affair demonstrated rather the ability of King and others to exploit the errors of the whites and to unify the Negroes for an effective boycott. There is no evidence that whites react to philosophy, but they do react to what happens. King's philosophy did not exist before the fact; rather, it was adopted after it was found to be working.

167

The development of philosophical and religious support for the method did, however, help to gather support for future action by focusing and refining a tactic and by an appeal to the conscience of Negro and white. King effectively turned the main weakness of the Negro, his numerical, economic, and political impotence, into a working strategy. Practically speaking, he could not seek redress by violence, but he did have available resources of nonviolence. Nietzsche said that Christ developed a philosophy of love because the Jews were weak; and that only when Christianity becomes strong can love become powerful. King's philosophy is actually a response to the behavior of others, effective directly in terms of the ferocity of the resistance it meets. It is not only nonviolent; it is also assertive. It depends on the reactions of others for its own strength. King and SCLC sometimes appear, indeed, to be satisfied, as in the case of Birmingham, with negotiations leading to minimal concessions. King does not insist upon total change in the status of Negroes in a community but considers partial change temporarily satisfactory. What he settles for can be questioned in terms of the energy expended and the risks taken.

One cannot understand SCLC solely in terms of its organization, which is amorphous and more symbolic than functional, even though the national headquarters in Atlanta, Georgia, has sixty-five affiliates throughout the South. To understand this organization, one has to understand King, because SCLC *is* Martin Luther King, Jr. King is a national hero, a charismatic leader, portrayed in America and through the world as a man of quiet dignity, a personification of courage in the face of racial danger. He has the ability to articulate a philosophy and ideology of race relations clearly acceptable to the larger society. As far as the general public is concerned, the civil rights movement has converged in his personality. His ability to portray selflessness and to understand other civil rights leaders has made him a suitable person for his role. In the complexities, tensions, and frustrations of the civil rights movement, King fills an important function of simplification through personalization.

168

The presence of King and SCLC indicates something about the inadequacy or the inappropriateness of the methods and techniques used by the NAACP and the Urban League in the South today. If either the NAACP or the Urban League had been sufficient, King could not have been so successful as he is. King moved into a vacuum that existing civil rights groups did not fill. He mobilized people not in protest against the entire system but against specific injustices. Concrete successes, in turn, raised Negro morale. But SCLC's program, as a means to transform society, is more apparently than actually successful. The dramatization of the direct-action, SCLC-King technique over the mass media leads to the impression that the civil rights movement in the South is in fact a mass movement. In those situations in which white police and political officers do not exacerbate the resentment of Negroes by acts of cruelty and hostility, even King's appeal does not actively involve more than a fraction of the Negro population. It can, of course, be said of any "mass" movement that it rarely involves more than a small minority in direct action, at least in its initial stages.

King himself seems to realize the limitations of his method as shown by his unsuccessful attempt to encourage a less concrete strategy, a general boycott of the state of Alabama. In his plans to extend his program into Northern cities he seems likely to be less successful. In the future phase of the civil rights movement where Negroes confront not direct tyranny but pervasive oppression, King's strategy and charisma may be less effective. Furthermore, it would probably be all too easy to abort and to make impotent the whole King-SCLC approach, if white society could control the flagrant idiocy of some of its own leaders, suppress the more vulgar, atavistic tyrants like Sheriff Jim Clark, and create instead a quiet, if not genteel, intransigence. Such intransigence presents a quite different problem to the civil rights movement. A philosophy of love or techniques which seem compatible with such a philosophy would seem effective only in a situation of flagrant hate or cruelty. When love meets either indifference or passive refusal to change, it does not seem to have the power to mobilize the reactions of potential allies. Nor does it seem to affect the enemy—it appears irrelevant to fundamental social change.

Gandhi, of course, whose philosophy was one of nonviolent resistance, was the leader of a *majority* in the fight for Indian independence, King of a *minority;* this fact, important in an analysis of power, may be the decisive one in determining whether King can achieve a transformation of American society as deep and real as the Gandhian victory in India. The willingness of an oppressed people to protest and suffer, passively or assertively, without bitterness or with "love for the oppressors" seems to have influence only where the conscience of the majority of the society can be reached. In Hitler's Germany the Jews suffered nonviolently without stirring Nazi repentance; the early Christians who were eaten by lions seem to have stimulated not guilt but greed in the watching multitudes. King's strategy depends therefore for its success not only upon the presence of flagrant cruelty in a society but also upon the inherent good will, the latent conscience of the majority of the American people, as Gandhi's did upon the British commitment to justice.

In a situation of benign intransigence—like New York City—or a society of gentlemen—North Carolina, for example—a philosophy of love for the oppressor may be less effective than in Alabama. There Negroes do not face overt cruelty but rather the refusal to alter their status. What do you do in a situation in which you have laws on your side, where whites smile and say to you that they are your friends, but where your white "friends" move to the suburbs leaving you confronted with segregation and inferior education in schools, ghetto housing, and a quiet and tacit discrimination in jobs? How can you demonstrate a philosophy of love in response to this? What is the appropriate form of protest? One can "sit-in" in the Board of Education building, and not a single child will come back from the suburbs or from the private and parochial schools. One can link arms with the Mayor of Boston and march on the Com-

169

mons, but it will not affect the housing conditions of Negroes in Roxbury. One can be hailed justifiably as a Nobel Prize hero by the Mayor of New York City, but this will not in itself change a single aspect of the total pattern of pathology which dominates the lives of the prisoners of the ghettos of New York.

The Student Nonviolent Coordinating Committee

The rise of the Student Nonviolent Coordinating Committee intensified and sharpened the dramatic confrontation begun by CORE in the 1940's and developed by Martin Luther King, Jr., in the late 1950's. The restless young students who originally led the movement used direct assertive defiance and resistance, nonviolent in tactic and yet militant in spirit. They had gone beyond the quiet, stubborn, passive resistance of the bus boycott in Montgomery to a new stage of challenge—no less stubborn but considerably less passive. The first demonstrations in Greensboro, North Carolina, and Nashville, Tennessee, were appropriately in college towns. It was as a result of these that the Student Nonviolent Coordinating Committee was formed.[5] SNCC was organized in April 1960 at a meeting at Shaw University in Raleigh, North Carolina. It took as its original function the coordination of the protest work of the many student groups conducting sit-ins.[6]

This program, representing the impatience of a younger generation, came at a time when more established civil rights groups seemed ready to settle for post-Little Rock tokenism and moderation. During the years since 1954 and up to that time, the letter and spirit of the Brown decision had been effectively eroded. "All deliberate speed" had been translated into "any perceptible movement," or mere verbalization of movement. The presence of a single Negro child in a previously white school was considered a famous victory. But the SNCC "kids" in their worn denims brought new verve, drive, daring, and enthusiasm—as well as the brashness and chaos of youth—to sustain the dynamism of direct-action civil rights tactics. They propelled more orderly and stable groups like the NAACP and Urban League toward increasing acceptance of direct-action methods not only because some of the older leaders found the ardor of youth contagious but also because, after the manner of experienced leaders, they sensed that bolder programs would be necessary if their own role were not to be undermined. The intervention of youth revitalized CORE and sustained the intensity of the direct involvement of King and SCLC. It has helped make possible—indeed it may have played a vital part in—the continuation of King's role as charismatic leader by arousing weary and apathetic Negroes to the imminence of justice, thereby stimulating an atmosphere sympathetic to crusade and sacrifice.

The SNCC uniform of blue denims and the manner of defiance were far removed from the neat white shirt and tie and Ivy League jacket of Urban League workers and the courteous, Biblical eloquence of King. After SNCC's initial stage of urban protest, it decided to move into the deep South and consciously attempted to express through dress, manner, and method a direct identification with working-class Southern Negroes. Nonetheless, many of the SNCC leaders were actually even closer than the SCLC, NAACP, and Urban League leadership to sophisticated Northern campuses where militance previously had been less action-oriented than intellectual.

SNCC seems restless with long-term negotiation and the methods of persuasion of the Urban League, and it assumes that the legislative and litigation approach of the NAACP has practically attained its goals. SNCC has not overtly repudiated King's philosophy of nonviolence, but it does not root its own acceptance of this strategy in love of the enemy. Rather SNCC leaders seem almost nationalistic in spirit, in the sense of pride that they hold, not so much in *being* black (an appreciable number of SNCC workers are white) as in their conviction that justice and the future are on their side. SNCC welcomes dedicated whites and others who presumably share its concern for total justice. The style and manner of the SNCC leaders and workers are not consistent with any overt display of gratitude even to those whites who share their dangers and daily risks. The underlying assumption of the SNCC approach appears to be that the struggle for political and social democracy in the South is the responsibility of all Americans. They approach their programs and tasks with pride, courage, and flexibility and with an absence of sentimentality which those seeking gratitude or deference might view as disdain. They do not seem to be so concerned with the careful political screening of co-workers and exclusion of "radicals" as are the more experienced and "respectable" civil rights organizations. But it would be a mistake to interpret the SNCC style and method of challenge to the racial hypocrisies of the South as evidence of "left-wing" or Communist domination. SNCC is flexible and inclusive—not doctrinaire and dogmatic. Being loosely organized, SNCC has practically no hierarchy or clear lines of authority. The discipline of its workers seems to be determined by each individual's identification with the "cause" and the direct confrontation approach rather than by external controls or organizational structure.

Instead of a single leader, SNCC has many "leaders." Nominally, John Lewis is president of the Board of Directors and James Forman is executive director of SNCC. Actually "policy" and "operational" leadership is not only shared by Lewis and Forman but must be shared with others. Robert Moses, who plays a key role in the SNCC leadership team, directed the activities of the Council of Federated Organizations (COFO) in Mississippi during the summer of 1964. The individuals who coordinate SNCC activities for such Southern states as Georgia, Louisiana, and South Carolina also insist upon being heard in the leadership councils of SNCC. So far no single personality has emerged to speak for SNCC. John Lewis and Bob Moses seem deceptively retiring and soft-spoken in manner, but each is doggedly determined, assertive, and courageous in pursuit of the goals of unqualified equality. James Forman and Donald Harris, formerly SNCC coordinator in Georgia, are more overtly assertive and articulate but are no less likely to assume personal risks. The essence of SNCC leadership appears to be this willingness to assume personal risks, to expose oneself to imprisonment and brutality, and thereby to dramatize the nature of American racism before the nation and the world. Its members play the important role of commando raiders on the more dangerous and exposed fronts of the present racial struggle. This is not to be understood as mere adolescent bravado or defiance. It must be understood as an insistence upon total honesty, unwillingness to settle for anything less than uncompromised equality. It is an impatience with the verbalizations and euphemisms of "the accommodations" of more "realistic" or "strategic" leaders and organizations. This stance could be and has been described as "unrealistic" and "radical."

A Variety of Methods, the Same General Goals, and Contemporary Relevance

There are obvious and subtle problems in any social movement when a variety of organizations with different philosophies, strategies, tactics, organizational structure, and leadership all seek the same broad goals. All civil rights organizations are committed to full inclusion of the Negro in the economic and political life of America, without restrictions based on race or color. But each differs from the other in its conception of how this commitment can best be fulfilled.

There is general agreement that the successes of the civil rights movement and organizations have catapulted the civil rights struggle into a new stage with more complex and difficult problems and goals. Martin Luther King, Jr., in an interview with this observer which included other civil rights leaders, sought to verbalize this growing awareness of the fact that the civil rights movement must now address itself to the problem of bringing about observable changes in the actual living conditions of the masses of Negroes. He said:

Well, aren't we saying, gentlemen, that a program has not yet been worked out to grapple with the magnitude of this problem in the United States, both North and South? Isn't there a need now, because of the urgency and the seriousness of the situation, to develop a sort of crash program to lift the standards of the Negro and to get rid of the underlying conditions that produce so many social evils and develop so many social problems?

I think this is what we face at this time, and I know it leads to the whole question of discrimination in reverse, and all of that. But I think we've got to face the fact in this country, that because of the legacy of slavery and segregation, and the seeds of injustice planted in the past, we have this harvest of confusion now, and we're going to continue to have it until we get to the root of the problem.[7]

The disturbing question which must be faced is whether or not the present civil rights organizations are equipped in terms of perspective, staff, and organizational structure to deal effectively with the present level of civil rights problems. And, if not, whether they are flexible enough to make the necessary changes in order to be relevant.

An examination of some of the concrete deficiencies in the organizations themselves shows that the NAACP and Urban League are under the handicap of experience. Committed to a method and a goal, they have not altered either in major ways since their founding. The sweep of the civil rights movement in the past two decades has not significantly affected these two elders of the movement. They still appear to function primarily in terms of personal leadership rather than staff competence. An exception is the expansion of the NAACP's legal and educational fund staff, which still remains

173

largely legal and pays little attention to education. A serious analy-sis of the way in which the NAACP has attempted to modify its structure to meet the current civil rights struggle would force one to conclude that it has done so to a minimal degree. For example, the staff concerned with the problems of housing is, practically speak-ing, nonexistent. As of June 1965, and for the previous two years, the position of housing secretary was unfilled. The NAACP staff con-cerned with labor consists of a director and a secretary. This is true also for education. The staff responsible for public relations, pro-motion, and propaganda has increased from five to seven persons within the past crucial decade of civil rights activity. These facts suggest that the NAACP has made virtually no organizational re-sponse to meet the present increased civil rights demands. The lo-cal branches are archaic and generally ineffective, with barely ade-quate communication and coordination of policy and procedures between the national organization and the local branches. Probably the NAACP's most glaring inadequacy in light of the present and future demands of the civil rights revolution is the lack of a fact-gathering and research staff.

The Urban League seems more modern and efficient in its fund raising, promotion, and public relations and in its relationship with its local groups. It also, however, seems weak in research.

One could speculate that this weakness—which is shared by the newer organizations as well—reflects the difficulty of moving from reliance on personal leadership to the more demanding, less dra-matic, less ego-satisfying but imperative staff approach. Now that the maximum gains have been obtained through legislation, litiga-tion, and appeals to conscience, the difficult problem of implemen-tation, of translating these gains into actual changes in the lives of Negroes, remains. This cannot be achieved by charisma alone. It requires adequate and efficient staffs, working, of course, under in-spired and creative leadership.

In spite of these objective limitations, the NAACP and the Ur-ban League are flourishing. In 1962, the NAACP was said to have a membership of 370,000 in 1,200 local branches in forty-four states and the District of Columbia.[8] By the end of 1964, its membership was given as 455,839 in 1,845 branches in forty-eight states and the District of Columbia. An unaudited budget indicates that income for 1964 was $1,116,565.68.

The picture for the Urban League is even more dramatic. Until Whitney Young became executive director of the organization in

1961, the largest fund-raising total in any one year was $325,000. In 1962, contributions were $700,000; in 1963, $1,441,000; and in 1964, $1,650,000. Of particular note is the fact that, prior to 1962, no corporate body had made a contribution of more than $5,000 to the Urban League. In 1964, several donations of $50,000 were received from corporations, and foundations have given as much as $150,000. These impressive accretions are, no doubt, a testament not only to the skill and eloquence of Young but also, as in the case of the NAACP's growth, to the dynamic momentum and strength of the entire civil rights movement. The success of both might be a reflection, at least in part, also of their relative respectability.

CORE's chief deficiencies are its weak organizational structure, the fact that its executive does not have sufficient power, and the problem that it has seemed at various times to be endangered by lack of discipline. However weak in discipline, it is nevertheless strong in enthusiasm and dedication among its members and its locals. It appears to be weak also in its fiscal arrangements, its fund-raising and systematic promotion. CORE is in serious financial difficulties. There is a serious question whether CORE's lack of organizational discipline and structure is an asset or liability in terms of the flexibility necessary for it to be relevant to the present civil rights problems.

Behind SCLC's inspiring reality lie some very real difficulties, many of them quite human. Financially, however, it seems strong; it seems relatively easy for SCLC, through King, to attract a majority of the nonselective contributions to the civil rights movement, despite the minimal organization of SCLC itself. It is reasonable to conclude that if King were not its leader there would be no SCLC. Indeed, it is difficult to understand the role of SCLC's Board of Directors. It and the organization seem to be dominated by the magnetic appeal of King, by the personal loyalty and reverence of his top aides and of the masses who respond to his leadership. It is reasonable to assume that most of those who respond most enthusiastically to King's and SCLC's leadership are not members of his organization. The burdens of this special type of personal leadership are great if not intolerable. Probably the most desperate need of King and SCLC is for an effective supporting working staff to provide King with the type of background information and program planning which are necessary if this organization is to be relevant and if the type of leadership held by King is to continue to be effective.

SNCC is probably the least organized of all the civil rights organizations, suggesting that the degree of organization is not necessarily related to effectiveness or to the appearance of effectiveness.

As movements become more structured, they fall prey to the problems that plague most organizations, namely, red tape, bureaucracy, hierarchical discipline restricting spontaneous and imaginative experimentation, fear of change and, therefore, of growth. In large industrial, economic, financial, and governmental bureaucracies, and in political parties, major decisions are not personal, in spite of the existence of a charismatic leader. Similarly in the civil rights movement, major decisions must now reflect painstaking, difficult staff work based on fact-finding, intelligence, continuing critical analyses of data and strategies. Institutions tend to repress the rebel and to elevate the businessman-diplomat, yet the civil rights movement is full of rebels and its goal is independence. It is possible that the vitality of all of the civil rights organizations will depend on sustaining certain respectable organizations like the NAACP and the Urban League while stimulating them to pursue new programs and encouraging the fluid realignment of younger, more restless forces from whom the momentum for change must certainly come.

Who Speaks for the Negro?

It would be understandable to succumb to the temptation to rank the civil rights organizations in terms of their degree of militance and effectiveness. And it has been argued persuasively that for maximum effectiveness the civil rights organizations should develop an efficient and disciplined machinery for coordination and genuine cooperation. This tendency and these suggestions, while understandable, would reduce the complexities of the present civil rights movement and the role of the organizations and leaders to a convenient oversimplification. The civil rights problems—the American racial problem—are historically and currently complex and multidimensional. Each approach has some validity and no one now knows which is more valid than others. The ultimate test of a given approach or pattern of approaches will be in the demonstration of observable and sustained changes in the status of Negroes— the evidence that the Negroes are included in all aspects of American life with the equal protection of laws and governmental power.

This goal is not likely to be obtained by a single agency, method, or leader. Certain approaches will be more compatible with the temperament of some individuals, Negro and white, than with others.

The civil rights groups vary in organizational efficiency as well as in philosophy, approach, and methods. The rank and file of liberal or religious whites might be more responsive to the seemingly nonthreatening, Christian approach of Martin Luther King, Jr. More tough-minded and pragmatic business and governmental leaders might find a greater point of contact with the appeals and approaches of the NAACP and the Urban League. The more passionate Negroes and whites who seek immediate and concrete forms of justice will probably gravitate toward CORE and SNCC. Obviously one would not offer financial or other support to an organization whose philosophy and methods made one uncomfortable or threatened one's status. Therefore, while the extent of financial support for a given organization may be seen as an index of the degree of the general acceptability of that organization's approach, it is not necessarily an index of the relevance or effectiveness of its program. One is tempted to hypothesize from these data that the financial success of an organization engaged in the civil rights confrontation is directly related to the *perceived* respectability of the organization and its nominal head. Correlative to this would be the hypothesis that the relative financial success of a civil rights group is inversely related to the *perceived* degree of radicalism of the organization and its nominal head.

The question "Who speaks for the Negro?" is real; perhaps no one group can speak for all Negroes just as no one political party can speak for all citizens of a democracy or no one religion can satisfy the needs of all individuals. The variety of organizations and "leaders" among Negroes may be viewed as a sign of democracy, health, and the present strength of the movement rather than as a symptom of weakness. This variety and loose coordination can help revitalize each through dynamic competition. Each organization influences the momentum and pace of the others. The inevitable interaction among them demands from each a level of effectiveness and relevance above the minimum possible for any single organization.

As Roy Wilkins said in response to a question from this observer:

We cannot promise you . . . that there will be a co-ordinated, organized, structural, formalized attack on these matters and that each will be apportioned a part of this task. But we will say this: like Martin (Luther King, Jr.) said, there is more unity than there ever has been before, there's more division of work, and there's more co-ordination and backing up of each other than there has been before. Maybe in 1975, or some other time, there will come an over-all organization, but no other group has managed that, and why should we?[9]

Direct observation and analysis of relevant data and events lead to the conclusion that the stresses and strains within the civil rights movement and within and among the various organizations are real and cannot be denied; and a great deal of energy is expended in preventing these difficulties from becoming overt and thus destroying the public image of unity. But these problems can be seen as symptoms of the irresistible strength of the civil rights movement rather than as signs of inherent flaws or fatal weaknesses of the organizations and their leaders. Furthermore, the power and the momentum of the movement itself seem able to compensate for the present deficiencies in the organizations and leadership. Probably, and paradoxically, the clearest indication of the solidity and rapidity of movement toward the goal of unqualified rights for America's Negro citizens is the fact that civil rights agencies not only have mobilized and organized some of the latent power of committed whites and Negroes necessary for social change, but, in so doing, have now achieved sufficient strength to risk the beginnings of public debate over philosophy, strategy, and tactics. The lie which supports racism is being supplanted by more forthright dialogue and honest confrontation between whites and Negroes, among various classes of Negroes, between Negro "leaders" and their white and Negro co-workers, and within the civil rights movement itself.

REFERENCES

1. For a thoughtful discussion of the Negro revolt, see Lerone Bennett, Jr., *Confrontation: Black and White* (Chicago, 1965).

2. E. Franklin Frazier, *The Negro in the United States* (rev. ed.; New York, 1957), pp. 524-525.

3. Louis Lomax, *The Negro Revolt* (New York, 1963), p. 145.

4. James Peck, *Freedom Ride* (New York, 1962), *passim.*

5. For an excellent study of SNCC, see Howard Zinn, *SNCC, The New Abolitionists* (Boston, 1964).

178

6. W. Haywood Burns, *The Voices of Negro Protest in America* (London, 1963), p. 44.

7. Kenneth Clark, Roy Wilkins, Whitney Young, Jr., James Farmer, Martin Luther King, Jr., and James Forman, "The Management of the Civil-Rights Struggle," in Alan F. Westin (ed.), *Freedom Now! The Civil Rights Struggle in America* (New York, 1964).

8. W. Haywood Burns, *op. cit.*, p. 19.

9. Kenneth Clark, *et al.*, in Alan F. Westin (ed.), *op. cit.*

179

Black Belt, Alabama

JERRY DeMUTH

Dallas County, Alabama. A Black Belt county, with Negroes in the majority though only a few registered to vote, and with no integrated facilities except the Trailways bus station. Birthplace of Alabama's White Citizens' Council and home of a unit of the National States' Rights Party. Target of four Justice Department civil suits against county and city officials and Citizens' Council leaders. Base of operations for a posse organized by the county sheriff which not only quells local demonstrations but ranges throughout the state in its activities.

Dallas County, Alabama, one of the most "Southern" of Southern counties. Circuit Judge James A. Hare summed up its creed last fall: "Any form of social or educational integration is not possible within the context of our society." And Chris Heinz, mayor of the county seat, Selma, said, "Selma does not intend to change its customs or way of life."

In fall of 1962, an organized attack on the county's customs of total segregation and discrimination began when the Student Nonviolent Coordinating Committee (SNCC) went into Selma to assist and encourage local leadership. The SNCC project itself began in February 1963 and continues this summer, though success is as slow coming as in the worst parts of Mississippi.

In June, the resumption of intensive voter registration activities immediately brought on increased arrests and intimidation. SNCC planned a Freedom Day—a period of heightened effort at registering Negro voters—for the week beginning July 6. Registration books would be open all that week, instead of the usual first and third Monday of each month. Then, with President Johnson's signing of the civil rights bill, came tests of its public

1

accommodations section. Violence and arrests, and the resulting tension, climbed to new heights.

Accompanied by a photographer, I went to Selma the first weekend in July. We were followed and watched by police as we entered the town and went to the main hotel. We called the local FBI agent, so he would know we were in town. When asked, he said he knew nothing about recent arrests and violence growing out of theater integration. Then as we wandered to the sheriff's office, we saw crowds of whites in front of some stores, waiting, staring at us with hostility.

About 25 possemen—deputized local citizens—milled around outside the county building. Others filled the offices and hallway inside. A few talked of "beating niggers." After emptying their office of possemen, Chief Deputy Sheriff L. C. Crocker and Circuit Solicitor Blanchard McLeod—both of whom have a number of Justice Department suits pending against them—conducted us inside. We introduced ourselves, and they refused to give us information of any kind. McLeod brought in a magazine with an article of mine which mentioned Selma and read and reread it, getting more upset each time. Crocker took down descriptive information on us. "So we can identify you, when we pull you out of the river in the morning." He had made the same comment to SNCC workers last spring when he asked them to fill out identification forms.

Crocker and McLeod said they knew nothing about Freedom Day and the voter registration drive. Two flyers announcing the drive were posted on their bulletin board and they had already begun a campaign of arresting all SNCC staff persons in town.

On Friday, July 3, Eric Farnum of SNCC spoke at the Catholic Mission about the literacy program. Head of the mission is Father Maurice Ouellet of the Society of St. Edmund. A friend of the movement, he often has visited civil rights workers in jail. Last fall, Sheriff Clark banned him from the county jail. The priest was also threatened with arrest and a warrant was made out but never served. Officials have asked the archbishop to remove him.

Farnum left the mission but before he could walk to the corner was picked up by police and arrested on charges of disturbing the peace. When an attorney and SNCC project director John Love went to the jail, the jailer tried to attack Love. On Saturday, four members of the literacy project were arrested on trespassing charges when they tried to eat in a downtown restaurant. A girl who carried a broken chain medallion in her purse was charged with carrying a concealed weapon. Clark described it as a weighted chain. The car they had driven downtown was towed off by police. Later a sixth SNCC staff person, Alvery Williams, was arrested too.

Saturday afternoon, local Negroes went to the two theaters in Selma, the Walton and the Wilby. At the Wilby, where the balcony was filled, Negroes asked manager Roger Butler if they could sit downstairs. He said they could; the owner of the chain had told Butler to seat persons regardless of race. Despite the angry departure and verbal objections of some whites the group of thirteen sat on the main floor, but not for long. Sheriff Jim Clark and his possemen soon invaded the theater, chasing the Negroes out. Meanwhile a mob of whites assisted by Clark's posse attacked Negroes in line outside. At 6:40 Clark ordered the theater manager to close both box offices and not admit anyone, white or Negro.

183

That night two crosses were burned on the edge of town, and the Dallas County unit of the National States' Rights Party held another evening meeting. Fifty to 150 persons had been meeting nightly since civil rights activities increased.

On Sunday, police arrested Rev. Ben Tucker who had just returned from Memphis with a station wagon donated to the Selma project. That night, as a prelude to the next day's Freedom Day, a mass meeting was held at the AME Zion Hall.

Five local officials in street clothes—one identified by a local Negro as a Klan leader—attended the meeting. They watched the last thirty minutes from outside a window. Charles Robertson told of SNCC's plans: "We're not going to sit-in. We're going to go and eat at a public place. We're going to tell the police what we're going to do and ask them to protect us." One of the officials, leaning on the window sill, chewed a cigar, and smiled cynically.

Outside, these five were backed by over sixty men in brown uniforms and white helmets, who lined up elbow to elbow across the streets, night sticks in hand, pistols at their sides. This was the posse of deputized local citizens that Sheriff Clark had organized several years ago when racial demonstrations began in Montgomery, fifty miles away. Since that time, it has traveled with Clark to Birmingham, Tuscaloosa and Gadsden, helping quell racial demonstrations. The posse has often assisted Col. Al Lingo and his state troopers—Lingo is an old friend of Clark's—and Lingo in turn has frequently come to Selma to help Clark. Last February, Clark joined Lingo 100 miles away in Macon County where free-lance photographer Vernon

Merritt III was beaten near the Notasulga High School. In Selma and Dallas County, the posse has been used not only against racial demonstrations but also to hinder union activity.

Chief Deputy Crocker told the local paper that he had forty possemen there, that there were 200 Negroes outside the hall, 300 Negroes in the hall and that John Lewis, SNCC chairman, "had them pretty worked up." But Lewis wasn't even there, let alone spoke; and the small hall (which was filled) held no more than 160 Negroes, while only twenty-five to fifty were outside. Shortly after the meeting ended and the hall emptied I heard yelling and screaming from a crowd of Negroes to my right. Turning, I saw possemen charging through the crowd, night sticks swinging. Among the possemen's first targets were my photographer-companion and myself. He was beaten and shot at. I was clubbed over the head—seven stitches were required to close the gash—and struck and shoved with night sticks. Three separate times possemen smashed the photographer's camera. After threatening us, McLeod ordered us out of the state. Later Crocker and a state investigator told newsmen and Justice Department officials that we had reported being grabbed and beaten by Negroes. Clark informed the local newspaper he was proud of his possemen and of how they conducted themselves.

Then came Freedom Day. Over 75 Negroes lined up at the courthouse to take the registration test. Each was given a number and made to wait in the alley behind the courthouse which would thus be entered through the back door. Possemen posted at the alley entrance kept away newsmen and anyone else not attempting to register. Even one Selma resident, James Austin, formerly on SNCC's staff, was not permitted to join the line.

Fifty-five Negroes, including SNCC chairman John Lewis, were arrested on orders from Clark. Newsmen were chased away from the arrested group, and two photographers were roughed up by officers. Six whites were also arrested for carrying an assortment of clubs in their car. The local paper printed their names and residences the next day; four were identified as residents of Selma, the other two from nearby Suttle. A newsman confirmed the fact that they were local youths. But an AP report in the Montgomery *Advertiser* stated: "The sheriff exhibited the clubs to newsmen and said the weapons were examples of what 'outside agitators' bring into the city. He said their car had an Alabama license tag fastened over a Virginia tag. Their identity was not released."

Only five Negroes were allowed to take the test that day. The remainder of the week, twelve persons were permitted to take the registration test each day, some of them, however, whites.

That night, the Rev. Ralph Abernathy spoke at the mass meeting. "I come to pledge the full support, full resources of Martin Luther King and the Southern Christian Leadership Conference," he told the 250 Negroes attending the meeting. "We are behind you, with you and even in front of you every step of the way."

Three officials sat inside, listening to his speech. Outside two school buses and ten cars deposited 150 city police, county deputies, possemen and state troopers. (Col. Al Lingo, in town Saturday and Sunday nights conferring with Clark, had brought his men into Selma on Monday.) Nonetheless, the meeting ended peacefully. But Clark told James Gildersleeve of the Dallas County Voters League that he would break up all mass meetings from then on.

185

Although leaders of the registration drive determined to hold more meetings, no location could be found because of threats. Even a meeting already set for Wednesday night had to be cancelled. Finally on Thursday a mass rally attended by almost 300 was held. In the meantime, more than twenty-seven additional arrests had been made, including the president of the Voters League, Rev. F. D. Reese, arrested while taking photos of demonstrators; white youths attacked Negro employees leaving work at the Plantation Inn restaurant; three SNCC workers were reportedly beaten in jail; police towed away another SNCC worker's car leaving the project carless; and ten fresh carloads of state troopers arrived in town.

The next day, Friday, the county got an injunction prohibiting assemblies of three or more persons in any public place. Named in the injunction were fourteen organizations, including SNCC and the Southern Christian Leadership Conference, and forty-one individuals.

The combination of arrests, intimidation, violence and the injunction brought civil rights activities to a temporary halt in mid-July. But it did not bring to a halt the determination to create change in this old Southern city, although the past as well as the present in Selma has not created a situation in which change is easy.

Selma was founded 40 years before the Civil War and became an important military depot during the war. Industries that manufactured arms and other war equipment were established then. The four noted gunboats—Tennessee, Selma, Morgan and Gaines—that formed Buchanan's fleet at Fort Morgan were built in Selma. And the county furnished the Confederate army with ten infantry, six cavalry and four artillery companies.

Dallas County has long had a plantation economy and even today the county is 49.9 percent rural. Two-thirds of the rural population is Negro. Though some industry has come to the area, population growth is almost static. In fact, the Negro population of the county is declining—in 1950, Negroes comprised 65 percent of the population, today only 57 percent.

Median family income in Dallas County is $2846 (compared to $3937 for the state), but median family income for Negroes is only $1393. Median school years completed in the county is 8.8 (compared to 9.1 for the state), but median school years completed for Negroes is 5.8.

186   Only 1.7 percent of 14,509 voting-age Negroes (242 Negroes) were registered in the county as of September 1963 according to the U.S. Commission on Civil Rights. (Fewer Dallas County Negroes could vote in 1963 than in 1956, when 275 Negroes were registered!) But 63 percent of the 14,400 voting age whites (or 8,953 whites) were registered. (In the two adjoining Black Belt counties, Wilcox and Lowndes, none of the 11,207 voting age Negroes were registered in 1962 according to the Civil Rights Commission.)

The first voting suit filed by the Kennedy Administration, in April 1961, was filed against the Dallas County registrar. "It sought an injunction against systematic discrimination against Negro registration applicants," according to Burke Marshall of the Justice Department. The district court denied the injunction, but did order the registrar to reduce from one year to sixty days the period an applicant who fails the registration test must wait before he can take the test again. Eventually, by direction from the Fifth Circuit Court of Appeals an injunction was issued. But it has had little effect on registration. An enforcement proceeding has now been filed and a hearing on that has been set for October 5.

On June 26, 1963, the Justice Department filed the suit, *U.S. vs. Dallas County, et al.*, including Sheriff Clark. According to the Civil Rights Commission the charge was "intimidation of voter registration workers by sheriff and county prosecuting attorney by means of baseless arrests."

Then on November 12, the Justice Department filed two more suits—*U.S. vs. McLeod, et al.* (again including Sheriff Clark) and *U.S. vs. Dallas County Citizens Council*. At this time the department pointed out that from June 1954 to 1960 the Dallas County Board of Registrars registered more than 2,000 whites and only 14 Negroes. It said the board rejected many qualified

6

Negroes, including school teachers with college and advanced degrees, and accused county officials of threatening, intimidating and coercing Negro citizens of voting age "for the purpose of interfering with the right to register and vote."

The Citizens' Council was accused of preventing Negroes from registering and attending voter registration meetings, of using economic sanctions against Negroes and of resisting federal attempts to enforce the civil rights act of 1957 and 1960. Last March 19, the district judge ruled against the federal government in the second and third suits; they are now in the appeals court. The suit against the Citizens' Council has not gone to trial yet.

Selma is the birthplace and stronghold of the Citizens' Councils of Alabama. The Dallas County council was organized in 1954 by Attorney General Patterson of Mississippi and is partly subsidized by the state and large industries nearby. In April, 1960, Birmingham Police Commissioner Eugene Connor, who hails from Selma, told a Citizens' Council rally in Selma, "We are on the one yard line. Our backs are to the wall. Do we let Negroes go over for a touchdown, or do we raise the Confederate flag as did our forefathers and tell them, 'You shall not pass'?" 187

This last cry has been the attitude of the council and of county officials. In a full-page ad in the Selma *Times-Journal*, June of last year, the council said its "efforts are not thwarted by courts which give sit-in demonstrators legal immunity, prevent school boards from expelling students who participate in mob activities and would place the federal referees at the board of voter registrars." The ad asked, "Is it worth four dollars to you to prevent sit-ins, mob marches and wholesale Negro voter registration efforts in Selma?" In October 1963, the Dallas County Citizens' Council was the largest in the state with 3,000 members. A lot of citizens must have thought the four dollars worthwhile.

Last summer, like this summer, there were increased voter registration and integration activities in Selma and Dallas County, leading a Citizens' Council spokesman to comment in October, "I never thought it would happen in Selma. But I tell you this. We are not going to give in. If we let them have an inch, they would want to go all the way."

Nine months have passed since that statement—nine months of determined and hard work by hundreds of Negroes in the face of threats, beatings and arrests—and Selma still has not yielded that inch.

Negro Demonstrations and the Law: Danville as a Test Case

James W. Ely, Jr. *

The hectic events of the summer of 1963 abruptly shattered the prevailing domestic calm of the United States. Widespread Negro demonstrations that summer contrasted sharply with the peaceful 1950's and heralded the advent of the major disorders and urban riots which characterized the late 1960's. Growing directly out of the civil rights movement, the 1963 demonstrations reflected the impatience of black Americans with the leisurely implementation of *Brown v. Board of Education*[1] and the other equal rights decisions. Moreover, they indicated that Negroes were no longer content to await executive and judicial action, the impact of which had too often proved minimal or illusory in the past. The era of direct action had begun in early 1960 with the lunch counter sit-ins. By the spring of 1963, however, racial disturbances in Birmingham raised the level of violence and spawned numerous lesser protests across the South. The protest movement presented a serious crisis in law enforcement and respect for the law.

189

Perhaps the most significant of these secondary demonstrations occurred in Danville, Virginia. Overshadowed by the massive national publicity accorded the Birmingham affair, the Danville disturbances have not received a careful study.[2] The Danville experience, however, is instructive in several areas. Its study raises a series of important questions. How did the law, both state and federal, respond to the outbreak of racial demonstrations? What was the role of the courts, and of the Kennedy administration, in handling the Negro protest movement? What does the Danville imbroglio suggest about the feasibility of the resort to direct action tactics? Considered in a broader context, a study of the Danville demonstrations

* Assistant Professor of Law, Vanderbilt University. Member, Bar of State of New York. A.B. 1959, Princeton University; LL.B. 1962, Harvard Law School; Ph.D. 1971, University of Virginia. The author wishes to express his appreciation to the National Endowment for the Humanities and the Vanderbilt University Research Council for grants assisting part of the research on which this study is based.

1. 347 U.S. 483 (1954).

2. Two attorneys and civil rights activists have described their experiences in Danville: L. HOLT, AN ACT OF CONSCIENCE (1965); W. M. KUNSTLER, DEEP IN MY HEART 211-32 (1966). For other accounts of the Danville demonstrations see A BUNI, THE NEGRO IN VIRGINIA POLITICS, 1902-1965, at 214-16 (1967); G. Powell, Jr., Black Cloud over Danville—the Negro Movement in Danville, Virginia, in 1963, 1968 (unpublished thesis in University of Richmond Library); "Danville on Trial," New Republic Nov. 2, 1963, at 11-12.

illustrates a major, and surprisingly successful, chapter in Virginia's resistance to any change in the racial status quo.

The City and the Demonstrations

The City of Danville is located on the Dan River in Southside Virginia, just north of the boundary with North Carolina. In 1960 the city contained a population of 46,577, of which 11,558 or 24.73 per cent were Negroes.[3] Danville was governed by nine councilmen elected at large, and the council in turn named the city manager. The largest industry was Dan River Mills, which employed about 9,500 people in Danville alone.[4] In addition, there were tobacco processing and storage plants, and factories of Corning Glass Works. Two institutions of higher education, Averett College and Stratford Junior College, were located in the city. Danville's newspapers, the morning *Register* and the afternoon *Bee*, followed a staunchly conservative editorial line.

Although Danville appeared a bustling commercial center, the past weighed heavily on the city as it did upon so much of the South. Danville had been the site of prisons for Union soldiers during the Civil War. For a week in April, 1865, the city served as the last capitol of the Confederacy after Jefferson Davis fled there from Richmond.[5] Located in the heart of the Virginia black belt, Danville had long maintained a rigidly segregationist line in the area of race relations. These racial tensions were demonstrated most vividly by the serious Danville riot of November, 1883. That disturbance developed out of the exceedingly bitter political struggle between the Virginia Democrats and the Readjusters, a relatively liberal state political faction that included blacks and Republicans.[6] During the 1880's a majority of Danville's population was black, and in 1882 Negro voters elected a Readjuster majority to the city council. The Readjuster city administration appointed black policemen and named Negroes to important municipal posts. Although the mayor and chief of police were white, Danville whites became increasingly restive. As part of their campaign in the forthcoming legislative elections, the Democrats seized upon the race issue, and particularly the situation in Danville, as a stratagem to boost the fortune

190

3. U.S. Census of Population, Virginia: General Population Characteristics, 1960.

4. For the growth of Dan River Mills see R. SMITH, MILL ON THE DAN: A HISTORY OF DAN RIVER MILLS, 1882-1950 (1960).

5. L. HAIRSTON, A BRIEF HISTORY OF DANVILLE, VIRGINIA, 1728-1954 (1955).

6. The Readjusters breached Virginia political tradition by their efforts to lure black votes. *See* J. Moore, To Carry Africa into the War: the Readjuster Movement and the Negro, 1968 (unpublished thesis in University of Virginia Library); C. PEARSON, THE READJUSTER MOVEMENT IN VIRGINIA (1917).

of their party. On Saturday, November 3, 1883—just four days prior to the election—armed whites, inflamed by Democratic campaign propaganda, fired indiscriminately into a crowd of Negroes, killing four blacks and wounding ten. The governor called out the militia and the city was subsequently placed under martial law. Both in Danville and throughout Virginia, the Democrats effectively used the Danville riot and appeals for white supremacy to regain political ascendancy.[7] No one was ever arrested or punished for the shootings. Hence, a resort to violence to defend white rule was nothing novel in Danville.[8] Subsequently, in 1906 the city was the scene of a short-lived and unsuccessful Negro boycott against the introduction of segregated streetcars.[9]

191

Racial attitudes in the Old Dominion had not changed appreciably when the Supreme Court decided the *Brown* case in 1954. After a brief period of indecision, the state political leadership, headed by United States Senator Harry F. Byrd, adopted a policy of massive resistance to school integration. Space does not permit an exhaustive discussion of the many legal and practical problems posed by massive resistance. Briefly stated, massive resistance was a program which sought to halt school integration anywhere in Virginia by erecting a series of defensive rings: a statewide pupil assignment plan administered by a Pupil Placement Board that would try to forestall integration by elaborate criteria and cumbersome proce-

7. Ten days before the election a circular entitled "Coalition Rule in Danville" appeared over the signature of several Danville businessmen. The circular was addressed to the citizens of southwest Virginia and described in lurid detail the alleged conditions of Negro domination in Danville. The purpose of the Danville circular was to solidify the white voters behind the Democratic Party. *See* "Coalition Rule in Danville" 1883, (circular in Virginia Historical Society).

8. Concerned about the adverse publicity given Danville in the northern press, a meeting of white citizens appointed a committee to investigate the riot. The committee report blamed the riot on Negroes and the Readjuster city administration; " . . . there was engendered in the minds of the Negroes of Danville a belief that as against the white men they would receive the support and protection of the municipal government. In consequence of which belief they became rude, insolent and intolerant to the white citizens of the town, and the bad temper and ill-feeling between the races thus generated continued to increase and was of late greatly aggravated by the heated political canvass preceding the election. . . ." *Report of the Committee of Forty* (Richmond, 1883). A committee of the United States Senate also investigated the Danville riot. The majority report, adopted by a 5-4 vote, attributed the disorders to the efforts of the Democratic Party to excite the race issue. SENATE COMM. ON PRIVILEGES AND ELECTIONS. REPORT UPON DANVILLE, VIRGINIA RIOT (Washington 1884). For scholarly treatment of the subject see C. WYNES, RACE RELATIONS IN VIRGINIA, 1870-1902 (1961); Calhoun, *The Danville Riot and Its Repercussions on the Virginia Election of 1883*, in 3 EAST CAROLINA COLLEGE PUBLICATIONS IN HISTORY, at 25-51 (1966); J. Melzer, The Danville Riot, November 3, 1883, 1963 (unpublished thesis in University of Virginia Library).

9. Meier and Rudwick, *Negro Boycotts of Segregated Streetcars in Virginia, 1904-1907*, 81 VA. MAGA. HIST. AND BIOG. at 479-87 (1973).

dures, and a statutory mandate that the governor close any school confronted with a final integration order and attempt to reorganize such school on a segregated basis. If all else failed, the governor was authorized, in his discretion, to permit a closed school to reopen with racial integration, but all state appropriations were automatically cut off to any integrated schools. A program of tuition grants was established to facilitate attendance at private schools by students adversely affected by the public school closings.[10]

192

The Byrd organization, as the senator's political friends were known, completely dominated the agencies of state government in the 1950's and enacted the massive resistance legislation at a special session of the Virginia legislature in September of 1956. Byrd represented the interests of white, conservative, property-owning Virginians, and, although never a race-baiter, he was personally antagonistic to racial integration. Convinced that the *Brown* opinion was "illegal and a usurpation of power," Byrd admitted that the opinion "has disturbed me more than anything that has occurred in my political career."[11] Pursuant to massive resistance, white schools in three Virginia localities were closed during the fall semester of 1958. The policy expired in January of 1959 when the Virginia Supreme Court of Appeals and a three-judge federal district court declared massive resistance unconstitutional.[12]

While there was considerable unease about the school closing aspects of massive resistance, there was at the same time no white support for racial integration. Through their elected representatives in the legislature, Danville whites gave enthusiastic support to massive resistance and bitterly battled the modification of the state's policy in the spring of 1959. Delegate C. Stuart Wheatley of Danville declared: "What some of the people do not realize and will never realize until it has been [sic] too late is that an integrated school is worse than a closed school."[13] Despite the tactical retreat from

---

10. For recent scholarship on the topic see J. Ely, Jr., The Crisis of Conservative Virginia: The Decline and Fall of Massive Resistance, 1957-1965, 1971 (unpublished dissertation in University of Virginia Library); A. Grundman, Public School Desegregation in Virginia from 1954 to the Present, 1972 (unpublished dissertation in Wayne State University Library); N. BARTLEY, THE RISE OF MASSIVE RESISTANCE: RACE AND POLITICS IN THE SOUTH DURING THE 1950's (1969). *See also* B. MUSE, VIRGINIA'S MASSIVE RESISTANCE (1961); R. GATES, THE MAKING OF MASSIVE RESISTANCE: VIRGINIA'S POLITICS OF PUBLIC SCHOOL DESEGREGATION, 1954-1956 (1964).

11. Letter from Harry F. Byrd to Samuel M. Bemiss, September 24, 1956 (Samuel M. Bemiss Papers in Virginia Historical Society).

12. Harrison v. Day, 200 Va. 439, 106 S.E.2d 636 (1959); James v. Almond, 170 F. Supp. 331 (E.D. Va. 1959).

13. Letter from C. Stuart Wheatley to J. Lindsay Almond, September 22, 1958 (Almond Executive Papers in Virginia State Library).

massive resistance to a program of containment, the Old Dominion was successful in holding school integration to token levels during the early 1960's.[14]

Danville's first modern experience with racial integration took place during 1960 in the city's public libraries, and the degree of municipal opposition did not bode well for more ambitious integration plans. The city had long maintained two libraries: the main library—the Confederate Memorial Library—reserved for whites, and a small branch library for Negroes. Each library issued its own cards, which were restricted to use in the issuing library. On April 2 a group of black students attempted to use the facilities of the Confederate Memorial Library. The city manager responded by temporarily closing the main library. Two days later, the city council reopened the main library but limited access to the present holders of library cards.[15] The Negroes filed suit in federal district court alleging that they were subject to unlawful discrimination in their use of the municipal library facilities. In May, Judge Roby C. Thompson directed Danville to cease practicing racial discrimination in the operation of its libraries and to permit all persons with library cards to use the main library.[16] Responding unanimously to the decision, the city council closed both libraries on May 20, just prior to the effective date of the court order, and scheduled a June advisory referendum to consider the fate of the libraries. The referendum produced a vigorous campaign by Negroes and a small number of whites who urged voters to keep the libraries open. The June 14 balloting showed the strong segregationist convictions of Danville whites: 2,829 votes were cast for keeping the libraries shut, 1,598 votes supported reopening on an integrated basis. Armed with the referendum results, the council voted five-four the following day to keep the libraries closed. Here the matter rested until September when the council, by another five-four vote, reopened the libraries but removed all the chairs and tables.[17]

Although the battle of the library ultimately was resolved in favor of racial integration, similar movement did not take place in

193

----

14. By the fall of 1963 only an estimated 3,721 Virginia Negro pupils, or 1.57% of the total, were in school with white students. SOUTHERN SCHOOL NEWS, (Dec. 1963).

15. For the municipal ordinance of April 4 restricting use of public library facilities see 5 RACE REL. L. REP. 528 (1960).

16. Giles v. Library Advisory Committee, 5 RACE REL. L. REP. 1140 (W.D. Va. 1960).

17. For the library controversy see G. Powell, Black Cloud over Danville—the Negro Movement in Danville, Virginia, in 1963, (unpublished thesis in University of Richmond Library) [hereinafter cited as Powell, Black Cloud Over Danville]; SOUTHERN SCHOOL NEWS at 10-15, 75 (June-Oct. 1960); N.Y. Times, May 20, 1960, at 27, June 15, 1960, at 28, September 18, 1960, at 72.

other areas of municipal life. In the spring of 1963 the hotels, motels, motion picture theatres, hospitals, public schools, courthouses and prison farms remained rigidly segregated.[18] All agencies of municipal government and the entire seventy-man police force were white. Danville Negroes also charged that the city and private employers discriminated against blacks in employment practices. Negro petitions to city council seeking redress of their complaints were ignored. Nine years after the *Brown* ruling, the civil rights currents had somehow bypassed Danville. It appeared to be an example of effective nullification of an unpopular judicial trend, the very goal that Virginia's massive resistance had sought in vain.

194

The Birmingham demonstrations were the catalyst for the outbreak of similar disturbances in Danville as Negroes took to the streets in this segregationist stronghold.[19] The initial march took place on May 31; it was peaceful and no arrests were made. The local press ignored the first marches. During the hot and muggy month of June, however, the demonstrations grew more disorderly and took the form of marches, singing and chanting, mass picketing, trespass on private property, sit-ins (including one in the city manager's office), and impeding traffic and downtown business. Danville's Municipal Building became the focal point of the disturbances. These almost daily events soon exacerbated the already tense race relations in Danville. On the evening of June 5, the Negro demonstrators sat down on a main business street, blocking all traffic. At this point the police summoned Archibald M. Aiken, judge of the Corporation Court of Danville. Aiken addressed the crowd and asked the demonstrators to disperse.[20] This command

---

18.   The initial desegregation of Danville public schools was not the result of litigation. On June 19, 1963, the Pupil Placement Board assigned 10 Negro students to 4 white schools. When Danville schools opened August 26 this limited integration proceeded without incident. One can only speculate whether the demonstrations were a factor in the action of the Board. It seems unlikely that the demonstrations were a prime cause of school integration in Danville because, by 1963, Virginia had abandoned massive resistance and was following a policy of token integration. The Board made similar pupil assignments in other localities which did not experience racial disorders. School integration moved slowly in Danville for the balance of the decade. For a history of school desegregation in Danville see Medley v. School Board, 350 F. Supp. 34 (W.D. Va. 1972), *Rev'd* 482 F.2d 1061 (4th Cir. 1973), *cert. denied* 414 U.S. 1172 (1974).

19.   The Danville *Register* castigated the Birmingham disorders and praised the city authorities for maintaining order "in a responsible manner." Danville Register, May 14, 1963.

20.   Aiken appeared pursuant to § 18.1-247 of the Code of Virginia which provided:

Suppression of riots.—All judges and justices of the peace may suppress riots, routs, and unlawful assemblies within their jurisdiction. And it shall be the duty of each of them to go among, or as near as may be with safety to, persons riotously, tumultuously, or unlawfully assembled, and in the name of the law command them to disperse; and if they shall not thereupon immediately and peacefully disperse, such judge or justice of

was ignored and Aiken was jeered. The next day, upon application by the city, Aiken issued ex parte a temporary injunction limiting the scope of the demonstrations.[21] This injunction provided the principal ground for the numerous arrests made by city authorities in the course of the summer.

More than any other person, Judge Aiken symbolized the determination of Danville whites and the city administration to crush the Negro protests. A native of Danville and the son of a judge, Aiken received his undergraduate and legal education at the University of Virginia. He had served as a Circuit Court judge and as the city attorney before being named judge of the Corporation Court by the

195

---

the peace giving the command, and any other present, shall command the assistance of all persons present, and of the sheriff or sergeant of the county or corporation, with his posse, if need be, in arresting and securing those so assembled. If any person present, on being required to give his assistance depart or fail to obey, he shall be deemed a rioter.
VA. CODE ANN. § 18.1-247 (1950) (repealed 1968). This section was repealed in 1968 as part of a general revision of the laws dealing with riots.

21.   "This day came the plaintiff, by Counsel, and presented to the Court its motion for a temporary injunction and restraining order, which motion was verified and upon the presentation and consideration of said verified motion and affidavit of T. Edward Temple, City Manager of the City of Danville;

"Upon due consideration whereof it appearing to the Court that the plaintiff herein is entitled to the temporary injunction and restraining order prayed for and that under the circumstances of this case, no notice to said named defendants herein is necessary or practicable, it is ADJUDGED, ORDERED and DECREED as follows:

"1.   That said named defendants, their servants, agents and employees, their attorneys and all other persons acting in concert therewith be, and they hereby are, enjoined and restrained until the further order of this Court from participating in the following actions or conduct:

(a)   Unlawfully assembling in an unauthorized manner on the public streets and in the vicinity of the public buildings of the City of Danville;

(b)   Unlawful interference with the lawful operation of private enterprises and business in the City of Danville;

(c)   Unlawfully obstructing the freedom of movement of the general public of the City of Danville and the general traffic of the City of Danville;

(d)   Unlawfully obstructing the entrances and exits to and from both private business concerns and public facilities in the City of Danville;

(e)   Participating in and inciting mob violence, rioting and inciting persons to rioting;

(f)   Unlawfully carrying deadly weapons, threatening to use said deadly weapons, assaulting divers citizens in this community;

(g)   Unlawfully using loud and boisterous language interrupting the peace and repose of the citizens of the community, business establishments of the community and the public works of the community;

(h)   Creating and maintaining a public nuisance by reason of unlawful and unauthorized gatherings and loud, boisterous and concerted demonstrations interferring with the peace and quiet and enjoyment of the citizens of the City of Danville.

"2.   This temporary injunction and restraining order shall be effective immediately and shall continue from day to day until the further order of this Court until July 6, 1963, at which time it shall stand dissolved unless prior thereto it be enlarged or further temporary or permanent injunction granted herein.

"3.   And that a copy of this Order be served upon the named defendants herein."
8 RACE REL. L. REP. 435 (1963).

legislature in 1950.[22] As was the case with nearly all Virginia state judges, Aiken was an ally of Senator Byrd and held conservative social and political views.[23] Moreover, Aiken was unquestionably committed to the defense of racial segregation. In early 1959 he privately proposed a plan to "keep the public schools of Virginia permanently open and segregated, and be [sic] federal court proof."[24] Aiken's plan was designed to take advantage of the superior economic position of Virginia whites. The Judge suggested these specific steps:

196

1.   Repeal of Section 129 of the Virginia Constitution, the section which mandated public education.
2.   Repeal of the compulsory school attendance law.
3.   The legislature, or localities, should impose a school tax on every child, regardless of race, who attends a public school.
4.   This school tax should be a credit against the payment of state income taxes or local real property taxes.

"I imagine," Aiken explained, "most of the Negroes who have been getting a free education at the expense of the White people either could not and would not pay it." He further envisioned a limited scholarship plan for the poor, and white sponsorship of black pupils so long as they attended separate schools. Aiken reasoned that his proposal should be viewed as a revenue measure, not merely a device to prevent integration. Coming in the final, emotional days of the massive resistance controversy and raising a host of new problems, Aiken's ideas never had much chance of being adopted into law. Nonetheless, Byrd evidently found Aiken's proposal sufficiently intriguing to circulate it among his Virginia colleagues in Washington.[25] Later the same year Aiken criticized Virginia's tactical retreat from massive resistance and renewed his call for an amendment to the Virginia Constitution.[26] There can be no doubt

---

22.   Danville Register, November 28, 1971.

23.   In October of 1964 Aiken expressed his highest regards to Byrd and promised to do anything he could to assist Byrd's re-election bid. Aiken predicted that Byrd and Senator Barry Goldwater, the Republican presidential nominee, would carry Danville handily. Letter from Archibald M. Aiken to Harry F. Byrd, October 13, 1964 (Harry F. Byrd Papers in University of Virginia Library).

* 24.   Letter from Archibald M. Aiken to Harry F. Byrd, January 24, 1959 (Watkins M. Abbitt Papers in University of Richmond Library).

25.   William M. Tuck, congressman for Virginia's Fifth District (which included Danville), wrote to Byrd: "Many thanks for letting me see Judge Aiken's letter. I think he is undoubtedly hitting at them in the right way. His plan is worthy of serious consideration." Letter from Tuck to Byrd, January 28, 1959 (Watkins M. Abbitt Papers in University of Richmond Library).

26.   Letter from Archibald M. Aiken to Harry F. Byrd, March 25, 1959 (Watkins M. Abbitt Papers in University of Richmond Library).

that Aiken found the tactics and objectives of the Negro protesters very distasteful.

Despite Judge Aiken's temporary injunction, the disorders did not cease. On the night of June 10, after a full day of protest activity, a demonstration ended in violence as police attacked Negroes massed outside the city jail with nightsticks and fire hoses.[27] The quickening tempo of events in mid-June underscored the unyielding municipal resistance. First, a special seven-man grand jury summoned by Aiken indicted the demonstration leaders under a Virginia statute outlawing conspiracy "to incite the colored population of the State to acts of violence and war against the white population. . . ."[28] For those indicted Aiken set bail at 5,000 dollars apiece.[29] Secondly, on June 11 a heavily armed detachment of forty-eight state police moved into Danville to supplement the local force. Thirdly, the city council enacted an ordinance to limit the time, place, and size of picketing or demonstrations.[30] Lastly, Councilman

197

---

27. Len Holt makes a convincing case that the Danville police overreacted and unnecessarily beat Negro demonstrators with clubs on the evening of June 10. L. HOLT, AN ACT OF CONSCIENCE 23-25, 93-95 (1965). Burke Marshall, Assistant Attorney General, Civil Rights Division, seems to have agreed with this assessment. In a September 18, 1963 memorandum to the Attorney General Marshall declared: "However, I am trying to develop a broader kind of case against this sort of repressive and violent police action. We have one, for example, in Danville, Virginia." Memorandum, September 18, 1963 (Burke Marshall Papers in John F. Kennedy Library). The Fourth Circuit concurred in this evaluation. "On that occasion the police were guilty of excesses, as the demonstrators had been on earlier occasions." Baines v. City of Danville, 337 F.2d 579, 584 (4th Cir. 1964), *cert. denied* 381 U.S. 939 (1965).

28. VA. CODE ANN. § 18.1-422 (1950).

29. 60 Danville Common Law Order Book, Corporation Court at 111-12, 139-40.

30. "An Ordinance Limiting Picketing and Demonstrations; Providing Punishment for Violations Thereof.

"WHEREAS, large, noisy, lawless and rioting groups of people, there being among these armed persons with records as habitual criminals, under the pretext of picketing, have incited racial strife, caused personal injuries and destruction of property; and,

"WHEREAS, such groups have further disrupted the peace and convenience of this community, have placed the citizenry in fear of its safety and have disrupted the orderly flow of both vehicular and pedestrian traffic; and,

"WHEREAS, there are reasonable restraints which must be imposed upon freedom of speech and assembly when such freedoms are exercised in such a manner as to endanger the personal safety and property of the citizenry; and,

"WHEREAS, it is necessary to impose reasonable regulations upon assemblies and picketing,

"NOW, THEREFORE, BE IT ORDAINED, as follows:

"(1) All assemblies and picketing shall be peaceful and unattended by noise and boisterousness, and there shall be no shouting, clapping or singing of such a nature as to disturb the peace and tranquility of the community; and,

"(2) That marching shall be in single file and pickets or demonstrators shall be spaced a distance of not less than ten feet apart, and not more than six pickets shall picket or demonstrate before any given place of business or [public facility]; and,

"(3) That all picketing or demonstrating shall be during the business or work hours of

John W. Carter, a vitriolic segregationist who was determined to crush the protests, moved to the fore as the principal spokesman for the city administration. Playing to the racial attitudes of Danville whites, Carter's popular following undercut more moderate councilmen and rendered a compromise solution impossible. Carter also helped to represent the city in the voluminous litigation which emerged from the disorders.

As the demonstrations continued, so did the arrests for violation of the Aiken injunction and the newly enacted ordinance. By June 17 there were 105 persons under arrest and awaiting trial before Judge Aiken on charges of contempt. The defendants were represented by five Danville Negro lawyers affiliated with the NAACP, by Len W. Holt, a black attorney from Norfolk,[31] and by a shifting group of civil rights attorneys that included William M. Kunstler. The proceedings in the Corporation Court proved extremely controversial and figured prominently in the subsequent efforts to remove the injunction cases to the federal district court. Although a removal petition had already been filed, and although he was without jurisdiction in the matter, Aiken began to try the cases of persons charged with disobeying his injunction. A Justice Department official related the courtroom setting to his superiors:[32]

> The proceedings before Judge Aiken have been extraordinary. The judge has entered a formal written order excluding the public from the courtroom

---

the place of business or public facility being picketed, and upon such days as such facility may be open for the transaction of business; and,

"(4)   That no picketing or demonstrating shall be performed within any public building; and,

"(5)   That no person under the age of eighteen years shall be permitted to march, picket or demonstrate in the City; and,

"(6)   That no vehicles shall be used in any picket or demonstrating line, and that all picketers or demonstrators shall be afoot; and,

"(7)   That violation of the foregoing regulations shall constitute a misdemeanor, and be punished as provided in Section 1-6 of the Code of the City of Danville, 1962."
8 RACE REL. L. REP. 698 (1963).

31.   Holt was in the unique position of being both an attorney for the defendants and a defendant himself. He was arrested for violating the Aiken injunction and indicted under the racial conspiracy statute. Holt was already in trouble with the courts of Virginia. In January of 1962 he was found guilty of contempt of court and fined by the Circuit Court of the City of Hopewell. The Virginia Supreme Court of Appeals affirmed the sentence, 205 Va. 332, 136 S.E.2d 809 (1964), but the Supreme Court reversed on the grounds that, on the facts presented therein, Holt could not be punished for contempt consistent with due process. Holt v. Commonwealth of Virginia, 381 U.S. 131 (1965). Holt's conviction under the Aiken injunction was reversed by the Virginia Supreme Court of Appeals. Holt v. Commonwealth, 72 Danville Common Law Order Book, Corporation Court, 29-45.

32.   Memorandum, June 19, 1963 (Burke Marshall Papers in John F. Kennedy Library). For the text of the order excluding the general public from the courtroom on the grounds that "there is danger of unlawful interference with the lawful operation of this Court" see 60 Danville Common Law Order Book, Corporation Court, 131 (1963).

because of unrest and possible violence. The only ones admitted are city personnel, court attaches, the defendants, their attorneys, witnesses, and the
parents of juvenile defendants.

Witnesses, and even attorneys, are frisked for weapons. All of the city
personnel, however, wear sidearms. The last two days there have been approximately 30 armed police in the courtroom. Judge Aiken has been wearing a
pistol while presiding on the bench.[33]

In the course of June 17 and 18 Aiken tried two cases and both
defendants were found guilty of contempt. The court imposed forty-
five- and sixty-day jail sentences on the convicted defendants, together with fines.[34] Aiken permitted no discussion of the legality of
his injunction and denied defense requests for an adjournment to
prepare its case. In passing sentence, the judge read from a written
memorandum prepared in advance of the trial. Aiken refused to
release the convicted defendants on bail pending appeal reasoning
that "any such suspension of the judgement would render the injunctive powers of the Court ineffective . . . . "[35] Without a stay of
execution, the defendants would be compelled to serve their sentences before an appeal could be heard by the Virginia Supreme
Court of Appeals, effectively denying appellate review. Moreover,
Aiken refused to allow out-of-state attorneys to practice in the Corporation Court unless they produced their certificates of admission
to the bar. He also conducted daily roll calls of all defendants and
their attorneys, forcing the latter to waste valuable time in court.
"Danville's Negroes," Kunstler wrote, "were in the grip of a reign
of judicial terror."[36]

On June 19, Aiken postponed further trials for the contempt
defendants, apparently planning to abide the outcome of the removal proceedings. With the trials stalled, Danville pressed other
tactics to disquiet the demonstrators. Up to half of the protestors
were of high school age and within the purview of the juvenile laws.
Parents of such young demonstrators were arrested on charges of
contributing to the delinquency of a minor by failing properly to
supervise their children. In late June the first administrative level
of the Virginia Employment Commission cut off unemployment in-

199

---

33. Aiken denied that he had ever worn a gun while on the bench, but he readily
admitted that, upon police advice, he traveled armed to his office. Indeed, virtually every
city official began wearing pistols in June. Although avowedly for protection, this policy of
going armed was likely to have a chilling effect on the Negro demonstrations. Martin Luther
King recalled: "Danville, Virginia—upright white citizens, concerned that police brutality is
unsufficient to intimidate Negroes, began wearing guns in their belts." M. KING, JR., WHY
WE CAN'T WAIT at 126 (1964).

34. 60 Danville Common Law Order Book, Corporation Court, 131-133 (1963).

35. *Id.* at 132.

36. W. KUNSTLER, DEEP IN MY HEART 218 (1966).

surance checks for those awaiting trial. The Commission reasoned that persons under arrest and facing possible jail terms were not "available" for work within the meaning of Virginia's unemployment insurance law. With seasonal unemployment falling heavily on Danville Negroes, the action of the Commission weakened the financial basis of the protest and tended to discourage new demonstrations.[37]

Although the Danville demonstrations were of spontaneous origin, the various civil rights groups promptly formulated a series of demands for city officials. The announced objectives of the protest included:

200

1. The appointment of a bi-racial committee to fix a schedule for the desegregation of schools and municipal facilities.
2. Desegregation of public accommodations, such as restaurants and hotels.
3. The employment of Negroes in municipal jobs, particularly the hiring of Negro policemen.
4. The hiring or upgrading of Negro employees by Danville merchants.
5. The dropping of all charges against the demonstrators who had been arrested.[38]

The demonstration leaders further charged that Dan River Mills had a discriminatory hiring policy under which blacks were confined to menial jobs. To dramatize this complaint against the textile company, in July civil rights organizations picketed the New York City offices of Dan River Mills demanding that the concern use its influence to end segregation in Danville.[39] Local blacks picketed and conducted sit-ins before the gates of Dan River Mills.

Obviously, several of the objectives of the demonstrators did not relate to state or municipal activities, but rather to private employers and privately owned accommodations. The city, of course, had no direct control over the operations of such private facilities. With respect to alleged private discrimination, the demonstrations both highlighted the problem and impeded its solution. Merchants, for example, worried that the white public was so angry at the demonstrators that the employment of Negro store clerks might become economically hazardous. Those demands directed squarely against the city raised a similar difficulty. Token steps

---

37. Powell, Black Cloud over Danville, *supra* note 17, at 43.

38. For the demands of Negro protestors in Danville see *id.* at 33; L. HOLT, AN ACT OF CONSCIENCE 142 (1965).

39. N.Y. Times, July 18, 1963, at 10.

might have been taken, especially in the employment area, to meet some of the protest goals. Danville officials, however, rejected any moves that might be interpreted as a concession to the racial disorders. Thus, while the demonstrations continued, the city offered no hint of a compromise solution and turned instead to a determined and ingenious effort to break up the protests. Benjamin Muse described the city's viewpoint:

> The whites feel that the Negroes should be punished for the June disorders rather than rewarded with concessions. They are not irrevocably opposed to the moves desired by the Negroes, but refuse to discuss them under pressure.[40]

In keeping with this philosophy, the city authorities never considered the demand that charges pending against the demonstrators be dropped.

201

A fair example of this municipal attitude is the handling of the demand for the hiring of black policemen. Muse reported in October that "[t]he city has no objection in principle, but it does not want to move while 'under the gun.' I gather that the Negro policeman will be hired shortly, but it must be in a routine way . . . ."[41] As if to confirm this assessment, later that same month, and with the disorders at an end, Danville employed a Negro policeman. In this anticlimactic fashion the demonstrators gained partial satisfaction of one of their major demands.

From the outset of the demonstrations Danville Negroes hoped for a visit from Martin Luther King, fresh from his seeming triumph in Birmingham. Indeed, King had spoken before a large crowd in this troubled city in March. After several postponements, King paid a return visit to Danville on July 11, ostensibly to lead a march in defiance of the Aiken injunction. "I have so many injunctions that I don't even look at them anymore," he declared.[42] Danville, however, was not to be a success for King. His mass demonstration on the night of July 11 drew only about eighty participants and King declined to lead the march. Coming at the very time that he was receiving massive publicity and was catapulting toward the apex of his civil rights career, King found that he could not devote sustained personal attention to the demonstrations. Historian David L. Lewis regards King's Danville campaign as a failure and compares the result there with Albany, Georgia, another disappointment for

---

40. Confidential memorandum entitled "Danville, Va." from Benjamin Muse to Burke Marshall, October 8, 1963 (Burke Marshall Papers in John F. Kennedy Library) [hereinafter cited as Muse, Danville, Va.]. Muse, an author and journalist of liberal racial views, prepared a series of reports for the Justice Department on the situation in various southern cities.

41. *Id.*

42. D. LEWIS, KING: A CRITICAL BIOGRAPHY 212 (1970).

King.[43] With King's inability to furnish effective assistance, the prospect for any meaningful success resulting from the Danville disorders was greatly lessened.

White attitudes, on the other hand, remained adamant throughout the period of the demonstrations. The disorders and marches failed to arouse support from any level of the city's white population. The local newspapers poured scorn on the protest at every turn, linking the demonstrations with crime and communism. Mayor Julian R. Stinson referred to the protestors as "hoodlums."[44] "The anti-Negro feeling at the middle-class and country club level is intense . . . ," Muse reported in October.[45] At the zenith of the controversy over Judge Aiken's conduct of the contempt trials, the Danville Bar Association adopted a resolution expressing "its support and admiration of the Honorable A. M. Aiken and of the extremely able and judicious manner in which he conducts his court, thus assuring a fair and impartial trial to every defendant, regardless of race, color, or creed."[46] No resident white lawyer took any part in the defense of the demonstrators. Likewise, the white textile workers were hostile to the civil rights campaign. Holt explained:

202

> For the most part the Danville textile workers are complacent members of a complacement textile workers union who consider themselves well off. . . . The Negro is both their standard and their *enemy*. Realizing this, they are told by *City Hall* that Negroes are trying to force their way into the union and thus destroy the seniority rights of the white members and their right to pass on their trades to their sons, along with forcing their daughters to sit beside Negro children in the public schools.[47]

The reaction of whites elsewhere in Virginia to the Negro demonstrations paralleled that of the Danville leaders. Virginia had generally avoided mass demonstrations and civil rights violence, and the surprised state officials reacted with dismay and support for the City of Danville. Congressman William M. Tuck commended Danville authorities for "the forthright manner" in which they dealt with the protest. Tuck was confident that the disorders could "be traced directly to troublemakers in Washington and elsewhere who have been preaching enforced integration against the will of the most thoughtful people of both races."[48] He was even moved to

---

43. *Id.* at 211-14; *see* HOLT, AN ACT OF CONSCIENCE 205-07 (1965); N.Y. Times, July 12, 1963, at 8.

44. N.Y. Times, June 11, 1963, at 22.

45. Muse, Danville, Va.

46. "Resolutions of Bar Association of Danville," 109 Cong. Rec. 12211 (1963) (remarks of Senator A. Willis Robertson).

47. L. HOLT, AN ACT OF CONSCIENCE 227 (1965).

48. Powell, Black Cloud Over Danville, *supra* note 17, at 29.

introduce legislation that would bar persons from crossing a state line for the purpose of demonstrating in violation of law. "When I consider the disgraceful concerted defiance of law which has occurred in communities such as Danville, Va., in my own Congressional district," Tuck declared, "it is perfectly obvious that the participants are responding to incitation from outsiders . . . ."[49] Similarly, United States Senator A. Willis Robertson observed: ". . . the trouble you have experienced in Danville recently was the result of outside agitation . . . ."[50]

The response of the state government was largely determined by Albertis S. Harrison, Jr., the Old Dominion's cautious and quiet governor. Cognizant of the importance of maintaining the favorable national image of Virginia, Harrison characteristically followed a low-key path. He eschewed the flamboyant role and the defiant statements that became the trademarks of Governor George C. Wallace in Alabama. Harrison realized that a relaxed executive attitude would minimize the prospects for extensive national press coverage of events in Danville, and thereby give Danville officials a freer hand to deal with the demonstrations. As the prospect for sensational press coverage dimmed, so did the chance for federal intervention. While Harrison sent state police to Danville, he publicly emphasized that better education and understanding were the solution to racial harmony. He declined to encourage the formation of bi-racial committees in Virginia communities. Harrison's desire to call as little attention as possible to the Danville disorders is best illustrated by his correspondence with State Senator William F. Stone, who represented the embattled city in the legislature. Stone called upon the governor "to make very strong statements denouncing what is going on in Danville . . . ."[51] Harrison replied that "I am as deeply conscious of what is going on in Danville as you are," but he significantly added:

> There is a great deal that I would like to say publicly about this matter. However, a Governor cannot always indulge himself that luxury.[52]

He further advised the mayor of neighboring Farmville that he doubted "the wisdom of too much activity on our part when such might provoke demonstrations."[53]

---

49.   109 Cong. Rec. 13429 (1963) (remarks of Congressman Tuck).

50.   Letter from A. Willis Robertson to Landon R. Wyatt, July 11, 1963 (A. Willis Robertson Papers in College of William and Mary).

51.   Letter from William F. Stone to Albertis S. Harrison, Jr., June 17, 1963 (Harrison Executive Papers in Virginia State Library).

52.   Letter from Albertis S. Harrison, Jr. to William F. Stone, June 19, 1963 (Harrison Executive Papers in Virginia State Library).

53.   Letter from Albertis S. Harrison, Jr. to William F. Watkins, Jr., June 20, 1963 (Harrison Executive Papers in Virginia State Library).

Harrison's thinking on the racial disorders is most fully set forth in the draft of a statement prepared for delivery on television, a speech that the governor ultimately decided not to deliver.[54] In his draft remarks Harrison offered the following comments on the situation in Danville:

1.   He deplored the outbreak of racial violence in Virginia.

2.   He pledged to the Negro demonstrators that "Virginia will see to it that your rights of free speech and peaceable assembly are protected to the fullest extent of the law."

3.   He promised to protect the owners of private property against trespass or seizure of their place of business.

4.   He stressed that the fourteenth amendment applies only to state action.

5.   He defined the limits of freedom of speech:

> By this I mean to say that free speech will be protected, but the cursing and abusing of law enforcement officers will not be tolerated in this State. The right to peaceable assembly will be made fully secure, but we shall not permit mob violence to be masked as peaceable assembly. A right to demonstrate will not be equated, in Virginia, with some imagined right to take effective possession of private property. The right to petition for redress of grievances will not be converted into a license to intimidate, to coerce, and to extort. The right of protesting groups to walk the streets in freedom will not be made superior to the right of all men to walk the streets in safety.

6.   He alerted units of the Virginia National Guard for possible riot duty and, contrary to his earlier position, he now urged that cities and counties consider creating bi-racial committees.

7.   He concluded by saying that social "changes of this magnitude cannot successfully be imposed by compulsion, by coercion, or by the suppression of any of the rights with which free men are endowed."

Harrison's undelivered remarks indicate a painstaking effort to evaluate the first amendment rights of the Danville community and the owners of private property. Orderly, but not massive or riotous, picketing and demonstrations were to be permitted and protected. Although Harrison correctly emphasized that trespass and blocking the streets were not to be confused with freedom of expression,[55]

---

54.   "Draft of a statement, intended for use on television, that might possibly be delivered by Governor Harrison, dealing with the racial disorders" (Harrison Executive Papers in Virginia State Library).

55.   Compare Harrison's comments with a similar analysis of the Fourth Circuit: "Those First Amendment rights incorporated into the Fourteenth Amendment, however, are not a license to trample upon the rights of others. They must be exercised responsibly and without depriving others of their rights, the enjoyment of which is equally as precious." The court

204

nothing in the governor's comments constituted a threat to suppress reasonable speech and protest activities. Rather, his message called for mutual accommodation for the various legitimate interests involved in the controversy. Of course, Harrison's views did not necessarily reflect those of the Danville authorities, but they tend to establish that the state government was not itself a party to any design to crush the first amendment rights of the demonstrators. The most likely explanation for Harrison's decision not to deliver the speech is the governor's belief that any television talk, regardless of its content, would serve to highlight and possibly enflame the Danville situation.   205

By early July it was evident that the demonstrations had utterly failed to achieve their announced objectives. Although the disorders and consequent arrests continued on a sporadic basis, they gradually diminished. With bail money nearly gone and most potential protestors already awaiting trial, it became progressively more difficult to find Negroes willing to march. The reopening of the public schools in late August deprived the protest of a major source of demonstrators. Despite the flagging level of protest activities, city policy continued to be aggressive. On July 10, the city council amended the ordinance regulating permits for parades. The amendment specified that applications for a parade permit must be filed "not less than thirty days nor more than sixty days" before the date of the proposed parade.[56] Arrests for parading without a permit supplemented the city's other tactics. A special August report in the *New York Times* described Danville "as an example of successful resistance to Negro demonstrations demanding equality." The *Times* noted that Danville had developed "a defense strategy that is among the most unyielding, ingenious, legalistic and effective of any city in the South."[57]

The Resort to the Federal Courts

Almost immediately, the attorneys for the Danville demonstrators sought to enlist federal jurisdiction as a shield for protest activities. The proceedings before Judge Aiken and the other state and municipal actions indicated that defense efforts would not meet with success at the local state court level. Moreover, the inevitable

---

pointed out that Negro demonstrators did not have any right "to coerce acceptance of their demands through violence or threats of violence." Baines v. City of Danville, 337 F.2d 579, 586 (4th Cir. 1964), *cert. denied*, 381 U.S. 939 (1965).

56. The text of the parade permit ordinance may be found in York v. City of Danville, 207 Va. 665, 152 S.E.2d 259, 261 (1967).

57. N.Y. Times, August 11, 1963, at 71, col. 1.

delays and expenses of carrying hundreds of appeals to the Virginia Supreme Court of Appeals certainly would sap the energy and resources of the protest. One commentator has concluded that "the most prominent characteristic of state courts in the South is that a Negro will not voluntarily bring them a dispute involving his civil rights."[58] This was certainly true in Virginia, where the task of implementing racial desegregation was almost exclusively a federal court responsibility. Accordingly, the protesters attempted to fashion procedures that would produce federal court intervention. They filed a petition to remove the cases of those charged with violating the Aiken injunction to federal court on the ground that a fair trial could not be obtained in the Corporation Court. They filed original federal suits attacking the constitutionality of the Danville ordinance limiting picketing, attacking the Aiken injunction, attacking the Virginia racial conspiracy statute, and attacking the administrative decision to terminate unemployment compensation for demonstrators under arrest. In July the demonstrators brought suit to restrain enforcement of the parade ordinance, contending that it was used to suppress lawful demonstrations. Holt explained the strategy of the Negroes:

> We were fighting. This action had enhanced the probability of intervention of the federal government . . . . As Danville would pass or invoke a law, the lawyers would scamper to the federal courts with a suit.[59]

Hence, one of the principal legal questions posed by the demonstrations was whether the defendants could establish some theory to secure federal court intervention in the Danville situation. This struggle was confusing and prolonged, and ultimately the Supreme Court gave a negative answer.

The various applications for federal relief were presented to Judge Thomas J. Michie of Charlottesville. A graduate of the University of Virginia, Michie had practiced law in Charlottesville since the 1920's. A member of the Democratic Party, Michie had served as mayor of Charlottesville in the late 1950's, a period in which he gained the reputation of a moderate on racial integration. Michie had earned the enmity of the Byrd organization by opposing the school closings in Charlottesville pursuant to massive resistance and by supporting John F. Kennedy for the presidency.[60] In fact, when

---

58. Meltsner, *Southern Appellate Courts: A Dead End*, in SOUTHERN JUSTICE 138 (L. Friedman ed. 1965).

59. L. HOLT, AN ACT OF CONSCIENCE 177 (1965).

60. Letter from Francis P. Miller to Ralph A. Dungan, December 21, 1960 (Miller Papers in University of Virginia).

President Kennedy nominated Michie to the federal bench in 1961 Virginia conservatives urged their senators to defeat confirmation of the appointment. One constituent informed Senator Robertson that Michie had always been opposed to conservative government.[61] The president of the Defenders of State Sovereignty and Individual Liberty, a segregationist lobby in the Old Dominion, asserted that the appointment of Michie to a federal judgeship would be extremely unfortunate.[62] Such expressions of opposition were to no avail, and Michie was duly confirmed, but they do underscore the liberal image which Michie had acquired. As Kennedy's first appointment to the federal district bench in Virginia, one could reasonably expect that he would be more sympathetic to the plight of the Negro demonstrators than any other federal judge in the Old Dominion.

207

Acting first on the petition to remove the criminal proceedings to federal court, Michie declined to take immediate action on the city's motion for remand and scheduled a hearing in Danville on June 24 to receive evidence on the question. During the two day hearing, the protesters' attorneys called witnesses to show that their clients could not obtain a fair trial before Judge Aiken. Michie reserved judgment on the general removal problem, but granted writs of habeas corpus for the two defendants convicted by Aiken after their cases had been removed.[63] Yet the Aiken injunction and the municipal ordinance curtailing demonstrations remained in effect, and Michie's steps did not preclude further arrests. In a move without modern precedent, the Justice Department filed a brief supporting the removal effort. The brief reviewed the courtroom proceedings before Aiken and asserted that the trials were being "conducted in a most unjudicial atmosphere."[64] Contending that the Negro demonstrators could not receive a fair trial in the Corporation Court, the brief concluded:

> The combination of the trier of the fact who has apparently prejudged the issues and was a participant in the events culminating in the very charges to be tried, considered together with the general atmosphere of the proceedings and its inevitable result, make it quite clear, it seems to us, that a fair trial cannot be had in the Corporation Court. But that is not all. It is not simply that whatever rights defendants have to demonstrate for the equal protection

---

61. Letter from John B. Boatwright, Jr. to A. Willis Robertson, February 13, 1961 (Robertson Papers in College of William and Mary).

62. Letter from Robert B. Crawford to A. Willis Robertson, February 10, 1961 (Robertson Papers in College of William and Mary).

63. L. HOLT, AN ACT OF CONSCIENCE 6-40 (1965); W. KUNSTLER, DEEP IN MY HEART 221-22 (1966).

64. The Justice Department brief is reprinted in part in W. KUNSTLER, DEEP IN MY HEART at 219-21. *See also* N.Y. Times, July 3, 1963, at 10.

of the laws will be disregarded in the contempt trials. The situation is further aggravated by the fact that racial antagonism lies at the root of this denial. The entire controversy now before this Court stems from the conflict over Negro equality, and the proceedings in the Corporation Court which are here challenged are a direct result of this conflict. We do not suggest that Judge Aiken is racially prejudiced against the defendants; but a Court would have to close its eyes to the realities not to notice that the peculiar proceedings in the Corporation Court are the direct result of this racial conflict.

The Danville Bar Association responded to the Justice Department brief by denouncing the "unwarranted, irresponsible and unjust attack" on Aiken, and proceeded to censure the representatives of the Justice Department for making such statements.[65]

Judge Michie's next action absolutely stunned the demonstrators. News that Martin Luther King would lead a march in early July prompted Danville to seek a federal court order curtailing further demonstrations. On July 2 Michie rendered a federal injunction against the Negro protest movement on the ground that the disorders denied others in Danville federally protected rights. Almost as broad as the earlier Aiken order, the Michie injunction prohibited obstructing traffic, use of public facilities or private property, "unnecessarily loud, objectionable, offensive, and insulting noises," inciting any person to riot, and meetings at which violations of the laws of Virginia or Danville or of the federal court order were advocated.[66] The Michie injunction complicated the plight of the Negro protesters.[67] The Justice Department declined to "take any legal action to suspend issuance of the restraining order," and a representative of the Department advised Len Holt that "in my judgment, the defendants would be obliged to obey any order issued by Judge Michie whether they thought it legally sound or not and

---

65. "Resolutions of Bar Association of Danville," 109 Cong. Rec. 12211 (1963) (Remarks of Senator Robertson).

66. Powell, Black Cloud Over Danville, *supra* note 17, at 47.

67. Michie's course of action was perhaps influenced by a similar injunction issued by Federal District Judge J. Robert Elliott against mass racial demonstrations in Albany, Georgia. In a suit filed by the mayor of Albany, Elliott granted a sweeping temporary order on July 20, 1962 restraining demonstration leaders from continuing to incite or encourage unlawful picketing or parading, and from engaging in acts designed to produce breaches of the peace. The suit was brought under the federal civil rights act and alleged that organized breaches of the peace had prevented city authorities from carrying out governmental functions and from according equal protection of the law to all citizens. Chief Judge Elbert P. Tuttle of the Fifth Circuit set aside the restraining order on July 24 on the basis that no federal question was raised by the complaint. Evidently neither Elliott nor Tuttle prepared formal opinions to support their actions. The events in Albany, however, may be traced in Kelly v. Page, 9 Race Rel. L. Rep. 1115 (M.D. Ga., 1963), *aff'd in part, remanded in part,* 335 F.2d 114 (5th Cir. 1964). *See* N.Y. Times, July 22, 1962 at 32.

would have to pursue their remedies in the court."[68] Now confronted with two injunctions against the demonstrations, the protest leaders hurriedly asked Michie to dissolve his order. When Michie refused, Kunstler carried the matter before Chief Judge Simon E. Sobeloff of the Fourth Circuit. After hearing Kunstler, Sobeloff had a private telephone conversation with Michie, the substance of which was never disclosed. Apparently as a result of this conversation, Michie dissolved his injunction on July 10.[69]

This minor gain for the demonstrators was more than offset, however, by Michie's other actions. He remanded all the removed contempt cases to the Corporation Court.[70] Reasoning that the accused should exhaust their remedies in the state courts, he denied the request for orders restraining enforcement of the Aiken injunction and the city ordinance limiting picketing and demonstrations.[71] Virginia's political leaders were delighted with Michie's performance. Senator Robertson, for example, strongly approved Michie's course and viewed the removal proceedings as a political maneuver by Attorney General Robert F. Kennedy.[72]

In addition, Michie's actions highlighted the central role of the federal district court in determining the course of racial demonstrations. Time was a crucial factor for the demonstrators: as the period without effective federal intervention grew longer, the prospect of success became more remote. Whatever the outcome of subsequent appellate review, the district court judge was in a position to withhold or extend an immediate and hence effective federal remedy. Certainly Michie's decisions furnished no encouragement to the demonstrators while giving a legal and psychological boost to the city at a key time in the history of the Danville demonstrations.

The attorneys for the demonstrators had filed their wide array of petitions and suits on the theory that the best defense was an aggressive assault on the state court proceedings. A study of the response of the federal district judges, however, suggests that the strategy of multiple litigation backfired. It perplexed the judges and

209

---

68. Memorandums from Justice Dept. to Len Holt, July 3, 1963 (Burke Marshall Papers in John F. Kennedy Library).

69. W. Kunstler, Deep In My Heart 226-27 (1966).

70. For the order, dated July 11, 1963, remanding the criminal contempt cases see Baines v. City of Danville, Civil Action No. 574, Federal Records Center, Suitland, Maryland.

71. For Michie's opinion denying injunctive relief against arrests and prosecutions under the ordinance limiting demonstrations see Chase v. McCain, 220 F. Supp. 407 (W.D. Va. 1963). Michie evidently did not prepare opinions in his disposition of the other matters before him.

72. Letter from A. Willis Robertson to Walter L. Grant, July 12, 1963 (Robertson Papers in College of William and Mary).

caused them to downgrade, indeed, to desire to escape altogether, the Danville cases. Michie, for example, expressed a sense of relief that he was not required to deal with the thorny problems in "the numerous suits" growing out of the disorders: "Again, I am happy to say that I do not have to decide that issue in this case."[73] For further evidence of this skeptical judicial attitude consider the correspondence of Judge John Paul, who was named along with Michie to a three judge panel to hear the suit challenging Virginia's racial conspiracy statute.[74] Paul complained to Michie:

210

> The complaint is about as badly drawn as it could be. It attacks the Virginia statute forbidding the incitement of racial hostilities and then proceeds to list a lot of alleged grievances which the Negroes have, but which seem to have no connection with the statute which is attacked. It is charged that the Negroes have been prevented from registering as voters, have been subjected to police brutality and that they have been denied bail and several other things. These matters are those which are protected by various federal statutes designed to protect the civil rights of all citizens, but there is no allegation in this complaint which invokes the protection of these federal statutes or makes them applicable to the alleged wrongs. In other words, the attack made by the plaintiffs is solely on that section of the Virginia Code which is cited in the complaint and to which I have referred. As far as I can see, no federal question arises either by virtue of federal statutory provisions or by the terms of the Constitution.[75]

In August, Paul was even more explicit:

> I might say also that, with the numerous suits which have been instituted against the city of Danville and its officials, I am in quite a state of confusion as to what the real situation is there and I cannot make very much out of the complaint in the instant case, as I previously wrote you.

He revealingly added that "I know this whole Danville business has been a headache to you . . . ."[76] Since Michie and Paul conceived of the demonstrations as a legal headache, one is hardly surprised that they were disinclined to assert federal jurisdiction.

Stymied in the district court, Kunstler and the other attorneys

---

73. Chase v. McCain, 220 F. Supp. 407, 408 (W.D. Va. 1963).

74. John Paul (1883-1964) was a resident of Harrisonburg and a member of the Republican Party. Educated at the University of Virginia, Paul was named federal district judge by President Herbert Hoover in 1932. Paul had early and consistently enforced the *Brown* edict against Virginia localities. Allen v. School Bd., 144 F. Supp. 239 (W.D. Va.), *aff'd*, 240 F.2d 59 (4th Cir. 1956), *cert. denied*, 353 U.S. 910 (1957); Kilby v. County School Bd., 3 RACE REL. L. REP. 972 (W.D. Va. 1958). Although his judicial orders caused schools to be closed in two areas pursuant to the program of massive resistance, Paul remained on friendly personal terms with Senator Byrd and other leaders of the Byrd organization. Letter from Paul to Harry F. Byrd, June 20, 1958 (John Paul Papers in University of Virginia).

75. Letter from John Paul to Thomas J. Michie, July 30, 1963 (Paul Papers in University of Virginia).

76. Letter from John Paul to Thomas J. Michie, August 21, 1963 (Paul Papers in University of Virginia).

for the protest movement again applied to the Fourth Circuit for an immediate hearing on Michie's orders. Danville authorities were jubilant when on July 22 the court decided to take no action. This inability to gain federal intervention completed the paralysis of the waning protests. In early August, Aiken modified and made permanent his earlier temporary injunction and resumed the trials of the contempt and ordinance violation cases.[77] The number of contempt defendants had swollen to 346.[78]

At this point, however, the city overplayed its hand and finally provoked limited federal court intervention. Since each defendant demanded and was granted an individual trial, it was obvious that the trials would drag on interminably and clog the entire judicial calendar in the Corporation Court. The assignment of Judge Leon M. Brazile of Hanover County to assist Aiken in holding court provided only partial relief. To alleviate this problem, the prosecutor moved on August 5 for a change of venue for the trials of some defendants. He reasoned that the crowded docket would not permit the defendants to receive speedy trials and would burden the administration of justice. Over the objection of the defendants, the court granted the motion, and some 124 cases were transferred to other courts in Virginia from 80 to 200 miles from Danville.[79] The defendants, most of them poor, were now confronted with having to travel, and transport their witnesses, a considerable distance for trial. Pressure on the defense attorneys was, of course, greatly increased by the change of venue. The court's ruling was based on a misreading of Section 19.1-224 of the Code of Virginia authorizing a change of venue "for good cause" at the request of either the accused or the state.[80] It seems evident that the venue statute was intended to accord criminal defendants a fair and impartial trial free from local prejudice. The Danville court's action, then, was a grievous misapplication of the statute and hampered the accused

77. On August 2 Judge Aiken issued a permanent injunction against certain named defendants "and all other persons similarly situated" and "all other persons in active concert and participation with them." 38 Danville Chancery Order Book, Corporation Court 385.

78. L. HOLT, AN ACT OF CONSCIENCE 216-17 (1965).

79. Cases were transferred to courts in Lee County, the City of Bristol, Russell County, Fairfax County, Buchanan County, Hanover County, Chesterfield County, Cumberland County, the City of Hopewell, and the City of Virginia Beach. Danville Register, Aug. 6-8, 1963; 60 Danville Common Law Order Book, Corporation Court 274-83.

80. Section 19.1-224 provides in part as follows: "—A Circuit court may, on motion of the accused or of the Commonwealth, for good cause, order the venue for the trial of a criminal case in such court to be changed to some other corporation or circuit court. Such motion when made by the accused may be made in his absence upon a petition signed and sworn to by him, which petition may, in the discretion of the judge, be acted on by him in vacation . . . ."

in offering a defense. The transfer of the trials to distant points struck many observers as a naked display of judicial power designed more to intimidate the defendants rather than enhance their chance for a fair trial.[81]

Another application to the Fourth Circuit finally produced an order favorable to the demonstrators. Attorneys for the protest movement sought an order staying all arrests, trials, and other proceedings for violation of the Aiken injunction and the ordinance restricting demonstrations.[82] Reviewing the criminal prosecutions in the state court, and noting specifically the denial of bail to those convicted and the transfer of the cases, the circuit court restrained trials for violation of the Aiken injunction and the ordinance curtailing demonstrations. Temporary relief was granted "to protect the jurisdiction of this court pending disposition of the appeals before us . . . ." The court called upon "persons of good will of both races to establish communications and to seek eventually acceptable solutions to these problems out of which these cases arise."[83] It should be noted that the Fourth Circuit order, coming on August 8, was both too little and too late as far as the demonstrators were concerned.[84] The stay only halted trials for offenses against the Aiken injunction and the ordinance regulating demonstrations. Prosecutions for trespass, contributing to the delinquency of a minor, or

212

---

81. L. HOLT, AN ACT OF CONSCIENCE 217 (1965).

82. Chase v. Aiken, Civil Action No. 9084, Federal Records Center, Suitland, Maryland.

83. Baines v. City of Danville, 321 F.2d 643 (4th Cir. 1963).

84. The action of the Fourth Circuit was commended by an unlikely source, the *Richmond News Leader*. Under the editorship of James J. Kilpatrick, the *News Leader* had championed massive resistance and generally opposed the civil rights movement. Nonetheless, the *News Leader* was concerned about the manner in which Danville handled the protests and hailed the Circuit Court "for suspending the gold-plated, triple-bottomed, hand-tooled stupidity of these so-called Danville trials." Charging that Danville had abridged the right of free speech, the *News Leader* assailed "trumped-up ordinances, unwarranted arrests, drum-head trials, and autocratic decrees!" Richmond News Leader, Aug. 12, 1963. Reaction from Danville was swift. The *Danville Register* described the *News Leader* editorial as "half-baked comments based upon less-than-half accurate information . . . ." Danville Register, Aug. 13, 1963. Congressman Tuck told Kilpatrick that "I was sure that you had not familiarized yourself with all of the facts in respect to the situation in Danville." William M. Tuck to James J. Kilpatrick, Aug. 14, 1963, Watkins M. Abbitt Papers, University of Richmond. In turn, the *News Leader* explained that it was not defending the excesses of the demonstrators: "When racial demonstrators run in the streets, stop automobiles, swarm into public offices, block traffic, smash windshields, hurl bricks, shoot at police cars, carry concealed weapons, trespass upon private property, prevent access to stores, lie down on bridges, and engage in noisy disturbances of the peace—and they have done all of these things in Danville—the proper course of conduct is to lock 'em up on appropriate criminal charges." The newspaper insisted, however, that while the "professional troublemakers" from various civil rights groups may "have inflamed the problem," they "found a sickness to begin with." Richmond News Leader, Aug. 15, 1963.

violating the parade permit ordinance were unaffected. Further-more, the stay did not prevent continued arrests for all offenses, and the mass arrests were more effective than the trials in destroying the protest. In addition, by August the demonstrations were already dying in the face of the city's unyielding position. The protestors had lost the energy and will to extend their campaign and at this point, more than six weeks after the first application to Judge Michie, partial federal assistance did not suffice to revive the disorders. Danville had outlasted the demonstrators and won the victory.

On August 13 Aiken continued the criminal contempt cases until the federal appeal was determined.[85] In late 1963 and early 1964, however, he proceeded to hear cases of resisting arrest, disorderly conduct, violation of the parade permit ordinance, and trespass growing out of the summer disorders. Sentences for those found guilty typically imposed two to five days in jail and a fine, and the execution of the sentences was suspended pending an appeal.[86] Moreover, as a consequence of counsel's agreement to consolidate the injunction cases for trial, in September Aiken rescinded the orders transferring the venue of the 124 cases.[87]

213

While the demonstrations ended, the legal struggle over the fate of those arrested for contempt of the Aiken injunction was just beginning. That the relief held out by the Fourth Circuit was temporary as well as limited in scope became manifest a year later when the court, sitting en banc, dissolved the temporary injunction by a three-two vote.[88] The court considered the merits of the appeals from the various decisions of Judge Michie and the majority opinion by Clement F. Haynsworth, Jr. reached the following conclusions:

1.   As passions in Danville ebbed the court had no reason to conclude that "in the quieter atmosphere of the present" the contempt defendants could not obtain a fair trial.[89] The majority judges were particularly impressed by the fact that the order transferring cases away from Danville had been rescinded. They assumed that bail would be available pending appeal to the Supreme Court of Appeals of Virginia, "a court which merits the high reputation it enjoys."[90] Since the temporary injunction had served its purpose of protecting the justiciability of these appeals, the order was dissolved.

85.   60 Danville Common Law Order Book, Corporation Court 292 (1963).
86.   Id. at 401-07; 61 id. at 113-15, 232-34.
87.   60 Danville Common Law Order Book, Corporation Court 399 (1963).
88.   Baines v. City of Danville, 337 F.2d 579 (4th Cir. 1964).
89.   Id. at 594.
90.   Id.

2.   The actions challenging the ordinance limiting picketing and demonstrations, the parade permit ordinance, and the Aiken injunction were remanded to the district court for a hearing to determine whether injunctive relief against future prosecutions was appropriate. The district court was instructed to restrain further arrests under the ordinances and Aiken injunction "only if he finds that in combination they have been applied so sweepingly as to leave no reasonable room for reasonable protest, speech and assemblies."[91]

3.   Under the governing statute the court had no jurisdiction to review the remand of the contempt cases to the Corporation Court.[92]

4.   The suit against the Virginia Employment Commission for denying unemployment compensation benefits to defendants awaiting trial was dismissed because the Commission had never been made a party to the proceedings.[93]

Chief Judge Sobeloff and Judge J. Spencer Bell dissented in part. They raised no objection to the handling of the remand and unemployment insurance questions. The dissenters, however, were concerned about the suppressive effect of the ordinances and the Aiken injunction on attempts by the Negro defendants to express their grievances:

> The plaintiffs have alleged that the official and unofficial power structure of the white community has been successfully mobilized to deny them their First Amendment rights to protest their relegation to second class citizenship. They allege that the police, by means of violence and brutality exercised during wholesale arrests upon trumped up charges; the judiciary, by means of broad and vague injunctions; and the City Council, by means of its unconstitutional ordinances against picketing and parading, have succeeded in crushing the minority's carefully organized effort to express its discontent with the status quo.[94]

The dissenters argued that the court should have considered whether the ordinances and the Aiken injunction were "unconstitutional on their face." They felt that if the district judge should conclude that "a clear and imminent danger of irretrievable injury" to the first amendment rights of the protesters existed, then he should enjoin both pending and future criminal prosecutions.[95]

The majority and minority opinions parted company largely over the extent to which Danville had curtailed the freedom of as-

214

---

91.   *Id.* at 596.
92.   *Id.* at 596-98.
93.   *Id.* at 598-99.
94.   *Id.* at 599-600.
95.   *Id.* at 601.

sembly and protest. Judge Haynsworth ruled that the ordinances and the Aiken injunction "were far from absolute."[96] Moreover, the majority was aware of excesses committed by the demonstrators and consequently was inclined to balance the rights of the protesters against the rights of the Danville community. Lastly, the majority argued that the pending state court proceedings would provide an adequate legal remedy for the defendants. The dissenters, on the other hand, were clearly moved by the plight of the Negro demonstrators and by their fear that municipal actions had chilled all expression of racial grievances. They suggested that the present calm in Danville, on which the majority had relied, might mean that the demonstrators "have been so cowed that they no longer dare to express themselves. . . ."[97] Their opinion gave no attention to the rights of private property owners and others in Danville.

215

There is only a sketchy record of the action taken by the district court on the matters remanded for additional consideration at a hearing. In December of 1966, Judge Michie refused to restrain the trials for violation of the Aiken injunction on the ground that the demonstrators must first exhaust their state court remedies.[98] No federal injunction was ever issued against further arrests and trials for violation of the various municipal ordinances and the Aiken injunction. By August of 1964 the racial disorders in Danville were long since concluded, and judicial relief of this nature was unnecessary.

The removal of the contempt cases from the Corporation Court, however, was presented anew to the Fourth Circuit on a petition for rehearing. The Civil Rights Act of 1964 amended the removal statute to permit appellate review of remand orders in civil rights cases. The circuit court ruled that the Act should be applied to appeals pending on its effective date and proceeded to reconsider the removal problem. Sitting *en banc*, the Fourth Circuit again divided by a three-two margin.[99] Chief Judge Haynsworth, writing for the majority, held that the cases were properly remanded. The majority opinion primarily analyzed 28 U.S.C. section 1443(1), which provides for the removal of civil actions on criminal proceedings

[a]gainst any person who is denied or cannot enforce in the courts of such

---

96.   *Id.* at 594.

97.   *Id.* at 600.

98.   Danville Bee, Dec. 22, 1966.

99.   Baines v. City of Danville, 357 F.2d 756 (4th Cir.) *aff'd*, 384 U.S. 890 (1966) (5-4). The majority opinion briefly treated and rejected the contention that removal could be accomplished under 28 U.S.C.A. § 1443(2), holding that removal under that section only applied to federal officers performing their duties under federal law.

State a right under any law providing for the equal civil rights of citizens of the United States, or of all persons within the jurisdiction thereof . . . .

Haynsworth determined that the clause "a right under any law providing for the equal civil rights of citizens" did not furnish a basis for removal of first amendment claims.[100] He contended that the right of removal must appear in advance of trial and could not be predicated on supposition that the defendant would be unable to enforce a protected right during trial. Haynsworth also ruled:

216

> It would appear that the requirement of a showing of inability to enforce protected rights in the courts would require us to view all of its courts vertically, and that even a successful showing of unfairness in the trial court would not be sufficient unless it were also shown that the appellate court was unfair, too, or that the unfairness of the trial court was not correctable on appeal or avoidable by a change of venue.[101]

Hence, the contention of the protesters that they could not obtain a fair trial before Judge Aiken in the Corporation Court was not enough to sustain removal. Haynsworth stressed that there was no allegation of unfairness on the part of the Virginia Supreme Court of Appeals, "a court which showed its courage and faithfulness to constitutional principles when . . . it struck down Virginia's massive resistance laws . . . ."[102]

Once again Judges Sobeloff and Bell dissented in a lengthy opinion which accused the majority of giving an "extremely narrow construction" to the removal statute. Sympathetic with the aims and aspirations of the Negro protest movement, the dissenters saw the problem in the light of contemporary racial problems:

> Completely ignored in the majority opinion are the broader considerations unfolded by recent events and expounded in the latest decisions of the Supreme Court. In the full century since the Civil War, Congress has enacted ten civil rights statutes, three of them within the past ten years. The national purpose, as declared by Congress and the Court, has been made manifest. It is to make freedom a reality for the Negro, to secure him against the destruction of his most precious constitutional rights, and generally to permit him to enjoy the guarantee of citizenship equally with members of the white race. Nothing compels the continuance of a narrow legalistic interpretation of the removal provision, a statute which forms an indispensable link in the congressional plan to effectuate equal rights. It is stultifying to the recently enacted 'section 901, permitting appellate review of remand orders, to persist in the devitalizing construction of section 1443. Legislating a right of appeal would be of little worth if Congress did not mean to give section 1443 new force.[103]

Finding that the state appellate process was inadequate to guarantee that constitutional rights would be protected, the minority de-

---

100. *Id.* at 764.
101. *Id.* at 769.
102. *Id.*
103. *Id.* at 788.

clared that the Negro protesters were entitled to removal and a "fair trial" in the federal district court.

The Supreme Court affirmed the Fourth Circuit decision by a five-four margin[104] on the strength of its opinion in *City of Greenwood v. Peacock*.[105] Justice Potter Stewart's majority opinion closely paralleled the reasoning of Judge Haynsworth. Stewart held that the first amendment rights of free expression were not rights arising under a "law providing for . . . equal civil rights" within the meaning of 28 U.S.C. section 1443(1).[106] He further ruled that

> The civil rights removal statute does not require and does not permit the judges of the federal courts to put their brethren of the state judiciary on trial. Under § 1443(1), the vindication of the defendant's federal rights is left to the state courts except in the rare situations where it can be clearly predicted by reason of the operation of a pervasive and explicit state or federal law that those rights will inevitably be denied by the very act of bringing the defendant to trial in the state court.[107]

217

Stewart emphasized that any denial of federal constitutional rights uncorrected by the state courts could be remedied by Supreme Court review or federal habeas corpus. His opinion concluded with a consideration of the immense practical problem that would be placed upon the federal courts if thousands of criminal removal cases were tried annually before federal judges.[108] Justices Douglas, Brennan, Fortas, and Chief Justice Warren dissented, maintaining that the Court gave a narrow reading to the removal statute.[109]

The Kennedy Administration and Danville

Victor S. Navasky has charged that the Kennedy administration came into office with a civil rights program that was considerably more limited than the President's campaign rhetoric suggested. It was willing to encourage racial integration, but not at the price of social tranquility. Contrary to the white South's image of Attorney General Robert F. Kennedy, Navasky observed, "he was cautious to the point of timidity when it came to risking any kind of confrontation with an escalation potential."[110] Although this is how the Kennedy years appear in retrospect to the civil rights activist, the white South did indeed see Kennedy's record very differently.

President Kennedy had little choice but to maintain as cordial

---

104. Baines v. City of Danville, 384 U.S. 890, *rehearing denied*, 385 U.S. 890 (1966).

105. 384 U.S. 808 (1966).

106. *Id.* at 825.

107. *Id.* at 828.

108. *Id.* at 832-34.

109. *Id.* at 835-54.

110. V. NAVASKY, KENNEDY JUSTICE 228 (1971).

relations as possible with Virginia leaders. Byrd and Robertson headed the Senate Finance and Banking Committees respectively. Congressman Howard W. Smith was chairman of the House Rules Committee, which handled all legislation cleared for action in the House of Representatives. These powerful Virginians were in posi⁻ tions to delay or even block much of the New Frontier legislation, and Kennedy was understandably anxious not to alienate them if it could be avoided. Efforts by the administration to compel a reopening of public schools in Prince Edward County, although not immediately successful, had already severely strained Kennedy's dealing with Byrd and other Virginia leaders.[111]

Further, the political climate in the Old Dominion necessarily inhibited any move by the Kennedy administration to enter the Danville situation. John F. Kennedy had never been especially popular in Virginia. Richard M. Nixon had carried Virginia in 1960, with the tacit assistance of the Byrd organization, and nothing in the next few years improved Kennedy's image in the state. The administration, of course, was tarnished in Virginia by the onerous task of enforcing the *Brown* edict. More to the point, the Virginia leadership was convinced that by 1963 the administration was promoting racial demonstrations across America in order to marshall national backing for the Kennedy civil rights proposals submitted in June of that year.[112] Governor Harrison charged that "these mass demonstrations and disorders" were "given encouragement by the President himself."[113] Delegate C. Harrison Mann, Jr. complained directly to the President that members of his administration were inciting riots and bloodshed.[114] Senator Robertson likened the demonstrations to extortion and asserted that many irresponsible officials of government . . . were inciting Negroes to riot.[115]

218

---

111. Department of Justice press release, April 26, 1961, Byrd Papers; Richmond News Leader, April 27, 1961.

112. For example, the *Danville Register* charged that the Kennedys were promoting violence in Birmingham. "The sad conclusion of the action by the Kennedys and Dr. King is that the Government of the United States, as the tool of the Kennedys, cannot stand law and order in the South. Only by shattering enforcement of law and order, or by actions lending an impression that law and order has been shattered, can the full and brutal forces at the command of the Kennedys be applied against the people in the South who defend themselves against extra-legal action to bring about immediate total and complete race-mixing in any locality chosen by Dr. King and his colleagues in riot-making." Danville Register, May 14, 1963.

113. Harrison draft statement, *supra* note 54. *See also* letter from Harrison to Sam J. Ervin, Jr., Aug. 12, 1964 (Harrison Executive Papers).

114. Letter from C. Harrison Mann, Jr. to John F. Kennedy, June 7, 1963 (Robertson Papers in College of William and Mary).

115. Letter from A. Willis Robertson to C. Harrison Mann, Jr., June 10, 1963 (Robertson Papers in College of William and Mary).

The Kennedy strategy in Danville infuriated the Byrd leaders while, ironically, furnishing support for the Navasky assessment of the administration's limited civil rights program. Already aggravated over federal enforcement of *Brown*, the Virginians were hypersensitive to any federal action in the racial area. They saw every step by the Justice Department, however modest, as a politically inspired effort to prevent local law enforcement officials from keeping order in the state. Yet, from the point of view of Danville blacks, what did the Kennedy administration really do to assist them? There was no Justice Department intervention of any sort in June, the most tense month, and no suit was ever brought to redress police violence in Danville.[116] A brief in support of the removal petition was the only tangible move undertaken on behalf of the demonstrators. To be sure, Justice Department representatives monitored events in the troubled city closely. Department officials profitlessly urged the city and the demonstrators to negotiate their differences. This was the full extent of Kennedy administration involvement in Danville. Danville blacks were distressed at this lack of interest in their problems. Negroes intermittently picketed the FBI office in Danville, and one protester carried a revealing placard reading "What has the Justice Department Done?"[117] Holt explained:

> . . . the Kennedy administration responded in characteristic fashion . . . . First it brought about a cessation of demonstration, if possible, and then it wielded pressure on city hall or local merchants to make minor concessions. The third step consisted of convincing the persons involved in racial protest that they had gained a great victory while simultaneously persuading city hall or the merchants that they had given up nothing important.[118]

The Danville experience illustrates the central paradox of the Kennedy civil rights intervention in the South—that the rage of southern conservatives and the disappointment of Virginia Negroes was equally merited. By justifying and seeking legal protection for the demonstrators, and by incorporating their demands in his legislative program, Kennedy inevitably, but perhaps inadvertently, encouraged and dignified the disorders. In some measure, then, Kennedy must be held responsible for the wave of urban unrest and the tendency to direct physical action which appeared in the late

219

---

116. In September of 1963 Burke Marshall wrote: " . . . I am trying to develop a broader kind of case against this sort of repressive and violent police action. We have one, for example, in Danville, Virginia, but I think it would not be wise to bring it there." Memorandum for the Attorney General, Sept. 18, 1963 (Burke Marshall Papers in John F. Kennedy Library).

117. Danville Register, Aug. 6, 1963.

118. L. Holt, An Act of Conscience 177-78 (1965).

1960's.[119] On the other hand, while he aroused heightened expectations by blacks in America, Kennedy was nonetheless too deliberate to satisfy rapidly the promises fired up by his gestures and pronouncements. In short, his moralistic rhetoric vastly outstripped his performance, a gap that was bound to fuel the very disorders that he claimed to disapprove.

This interpretation accords with the highly suggestive study of Henry Fairlie, in which he argues that Kennedy relied upon the politics of expectation.[120] Fairlie contends that the Kennedy administration governed by keeping people in a constant state of expectation and by encouraging an exaggerated notion of what politics could achieve. When the aroused hopes were necessarily unrealized, the public mood turned to the frustration and disillusionment of the 1960's. Fairlie points out that Kennedy moved on civil rights only after Negroes had taken to the streets, and concludes:

220

> It is false to try to manufacture a "consensus" in such a situation; and it was false in the 1960's to try to do so in the cause of civil rights. It could only be a distraction, certain in the end to provoke the frustration as much of the advocates of the cause, whose expectations had been aroused, as of its opponents, who felt with some justice that the political processes of the country had been bypassed.[121]

Disposition in the State Courts

In December of 1966 Aiken resumed the long-stalled trials of the persons accused of violating his injunction. By consent of the state and the defendants, groups of cases were consolidated and tried together by the court without a jury.[122] The trials now pro-

---

119.   In his January 1963 State of the Union message Kennedy did not mention new civil rights legislation. The disorders of April and May in Birmingham induced the administration to propose a sweeping civil rights bill, which eventually became the Civil Rights Act of 1964. The Kennedy recommendations fit neatly into the administration pattern of seeking to manage the civil rights movement and channel its energy into peaceful courses. "Even the proposed new civil rights legislation . . . ," Navasky contended, "was designed to cool down trouble as much as to correct injustice." V. NAVASKY, KENNEDY JUSTICE 205 (1971). Of course, it seems most likely that there would have been no Kennedy civil rights proposal in 1963 but for the Birmingham disturbances. Thus, one could surely argue that Kennedy did in fact yield to pressure generated by mob activities in the street. In other words, the Kennedy concern about halting the demonstrations took the form of granting the demands of the protestors, a certain prescription for renewed street violence.

120.   H. FAIRLIE, THE KENNEDY PROMISE: THE POLITICS OF EXPECTATION 13-16 (1973). In a similar analysis of contemporary urban problems, Edward C. Banfield has stressed the major role of expectancy in our understanding of city life. "The answer," he observed, "is that the improvements in performance, great as they have been, have not kept pace with rising expectations. In other words, although things have been getting better absolutely, they have been getting worse relative to what we think they should be." E. BANFIELD, THE UNHEAVENLY CITY: THE NATURE AND THE FUTURE OF OUR URBAN CRISIS 19 (1970).

121.   FAIRLIE, *supra* note 120, at 255.

122.   65 Danville Common Law Order Book, Corporation Court 316; Commonwealth v. Burrell, transcript, 4.

ceeded expeditiously, and on some days Aiken heard three sets of cases.[123] As many as twenty-nine defendants were tried in a group, many of them for multiple offenses.[124] It was stipulated that when a defendant failed to appear on the date of his trial, the state could present its evidence against the defendant and that such could be used at a later trial.[125] Not all the accused were convicted. The Commonwealth's Attorney announced that he was not going to prosecute certain defendants, presumably for lack of evidence, and they were ordered discharged.[126] Additionally, Aiken dismissed other cases after hearing the evidence.[127] Numerous defendants failed to appear, and Aiken declared as many as eleven 500-dollar bonds forfeit in a single day.[128]

221

In the course of the trials, defense counsel routinely moved to strike the evidence of the prosecution on the following grounds:

1. that there was no showing of service of the Aiken injunction, or that the defendants had actual notice thereof;
2. that even if service had been made, the defendants were not named or described in the order and hence not within its coverage;
3. that the acts committed by the defendants were not in violation of the injunction;
4. "that the injunction denied due process of speech and assembly in violation of the First and Fourteenth Amendments to the Constitution of the United States."[129]

As would be expected, Aiken consistently overruled the motions. The leaders of the demonstration received relatively severe sentences, with Rev. Lawrence Campbell drawing the stiffest punishment of 250 days and a fine of 2,500 dollars. The usual sentence for a single violation was a ten day term at the city prison farm, of which eight days were suspended, and a fine of twenty dollars.[130] Those convicted were admitted to 500- or 1,000-dollar appeal bonds. Aiken refused to release them on personal recognizance, noting the poor experience with defendants appearing for trial.[131]

123. 66 Danville Common Law Order Book, Corporation Court 21-27, 32-41.
124. *Id.* at 9-11.
125. *Id.*; Commonwealth v. Burrell, transcript, 3a.
126. 65 Danville Common Law Order Book, Corporation Court 304-05; 66 *id.* at 15, 53.
127. 66 *id.* at 46, 53-56.
128. 65 *id.* at 333-37.
129. *Id.* at 305-06, 317-19; Commonwealth v. Burrell, transcript, 126-27.
130. 65 Danville Common Law Order Book, Corporation Court 317-19.
131. Commonwealth v. Bethel, transcript, 217.

Judge Aiken felt that his sentences were very mild. "I realize," he declared from the bench, "that I am being rather lenient on these people. I don't know but what I am being too lenient on them."[132] Even Samuel W. Tucker, NAACP attorney and one of the defense counsel, agreed that "the court has imposed a nominal fine and a short jail sentence."[133] Aiken's analysis of the question of sentences was most fully elaborated at the end of the first group of trials:

222

> The Court is considerably disappointed about these defendants. As Mr. Ferguson pointed out, not a single defendant has expressed any regret for disobeying the Court's orders. Not a single lawyer representing these defendants has expressed any regret about it that I know. They are not willing to say that they were mistaken and misguided in doing what they did, and maybe they don't think so. I don't know. I am disappointed too in the attitude of some of the leaders of this movement, especially the ministers . . . . and the Court thinks that he [defendant Reverend McGhee] ought to have been advising the people that he was leading there that night to obey the Court's order rather than leading them in demonstrations . . . . The Court feels that it is its duty to uphold the dignity and self-respect of this Court, and when this Court makes an order, it's got to be obeyed and anybody who violates it has got to pay some penalty for it even though it may be small.[134]

Assuming that the evidence supported a determination of guilt, then Aiken was unquestionably correct in passing sentence on the convicted defendants. The sentences were hardly onerous, and they served to uphold the rule of law over the resort to the streets. Surely the delay between the disorders and the time of the trial—a delay caused in large part by the futile efforts at removal—could not be considered as an excuse for criminal conduct. A contrary outcome would have permitted the demonstrators to evade the consequences of their illegal activities by the mere passage of time.

Although his punishments were moderate, Aiken's handling of defense counsel and private criticism was inexcusable and again showed all too clearly his overbearing character. On December 20, 1966, he found Ruth L. Harvey, a Danville attorney representing the defendants, guilty of contempt for allegedly misleading the court with respect to her representation of defendant Leonard Holt. At a pre-trial conference she advised Aiken that she represented Holt and that he would appear for trial. Holt subsequently failed to attend, and Miss Harvey explained that she was no longer his attorney. Aiken fined her twenty-five dollars.[135] The Virginia Supreme Court of Appeals unanimously reversed this absurd judgment, hold-

---

132. Commonwealth v. Burrell, transcript, 185.
133. Commonwealth v. Bethel, transcript, 217.
134. *Id.*
135. Danville Bee, Dec. 21, 1966.

ing that the statements of Miss Harvey "were not sufficient to warrant the finding of contempt against her."[136]

Even more controversial was the Taylor affair. Shortly after the trials resumed, W. Leigh Taylor, the director of education and training at Dan River Mills, wrote a personal letter to Judge Aiken in which he charged that the Judge's imposition of jail sentences "served to aggravate a situation which has been improving constantly."[137] He referred to "petulance on the part of the judge" and characterized Aiken's disposition as "an inane decision." Aiken reacted swiftly, ordering the arrest of Taylor on a charge of contempt of the judge of the court. Arrested at his mill office, Taylor admitted writing the letter and apologized to Aiken. The apology was to no avail, and Aiken found Taylor in contempt, sentencing him to ten days, eight of which were suspended, in the city prison farm and a fine of fifty dollars.[138]

223

In a free society, judges are not immune from criticism, and there can be no doubt that Aiken's behavior toward Taylor was a serious error which curtailed constitutionally protected freedom of speech and reflected negatively on his judicial temperament.[139] Returning to an old target, the Richmond *News Leader* declared that Aiken "has grossly abused his powers. In our opinion, he ought to be impeached."[140] In the resulting furor the Danville Bar Association once more came to Aiken's defense with a resolution which described the *News Leader* editorial as "irresponsible, despicable, thoroughly unjustified and designed to hold the dignity of the Court up for public ridicule."[141] The lawyers recorded their "highest respect for and confidence in Judge Aiken." By February of 1967, Aiken evidently thought better of his hasty action and suspended Taylor's entire jail sentence.[142]

As the federal courts anticipated, the constitutional issues raised by the Negro protest movement were resolved by the state courts. Under the rationale of the federal deference policy, as expressed by the *Peacock* opinion, it was incumbent upon the state courts to decide the criminal cases in good faith and not to permit the law to become a hindrance to the expression of unpopular views.

---

136. Harvey v. Commonwealth, 209 Va. 433, 437, 164 S. E. 2d 636, 638 (1968).

137. For the text of Taylor's letter see Danville Bee, Dec. 20, 1966.

138. 65 Danville Common Law Order Book, Corporation Court 319-20.

139. Taylor's action in sending a personal letter to Aiken scarcely presented a danger to the administration of justice. Wood v. Georgia, 370 U.S. 375 (1962).

140. Richmond News Leader, Dec. 21, 1966.

141. Danville Bee, Dec. 23, 1966.

142. 66 Danville Common Law Order Book, Corporation Court 14.

The Fourth Circuit had repeatedly expressed its confidence in the judicial integrity of Virginia's highest court. Its conscientious and deliberate treatment of the varied issues posed by the disorders amply vindicated the trust of the Circuit Court.

In early 1967 the first of a long series of appeals from the Danville Corporation Court were decided by the Supreme Court of Appeals. The most important device used by the city to halt the demonstrations was the Aiken temporary injunction of June 6, later made permanent. This injunction was considered by the Supreme Court of Appeals in *Thomas v. City of Danville.*[143] On appeal from the order entering a perpetual injunction, the defendants raised no factual or procedural questions and pressed the contention that the order was contrary to the protections of the first and fourteenth amendments. The Court ruled that a court of equity had jurisdiction to enjoin acts that were a menace to the public rights or welfare.[144] Indeed, the defendants conceded that Aiken could properly restrain obstruction of traffic and the obstruction of the use of public and private facilities. They asserted, however, that the remainder of the Aiken injunction violated their freedom of speech and assembly. The Supreme Court of Appeals unanimously disagreed and upheld the permanent injunction in the main. Relying upon *Adderly v. Florida,*[145] the court pointed out that the Constitution does not guarantee that individuals can protest whenever and however they please. Concerned about the rights of the community as a whole, the court declared: "The rights guaranteed to the defendants under the Federal Constitution were not a license for them to trample upon the rights of the public, as was done in some of the incidents in the present case."[146]

Thereupon the Supreme Court of Appeals examined each item of the Aiken injunction. It had no difficulty upholding the prohibitions against assaults on persons and damaging property, against inciting persons to riot or violation of law, and against participation in mob violence or riot. Two items of the injunction were declared invalid on the ground that freedom of speech was protected unless shown likely to produce an evil greater than mere public inconveni-

224

---

143. 207 Va. 656, 152 S.E.2d 265 (1967).

144. The defendants also contended that certain items in the injunction enjoined violations of criminal law and thus deprived them of the right to trial by jury with respect to such violations. The court rejected this argument, pointing out that "such injunctive restraints are not criminal in character but are civil; that their purpose is not to convict and punish for violation of the law, but to prevent such violation." 207 Va. at 664, 152 S.E.2d at 270.

145. 385 U.S. 39 (1966).

146. 207 Va. at 661, 152 S.E.2d at 269.

ence.[147] The deleted portions of the order read as follows:

4.   From creating unnecessarily loud, objectionable, offensive and insulting noises, which are designed to upset the peace
and tranquility of the community.

6.   From engaging in any act in a violent and tumultuous
manner or holding unlawful assemblies such as to unreasonably
disturb or alarm the public within the City of Danville.

Lastly, the court modified the provision which restrained the defendants from participating in meetings where violations of the law or
the injunction "are suggested, advocated or encouraged." The court
eliminated the word "suggested," fearing that it would inhibit the
mere discussion of the validity of such laws and the injunction.[148] No
act that could legitimately be described as an exercise of free speech
was prevented under the Aiken injunction as modified.[149]

225

The parade permit ordinance posed the second constitutional
problem for Virginia's highest court in *York v. City of Danville*.[150]
The court's opinion, again unanimous, declared that the right to
conduct a parade was "subject to reasonable and nondiscriminatory
regulation."[151] Nonetheless, the court held that the Danville ordinance, requiring an application for a parade permit to be filed "not
less than thirty days nor more than sixty days" before the date of
the parade, was arbitrary and oppressive.[152] The practical effect of
this ordinance, enacted while the disorders were continuing, was to
prevent the defendants from demonstrating during the thirty day
waiting period. Hence, the parade ordinance was held to constitute
"an arbitrary and unreasonable prior restraint upon the rights of
freedom of speech and assembly . . . ."[153] The *York* opinion indicates
anew that the court was prepared to uphold first amendment rights
to express grievances.

The Supreme Court of Appeals readily disposed of some lesser
matters emanating from the disorders. Convictions for trespass on

147.   *Id.* at 662-63, 152 S.E.2d at 269-70.

148.   *Id.* at 664, 152 S.E.2d at 270.

149.   In December of 1963 Burke Marshall expressed a contrary view with respect to the
Aiken injunction: "In Danville . . . there has been repressive police action, and the use of
state and federal injunctions against demonstrations which will eventually be held to be
unconstitutional." Memorandum for the Attorney General, Dec. 2, 1963 (Burke Marshall
Papers in John F. Kennedy Library).

150.   207 Va. 665, 152 S.E.2d 259 (1967).

151.   *Id.* at 669, 152 S.E.2d at 263.

152.   For the text of the parade permit ordinance see 207 Va. at 667-68, 152 S.E.2d at
261-62.

153.   *Id.* at 671, 152 S.E.2d at 264.

private property and blocking ingress and egress to Dan River Mills were sustained.[154] In another action, the court affirmed a forfeiture of a bail bond when a defendant failed to appear for his trial, scheduled some three and one-half years after the demonstrations had occurred.[155]

An appeal dealing with arrests under the June 6 temporary injunction reached Virginia's highest court in 1970. The court regarded the constitutionality of the order as having been settled by the *Thomas* opinion, and considered the case solely in terms of notice and the sufficiency of the evidence upon which the defendant was convicted. Since the defendant was not named in the injunction, the court ruled that the state must prove "that he had actual notice or knowledge of the injunction before he committed prohibited acts."[156] Concluding that the evidence sustained a finding of actual notice on the part of the defendant, the contempt conviction was affirmed.

Finally, in January of 1973, the Supreme Court of Appeals decided the last batch of cases emanating from the Danville disorders. The high court asked the Commonwealth's Attorney for Danville to review the pending appeals in light of the *Thomas*, *York*, and *Rollins* rulings.[157] He conceded that in many of the contempt cases the state had failed to prove notice as required in *Rollins*. Violations of the parade permit ordinance had to fall as a consequence of *York*. The Commonwealth's Attorney further stipulated that there was inadequate evidence to uphold many of the convictions for resisting arrest, disorderly conduct, and trespassing.[158] Thus, without contest the Virginia Supreme Court overturned the convictions of nearly 270 persons.[159] At the same time, the court upheld the contempt convictions of the persons named in the injunction and served with a copy thereof. Sentences for illegal picketing, trespassing, and obstructing traffic were also sustained.[160]

A month later, and nearly ten years after the demonstrations, the prolonged legal proceedings reached their anti-climactic end. Aiken having died in 1971, and the new Danville judge having disqualified himself, Judge Glynn R. Phillips, Jr. of Clintwood was assigned to hear a defense motion to suspend the fines and jail

226

---

154. Hubbard v. Commonwealth, 207 Va. 673, 152 S.E.2d 250 (1967).
155. McGhee v. Commonwealth, 211 Va. 434, 177 S.E.2d 649 (1970).
156. Rollins v. Commonwealth, 211 Va. 438, 441, 177 S.E.2d 639, 642 (1970).
157. Letter from William H. Fuller III to author, Apr. 25, 1973.
158. 75 Danville Common Law Order Book, Corporation Court 428-39.
159. *Id.*; Richmond News Leader, Jan. 13, 1973.
160. 75 Danville Common Law Order Book, Corporation Court 439-43.

sentences of those persons whose convictions were affirmed. Over the heated objection of the Commonwealth's Attorney, Judge Phillips suspended the jail terms, conditioned on good behavior for two years, but directed payment of fines totalling more than 5,000 dollars.[161]

Conclusion

The Danville demonstrations of 1963 were a failure. Municipal authorities made only modest concessions to the demands of the protest movement and life resumed its traditional pattern. White racial attitudes were unchanged.[162] The legal aftermath of the hectic summer events was, in an important sense, irrelevant to the successful crushing of the disorders. Probably the principal reason for the collapse of the protests was the inability of Danville Negroes to enlist meaningful assistance from either the Kennedy administration or the federal courts. During the critical months of June and July, the city was able to harass and arrest the demonstrators at will under a host of state and municipal provisions. While police violence was not a conspicuous feature of the Danville plan, the police excesses on the night of June 10 were calculated to discourage protest activities.

Judge Aiken significantly contributed to the chilling of the demonstrations.[163] His injunction provided the basis for hundreds of arrests, and the arrests in turn permitted the court to require bail of the accused awaiting trial. With many blacks unemployed or holding marginal jobs, this bail policy fell upon the poorest members of the Danville community. Moreover, Aiken's abrupt and arbitrary conduct in the first contempt trials unmistakably conveyed the impression that the demonstrators could expect swift and harsh judicial treatment at his hands. Faced with the certainty of arrest and consequent bail expenses and the likelihood of a jail term, many protesters came to have second thoughts. Aiken's deportment, then, furnished an excellent example of the utilization of the state court

227

---

161. 76 *id.* at 11.

162. In June of 1964 the first municipal elections after the disorders produced a complete triumph for supporters of a tough policy against demonstrations. Five candidates who defended the city's handling of the demonstrators and were allied to John W. Carter easily won all the vacancies on the city council, defeating Negro and moderate candidates. Richmond News Leader, June 10, 1964; N.Y. Times, June 10, 1964.

163. Aiken was re-named judge of the Corporation Court by the legislature in February of 1968. He was elected by a margin of 99-7, with only the Republican minority in the House of Delegates opposing him because of his advanced age. There seems to have been no open discussion of Aiken's role in the demonstration cases. *Journal of the Senate of Virginia,* Regular Session, 310-15 (1968); Richmond Times-Dispatch, Feb. 10, 1968.

trial bench as an additional club to undercut racial disorders. His stern resistance to the demonstrations exacted a heavy price in terms of judicial integrity. Aiken was all too obviously part of a municipal power structure dedicated to white supremacy and the racial status quo.

Nevertheless, it is entirely possible to offer a partial justification for the city's method of handling the unrest. In at least some measure, the Negro demonstrations of the 1960's were an attempt to create tensions and intimidate the white public into taking actions favored by the black minority, or, that failing, to provoke such a savage reaction from the whites as to arouse national public opinion. Violence and threats of violence were an integral part of this strategy. It is to the credit of Virginia leaders at all levels that they recognized this overt threat and refused to yield to extra-legal tactics. One of the most unhappy legacies of the 1960's was the widespread notion that questions of public policy should be determined by mobs in the street.[164] Not infrequently it seemed that even the federal judiciary viewed the behavior of Negro demonstrators as somehow above the law. At first glance the judicial receptivity to civil rights demands would appear to remove any necessity for protest activity, but in fact the judicial climate encouraged the belief that almost any conduct by blacks in the name of "civil rights," short of personal violence, would be upheld as a form of free expression. Whatever the flaws in Danville's handling of the demonstrations, Virginians correctly insisted upon obedience to law and established procedure. Illegal practices in Danville or errors by Judge Aiken could be corrected on appeal and did not furnish an excuse for street mobs.

Failing to coerce the whites, the Negro demonstrators sought to arouse some type of national support. Here, too, Danville Negroes were disappointed. The low profile of Governor Harrison was the decisive factor in keeping Danville out of the national headlines. Holt revealed the publicity consciousness of the protestors when he lamented that the press "had forsaken Danville, finding nothing spectacular about the routine arrests and demonstrations. . . ."[165] When some provocative events in Danville threatened to generate outside attention, national developments fortuitously overshadowed

228

---

164. Elliot Zashin has recently argued that the civil rights movement did not rely upon litigation or upon convincing the electorate, but "hoped to force southern whites to abandon segregation both by confronting them directly and by creating publicity that would apply still more pressure." Zashin, *Civil Rights and Civil Disobedience: the Limits of Legalism*, 52 TEX. L. REV. 285, 293 (1974).

165. L. HOLT, AN ACT OF CONSCIENCE 206 (1965).

the demonstrations. For example, the March on Washington by civil rights groups on August 28 and the maneuvers over the Kennedy civil rights proposals dominated the domestic news coverage in the summer of 1963. Without the kind of federal assistance that publicity could arouse, there was never much doubt that Danville would crush the disorders.

The demonstrators were unquestionably entitled to engage in peaceful picketing and orderly marches to express their dissatisfaction with the racial conditions in Danville. Indeed, the initial demonstrations were peaceful and without incident. Not surprisingly, the protestors soon found that the white citizens of Danville paid no attention to such activities. Accordingly, they resorted to extralegal tactics for which they erroneously claimed first amendment protection, thereby blurring both the constitutional issues and their own coercive and publicity-seeking aims. When the Corporation Court and the city council sought to halt these unlawful activities, the protestors promptly alleged that the judicial and municipal responses were overly broad and forbade conduct protected under the first amendment. Conveniently overlooked was the indisputable evidence that their own unlawful conduct had caused the prohibitions of which they complained.

Finally, the Danville imbroglio calls into question the image of the federal courts and the Kennedy administration as stalwart champions of the Negro protest movement. At no point were the demonstrators able to secure meaningful judicial relief. In the last analysis, the federal courts respected the traditional deference to the adjudication of criminal cases in the state courts. The remand of the Danville contempt cases was certainly appropriate as a matter of general policy, but it nevertheless allowed the state court to maintain the pressure against the disorders. The Kennedy administration, for its part, was simply not as aggressive on the racial front as either the Danville blacks hoped or the Virginia whites feared.

By February of 1973 the sentencing of the Danville demonstrators was finished and a violent chapter in Virginia's history closed.[166] The Danville experience suggests the limitation of mass demonstra-

229

---

166. The defendants indicted under Virginia's racial conspiracy statute were never brought to trial. Letter from William H. Fuller III to author, Feb. 23, 1973. Although the challenge to the constitutionality of the statute was referred to a 3-judge federal court, no action was taken after the death of Judge Paul in 1964 and the suit was dismissed in 1967 for failure to prosecute. Adams v. Aiken, Civil Action No. 584, Federal Records Center, Suitland, Maryland. A similar statute was held unconstitutional in Herndon v. Lowry, 301 U.S. 242 (1937).

tion as a tactic to encourage social change. Only under unique circumstances—favorable national publicity, clumsy and obnoxious local government authorities subject to ready vilification, timely federal assistance—could they succeed. In short, the Danville disorders show the ease with which the South could maintain racial segregation absent federal intervention.

230

The Southern Christian Leadership Conference and the Second Reconstruction, 1957–1973

Adam Fairclough

By any orthodox standard, the Southern Christian Leadership Conference was an unusual organization. Run, as Andrew Young put it, by "a bunch of Baptist preachers," its tangled structure and lax discipline made confusion a way of life. Although it had ambitious long-term programs, SCLC thrived on crises and prided itself on spontaneity. "When you are called upon to witness, you . . . can't always analyze what might happen," explained Ralph Abernathy. "You just have to go." This impulsiveness led to sudden changes of plan that exasperated outsiders: mass meetings would wait hours for the appearance or nonappearance of scheduled speakers; marches, demonstrations, and even whole campaigns would be announced and then abruptly cancelled. Its members accepted, even took a perverse pride in, administrative chaos. As Hosea Williams put it, "we are a movement, not an organization."[1]

Its critics took a less charitable view, and described SCLC as a bureaucratic shambles, a giant fundraising machine, and a vehicle for the glorification of its president, Dr. Martin Luther King, Jr. They found King's fame and SCLC's wealth irksome and ill deserved, for the conference represented but a fraction of the civil rights movement. The National Association for the Advancement of Colored People, founded in 1910, had won the stunning legal victories that culminated in the Supreme Court overturning the "separate but equal" doctrine in 1954. The Congress of Racial Equality, founded in 1942, originated the 1961 Freedom Rides and spearheaded most of the direct action in North

ADAM FAIRCLOUGH *took his degree in history at Balliol College, Oxford, and his Ph.D. from the University of Keele. Currrently he is a lecturer in Modern History at the University of Liverpool.*

South Atlantic Quarterly, 80:2, Spring, 1981. Copyright © 1981 by Duke University Press.

1. George Goodman, "He Lives, Man!" *Look*, April 15, 1969, p. 30; Pat Watters, *Down To Now: Reflections on the Southern Civil Rights Movement* (New York, 1971), p. 175; Charles Fager, *Uncertain Resurrection: The Poor People's Washington Campaign* (Grand Rapids, 1969), pp. 14, 20.

Carolina and Louisiana. The Student Nonviolent Coordinating Committee, organized in 1960, led the main voter registration drives in the rural Black Belt of the Deep South and began the protests in Selma which led to the passage of the Voting Rights Act. While others did the work, critics asserted, SCLC staged "a few showy projects" that reaped all the credit.[2]

That SCLC, an organization of clergymen, could become what Bayard Rustin called "the dynamic center of the civil rights movement" was all the more remarkable because the black church had been the despair of generations of activists. Although it enjoyed unequalled prestige and, in Gunnar Myrdal's words, had "the Negro masses organized," black ministers had traditionally accommodated to the racial status quo and, with few exceptions, displayed a complete lack of militancy. Critics of black Christians, from Booker T. Washington to Martin Luther King, complained that they were too other-worldly, so "absorbed in a future good 'over yonder' that they condition their members to adjust to their present evils over here."[3]

The outbreak in the mid-1950's of bus boycotts in half a dozen southern cities, all of them led by black ministers, signalled a momentous change. In 1944 Myrdal had predicted that leadership might pass by default to other middle-class elements within the black community. Organized labor, however, had been stifled in the South after the Second World War, while teachers and other professionals were too economically vulnerable to assume a militant stand against white supremacy. Ministers, financially independent of whites, remained the primary source of leadership. Those who became protest leaders shared the heightened postwar militancy of the black community as a whole—an impatience to abolish segregation that had been fuelled by recent victories such as the outlawing of the white primary, the integration of the armed services, and the Supreme Court's ruling against segregation in the public schools. Although only a small minority of the black clergy, the militant few, came to exercise disproportionate influence. The Montgomery bus boycott of 1955–56 epitomized the new kind of leadership. In addition to its leader, Martin Luther King, Jr., some twenty ministers took part in the Montgomery Improvement Association. Its close ties with the church gave the protest coherence, moral authority, and religious fervor.[4]

In early 1957 King and other like-minded clergymen formed the

2. August Meier, "New Currents in the Civil Rights Movement," *New Politics*, Summer 1963, p. 14.

3. Bayard Rustin, *Strategies for Freedom: The Changing Patterns of Black Protest* (New York, 1976), pp. 38–39; Gunnar Myrdal, *An American Dilemma* (New York, 1944), pp. 873–74; Martin Luther King, Jr., *Where Do We Go From Here: Chaos or Community?* (Boston, 1968), p. 124.

4. Myrdal, pp. 875–78; King, *Stride Toward Freedom: The Montgomery Story* (London, 1959), pp. 215–16.

Southern Christian Leadership Conference. SCLC had no members —unlike the NAACP, which had half a million—but consisted of a fluctuating number of affiliated organizations that were grouped together by state. Most of these affiliates comprised a number of ministers and their churches, although SCLC included some civic organizations, as well as northern affiliates that existed mainly to provide financial support. While this unusual structure had its problems— SCLC only became effective when it recruited a cadre of full-time organizers—it created a flexible network of popular local protest leaders.[5]

Its clerical leadership made SCLC uniquely equipped to communicate with ordinary blacks. For the most part excluded from politics, blacks had long used religion to sublimate or disguise their political aspirations. SCLC's leaders clothed political ideas in a religious phraseology that blacks readily understood and used Christian tenets to give the civil rights movement a divine sanction. As Ralph Abernathy, SCLC's vice-president, put it, "This is God's movement. There can be *no* injunction against God." Being preachers, they were adept at combining exhortation with entertainment, and provided what Bayard Rustin called "an emotional dimension to whip up the enthusiasm of the people." SCLC's identification with the church was invaluable when it came to organizing local protests, for churchgoers attended its mass meetings as they would Sunday services.[6]

233

SCLC's first few years, however, were disappointing and revealed important weaknesses. The fame that King had garnered from the Montgomery bus boycott gave an exaggerated impression of his leadership abilities. In fact, King had neither instigated the boycott nor sought its leadership, and the protest's success owed as much to the collective efforts of the Montgomery Improvement Association as it did to King himself. As president of SCLC King lacked the same kind of organized and dedicated support: as late as 1960 the Conference had a full-time staff of only three. There was also confusion about SCLC's precise role. Founded to promote nonviolent direct action—boycotts, demonstrations, sit-ins, and so forth—it launched intead an ambitious but unrealistic scheme to double the number of registered black voters in the South. Voter registration drives, however, required an extensive local organization, something that SCLC, unlike the NAACP, did not yet possess. Its "Crusade for Citizenship" staged some enthusiastic rallies but failed to register many new voters.[7]

5. David L. Lewis, *King: A Critical Biography* (Baltimore, 1970), pp. 88–89; SCLC, *This Is SCLC* (Atlanta, 1963). The number of affiliates rose from 65 in 1962 to 270 in 1967.

6. Watters, pp. 24, 203; Rustin, p. 40.

7. Lewis, pp. 48–56; Lawrence D. Reddick, *Crusader Without Violence* (New York, 1959), pp. 117–27, 216.

By 1959, SCLC's future appeared uncertain. Ella Baker, its first executive director, complained of an absence of "reflective thinking and planning" and criticized the failure to develop a distinctive program. When a student sit-in movement to protest segregated lunch counters swept the South in 1960, it did so spontaneously, with only slight assistance from the conference. The daring and imaginative "Freedom Rides" launched by CORE in 1961 pushed SCLC further from the limelight. The question of purpose still plagued the new organization. Should it assist local actions or should it instigate its own protests? Should it concentrate on voter registration or promote direct action to desegregate public accommodations?[8]

234

Primarily a strategist and a thinker, King was handicapped by his own ignorance of the practical techniques of nonviolent direct action, and only when he recruited knowledgeable tacticians and organizers did SCLC really come into its own. The staff members added between 1960 and 1963 provided this body of experience. James Lawson, C. T. Vivian, and James Bevel, ministers all, were veterans of the Nashville sit-ins and had taken part in the first "Freedom Ride" to leave that city in 1961. The Rev. Wyatt T. Walker was a long-time activist from Petersburg, Virginia, where he had served in the NAACP and organized the Petersburg Improvement Association. Hosea Williams, from Savannah, headed the Chatham County Crusade for Voters, probably SCLC's most successful affiliate in terms of both voter registration and direct action. Beneath these and the half-dozen other members of the executive staff, SCLC recruited a cadre of field organizers. As its full-time staff grew from five in 1960 to sixty in 1964, it developed the ability, working with local leaders and other volunteers, to mount large-scale protests that sent thousands to jail.[9]

Wyatt Walker, Hosea Williams, and James Bevel played especially noteworthy parts in perfecting SCLC's tactics. All three had a flair for inventive direct action and were willing to take risks when King hesitated to act. Walker's plans for the Birmingham protests, mapped out with Fred Shuttlesworth, called for gradually escalating demonstrations calculated to engineer a potentially explosive level of tension. Williams took a similarly hard-headed approach, scorning negotiations and biracial committees. The tumultuous protests he led in Savannah brought desegregation to that city a full year before the 1964 Civil Rights Act, and one of his tactics, the dangerous night march, became a

8. Ella Baker, "Report of the Executive Director," "Memo to Administrative Committee," October 1959, King Papers, Boston University, file VI, folder 153.

9. Watters, p. 102; *SCLC Newsletter*, July, August 1963, 8 March 1964; Coretta King, *My Life With Martin Luther King, Jr.* (New York, 1969), pp. 207–8. The full-time staff reached a peak of about 150 in 1966.

standard part of SCLC's repertoire. Bevel devised equally ingenious tactics, involving young children in the Birmingham demonstrations and originating the ploy of a fifty-mile march from Selma to Montgomery. Fred Shuttlesworth and C. T. Vivian shared the same combative approach toward direct action.[10]

The role of the Rev. Andrew J. Young, who joined SCLC in 1961, differed from that of the direct action specialists. Like King, Young realized that the sledgehammer tactics favored by Bevel and Williams could rarely force change by themselves, for a policy of mass arrests, if vigorously enforced and backed by court injunctions, could usually baffle nonviolent protests. Young believed that direct action was best used as a means of opening the door to negotiation. Well versed in the art of the possible, he proved adept at extricating the Conference from tactical quagmires. Conciliatory in manner and reasonable in argument, he became SCLC's principal negotiator, playing a key role, for example, in the talks that ended the Birmingham protests.[11]

To many outsiders, SCLC still looked like a one-man band. Unlike CORE and the NAACP, SCLC was not organized along democratic lines. Annual conventions and twice-yearly board meetings had little control over policy, and in practice merely approved King's proposals. Only once, when the 1965 convention refused to endorse his statements about Vietnam, did King fail to carry his organization with him. King's position at the apex of the SCLC hierarchy was unassailable, for nobody could rival his popularity or effectiveness as a publicist and fundraiser.

But despite its autocratic structure, King did not keep SCLC under his thumb, as some have asserted. His caution, tactical indecisiveness, and distaste for administration led him to delegate authority freely. As Willie Bolden, one of the field staff, recalled, "He never did believe in pulling rank. He did it only if it was necessary." Moreover, King did not surround himself with ciphers or sycophants but, as program director Randolph Blackwell admitted, with "egotistical, stubborn, arrogant people." Transcripts of staff meetings reveal spirited debates among, in Andrew Young's words, "driving, ambitious" individuals. Indeed, discussions often degenerated into shouting matches, with participants smashing furniture in their frustration. King did not hand down decisions from an Olympian height; after consulting trusted advisers outside SCLC, he hammered them out with his colleagues.[12]

10. Howell Raines, *My Soul Is Rested: Movement Days in the Deep South Remembered* (New York, 1977), p. 435; Robert Terrell, "Discarding the Dream," *Evergreen Review*, May 1970, pp. 75–76; Charles E. Fager, *Selma, 1965* (New York, 1974), p. 170; *Sunday Times* (London), 6 Feb. 1977; Lewis, pp. 137–38.

11. *Norfolk Journal and Guide*, 21 Aug. 1965.

12. John A. Williams, *The King God Didn't Save: Reflections on the Life and Death of*

235

It was true that King permitted, in journalist Paul Good's words, "a godlike myth to surround him." SCLC's much-criticized "cult of personality," however, was to a large extent a deliberate policy, "a careful, methodical process of image-building." His aides, particularly Ralph Abernathy, praised King extravagantly and ascribed to him almost superhuman powers. This was partly a fundraising strategy, enabling SCLC to translate King's "unique symbolism," as Wyatt Walker put it, into dollars and cents. More important, SCLC lacked a mass membership and had no political base; its effectiveness as a pressure group depended in large part on King's personal prestige or charismatic authority. It was also much easier, especially for unlettered blacks who lived in the rural Deep South, to identify with a larger-than-life individual like King than with an amorphous organization like SCLC.[13]

While Abernathy's exaggerated encomiums should be discounted, it would be wrong to err in the opposite direction by underestimating King's influence. His intellectual gifts and powers of expression surpassed those of his colleagues. In an organization of preachers, King was a preacher par excellence, and although some found his style pompous and repetitive, few denied his ability to inspire audiences. "King brought to life . . . a tangible God," wrote one journalist, "not some metaphysical concept." And although outsiders criticized SCLC's habit of depicting him as a latter-day Moses and emphasized the multiplicity of black leaders, opinion polls consistently recorded King as the most popular black leader by far. He swelled the ranks of demonstrations and filled churches and meeting halls to overflowing. As the church secretary of the NAACP admitted, "King packs them in."[14]

Some argued that blacks admired King despite, rather than because of, his commitment to nonviolence as a philosophy. The ideas of Gandhi, wrote sociologist E. Franklin Frazier, had "nothing in common with the social heritage of the Negro." The psychologist Kenneth B. Clark went so far as to call King's philosophy "pathological," because it demanded an unnatural response to oppression. King and his aides readily admitted that blacks had trouble understanding and accepting Gandhian doctrines. "Birmingham was probably the most violent city in America," Andrew Young recalled, "and every black

236

Martin Luther King, Jr. (London, 1971), p. 168; Raines, pp. 426–27, 478–52; Barbara A. Reynolds, *Jesse Jackson: The Man, The Movement, The Myth* (Chicago, 1975), p. 188.

13. Paul Good, *The Trouble I've Seen: White Journalist / Black Movement* (Washington, 1975), p. 226; Fager, *Uncertain Resurrection*, pp. 25–26; Robert Penn Warren, *Who Speaks for the Negro?* (New York, 1966), p. 231.

14. Good, pp. 18–20, 100–101; William Brink and Louis Harris, *The Negro Revolution in America* (New York, 1964), pp. 106–24.

family had an arsenal." Many activists came to view the philosophy of nonviolence as demeaning—even cowardly—and politically naive. Both SNCC and CORE would officially renounce it in 1966.[15]

In the early years of the civil rights movement, on the other hand, a small but influential minority of activists proved eagerly receptive to the Gandhian philosophy, which was propagated not only by SCLC but also by CORE and its pacifist progenitor, the Fellowship of Reconciliation. Nonviolence as a philosophy offered the stirring ideal of a "beloved community" as well as a cogent justification for the transgressions of the law that direct action involved. Moreover, King framed Gandhian ideas within traditional Christian dogmas, and, as John Lewis of SNCC has argued, was remarkably successful in attuning them to the religious beliefs of black southerners. Even those who scorned nonviolence as a philosophy accepted it as a sound method of social protest. As Stokely Carmichael admitted in 1970, "nonviolence was the only possibility."[16]

237

For most blacks, King's appeal was simple and direct. Involvement in the civil rights movement, especially in the Deep South, could bring economic reprisals, incarceration, physical injury, and even death. King instilled the fortitude and confidence to brave those threats. Stressing the dangers he faced himself, he urged blacks to develop "that quiet courage to die if necessary." Insisting that they had the power to mold their own futures if they replaced "pity with self-respect," he exhorted them to "straighten their backs up." It was a message that most blacks wanted to hear. When King went to jail, thousands followed him. "He was a symbol of all their hopes for a better life," wrote Cleveland Sellers of SNCC. "By being there and showing that he really cared, he was helping to destroy barriers of fear and insecurity."[17]

Despite King's popularity, SCLC never lacked critics. Older, accommodationist black leaders echoed the charge of white segregationists that King and his crew were irresponsible troublemakers. The Rev. Joseph H. Jackson, president of the five-million-strong National Baptist Convention, cared little for King's version of the social gospel and did not hide his aversion to SCLC's leader. Most black clergymen probably shared Jackson's views: Wyatt Walker estimated that as many as 90 percent of the black ministers in Birmingham shunned SCLC's campaign there. Many black-owned newspapers showed a

15. E. Franklin Frazier, "The Negro Church and Assimilation," in Hart M. Nelson, ed., *The Black Church in America* (London, 1971), p. 137; Warren, p. 23; Flip Schulka, ed., *Martin Luther King, Jr.: A Documentary* (New York, 1976), p. 66.

16. Watters, p. 24; Stokely Carmichael, *Stokely Speaks* (New York, 1971), p. 190.

17. Watters, pp. 98, 198; King, "Our Struggle," *Liberation*, April 1956, p. 3; Cleveland Sellers and Robert Terrell, *River of No Return* (New York, 1973), p. 165.

similar hostility. The *Birmingham World*, for example, denounced
SCLC's protests as "wasteful and worthless," and urged King and his
cohorts to go back to Atlanta.[18] Within the civil rights movement itself,
many regarded SCLC's tactics as ineffective. The NAACP remained
convinced that the really substantial victories were won in the federal
courts. SNCC was skeptical of direct action for different reasons. Having sent organizers into the Black Belt only to see their protests
crushed, it concluded that voter registration and the development of
political power was the path to change. By 1965 SNCC scorned direct
action and regarded SCLC's use of demonstrations as irresponsible.
The conference, SNCC charged, would organize dramatic but ineffec-
tual marches, win a few minor concessions, and then "proclaim a great
moral victory and leave town." It was certainly true that local leaders
in Birmingham and elsewhere felt that SCLC had exploited their protests for the sake of publicity and then abandoned them.[19]

Many believed that SCLC provoked white violence in an utterly
cynical fashion. According to SNCC's James Forman, the SCLC strategists were delighted when "Bull" Connor turned police-dogs and firehoses against peaceful demonstrators in Birmingham, and in their ela-
tion jumped up and down chanting, "We've got a movement. We had
some police brutality!" Journalists such as Pat Watters and Paul Good
also noted such behavior. SCLC, wrote Good, "is frankly opportun-
istic, sometimes dissembles, and does not particularly care if innocents
get hurt in the process."[20] King admitted that the success of SCLC's
tactics often depended on whites unleashing violence against nonviolent demonstrators. White violence not only provided the civil rights
movement with what Bayard Rustin called "an organizing dynamic,"
but also provoked, in extreme cases, federal intervention—it had
brought paratroopers to Little Rock in 1957 and marshals to
Montgomery during the 1961 Freedom Rides. After the dismal failure
of its protests in Albany, Georgia, in 1961–62, King and his staff concluded that without such federal involvement direct action would be
unable to effect fundamental change. Nonviolent protests had, it was
true, had some success in the Upper South and the Border States, but
even there the process of desegregation was slow and uneven. And in
the Deep South, with few exceptions, direct action had failed completely as the police, armed with court injunctions, locked up protesters and intimidated their supporters.[21]

In its Birmingham and Selma protests SCLC exploited white vio-

18. Lewis, pp. 157–58; Brink and Harris, p. 108; *Birmingham World*, 20 April 1963.
    19. James Forman, *The Making of Black Revolutionaries* (New York, 1972), p. 442;
Sellers and Terrell, p. 117.
    20. Forman, p. 312; Watters, p. 130; Good, p. 87.
    21. King, "Behind the Selma March," *Saturday Review*, 3 April 1965, pp. 16–17;
Rustin, p. 43.

lence to dramatize "before a national audience . . . the inhumanity of the Jim Crow system." Its strategy assumed that racism, at least in its most virulent form, was a southern anachronism, "an idea that is out of harmony with the basic idea of the nation." If its full depravity could be exposed, King contended, the "great decent majority" would bestir itself to demand protective legislation. SCLC therefore subordinated local demands to this larger goal, using Birmingham and Selma as arenas in which to stage what David Halberstam described as "a great televised morality play." As Samuel Lubell noted, "getting bloodied and beaten" was an essential part of the strategy.[22]

The charge that SCLC manipulated local movements clearly had substance. Yet the conference justified its tactics on both moral and practical grounds. Direct action might not bring about immediate changes, but the very act of defiance was necessary to "dissolve the stereotype of the grinning, submissive Uncle Tom." More important, SCLC contended that violence was intrinsic to the system of white supremacy and that direct action merely made it visible. As Andrew Young put it, SCLC made sheriffs like Jim Clark inflict their beatings "on Main Street, at noon, in front of CBS, NBC and ABC television cameras." If, as Pat Watters believed, SCLC adapted its tactics to "what the liberals in Washington wanted," those tactics paid off handsomely. President Johnson, in full-blown rhetoric, described Selma as "a turning-point in man's unending search for freedom"; and President Kennedy, in his more restrained prose, acknowledged that "the events in Birmingham" had "so increased the cries for equality that no city or state or legislative body can prudently choose to ignore them."[23]

As August Meier pointed out in 1965, SCLC's campaigns gave the civil rights movement a certain unity, coherence, and common focus. The tactical unity achieved by the "Big Five" civil rights organizations between 1963 and 1965 owed much to SCLC's ability to act as a bridge between the militant and conservative wings of the movement. On the one side, SCLC agreed with the NAACP and the National Urban League about the wisdom of working alongside sympathetic whites and within the national Democratic party. On the more militant side, SCLC shared with CORE an emphasis on Gandhian direct action, and the fact that they concentrated their efforts in different states made for a good working relationship.[24]

239

22. Earl Black, *Southern Governors and Civil Rights* (London, 1976), p. 322; Warren, p. 218; King, *Stride*, p. 205; David Halberstam, "The Second Coming of Martin Luther King," *Harper's*, August 1967, pp. 42–43; Samuel Lubell, *Black and White: Test of a Nation* (New York, 1964), p. 103.

23. King, *Where?*, p. 18; James H. Lane, "Power, Conflict, and Social Change," in Don R. Bowen and Louis H. Masotti, eds., *Riots and Rebellions* (Beverly Hills, 1968), p. 90; Watters, pp. 124–25.

24. August Meier, "On the Role of Martin Luther King," in Melvin Drimmer, ed., *Black History: A Reappraisal* (New York, 1968), p. 449.

SCLC's relationship with SNCC was more complex. SNCC resented the fact that when they conducted joint protests in Albany, Selma, and elsewhere, SCLC received most of the publicity although SNCC had laid the vital organizational groundwork. In addition, many SNCC workers disliked the religiosity of SCLC's style and the authoritarianism of its structure. They regarded SCLC as too bourgeois, too compromising. As one SNCC worker said of King—perhaps unwittingly pinpointing the secret of his success—"He's got one foot in the cotton field and one in the White House."[25] Even so, although some of his lieutenants reciprocated SNCC's hostility, King himself viewed SNCC with fatherly affection and was quick to defend its often intemperate militancy. For this and other reasons he commanded the respect of critics like Cleveland Sellers and Stokely Carmichael and enjoyed a close rapport with John Lewis, SNCC's chairman. Until 1966 the two organizations kept up a fruitful collaboration, and although SNCC complained that the conference stole its glory at Selma, its work there would probably have been inconclusive had not SCLC's intervention forged a tactical coalition that included the Urban League, the NAACP, and organized labor—groups that SNCC scorned.

Unlike SNCC, SCLC believed strongly in the strategy advocated by King's unofficial political adviser, Bayard Rustin, of constructing the broadest possible alliance of "progressive" forces. King and his colleagues determinedly courted white liberals, labor unions, church organizations, and university people and did much to strengthen the "coalition of conscience" that indirectly brought about what historians now see as a "Second Reconstruction" of the South. SCLC's ability to mobilize clerical support was especially noteworthy: when King appealed to the churches from Selma, some four hundred nuns, priests, rabbis, bishops, and denominational heads converged on the Alabama town. Richard Hofstadter's description of Progressivism could be applied with even greater accuracy to the civil rights struggle: "No other major movement in American political history . . . had ever received so much clerical sanction."[26]

As an individual, King was an enormously effective spokesman for the civil rights movement. He proved adept at adjusting his rhetorical style to suit different white audiences; and while his message evoked white guilt, it also, as King's biographer David Lewis pointed out, left "deeply pleasurable emotions." His emphasis on nonviolence helped to allay white fears and clothed the civil rights movement in what

25. Raines, p. 214; Forman p. 419; *Newsweek*, 15 May 1967, p. 23.
26. John Cogley, "The Clergy Heeds a New Call," *New York Times Magazine*, 2 May 1965; Fager, *Selma*, pp. 113–14; Richard Hofstadter, *The Age of Reform* (New York, 1955), p. 152.

Lerone Bennett called "the comforting garb of love and forgiveness." By defining the movement's goals in terms of universal values like democracy, Christianity, and "the best in the American dream," he maximized white support and involvement. His intellectual and oratorical gifts plus SCLC's flair for publicity made him the leader who, in Meier's words, "symbolized for most whites the whole program of Negro advancement."[27]

King's failure in Chicago is often cited as evidence of SCLC's inability to adapt to the northern ghetto. The conference certainly underestimated the degree of white opposition and black anger it would encounter there. Viewing the South as the main bastion of racism and regarding discrimination in the North as a secondary, residual phenomenon, SCLC mistook the significance of the 1964 riots in New York and elsewhere, construing them as aberrations rather than portents. Only the massive riot in Watts brought home the depth of the problem in the North. Once in Chicago, conference workers soon discovered that the black preacher lacked the singular prestige he enjoyed in the South and that the church alone was an inadequate organizing tool. SCLC thrived on spontaneity and dramatic confrontations; it had little experience of the tedious job of community organizing. Many became dispirited by the apathy, cynicism, and hostility they encountered. Hosea Williams, whose voter registration drive got nowhere, complained that "here, the Negro has been so plantationized that he feels there's no hope of ever breaking the stranglehold." The sheer size of its task overwhelmed SCLC's resources—as Coretta King plaintively recalled, "Chicago is such a big city, and we were so few." The hostility of the Daley machine, which included many of the established black leaders, was equally daunting.[28]

Even so, SCLC's efforts in Chicago were far from inept. Some of the staff, notably James Bevel and Jesse Jackson, showed great aptitude for working in the ghetto and organized neighborhood associations, tenant unions, and consumer boycotts. The conference also embarked upon slum rehabilitation and adult education programs. When it finally turned to direct action, moreover, it forced Mayor Daley to the negotiating table and extracted an open housing agreement which, as David Lewis pointed out, was "considerably more comprehensive" than the settlement it had won in Birmingham in 1963. _Newsweek_ even termed it a "solid vindication of Southern style nonviolent protest in a Northern city."[29]

241

27. Lewis, p. 394; Lerone Bennett, Jr., _The Negro Mood_ (Chicago, 1964), p. 30; Meier, p. 446.

28. _Newsweek_, 13 Feb. 1967, p. 18; Coretta King, p. 287.

29. SCLC, _Project Report_ (Atlanta, 1 March 1967), p. 2; Lewis, p. 352; _Newsweek_, 5 Sept. 1966, p. 19.

Unfortunately, Mayor Daley never made a serious effort to implement this agreement and, after his easy reelection in April 1967, openly
repudiated it. More important, SCLC's dramatization of discrimination
in the housing market did not prevent Congress from rejecting fair-
housing legislation in 1966 and 1967. The evidence of opinion polls, as
well as the North's long history of race riots, demonstrated that most
whites accepted with equanimity the exclusion of blacks from "white"
residential areas. Fear of economic competition coalesced with this
racism to produce an aggressive resentment against black demands
that led to the rejection of fair-housing laws in California and other
states, growing support for George Wallace, and a swing towards the
Republican party. Democratic leaders were terrified by the prospect of
a mass defection of white voters in the Northern cities and suburbs. As
Lyndon Johnson recalled, "the open housing issue had become a
Democratic liability." Political support for the civil rights movement
melted away.[30]

The wave of urban riots that started in Watts in 1965 hastened the
decline of SCLC's influence. Contrary to King's belief, most whites
detested direct action, but the fear of black violence, and the confidence that King's moderate leadership would prevent it, had given
many a pragmatic reason for backing SCLC's nonviolent crusade.
When King proved powerless to curb urban rioting—as dramatically
illustrated by the eruption that occurred in Chicago during SCLC's
campaign there—much of his white support fell away. In this context,
many black activists in the North agreed with Bayard Rustin that further direct action would only intensify the white backlash. The riots,
moreover, cast doubt upon the very feasibility of nonviolent protest in
the North: studies showed that significant numbers of blacks were in-
clining toward violence as a method of self-assertion and that the harsh
suppression of the outbreaks was creating a backwash of sympathy for
the rioters. King continued to argue that nonviolent "mass civil disobedience" in northern cities could be a "constructive and creative
force," but privately he admitted that "people expect me to have answers, but I don't have any."[31]

Tactical disagreements mirrored a deepening split within the civil
rights movement. The "Black Power" slogan, adopted by SNCC and
CORE in 1966, made unity among the "Big Five" impossible. Al-

30. Ben Van Clarke, "The Summit Follow-Up," undated, King Library; Mike
Royko, *Boss: Mayor Richard J. Daley of Chicago* (London, 1972), p. 149; William Brink
and Louis Harris, *Black and White: A Study of U.S. Racial Attitudes Today* (New York,
1967), pp. 41, 105–13; Lyndon B. Johnson, *The Vantage Point: Perspectives of the Presidency, 1963–1969* (New York, 1971), p. 178.

31. Rustin. pp. 41–42; Brink and Harris, pp. 260–65; King. "The Crisis in America's
Cities." text of speech. 16 Aug. 1967, p. 10, King Library; Coretta King, p. 298.

though defined in many ways, "Black Power" clearly meant the rejection of nonviolence, coalitionism, and integration. It also had unmistakable antiwhite overtones. SCLC tried to be positive about the slogan, but a split in the movement could not be avoided. The NAACP and the Urban League denounced "Black Power" and anathematized SNCC and CORE. Vainly struggling to keep the two sides together, King suspected that the NAACP welcomed the split "because they think they are the only civil rights organization"; but SNCC and CORE were equally obdurate.[32]

The war in Vietnam widened the divisions. Whereas SNCC and CORE denounced the American involvement, the Urban League and the NAACP stoutly defended it. King himself was appalled by the rapid escalation of the war, but fear of alienating President Johnson and lack of support from his own organization prevented him from speaking with his customary frankness. By early 1967, however, with his wife and many of his colleagues—notably James Bevel—already in the forefront of the antiwar movement, he could keep silent no longer. King's decision to denounce the war, this time with SCLC's backing, brought a storm of criticism from erstwhile supporters. Whitney Young, publicly castigating King, replied that "the greatest freedom that exists for Negroes . . . is the freedom to die in Vietnam." The NAACP insisted that civil rights leaders should stay away from foreign policy. Bayard Rustin defended King's "ride to debate" Vietnam but advised blacks to shun the peace movement. From the *New York Times*, *Washington Post*, and *Atlanta Constitution* came excoriating editorials.[33]

King searched for an issue that might bridge these divisions. By the end of 1967 he believed he had found one. A campaign in Washington to dramatize poverty, he contended, would resurrect the civil rights coalition and, he hoped, attract the young opponents of the war in Vietnam. Moreover, whereas "Black Power" alienated whites and other minorities, the concept of "Poor People's Power" would unite the dispossessed of all races. King believed that SCLC could serve as the "radical middle" of a resurgent movement for social reform and predicted that the proposed protests would "create new alliances, wake new forces."[34] Most black leaders, however, regarded the plan as dangerously misconceived. John Morsell of the NAACP warned

243

32. *New York Times*, 9 July 1966. For King's critique of Black Power, see *Where?*, pp. 44–46.
33. *New York Times*, 7 Sept. 1967; Rustin, *Down The Line* (Chicago, 1971), pp. 109, 167; *Current* (May 1967), pp. 39–40.
34. José Yglesias, "Dr. King's March on Washington, Part II," in August Meier and Elliott Rudwick, eds., *Black Protest in the Sixties* (Chicago, 1970), p. 274; *New York Times*, 22 Jan. 1968.

that protests in Washington would be "met with as an insurrection." Bayard Rustin thought they would attract "the most irresponsible and uncontrollable elements," and argued that direct action "can only lead . . . to further backlash and repression." King's top aides expressed other doubts. James Bevel contended that the war was now the most urgent issue and doubted that a campaign against poverty would excite the enthusiasm of students and young people. Then there was a tactical problem: would President Johnson "give enough opposition for us to build up steam and momentum?"—he was hardly likely to respond in the manner of "Bull" Connor. Hosea Williams and Jesse Jackson shared Bevel's skepticism and wanted SCLC to develop programs rather than pursue panaceas. Andrew Young believed that "with an asinine Congress like this," most of the campaign's goals would be unattainable.[35]

Would the Poor People's Campaign have been more successful if King had lived? Despite King's still-considerable prestige, the campaign's stated demands seemed to doom it to failure at the outset. SCLC sought the passage of an "Economic Bill of Rights" along the lines of John Conyers' Full Opportunity Bill, which called for an expenditure of $30 billion over three years. Yet Congress had slashed the War on Poverty and only grudgingly appropriated $40 million for rat control. President Johnson regarded demands for new multi-billion dollar social programs as completely unrealistic. King admitted that "we're riding on the forces of history and not totally shaping things," but those forces—the mood of white opinion, the hostility of president and Congress, the primacy of the war issue—were working against SCLC. King probably realized this and might well have cancelled the campaign lest it endanger the presidential candidacy of Robert Kennedy. More likely, he would have been satisfied with minor concessions from the government. As Andrew Young later admitted, "we were trying to hold ground we had won. We weren't trying to win new victories."[36]

King's assassination and the fiasco of the Poor People's Campaign exacerbated fundamental weaknesses in SCLC's structure. In 1967 King had attempted to place the conference upon a firmer organizational foundation. Operation Breadbasket, the consumer boycott apparatus which had proved successful in Atlanta and Chicago, became a nationwide program under the direction of Jesse Jackson. To improve

35. *New York Times*, 18 Dec. 1967; Rustin, *Down The Line*, p. 203; transcript of executive staff committee meeting, 21 Dec. 1967, pp. 7–8, King Library; *Wall Street Journal*, 29 May 1968.
36. Yglesias, p. 274; Lewis, pp. 384–85; Goodman, p. 29.

SCLC's overall efficiency and organizational discipline, King appointed a management consultant executive director, promoted Andrew Young to the new post of executive vice-president, and set up a central steering-committee comprising himself, Young, Ralph Abernathy, and two others.[37] But these reforms did not change SCLC's basic character. While Andrew Young and Hosea Williams wanted to orient the conference toward long-term political action, King took his own role as a prophetic leader increasingly seriously. A decade earlier, he had joked that "people will be expecting me to pull rabbits out of the hat for the rest of my life"; yet by 1967-68 he felt impelled to win fresh victories in order to avert what he saw as the threat of a right-wing takeover. His belated interest in developing SCLC as a permanent organization did not alter the fact that it remained King-centered. It never managed to establish its own identity. Dependent on King for leadership, publicity, and much of its financial support, it was ill equipped to carry on without him.[38]

245

By the end of 1968, SCLC was a demoralized organization. "The toll of some ten years of constant pressure is beginning to tell on all of us," admitted Andrew Young. Without King to enforce unity, personal antagonisms and policy differences became increasingly destructive. The tension and frustration became so acute that the senior staff underwent two lengthy sessions of group psychoanalysis. "We've never buried Dr. King," explained Young, "and we won't be able to do anything until we do." But this failed to keep the staff together. James Bevel, unable to win backing for a plan to intensify opposition to the war in Vietnam by using civil disobedience, left in 1969. Andrew Young resigned in 1970 to run, unsuccessfully at first, for Congress.[39] By that time, SCLC's activities had become too thinly spread and lacked a central focus. Since 1966, SCLC had ceased to be a purely southern organization, yet had failed to develop an adequate national structure. In practice, its move to the northern cities had meant temporarily abandoning the South, a fact which, combined with SNCC's collapse and CORE's decline, caused a dramatic slowdown in civil rights activity in that region. In 1965 the three organizations had fielded about one thousand workers in the South. Two years later fewer than fifty remained, and observers were pronouncing the civil rights movement dead or, at best, "fighting a last-ditch battle for survival." This collapse stunted black political growth and dulled the cutting edge of the recent civil rights laws. As Vernon Jordan of the Voter

37. SCLC, *North and South: Staff News* (Dec. 1967), pp. 1–10.
38. Lerone Bennett, Jr., *What Manner of Man* (Chicago, 1964), p. 64.
39. *New York Times*, 25 Dec. 1969; Goodman, p. 30.

Education Project put it, "the trouble is, the Movement never reached most counties in the South."[40]

SCLC tried to penetrate these neglected areas after King's death, and the years 1968–1970 saw a minor revival of its activities in the South. Its successful intervention in the Charleston, South Carolina, hospital workers' strike of 1969 was especially notable. Its efforts to become a viable national organization, however, foundered on the internecine leadership struggle that broke out between Ralph Abernathy, King's chosen successor, and Jesse Jackson, the rising star of SCLC's expanding economic wing, Operation Breadbasket. Jackson's resignation in 1971 removed SCLC's ablest and most popular northern spokesman and wrecked Operation Breadbasket. With the launching of Operation PUSH, Jackson became a national civil rights leader in his own right, with an organization that appropriated SCLC's northern role.[41]

This blow rendered SCLC's attempts to mount ambitious national projects increasingly futile, and critics complained that the conference engaged in an endless round of rallies and marches that produced little save angry rhetoric. Its involvement with the antiwar movement, its alliance with the National Welfare Rights Organization, and its support for such causes as the California grape workers overextended its declining resources and diluted their impact. By taking on too much, SCLC neglected its southern base and became swallowed up among other national movements. By 1972, SCLC's financial problems forced it to reduce its staff from sixty-one to twenty. A year later, Ralph Abernathy renounced the leadership, blasting those who "now occupy high positions made possible through our struggle . . . but will not support the SCLC financially." At the annual convention, however, he agreed to pick up King's mantle once again, and soldiered on for four more years.[42]

Waning black support paralleled a decline in white financial backing. Although SCLC argued that "marching is never outdated," faith in the ability of nonviolent direct action to bring about change had all but evaporated. By 1970 the election of Richard Nixon, the widespread white hostility to black demands, and the tendency to answer black protests with "massive police and military force" had driven down black expectations and ushered in a period of quietism and disillusionment. A 1970 opinion poll disclosed that most blacks expressed "profound cynicism about the American political system."[43]

40. *New York Times*, 1 Aug. 1965; 7 Feb.; 29 May 1967.
41. Reynolds, *Jesse Jackson*, passim.
42. *Christian Century*, Sept. 1970; *Washington Post*, 10 July 1973; SCLC, *Soul Force*, 14 Aug. 1973, pp. 12–13.
43. *Time*, 6 April 1970, pp. 18–21.

Part of this pessimism may well have been a reaction against the extravagant optimism preached by King and SCLC in the previous decade. As late as 1964, when the prevalence of segregation in the North was a matter of common knowledge, King predicted that "race and color prejudice will have all but disappeared . . . in the next five years." A year later, deceived by the sympathy aroused by the Selma protests, he argued that the "vast majority of Americans" supported the direct-action methods of the civil rights movement—an assertion which opinion polls plainly contradicted. As Samuel DuBois Cook has written, until the Chicago campaign King overestimated the white majority's "sense of guilt and shame over the dehumanized role of black people." Moreover, his claim that suffering could change the oppressor's heart by appealing to his conscience raised unrealistic hopes that inevitably gave way to bitterness and disillusionment. In short, SCLC did little to prepare blacks for a long and difficult struggle against tenacious white resistance.[44]

Ultimately, however, SCLC's decline can be attributed to its very success. The organizers of SNCC, CORE, and SCLC had furnished the leadership in the South that a small and fearful black middle class could not provide. With the opening of new opportunities, the expansion of the black electorate, and the gradual decline of white violence and intimidation, indigenous leadership grew stronger and more independent. The local church and voters organizations which had formed the social base of the civil rights movement progressed, with an increasingly sure step, along the path of political action. But if the 1965 Voting Rights Act moved the civil rights movement "from protest to politics" (SCLC itself sent Andrew Young and Walter Fauntroy to Congress) it also removed its basic raison d'etre. As James Bevel put it, "there is no more civil rights movement. President Johnson signed it out of existence."[45]

It would be misleading to blame SCLC for the still-birth of what C. Vann Woodward termed "the Third Reconstruction"—the tackling of northern, or national, problems of tacit discrimination, de facto segregation, and economic inequality. Although admittedly slow to understand the deep historical roots of racism in the North, the movement in which SCLC played such a vital part was, as Watters and Cleghorn pointed out, a southern movement with southern goals, "whose counterpart did not develop contemporaneously in the North." When King and his team went to Chicago in 1966, they had little chance of filling

247

44. Elliot M. Zashin, *Civil Disobedience and Democracy* (London. 1972), pp. 209–10; Samuel DuBois Cook, "Is Martin Luther King, Jr., Irrelevant?" *New South* (Spring 1971), p. 4.

45. August Meier and Elliott Rudwick, *CORE: A Study in the Civil Rights Movement, 1942–1968* (New York. 1973), p. 329.

the northern leadership vacuum, or of mitigating in any real way the cumulative damage of generations of discrimination and neglect. SCLC's greatest achievements were in the South: these alone made it one of the most successful—and unusual—reform groups in recent American history.[46]

46. C. Vann Woodward, *The Burden of Southern History* (New York, 1969), p. 128; Pat Watters and Reese Cleghorn, *Climbing Jacob's Ladder: The Arrival of Negroes in Southern Politics* (New York, 1967), p. 312.

The
Voter-Registration
Drive
in Selma, Alabama

JOHN R. FRY

1963 will be remembered as the year of John F. Kennedy's assassination *and* the year when the Negro revolt broke fully into the open. Literally hundreds of thousands of American Negroes joined mass demonstrations against the full range of injustices to which they have customarily been subjected. Some of those demonstrations were placid, and some were angry. Whether their protests were violent or nonviolent, thousands upon thousands of Negroes in many states risked jail, beatings, abuse by police dogs, fire hoses, shotguns, tear gas, nightsticks, and electric cattle-prods.

The demonstrations were not alike because there is no master plan being operated by master operators. Negro demonstrations have for the most part been locally instigated, do-it-yourself affairs; they have met an equally local and varied reception. And for the most part, the result of the demonstrations has been an aroused, committed, and cemented Negro community. Usually the demonstrations have brought about specific local changes, often small changes, but almost always something that can be called a victory.

The little gains, the small victories were hailed by Negro leaders as *signs* of the larger victories yet to come. By and large the white communities looked upon the minor alterations in the pattern of segregation as inexpensive *concessions* aimed at shutting off the demonstrations. Such major disagreement in estimating the result of the demonstrations points to a larger disagreement between Negroes and white leaders about the timing and possibility of the attainment of the full range of Negro goals. The problems created by so complicated a conflict do not fade away on a single day of victory and surrender.

In fact, there will be no one day of victory for the nation. Communities are too self-contained, too bound by their own histories, too different from one another, for that kind of once-for-all nationwide crisis and resolution. But crises and changes are sure to come about in these various local communities. It is difficult to generalize about what is going to take place everywhere. And Americans would be greatly helped to know that. We might more modestly and realistically reflect at some length and detail on certain experiences of one community in order to win some perspective amidst the chaotic events that made 1963 a year to be remembered and pondered.

When the United Presbyterian Commission on Religion and Race met in Birmingham—October 8 and 9—one of its members from Birmingham, Peter A. Hall, made an impassioned speech about the critical situation in Selma, Alabama, and then asked to be excused for the remainder of the day so he could go there. As he left, I followed him outside and asked to be taken along. "Fine," said Mr. Hall, "It's about time someone sees Selma. If you don't mind riding in this old truck." He pointed to a well-used '56 Chevrolet sedan. I didn't mind, and we were off. Peter Hall is a United Presbyterian elder. He is also a Negro. He is also an attorney. As an attorney he has been handling civil rights cases for fifteen years, and most recently has masterminded the legal strategy in Selma. On the ninety-mile drive to Selma he tried to fill me in on the tumultuous three weeks that had just passed.

"Yesterday," Peter Hall said, "there were more than three hundred Negroes who came down to the courthouse to register to vote (they only register every other Monday). Three hundred. The line went around the courthouse. This is a city with fifteen thousand Negroes, less than 1 percent of whom are registered. Three hundred is a lot of people. They called yesterday 'Freedom Monday.' If someone left the line, he couldn't get back in, and it was hot. The people were naturally hungry and thirsty. Two 'Snick' kids [field secretaries of the Student Non-violent Coordinating Committee: SNCC = Snick] brought some sandwiches and soft drinks to the people in the line and were arrested on the spot for *molesting* the hungry, thirsty voter applicants. Arrested right there on the street before the eyes of God and everybody."

Ninety miles of intense, detailed briefing prepared me to expect barbed wire, tanks, and flamethrowers ringing the town. Instead, we eventually drove into a pleasant, hot, tree-lined, moderately prosperous city, spread languorously along the banks of the twisting Alabama River. Business among its 28,000 residents was going on, I presume, as usual. We swung off the main street three blocks, and there was the Negro business district that didn't look nearly so prosperous as the main street but was far busier. In the middle of a series of Negro establishments was a more fantastic office than mere imagination could ever devise. The simple two rooms in a total space of 15 x 40 feet simultaneously house the Boynton insurance, real estate, and employment office; the office of James Chestnut, local attorney; the temporary headquarters for the voter-registration effort among Selma's Negroes, including the Snick operation. Never less than twenty people were in these two rooms all afternoon, or less than both telephones in continual use. Here, obviously, was the heart of "the movement" (as Negroes refer to concentrated civil-rights activity) in Selma.

251

Attorneys Hall and Chestnut hustled right off to the County Courthouse in order to request postponement on the trials of a dozen people slated for that afternoon (all were out of jail on peace and appearance bonds). When we returned to the office, we discovered that the Snick workers had arrived, and among them, the fabled executive secretary, James Forman, himself.

I was shocked by Forman. He wears bib overalls that are dirty enough not to look affected, but it is clear that he wears the clothing of field hands in order to identify with them. He does not look like a field hand, or act like one. He speaks in a tenor voice that is calm in conversation but that would be loud and clear from a speaker's platform. Forman displays a constant and intense dedication. "The problem" is always with him. He drives himself through days and nights without end in pursuit of the appropriate next step, whether he is in a field situation, such as Selma, or in New York, or Atlanta, or Washington.

Much later on that day, I asked Jim Forman for his history. "I was born black," he said.

"Cut out the poetics," I countered.

"That isn't poetics," he said; "that is the only important fact in my history. I was born in Mississippi, black. I was raised there and in Chicago, where I went to school. Later I went to school in Boston and did some graduate

3

work in political science. I taught some before this thing came up. Now I'm in it until every Negro in this country has what he's got coming to him."

With the Snick workers in the office, and the two attorneys on the scene, there was a three-hour strategy session, broken by long-distance calls, private conversations, greetings from citizens who just dropped by, hellos from some schoolgirls who had been in jail and felt that they belonged, and did. The Snick people had one dinner brought in on a tray for all ten of them. Mr. Hall and I still had not stopped for luncheon by the time dinner might be reasonably expected, but this was for lack of time, not as with the others for lack of funds. News came into the office that Wilson Brown, one of the field secretaries in the city jail across the street, was in solitary confinement. John Lewis (*the* John Lewis who made a major speech during the Washington March, and who is chairman of Snick), also in the city jail, wanted to know, after seven days, what was going on. Lewis meant, what was going on in South Vietnam? Was Kennedy going to dump the civil-rights bill? What was the news in Mississippi? and please send something to read.

While Peter Hall made the rounds at the jail, and since I couldn't accompany him, I talked with Jim Forman, who began drilling me full of holes for not writing the news. "You're a news editor, aren't you? Here's the news. I don't mean Birmingham, man, I mean the *South*. Why don't you write news about Selma?"

So I returned to Selma. Ten days later the situation had changed dramatically. No one was in jail on civil-rights charges. The voter-registration drive had entered a new and quieter phase. People had the time, and were generally willing to talk about what had happened and to speculate about what was going to happen.

Let this be understood at the outset: Selma is a definite, single Alabama city, but in talking to dozens of Selma residents, I soon discovered two distinct and very different cities. When I talked with white residents, a white Selma was described. When I talked with Negro residents, a Negro Selma was described. The true Selma does not lie somewhere beneath both descriptions. The true Selma is composed of radically opposite points of view.

White Selma has erected a sign by the side of the road at its southern entrance announcing proudly that this city is the birthplace of the Alabama Citizens Council. One gets the impression that everybody who is anybody or who aspires to be anybody belongs to the Council and favors its program. McLean Pitts, a Selma attorney who was counsel for the defense in an injunction suit initiated by the United States of America through its Justice Department, said of the Dallas County Citizens Council (whose main officers were named as defendants in the case):

"There is nothing wrong with an organization that wants to maintain segregation. The NAACP wants integration. The Dallas County Citizens Council wants segregation. I submit to the Court that if the Negro can contend for integration, nothing in the world can prevent the Dallas County Citizens Council from contending for segregation. . . ."

In white Selma absolute segregation is taken for granted as a fact of life. Water fountains are labeled "Colored" and "White." So are rest rooms, and those unmarked bear an invisible sign reading "White." All eating establishments and transient accommodations are rigidly segregated by local custom as well as by geographic location in the city. A colored motel is so marked. Seats in the public library have been removed. Now neither Negroes nor whites can sit down there.

253

In white Selma pride is expressed in the traditions of racial harmony that had, until the middle of September, existed for 150 years. Negroes work as maids, porters, janitors, handymen, flunkies, charwomen, busboys; and perform other menial tasks. A rare few have risen to the rank of junior white-collar workers. Some own their own businesses. In the eyes of the white community a happy arrangement existed. Until the recent disturbances the Negroes gave every evidence of being happy about the arrangement. They had houses, food, clothing; many Negroes owned their own homes, good automobiles, and television sets.

White Selma also takes pride in the fact that, as one resident put it, "There hasn't been a lynching around here for fifty years." His pride in such an accomplishment was genuine. He meant that no Negro had so trespassed law and custom in those fifty years that he deserved to be lynched *and* that the white people in Selma were humane folks, kindly disposed toward the Negroes.

When compared to Jackson, Mississippi; Americus, Georgia; or Plaquemine, Louisiana, white Selma is a land of peace and contentment, where excellent race relations abound. Mayor Chris B. Heinz explained to me that "you can walk any place in Selma at any time of day or night without fear of being clubbed, which is more than you can say for Washington, D.C." This is the city as it looks to white residents.

But the white Selma is only one part of the real Selma. Negroes live there and can articulate what they see. They see all-white political officeholders.

They see less than 1 percent of their number registered to vote, and among those registered are some of the obviously well-educated, clearly superior Negroes who are qualified to vote by any standard. They also see some clearly superior Negroes who are not registered and, among those who are registered, some who are "Uncle Toms" and "Aunt Tomasinas"—terms of scorn and derision used by Negroes to describe those who are thought to be "good niggers" by the white community.

The Negroes also see the signs marking out segregated water fountains and rest rooms, and even different entrances to the Dallas County Health Clinic. But these signs are not taken for granted. They are daily considered degrading and grossly unfair. The Negroes are not happy about the signs, or

254   with their jobs, or with their employers, or with their education, or with their economic opportunity.

Selma Negroes are the first to agree that relations between the races are marked by more understanding and far less violence than in Plaquemine or Jackson. But, nonetheless, an exhibit introduced as evidence in the Federal Court case of the Unites States of America vs. Dallas County and Others (Civil Action No. 3064-63) shows the handwritten notes of Deputy Sheriff Bates, taken at a voter-registration meeting. The notes indicate that Bernard Lafayette, addressing the meeting, ". . . spoke of a Negro that was killed and brought in tied on a car like a deer. (This happened several years ago)."

And in the State of Alabama vs. Bosie Reese, defendant, before Hon. Hugh Mallory, Jr., on July 11, 1963, the Negro voter-registration worker was questioned by his attorney about his arrest in the doorway of the Dallas County Courthouse:

Q: Did you hold back?
A: No, I didn't.
Q: Did the Sheriff strike at you?
A: He did.
Q: Did he miss you or hit you?
A: He hit me.
Q: How many times?
A: He hit me on the head three times.
Reporter Bailey: What did you say . . . out loud.
A: Hit me over the head three times, punched me in my stomach two times, punched me in my side once, and then kicked me in the chest."
(Page 81 of the Transcript.)

The Court found the defendant guilty of breach of peace and resisting arrest. It fixed punishment at $200 and costs. The case is being appealed.

Grisly stories are told by the Negroes to one another about what happens to them when "they get out of line," but no ready means for substantiating or disproving them is available. The stories do exist, however, as a part of the Negro Selma.

Even though Selma is once more a quiet city, it still has two sides that display an even wider gap between them than before the demonstration began. The quietness itself is strange, considering the fact that for three weeks the celebrated racial harmony was openly and repeatedly shattered. The white people still believe, more passionately than ever, in racial harmony. The Negroes believe that, beyond all doubt, the price for racial harmony is one they inevitably have to pay. If the Negro steps out of his place and asks for his simple constitutional rights, he believes—from his own direct experience—that the racial harmony will be broken by speedy arrest. To the Negro, accordingly, the events surrounding the demonstrations vindicate his view of Selma, and to the white, the swift return of racial tranquility vindicates his view.

255

From either point of view the time between September 15 and October 7 was an unusual and turbulent period. In essence the story is very simple. Negroes of all ages demonstrated in street parades, sat-in white eating establishments, picketed the Courthouse, and sought entrance to white churches (one of which allowed them in); many of the students at Hudson High School and Selma University, both of which are Negro schools, boycotted classes in protest of segregation. All of these activities were secondary to the chief concern of the demonstrators: to secure the vote for Negroes.

It all began a year ago when a Snick field secretary and his wife arrived in Selma to look over its possibilities as a place for a major Deep South voter-registration effort. His name is Bernard Lafayette. He had become a member of Snick in 1961 at Jackson, Mississippi, and had already known a lot of trouble before he came to Selma. He found a fledgling voter-registration league and an apparently insurmountable resistance among Negroes to the idea of attempting to register. His preliminary research marked Selma as an all but impossible location for a full-scale registration drive. So Lafayette concluded: *This is the place.* He and his wife, Colia, returned in February, 1963, and the city and the county have not been the same since.

"We didn't want to create new organizations," Lafayette reflects. "We tried to make existing organizations strong and to beef up the local Negro leadership. Our big problem was the Negro himself who wouldn't risk the possible loss of his job and other kinds of hardship just to vote. We had to convince him that he wouldn't ever get any place until he could vote. And the way we had of convincing him was to teach him at clinics the mechanics of registering. We introduced him to the registration application, which is three pages long, and tried to prepare him to answer the oral questions that the board of registrars might ask him. Theoretically, these questions should be directed at the applicant to determine his competency. Actually, we found from the feedback of applicants who had failed that the questions had the effect of intimidating the Negro. ('Does your employer know you are here?') Often the questions had nothing to do with civics. For instance, 'What is your opinion of the man on the street?' Now, what kind of question is that? How would you answer it?

256

"The more people we could convince to go down to register, the more we could arouse the whole community. And while this was going on, we weren't sure of being able to stay in Selma. We had a hard time even finding a place to stay. The people didn't want us because they suspected that they might have a bomb in their front room some evening. We were always being warned that we had better leave, or that we were going to get into trouble."

On June 12 trouble did come. Lafayette was severely beaten by two unidentified (and uncaught) men who had asked him to help them push their stalled automobile. He was asked to get out of his car and see that the bumpers of the two automobiles matched. While he was bent over, he was hit with a tool.

Eventually he did leave Selma but not in flight. He and his wife have returned to Fisk University where they are presently juniors and are awaiting their first child. He says that he will work with Snick until the struggle is over, which is a break for Snick because Lafayette's admirers in Selma call him "a natural-born genius at community organization." Of Bernard Lafayette, Father Maurice F. Ouelett, pastor of St. Elizabeth Mission, said, "He took me by the hand as though I were in kindergarten and led me to understand community relations."

The voter-registration drive was moving along briskly during the late summer. Mass meetings were being held almost every week in various Negro church buildings to capacity or near-capacity crowds. A petition was sent to the Mayor for the appointment of a biracial committee to look into a series of Negro complaints about features of segregated life in Selma. A time limit was placed on the petition so that it was understood that if the petition was not favorably received by September 15, demonstrations would begin. The time limit expired, so plans for demonstrations were already in operation on Sunday, the fifteenth, when news of the bombing of the Sixteenth Street Baptist Church in Birmingham was received. This news added to the determination of the demonstrators, most of whom at that point were students at Selma University and Hudson High School. Later, adults were involved in the demonstrations, or in securing bail-bond money or in mass meetings that were being held almost every night. Before the direct-action demonstrations had come to a halt, it is estimated that more than three hundred different people had been jailed for periods of time between one hour and two weeks. Some of the demonstrators when released from jail immediately joined new demonstrations. The jails were at one time so crowded that demonstrators were housed in Wilcox County facilities.

257

October 7 (the day before I first went to Selma with Peter Hall) was the big day when an estimated three hundred Negroes celebrated "Freedom Monday" by standing in line all day, waiting to register. Selma had seen nothing like it before. One hundred law-enforcement officers were on hand in case some of the nonviolent suddenly repudiated their way of life and became violent. That was the biggest demonstration mounted during the three-week period, and the last. Selma has since been picking up the pieces.

The Negroes in Selma claim that the arrests, high bail, and what they call "harassment" by the Dallas County Sheriff, his deputies, and his special deputies (popularly known as Sheriff Clark's "posse") were needless and unfair. The Justice Department in its pleading before Federal Judge Daniel Thomas (Civil Action 3118-63, December 5), sought temporary, preliminary, and permanent injunctions against the Sheriff on the following allegation:

54. The defendants have threatened, intimidated, and coerced and attempted to threaten, intimidate and coerce Negro citizens of voting age of Dallas County, Alabama for the purpose of interfering with their right to register and to vote. Such threats, intimidations, and coercions and attempted threats, intimidations, and coercions presently known to the plaintiff are the following:

A. *The Defendant James G. Clark, Jr.*
1. Stationing deputies inside each and every voter registration mass meeting and recording everything said by the speakers at the meetings as well as the names of many persons who attended the meetings.
2. Stationing large number of deputies and special deputies outside several of the mass meetings and copying the license numbers of automobiles of persons who attended the meetings.

3. Arresting, detaining, participating in the setting of unreasonable bail, and participating as a witness for the State of Alabama in criminal prosecution of Negro citizens who were engaged in voter registration activities in Dallas County. 4. Arresting, detaining, participating in the setting of unreasonable bail, and participating as a witness for the State of Alabama in criminal prosecution of Negro citizens who attempted, by peacefully picketing in small numbers at and near the Dallas County Courthouse, to urge all Negro citizens to register to vote. 5. On October 7, 1963, when a large number of Negro citizens went to the Dallas County Courthouse to register, issuing orders to his deputies and other police officers under his command that no person would be permitted to leave the registration line for any purpose without losing his place in line; stationing a large number of police along the registration line and preventing anyone from bringing food or drink, or from talking to the Negro citizens waiting in the line.

258

Judge Thomas has not at this writing made a ruling on the suit against Sheriff Clark and others.

In spite of these three weeks, Mayor Heinz told me in an interview that "we have no problems in Selma." He went on to show that the *we* in his statement referred to all of the white people and "our Negroes." There had been trouble. He couldn't pretend otherwise. But the trouble could be easily and finally explained as the work of outside agitators. They were the ones who had upset the racial peace. "If they would all get out and stay out, we'd work things out here in our own way."

Since the charge of outside agitation was made by every white person I talked with, and since it is used in almost every community that has lately experienced racial strife, it deserves careful and full analysis. One cannot understand Selma without understanding what the charge means and against whom it is leveled.

First, the Snick workers. They are the deluxe outsiders. The majority of Snick workers in Selma are Selma residents or students at Selma University. The ones who come from outside Selma come from such outside places as Mississippi, Arkansas, Georgia, and Birmingham. One hails from New York City, and another who was on the scene for two weeks calls Philadelphia her home. Where they came from is not the important fact in the charge. The syllogism is: A. Outsiders cause trouble. B. Snick people cause trouble. Therefore: Snick workers are all outsiders (even if they have been life-long residents).

Second on the list is the Negro comedian Dick Gregory, who appeared in Selma on September 27 and 28 during the height of the Negro demonstrations. Gregory addressed a mass meeting; said some unkind things to the sheriff who was inside the church building at the time, monitoring the

10

meeting; participated in a demonstration; and along with his wife and personal secretary, Wolf Dawson, was arrested. Gregory is a "Yankee nigger," but more than that he is considered "uppity" and "smart." "What was Mrs. Gregory doing with a sign in her hand asking for the vote?" questioned Mayor Heinz. "She is not even a resident of Dallas County."

Third on the list is the author James Baldwin, who came to Selma just in time to witness the events of October 7 and who addressed a mass meeting that evening.

White people told me that Dr. Martin Luther King, Jr., and the Reverend Fred Shuttlesworth have little influence in the Negro community because they collect funds and leave town. These leaders of the Southern Christian Leadership Conference did address breathing-room-only crowds, and if the Negroes have become disenchanted, they have kept that fact beautifully hidden.

259

It is obvious that the *charge* of "outside agitation" can be readily supported. But why has it been made? Because it offers a rational explanation for the Negro revolt. It tells why Selma Negroes have picketed, sat-in, prayed-in, paraded, boycotted schools, and attempted to register as voters. These activities have shattered the racial harmony. And, also, the charge of "outside agitators" is flexible enough to include Yankee reporters and television crews, who, in reporting the Selma news, seemed to give the authorities a black eye and thus "take the side of the niggers" as numerous Selma residents say. Thus reporters are agitators, too, and outsiders who don't know "our traditions or our niggers."

Once the plantation ethos of the Selma white man has been accepted, it is perfectly easy to see the validity of argument, made by almost all whites, that "this thing wouldn't have happened if those troublemakers hadn't come in here and riled up the Negroes." The inconsistency, and flagrant disregard for open facts, contained in such a statement is that the Negroes who are referred to as "our Negroes" have abdicated that title. The Negroes of Selma are the demonstrators. Local Negroes have filled all available space at every mass meeting. These people with whom such previously harmonious relations existed are the ones, not the outsiders, who have been filing down to the Courthouse by the dawn's early light to get in the voter-registration line. Free men don't have "to rattle their chains to show that they are free."

In fact the so-called agitators came with a plainly stated idea: "One man, one vote." They agree reluctantly and privately that not every Negro presently has the qualifications to vote because his educational opportunities

11

have been limited or inadequate. They argue, then, that through no fault of his own he has been disenfranchised because he did not receive a basic education which would equip him to pass qualification tests. Theoretically, they say, a fully functioning democracy gives one vote to every eligible citizen, and every citizen of appropriate legal age should be eligible. That is the democratic idea brought to Selma by the so-called outside agitators.

The "agitators" have said in public and private that if a majority of citizens believe that a county sheriff has not served law and order well throughout the community, the majority should be able to vote him out of office and vote in a man who would more impartially keep the peace. Since that is being done in thousands of counties in the United States every year, it does not seem to be a necessarily bad, provocative idea.

The "agitators" have said that if all people pay taxes, some of which are used for road maintenance, all of the streets should be paved and not just some of the streets. Why should only Negro mothers have to fight a constant layer of dust settling on everything in their houses because the white community can't find the money to pave the streets in front of Negro houses? Few white people live on unpaved streets in Selma, and few Negroes live on paved streets. All pay taxes.

The "agitators" have said, furthermore, that all the children of a community have a right to an equal education, provided indiscriminately by the administrators of public-education money. On no other issue have the U.S. Supreme Court, national Church groups, educators, and town after town in the nation, made such clear witness. Yet in Selma, Alabama, the idea itself is inflammatory; some who have articulated this idea and have demonstrated for it have been arrested.

Those who live in Yankeeland simply cannot, without firsthand experience, imagine the suspicion instinctively felt by a Selma resident of any other white person who does not profess *exactly* and *fully* the prevailing doctrine of total segregation of the races. Likewise, they would find unbelievable the anger and abuse heaped on the heads of Negroes, whether from Selma or anywhere else, who dare to challenge the "racial harmony" of Selma.

Father Ouelett (the same priest who had spoken highly of Bernard Lafayette) is the only white man in town who has identified himself publicly as a supporter of the voter-registration drive. Although his Archbishop has been requested to remove Father Ouelett from St. Elizabeth Mission, the Archbishop has refused and Father Ouelett stays with his blessing. Selma does not agree with the Archbishop, however. Ouelett has been ostracized,

260

vilified, and threatened by an uncomprehending white community. "I have no family and am not economically dependent on the white politicians or merchants, so they have no way to get at me in the way that they can hurt others. But they can show what they think of me, and I can tell you, it isn't good." He is a Yankee, a *Catholic* Yankee, and more than that a troublemaker because he has espoused the ideals of the voter-registration drive.

After patiently and fully testing the charge of outside agitation, one concludes that it is partly true. Had not Snick entered Selma, it is doubtful that such a full voter-registration effort would have been mounted or that the demonstrations would have taken place when they did. It is equally doubtful to assume that without Snick workers there would have been no enthusiasm for voter registration and no demonstrations.

261

One also concludes after examining the charge of outside agitation that the white man in Selma has little capacity to see Selma imaginatively through the eyes of a black man. Even though he is psychologically unable to see Selma as a Negro man sees Selma, were the white man to make that imaginative change of skin, he might then be enabled to see why, *really why*, the demonstrations occurred. He would then see what it means to be denied simple entrance to churches, theaters, restaurants, and most rest rooms. He would feel the helplessness in being unable to have any say at election time about how the house on which he pays taxes will be protected. He would feel, also, the helplessness of raising children who cannot compete favorably with white children in secondary and college-level education. He would feel, more than anything else, the crowning indignity of being called "boy," and being crowded into a limited and depressed spectrum of job opportunities.

With some sensitivity white citizens in Selma might not so easily explain the recent disturbances as wholly the work of "outside agitators." That sensitivity may well exist in many white citizens. It is not reflected, however, in the prevailing doctrine of segregation.

When I first heard the accepted ideological position fully stated, I said to myself that it was probably fifty years out of date. Later, on reading a history of Selma, I encountered a statement made on the floor of the Alabama State Constitutional Convention that sounds as up to date as the morning newspaper. John B. Knox made this statement in Montgomery:

> In my judgment, the people of Alabama have been called upon to face no more important situation than now confronts us, unless it be when they, in 1861, stirred by the momentous issue of impending conflict between the

North and the South, were forced to decide whether they would remain in or withdraw from the Union.

Then, as now, the Negro was the prominent factor in the issue.

The Southern people, with this grave problem of the races to deal with, are face to face with a new epoch in Constitution-making, the difficulties of which are great, but which, if solved wisely, may bring rest and peace and happiness. If otherwise, it may leave us and our posterity continually involved in race conflict, or what may be worse, subjected permanently to the baneful influences of the political conditions now prevailing in the state. . . .

Some of our Northern friends have even exhibited an unwanted interest in our affairs. . . .

262

The Southern man knows the Negro, and the Negro knows him. The only conflict which has, or is ever likely to arise, springs from the efforts of ill-advised friends in the North to confer upon him, without previous training or preparation, places of power and responsibility, for which he is wholly unfitted, either by capacity or experience. . . .

But if we would have white supremacy, we must establish it by laws not by force or fraud. . . .

(*The Story of Selma*, by Walter M. Jackson, 1954; The Birmingham Printing Co.: pages 429-30).

Mr. Knox's statement was made fifty-three years ago, and the fact that it expresses so neatly the current position is the real indication of how one-sided and, hence, misrepresentative is the accepted position of Selma in the fall of 1963. Stephen Foster plays on, but the "darkies" have all left the stage.

In contemporary Selma, Negroes have begun acting vigorously, in spite of opposition and disfavor. A merchant in nearby Beloit, for instance, was forced out of business because white suppliers wouldn't sell to him—a retaliation, presumably, against his "civil-rights" activities.

A revealing vignette of contemporary Selma was drawn for us by James Gildersleeve, a teacher in a local Lutheran academy. Gildersleeve's father was shot before his eyes in cold blood thirty years ago for daring to own not only his own farm but his own expensive automobile. James Gildersleeve told us of an incident when feelings were running highest during the direct-action campaign. After a mass meeting on September 18, Negroes were boiling out of the church "to the streets" but were not allowed off the sidewalk onto the street. There was considerable jamming of people when into the crowd walked a white man with an eighteen-inch nonpoisonous snake that he tried to stuff into people's mouths. Gildersleeve recalls shutting his own teeth tightly together to keep the snake out. Soon a Negro man knocked the snake out of the white man's hands. The Negro was instantly arrested.

Selma in 1963 bears little resemblance to the faded Stephen Foster-type image used by white citizens to depict a nostalgic way of life which they decline to believe is a thing of the past. The principal difference does not lie in the reports of recrimination against Negro civil-rights workers. The giant difference is in the Negro himself who has long ago shed himself of the "darkie" image. The whites have not apparently noticed the stunning change, and thus have registered astonishment at these freedom-singing "darkies" whose commitment to freedom is deepened by every trip to jail.

Snick workers are the antithesis of Stephen Foster's accepted perceptions of "darkies." Worth Long offers a notable example. He was educated in Philander Smith College in Little Rock, Arkansas, and joined Snick while participating in the direct action that finally won for Negroes in that city 263 some of the rights they had been working for during the past seven years. He has been involved in almost every troubled area in the South and came to Selma on September 16 at high noon, went directly into a mass meeting, began to protest with the students, as an observer, and was in jail before nightfall.

One never sees Worth ruffled, or bitter, or blue. His wife and newborn baby live in Durham, North Carolina, and he sees them only on rare occasions and then only briefly. Occasionally he receives a check from Snick headquarters in Atlanta that represents a partial payment on the ten-dollars-a-week subsistence wage that he is supposed to receive. He is thirty hours away from the completion of his A.B. degree, and "cannot even look far enough ahead into the future to see a time when life will be normal again and I can begin to contemplate what it is I want to do."

The life of Worth Long and his colleagues is filled with plain hard work. "Working persuasively with people is the hardest work a man can do, because people can change their minds on you, or goof up as they please." Inside a Snick worker two forces mount daily attacks. The one force is a faint, ever-present, gnawing hunger that only on occasion is pacified fully. The other force is tension. The high incidence of ulcers among Snick workers can be attributed to the tension as much or more than to their irregular eating habits. And tension is a polite word for fear. For the benefit of the tape recorder, I asked, "What are you afraid of?"

"Afraid of?" Worth answered in disbelief that the question even needed asking. "We're afraid that some drunk will get to thinking and all of a sudden say to his buddies, 'What are we waiting for?' and will give us an old-fashioned shotgun party.

We are afraid that along about one o'clock when the town's nice and asleep and dark, just about when we're closing up the office or going to bed over at Freedom House (their rented apartment), a bomb will go off. Sure enough, I'm surprised to see that place still standing *every* morning.

We are afraid that one day we'll be driving out to Orrville to Boque Chito, or down to Camden to get some people to vote, or to have a clinic, and in the middle of nowhere, with no witnesses, we'll run into a couple of automobiles blocking the highway, and that will be the end of us.

We are afraid of this all of the time. It never lets up. Say that somehow we do get fifteen hundred or two thousand voters registered in Dallas County. The more successful we are, the more vulnerable to personal danger."

The Snick workers who are from Selma do not seem to be so fearful, and they have no ulcers among them. But they are no more typical "darkies" than Worth Long or his New Yorker colleague, Bruce Gordon. Claude Porter, for instance, is a twenty-four-year-old Snick worker who has lived in Selma all of his life; who consequently knows everyone in Selma, and everyone knows him. He is almost obsessed with the subject of the Negro franchise. He made ninety-five visits on foot on Saturday in less than six hours, gathering facts, urging appearance in the registration line, and noting complaints of people whose applications had been rejected. He couldn't go in his car because someone had playfully immobilized the engine by putting sugar in the gas tank. Claude Porter has a wife and two children, with a third on the way. He is *not* frightened. "Why, man, we used to throw rocks at the Klan parades when we were kids. We never were fooled or scared."

Along with his quick speech and constantly aggressive activity goes a studied disbelief in a lot of talking. He has little use for long-winded strategy sessions, or for discussions of national objectives, or the general civil-rights philosophy. As a native of Selma, his whole being is intense focused on one thing only: getting the vote in Selma.

Taken together, the Snick workers might challenge the sanity of white people who still believe in "darkies."

The future has already broken in on Selma, for those who have eyes to see it. Almost unanimously the white citizens believe, with their heads if not with their hearts, that the Negro protest movement will somehow, like a head cold, dry up and go away. It won't. The fact is that Snick is more than a sneeze in Selma's nose, and the protest movement will continue, changing every day to meeting changing situations.

Presently The Voter Registration League, the Dallas County Improvement Association, and Snick (who have combined forces in a real coalition) have decided to eschew direct action in favor of encouraging as many Negroes as possible to attempt to register. A schedule of every-other-Monday registration days had been maintained throughout the summer. But beginning on October 16 the registrar's office was open in the Courthouse Monday through Friday until November 18. On the first day of the Courthouse registration, the first sixty people in the line were given numbered tickets on the theory that the registrars could not possibly receive more applications than that in one day. At four-thirty in the afternoon the numbers were redistributed so that those still in line received the lowest numbers for the next day's registration. This procedure taught Snick the lesson of disciplined hard daily efforts to make sure that enough and more than enough Negroes were in the line every day so that even with alleged irregularities that have been reported, and despite an order which bars a constant observer from the Courthouse, it is conceivable that 800 Negroes applied for registration before that period ended.

265

Inasmuch as the sheriff and the board of registrars have been enjoined by a Federal Court not to practice discrimination in voter registration, every application that is refused and all instances of questions asked by the registrars thought to be intimidating, unfair, or irrelevant are being carefully compiled so that when the Federal Courts do hear the Selma case there may be a mass registration such as occurred in Montgomery, Alabama, when a Federal judge ordered 1,000 names entered on the books at once.

No one can predict the eventual numbers of Negroes who will vote in Dallas County. Even if they never represent a simple majority of all voters, even if they have but 2,000 votes, it is clear that no politician could afford to run on a platform that is based on his promise to be more racist than his opponent.

And when a majority of all eligible citizens is registered, a vitally important precedent will have been created which will have great impact in the entire South.

Peter Hall believes that the destiny of Selma, Dallas County, and through them, surrounding counties, has already been altered by the voter-registration effort. "Those people who sound off that we want integration so we can have intermarriage just don't know what they are talking about. We want equal treatment before just laws, administered by just courts, and by just law-enforcement officers. We want Alabama to be a law-abiding state in the United States of America. We Negroes can't have the law as an ideal if we abandon the courts or give up belief in the courts. That's what we were guilty of for too many years. We just can't sing freedom; we have to do the job of securing the freedom through court decisions. We have begun to do that. It's paradoxical and a little ironic that the Negroes should be the instrument which brings the law back to the South, but that is exactly what has been happening, and will, to an even greater extent, continue to happen."

266

It is easy to lose one's perspective after an extended visit in Selma, and the future indeed looks at best blurred. It seems easy to overestimate the importance of the vote, or to stress too much the value of court decisions when there are no visible economic opportunities available to Negroes and fewer cultural opportunities. But never having been denied the vote, and never having been disqualified from economic opportunity solely because of my color, I really am not qualified to pass on the quality of Negro enthusiasm in Alabama for the vote. The Negro is the one who must pay the high price for it, in life, in earning power, in physical suffering, and at times in tragedy. The greater tragedy is that he already, as an American citizen, *has* the vote.

Even though John Fischer in a recent *Harper's* article ("The Editor's Easy Chair," November, 1963, pages 16-28) identifies the new heroes in the South as the Snick field secretaries, and they are, at the best, *heroes*, the greater heroes are as yet unnamed. They are the hopeless, helpless, colored poor in the plantation country who will come out of the cotton patch after all these years to claim their vote. Sophisticated analysts point out that even with the vote they will still have exactly nothing. What the analysts should do is examine minutely where these poor sharecroppers presently live, what they presently do, the system by which "the man" deprives many of them of some of what is rightfully theirs. They already have nothing. To walk out of the cotton patch and stay out may indeed mean more "nothing," but with one decisive difference; they would have overcome.

White churches in Selma are identified with the white idea of total segregation. Christendom is split. The Jesus Christ of the white man is different from the Jesus Christ of the Negro. The sacraments are split, as surely and along the same lines as the vote once was. Perhaps it is enough that courageous Negro pastors work for the elementary necessities of justice, or that a United Presbyterian attorney from Birmingham argues the cases of the jailed in Selma's courts. Jesus Christ's name has not been forgotten, but some people seem to have forgotten his mercy, his death and Resurrection. He nevertheless, cannot be kept out of Selma. He subtly and powerfully is teaching anew what it means to be human beings and what it means to have a neighbor. In him rests the future of Selma and the future of all the Selmas of the land whose good may yet be crowned with "brotherhood from sea to shining sea."

267

BLACK CIVIL RIGHTS DURING THE
EISENHOWER YEARS

David J. Garrow*

Professor Burk, in publishing a revision of his doctoral dissertation at the University of Wisconsin, says his book is "an account
of the racial policies of the Eisenhower administration and an effort
to explain why particular approaches were adopted by the executive
branch in the 1950s and others were not."[1] At that rather modest
level, Burk's volume is an adequate and workmanlike discussion of
a half-dozen different policy subjects—desegregation of the armed
services, racial issues in the federally-controlled District of Columbia, integration of the federal work force, equal employment rules
for federal contractors, and discrimination in federally-assisted
housing—plus a recounting of the Eisenhower administration's major civil rights events: the *Brown* decisions, the Little Rock crisis,
and the Civil Rights Acts of 1957 and 1960. However, it is not
thoroughly researched, nor a notable improvement over previous
scholarly surveys of civil rights developments of the 1950's. Besides
offering a critique of the Burk book, this essay will explore how
some newly released documents shed light on the political relationship between black America and the Eisenhower administration,
and particularly on some unusual financial arrangements involving
the White House and Adam Clayton Powell.

269

I

Burk devotes only a modest effort to providing any analytical
or thematic overviews of the Eisenhower administration's civil
rights policies. When he does voice such conclusions, however,
they are well-supported and accurate. He correctly identifies "a
consistent pattern of hesitancy and extreme political caution in defending black legal rights" by Eisenhower's executive branch, and
notes that "[m]uch of the blame for the administration's excessive

---

* Associate Professor of Political Science, City College of New York and the City
University Graduate Center.
1. R. BURK, THE EISENHOWER ADMINISTRATION AND BLACK CIVIL RIGHTS, at vi
(1984).

caution lay squarely with the President himself."[2] Burk gives two major reasons for that stance. Most important was Eisenhower's own conservative racial attitude; as Burk points out, yet fails to emphasize fully enough, "Eisenhower publicly waffled on the basic issue of the morality of segregation."[3] Second, there was Eisenhower's "strong aversion to the use of federal power as a coercive instrument" generally.[4] In combination, Burk says, these two significant influences left Eisenhower and his administration "incapable of moving beyond symbolism to an open confrontation with racial inequalities."[5]

The "symbolic" nature of the Eisenhower administration's few racial initiatives is a point that Burk makes repeatedly, but with only a pro forma citation of some of the traditional works on "symbolic politics." In that standard usage, a political actor employing "symbolic" conduct is seeking to convey the appearance of action, so as to reassure some constituency, rather than pursue any truly substantive policy. To say that the Eisenhower administration's racial policies were largely symbolic in this sense would be fully consistent with the historical record that Burk recounts. Burk also seems, however, to have another and much more original idea of symbolism. In his concluding paragraph, Burk suggests for the first time the idea that the long-term effect of the Eisenhower administration's passivity on civil rights was to strengthen Americans' supposedly prevailing assumption that the pursuit of racial equality would be relatively painless. That implicit reassurance, Burk seems to say, was the worst possible preparation for America's racial future. The 1960's brought home to all the fact that racial change would be far more problematic and painful than most Eisenhower administration policymakers supposedly assumed in the mid-1950's.[6]

Burk would have been well-advised to devote far more attention to fleshing out the idea that the Eisenhower administration did a very serious disservice to the subsequent course of American race

270

---

2. *Id.* at 263.
3. *Id.* at 193.
4. *Id.* at 16.
5. *Id.* at 127.
6. *Id.* at 266. Burk seems to believe, as he indicates several times, that Eisenhower and those around him believed in "the idea of an affluent, color-blind, democratic society" and assumed that it could be achieved without federal intervention. *Id.* at 127. Burk is on firmer ground, however, when he describes how Eisenhower and several top aides and close friends vocally opposed some forms of racial equality and harbored clearly racist thoughts. Although Burk is likely off-target in attributing any clearly thought-out egalitarian or even "color blind" ideals to either Eisenhower or most of his top aides, that point is neither necessary nor essential to his nascent argument about the longer-term effects of the administration's racial stance.

relations. From events large and small—particularly the administration's very grudging role in *Brown I* and its hesitant, tardy intervention in Little Rock—one could build a powerful argument that the administration's conduct gave important indirect assistance to the segregationist backlash that emerged as so powerful a political force across the South between 1955 and 1959. This point has often been made about President Eisenhower's equivocal remarks about *Brown*, but Burk could well have applied the point far more broadly. Similarly, he also could have expanded considerably, and interwoven with that theme, his description of the administration's indecisive support of what appeared to be the most politically uncontroversial civil rights initiatives, defense of the right to vote. As Burk notes, administration advocacy of voting rights statutes and support for a relatively powerless Commission on Civil Rights allowed Eisenhower to convey the appearance of taking meaningful civil rights initiatives while his administration's actual priority was to avoid civil rights involvement as much as possible and keep racial matters on the back burner for the indefinite future. Essentially the same strategy was pursued by the Kennedy administration until events in the late spring of 1963 forced it to change course.

271

Burk unfortunately does not consider such broader themes. He ends his brief, concluding description of the largely "symbolic" nature of Eisenhower administration policies by suggesting that they postponed and misled America about the inevitably traumatic racial changes that lay ahead, and in so doing helped produce a "bitter harvest of hypocritical national self-deception."[7] He treats this point so tersely, however, that even the careful reader has to work hard to extract Burk's likely meaning.

Burk is to be commended for adopting a clearly and deservedly critical attitude towards Eisenhower's racial policies, especially at a time when most recent scholarship on the Eisenhower administration is turning strongly commendatory and even some apologies for its civil rights conduct are being authored.[8] Another important theme, which Burk alludes to only in passing, would be a direct treatment of how that executive branch abdication of racial responsibility contributed so heavily to passing the initiative to the judiciary, particularly the Fifth Circuit.

If Burk does an adequate though unprovocative job of docu-

---

7. *Id.* at 266.
8. *See* F. GREENSTEIN, THE HIDDEN HAND PRESIDENCY (1982); M. Mayer, Eisenhower's Conditional Crusade: The Eisenhower Administration and Civil Rights, 1953-1957 (1984) (unpublished Ph.D. dissertation, Princeton University). *See also* Mayer, *With Much Deliberation and Some Speed: Eisenhower and the* Brown *Decision*, 52 J.S. HIST., Feb. 1986, at 43-76.

menting executive branch civil rights actions under Eisenhower, he does not even begin to describe the administration's dealings with black political and civil rights activists. He seems relatively unfamiliar with the original sources that could have given him a much richer understanding of the black political scene in the 1950's. A full understanding of administration policy cannot be achieved without a well-versed appreciation of the larger political context. In particular, Burk seems relatively unfamiliar with the importance of the major strategic concern that privately divided America's black leadership in the late 1950's, the question of whether civil rights proponents should continue to depend upon the lawyer-led litigation approach that had produced *Brown*, or whether mass boycotts and demonstrations could play an equal role in advancing black freedom. While the *Brown* triumph had pointed most strategically minded activists in the first direction, the remarkable success of the mass-based Montgomery, Alabama, bus boycott of 1955-56 gave great heart to those activists, particularly long-time Brotherhood of Sleeping Car Porters President A. Philip Randolph, who believed that the black masses, acting for themselves, could do as much as the courtroom efforts of a lawyerly elite.

Burk's relative blindness to important political themes such as this stems largely from his failure to draw on the archival papers of the major black groups of that time. Nor did he consult the major black newspapers and periodicals—*Jet* magazine, the New York *Amsterdam News*, the Pittsburgh *Courier*—that are truly invaluable sources for understanding the black political world of the 1950's. Although his bibliographical essay makes passing reference to the value of both types of sources,[9] the book reflects no actual use of them. Burk also did not interview any sources, nor did he apparently make much use of the Freedom of Information Act to obtain unreleased federal documents dealing with civil rights in the 1950's. Use of these sources would have helped produce a far richer and more original book.

Burk's research shortcomings contribute substantially to his less than adequate treatment of the major black political initiatives of the late 1950's. He devotes hardly a paragraph to the important 1957 Prayer Pilgrimage for Freedom,[10] organized originally to put pressure on Eisenhower to speak out against southern segregationist attacks upon black activists; gives only a few sentences to the sole meeting, in June 1958, that the black leadership had with the Presi-

---

9. R. BURK, *supra* note 1, at 270.

10. *Id.* at 220; Martin Luther King, Jr., et al. to Dwight D. Eisenhower (Feb. 14, 1957, GF 124-A-1, Box 912, Dwight D. Eisenhower Library, Abilene, KS) [hereinafter DDEL].

dent; and hardly mentions two significant but often-ignored national demonstrations in the nation's capital, the 1958 and 1959 Youth Marches for Integrated Schools.[11] These inadequacies not only lead to a seriously deficient portrayal of the political pressure that black leaders were attempting to place on the administration, but also lead Burk to understate the concern that often existed within the Eisenhower White House about the danger of public political embarrassment to the President by the black leadership, and the strategies for minimizing that danger adopted by Eisenhower's aides.

By early 1957 a number of significant black leaders, including A. Philip Randolph, NAACP Executive Secretary Roy Wilkins, New York Democratic Congressman Adam Clayton Powell, and Reverend Martin Luther King, Jr., President of the Montgomery Improvement Association, which had sustained the famous boycott of that city's municipal buses, all were becoming concerned about the administration's attitude toward the black leadership. Despite four years in office and a landslide 1956 reelection victory that had included substantial black support,[12] President Eisenhower had yet to meet with any significant group of America's black leaders. That failure, coupled with a strong upsurge in white terrorist violence in Alabama in late 1956 and early 1957, led King and several dozen other Southern activists, who were just beginning to form the organization that soon was named the Southern Christian Leadership Conference, to use their first organizing session to formulate three requests to the administration: that Eisenhower advocate peaceful compliance with *Brown*, that Vice President Richard M. Nixon come south to look into violence against blacks, and that Attorney General Herbert Brownell meet with black activists to discuss federal protection for civil rights activists. White House Chief of Staff Sherman Adams brushed aside the first two requests, and Brownell declined the third. Those rebuffs led King and his colleagues to repeat the demands a month later, and to announce that they would lead "a pilgrimage of prayer to Washington" if the administration continued to refuse their requests.[13]

The Prayer Pilgrimage for Freedom, as the demonstration came to be called, was scheduled for May 17, 1957, the third anniversary of *Brown I*. It drew the active support of Randolph, Wilkins, King's southern network, and a variety of black churchmen.

273

---

11. R. BURK, *supra* note 1, at 83, 238.

12. *Id*. at 170.

13. King to Eisenhower (Jan. 11, 1957), Sherman Adams to King (Jan. 18, 1957), and King et al. to Eisenhower (Feb. 14, 1957, GF-124-A-1, Box 912, DDEL).

The protest was the most significant political initiative undertaken by national black leaders since Randolph's 1941 threat of a march on Washington had led President Roosevelt to issue an Executive order banning racial discrimination by federal military contractors. The 1957 Pilgrimage was a direct outgrowth of the black leadership's dismay that the Eisenhower administration had little interest in either the growing turmoil in the South or the thoughts of black leaders.

The announcement of the Pilgrimage, and particularly the possibility that it would become an anti-Eisenhower demonstration, created considerable concern within the White House. Burk's relative inattention to the network of contacts that did exist between the Eisenhower White House and certain black leaders leads him to underplay the administration's sagacious and sophisticated response to the challenge that the Pilgrimage represented.

Burk does provide an excellent sketch of the valuable but often awkward role played by the Eisenhower White House's single black professional staff member, E. Frederic Morrow. Openly snubbed by some White House colleagues, Morrow had to cope with numerous black entreaties while often encountering substantial difficulties in getting his opinions taken seriously by higher-ranking staffers. Burk's sensitive portrait of Morrow is one of the strongest sections of his book.[14] Disappointingly, he does not show similar interest in other important black figures such as Republican National Committee staffer Val Washington and Archibald J. Carey, an early appointee to the President's Committee on Government Employment Policy. More importantly, Burk also gives insufficient attention to the very important role played by Maxwell M. Rabb, the racially liberal White House aide who, rather than Morrow, had primary responsibility for administration liaison with black organizations.

II

Perhaps the major reason for Burk's inadequate treatment is his general overreliance on secondary sources and insufficient mining of the rich original sources available at the Eisenhower Library. While Burk at times has made adequate usage of those materials, in many instances he has not; his second chapter, for instance, on the desegregation of the armed services, contains not one citation to unpublished sources.

This deficient utilization of the available original sources results in some substantial holes, none larger than Burk's failure to

---

14. R. BURK, *supra* note 1, at 77-88.

explore the fascinating relationship between the Eisenhower White House, particularly Max Rabb, and New York Democratic Representative Adam Clayton Powell. Burk notes almost casually, in his sole paragraph on the 1957 Prayer Pilgrimage for Freedom, that Powell had served as a White House "mole" within the black leadership during the time that the Pilgrimage was being organized.[15] Rather amazingly, Burk cites no original sources for this point; his only reference is an excellent book by Herbert Parmet which turns out to contain a considerably more extensive account of the Powell-Eisenhower White House relationship.[16] Surprisingly, Burk did not pursue this lead to see whether there were more revealing original sources unavailable to Parmet. If he had, Burk would have discovered that there are such items, and that the further leads they provide are most intriguing indeed.

275

Early in the Eisenhower administration, Powell had been a vocal public critic of the executive branch's lackluster efforts to eliminate racial discrimination in the armed services and in public schools housed on military bases. Rabb had taken the lead in assuaging Powell's anger and, thanks to his adept handling of the Congressman, Powell soon was publicly praising the administration's swift response to his complaints.[17]

Building on that success, Rabb proceeded to ingratiate himself with Powell in a fashion that repeatedly proved invaluable to the Eisenhower White House. Rabb, whom Morrow later characterized as "a very suave, smooth, able man" who "can really butter people up,"[18] skillfully commended Powell's various recommendations and suggestions in a warm series of personal letters that featured "Dear Adam" and "My dear Max" salutations.[19] Rabb proudly sent news clippings reporting Powell's public pro-Eisenhower comments to White House chief of staff Sherman Adams, noting how "a little friendly treatment" had paid off.[20] By the fall of 1956, with Eisenhower's reelection prospects looking quite rosy, the Harlem Democrat publicly endorsed the Republican President's

---

15. *Id.* at 220.

16. H. PARMET, EISENHOWER AND THE AMERICAN CRUSADES 505-08 (1972).

17. Powell to Eisenhower (June 3, 1953), Eisenhower to Powell (June 6, 1953), and Powell to Eisenhower (June 10, 1953, OF 142-A-4, Box 731, DDEL); R. BURK, *supra* note 1, at 29-31, 35-37, 39-40; M. Mayer, *supra* note 8, at 42, 47-49.

18. E. Frederic Morrow Interview with Thomas Soapes (Feb. 23, 1977, transcript p. 8, DDEL).

19. *See* Rabb to Powell (Sept. 18, 1953; Oct. 19, 1953; Sept. 2, 1954; and Dec. 9, 1954), Powell to Rabb (Dec. 10, 1954), Rabb to Powell (Feb. 3, 1955), Powell to Rabb (Feb. 4, 1955; Feb. 15, 1955; and Mar. 3, 1955), and Rabb to Powell (Mar. 17, 1955; June 2, 1955; June 21, 1955; and Oct. 17, 1955) (Powell Alpha File, Box 2485, DDEL).

20. Rabb to Adams (no date, attached to New York Herald Tribune clip, Oct. 12, 1953, Powell Alpha File, Box 2485, DDEL).

candidacy after a personal meeting at the White House.[21]

The Republican courtship of Powell left him vulnerable to sharp criticism from civil rights proponents troubled by his enthusiasm for a President who was unwilling even to endorse the correctness of *Brown*. But Powell was at least as much a self-promoter as a committed advocate for black freedom. Morrow accurately termed Powell "a flamboyant opportunist" in a confidential memo to Sherman Adams;[22] other staffers, particularly Rabb, appreciated how friendly relations with Powell could be used to the administration's advantage when prominent black assistance was needed to deflect civil rights criticism. The Prayer Pilgrimage represented just such a situation where that carefully cultivated relationship could be usefully employed.

276

Newly released documents also reveal some sub rosa financial relationships between Powell and the administration, stemming from the 1956 election campaign. In September 1957, more than ten months after the election, Powell asked Eisenhower's top White House staffers to provide at least several thousand dollars worth of funds to a number of Powell's political associates, funds that Powell asserted were needed to reimburse election expenses incurred on his behalf. "The leadership of the Republican party," Powell told White House Chief of Staff Sherman Adams in a September 27 letter, previously had promised to make good these sums, and Powell was now demanding immediate payment. When Powell's letter was forwarded to high-ranking presidential aides Bryce Harlow and Gerald Morgan, Harlow in puzzlement returned it to Adams. "Since, obviously, this letter concerns clandestine arrangements with which Mr. Morgan and I are unfamiliar," Harlow told Adams, "we are [at] a loss as to (1) what reply to make and (2) who should pay up."[23]

Powell's particular demands ranged from the mundane to the most intriguing. He wanted $900 for two of his secretaries to whom he owed overtime, $200 for a researcher he had retained, and $600 in personal reimbursement for funds he had advanced to another political aide. One other loose end concerned contacts Powell had made with black reporters. "Each one of the Negro newsmen in New York was promised one hundred dollars ($100)," Powell told Adams. "Each one received the money with the exception of James Booker of the New York Amsterdam News. In order to keep from

---

21. R. BURK, *supra* note 1, at 168-69.

22. Morrow to Adams (Feb. 27, 1956, OF 142-A, Box 731, DDEL).

23. Powell to Adams (Sept. 27, 1957), and Harlow & Morgan to Adams (Oct. 1, 1957) (Powell Alpha File, Box 2486, DDEL).

losing his friendship . . . I paid that money to him by check. This money should immediately be paid to me."[24]

Impatient to obtain the funds, Powell wrote Adams a second letter, adding a more specific request that $495 immediately be sent to one particular individual whom Powell had discussed in a more general way in his first letter. Within a week's time, White House and Republican National Committee staffers arranged to satisfy Powell's demands. Adams's secretary informed him that "checks to all the people involved with Adam Clayton Powell will go forward on November 15—these include those named in the second letter as well."[25] Apparently that resolved the matter to the full satisfaction of everyone concerned.

Given the existence of such intimate ties, it should come as no surprise that Powell worked closely with the Eisenhower White House, and Rabb in particular, when the threat of the Prayer Pilgrimage first loomed in the early spring of 1957. Powell informed his friend Rabb in advance about a major planning meeting that would take place on April 5, and volunteered to try and torpedo the entire Pilgrimage. "Powell is very much opposed to such a march and will do what he can to stop it," Rabb informed Chief of Staff Adams.[26] Powell recommended that Rabb also consult with NAACP Washington representative Clarence Mitchell. The next day, forty-eight hours in advance of the session, Rabb gave Adams an update on the situation.

> Congressman Powell will attend the meeting and will report to me what takes place. He is still a little fearful that, despite Clarence Mitchell's representations, Martin Luther King may still try to make a march on Washington. Powell and Mitchell will do their best to try to keep the meeting under control.[27]

In the wake of the meeting, Powell informed Rabb, who apparently took Powell's remarks at face value, that he, Mitchell and a third like-minded attendee at the April 5 planning session had been able to transform the Pilgrimage from an anti-Eisenhower demonstration into a purely celebratory event. Powell and his allies, Rabb told Adams, "successfully changed the entire character of this meeting into an occasion where there will be an observance of the anniversary of the school decision through prayer," and no criticisms of the administration. The fact that neither King nor any other major proponent of the Prayer Pilgrimage had pushed for any

277

---

24. Powell to Adams (Sept. 27, 1957); "Memorandum" (Oct. 16, 1957) (Powell Alpha File, Box 2486, DDEL).

25. Powell to Adams (Oct. 16, 1957), "Mary" [Burns] to "Governor" [Adams] (Oct. 24, 1957) (Powell Alpha File, Box 2486, DDEL).

26. Rabb to Adams (Apr. 2, 1957) (GF 124-A-1, Box 912, DDEL).

27. Rabb to Adams (Apr. 3, 1957) (OF 142-A, Box 731, DDEL).

anti-Eisenhower themes was unknown to Rabb, who instead accepted Powell's exaggerated claim. Rabb assured Adams that, thanks to Powell, "this matter is well in hand," but promised to keep a close eye on matters up through the May 17 event. "[W]e must keep constant vigil," Rabb said. "There is always the possibility that a prayer pilgrimage cannot be kept under control, and I am in constant communication with the leaders to ensure keeping it in hand."[28]

Two days before the Pilgrimage, NAACP Executive Secretary Roy Wilkins phoned Rabb "to assure [him] that there would be no demonstration against the Administration."[29] On May 17, Pilgrimage organizers were disappointed when the crowd that gathered amounted to only a third of the 50,000 to 75,000 turnout they optimistically had predicted. Speaking from the steps of the Lincoln Memorial, the march leaders focused their remarks on the need for further federal action to advance black civil rights, rather than on merely celebrating the third anniversary of *Brown*. In the first truly national speech of his young career, Martin Luther King, Jr., emphasized the importance of voting rights in the South, and called for federal government action to "[g]ive us the ballot." King's oration notwithstanding, press coverage of the Pilgrimage turned out to be disappointingly modest.[30]

Although the Eisenhower White House was pleased with the Pilgrimage's moderate tone and modest public visibility, the black leadership remained angry at the President's refusal to meet with them. Vice President Nixon, after a personal conversation with King during the early March independence ceremonies for the new nation of Ghana, had promised to receive King in Washington. In a letter to Eisenhower's appointments secretary at the time of the Pilgrimage, King emphasized that that commitment "can in no way substitute for the necessity of my talking directly with the head of our great government." A meeting with the President, King stressed, "would at least give persons of good will in general and Negro Americans in particular a feeling that the White House is listening to the problems which we confront."[31]

Eisenhower aides were willing only to inform King that the

28.   Rabb to Adams (Apr. 17, 1957) (GF 124-A-1, Box 912, DDEL).
29.   Rabb to Mr. [Jack] Toner (May 16, 1957) (GF 124-A-1, Box 912, DDEL).
30.   *Negroes Hold Rally on Rights in Capital*, New York Times, May 18, 1957, at 1, col. 8; *Prayer Pilgrimage to Washington*, 12 EBONY, Aug. 1957, at 16-22; H. PARMET, *supra* note 16, at 508.
31.   L. REDDICK, CRUSADER WITHOUT VIOLENCE 180-84 (1959); CHRISTIAN CENTURY, Apr. 10, 1957, at 446-48; letter from King to Bernard Shanley (May 16, 1957) (King Papers, Special Collections Dept., Mugar Library, Boston Univ., Boston, MA, Drawer IX) [hereinafter MLK].

President would at some future time see him and other black leaders. Despite repeated urgings from Max Rabb and especially Fred Morrow that such an audience not be greatly delayed, other White House staffers postponed any firm decision. A concerned Morrow bravely voiced a frank description of the situation to White House Chief of Staff Adams. "I can state categorically that the rank and file of Negroes in the country feel that the President has deserted them."[32] King and A. Philip Randolph each informed the White House of their willingness to be patient in waiting for a firm date to be chosen. The question dragged on through both the summer and fall without any resolution, despite a message from Vice President Nixon, following his own meeting with King, that the Montgomery minister was a most impressive man whom he believed the President would enjoy meeting.[33]

In late January of 1958, more than a year after King had first requested that the President signal his support for civil rights, King turned to Adam Clayton Powell for help. In a telegram to Eisenhower, Powell indicated that the President's evasiveness over meeting with the black leadership was beginning to make even him critical about the administration's indifferent attitude toward civil rights.[34] Even that was insufficient to generate any immediate progress, and not until May, when King publicly released a telegram to the President expressing "shock and dismay" over a recent Eisenhower comment that the enforcement of the law should not be allowed to create hardship, did the White House staff move into action. Presidential aide Rocco Siciliano, who had taken over the now-departed Max Rabb's minority liaison responsibilities, phoned King to promise that a meeting with Eisenhower would be speedily arranged. Following a preparatory conference on June 9 with Siciliano, Morrow, and Deputy Attorney General Lawrence Walsh, where King insisted that a broader black group than simply himself and Randolph would have to be invited, a June 23 presidential audience was scheduled for those two men plus Wilkins and National Urban League chief Lester B. Granger. Finally, after more than five years in the White House, Dwight D. Eisenhower personally met with a representative group of black American leaders.[35]

279

---

32. Rabb to Files (May 23, 1957) and Rabb to Shanley (May 23, 1957) (GF 124-A-1, Box 912); Morrow to Adams (June 4, 1957) (OF 142-A, Box 731, DDEL).

33. Rabb to Adams (June 5, 1957) (OF 142-A, Box 731), Rabb "Memorandum" (June 20, 1957) (GF 124-A-1, Box 912), Rabb to Adams (June 24, 1957) (OF 142-A, Box 731), "Memorandum" (June 25, 1957) (GF 124-A-1, Box 912, DDEL); Rabb to Morrow (July 13, 1957) (E. Frederic Morrow Papers, Box 10, DDEL); Morrow to Adams (Sept. 12, 1957) and Rabb to Adams (Sept. 27, 1957) (OF 142-A, Box 731, DDEL).

34. Powell to Eisenhower (Jan. 28, 1958) (Powell Alpha File, Box 2486, DDEL).

35. King to Eisenhower and "Statement" (May 29, 1958) (MLK Drawer VI); Siciliano,

Professor Burk is badly remiss in not giving far more extensive attention to both Representative Powell's relationship with the Eisenhower White House and the administration's indecisive dealings with the national black leadership. Even that presidential meeting itself did little to improve those badly frayed relations. When the four black leaders forthrightly voiced both black Americans' unhappiness at the administration's racial record plus specific calls for further action, including a White House conference on southern desegregation, Eisenhower brushed them off. "I don't propose to comment on these recommendations. I know you do not expect me to. But I will be glad to consider them. There may be some value to your idea of a conference. But I don't think anything much would really come of one."[36] Given that sort of presidential response, King and his colleagues were unsurprised when the White House staff over the ensuing several months turned a deaf ear toward Randolph's repeated requests for administration sponsorship of such a conference.[37]

280

Here again Burk errs badly in not giving greater attention to that presidential audience and its aftermath. He also all but ignores the double-barrelled response King and Randolph organized, namely the two Youth Marches for Integrated Schools, which took place in Washington on October 25, 1958 and April 18, 1959. More emphasis on these significant events, which drew crowds of 10,000 and 26,000, would again have drawn attention to the continuing unhappiness of black America towards the Eisenhower administration.[38] It also would have provided at least some indication of the ongoing mixture of disinterest and disdain with which the White House greeted these initiatives. When delegates from the first

"Memorandum for the Files" (June 9, 1958), Blanche Lavery, "Memorandum for the Files" (June 13, 1958), and Siciliano to James Hagerty (June 16, 1958) (Papers of the Office of the Special Assistant for Personnel Management [hereinafter OSAPM], Box 42, DDEL).

36. E. MORROW, BLACK MAN IN THE WHITE HOUSE 226-27 (1963); R. WILKINS, STANDING FAST 256 (1982); Lester Granger to National Urban League Board, "June 23rd Conference . . ."; King et al., "A Statement to President Eisenhower" (June 23, 1958), and Siciliano to Files, "Meeting of Negro Leaders with President . . ." (June 24, 1958) (OSAPM, Box 42, DDEL).

37. Lester Granger to Randolph (July 7, 1958) (Roy Wilkins Papers, Library of Congress, Washington, D.C., Box 4); Randolph to King (July 9, 1958) (MLK Drawer IV); King to Randolph (July 18, 1958) (A. Philip Randolph Papers, Library of Congress, Washington, D.C.) [hereinafter APR]; Randolph to Eisenhower (Aug. 1, 1958) (OSAPM, Box 42, DDEL); Randolph to King (Aug. 19, 1958) (APR); Siciliano to Randolph (Sept. 4, 1958) (OSAPM, Box 42, DDEL).

38. Pittsburgh Courier, Apr. 25, 1959, at 3; *Integration Rally Here Assured Ike Seeks End of Racial Bias*, Washington Post, Apr. 19, 1959, at B3, col. 3; Pittsburgh Courier, Nov. 1, 1958, at 2-3 and Nov. 8, 1958, at 3; *Harry Belafonte, Jack Robinson Lead Integrated Schools March*, Washington Post, Oct. 26, 1958, at A17, col. 1; Pittsburgh Courier, Sept. 13, 1958, at 2, and Sept. 27, 1958, at 4.

Youth March arrived at the White House gate to present copies of petitions calling for greater administration support for southern school desegregation, no official appeared to receive them. When, well in advance of the second march, A. Philip Randolph repeatedly requested that several students from it be allowed to call on the President, the White House responded by eventually providing only an audience with presidential counsel Gerald D. Morgan.[39]

All in all, Burk's inadequate attention to these important events and the larger story of the political interactions between America's principal black leaders and the Eisenhower White House underlines once again the narrowness of his book and the incompleteness of his research. Although his volume will be a useful resource for anyone seeking an adequate narrative account of federal civil rights policy initiatives during the 1950's, it reflects insufficient interest in black America's political climate during those years and incomplete study of the original source materials. A fully researched, politically informative, and analytically insightful study of the interactions between black America and the Eisenhower administration remains to be written.

281

39. J. Edgar Hoover to Gordon Gray (Oct. 27, 1958) (Papers of the Office of the Special Assistant for National Security Affairs, FBI Series, Box 2), Siciliano to Randolph (Oct. 29, 1958), Randolph to Siciliano (Nov. 19, 1958) (OSAPM, Box 42), Randolph to Eisenhower (Feb. 17, 1959), and Morrow to James Hagerty (Apr. 10, 1959) (OF 142-A-5, Box 732, DDEL).

THE RIGHT TO BE SERVED:
Oklahoma City's Lunch Counter Sit-ins, 1958–1964

*By Carl R. Graves**

On a hot day in August, 1958, thirteen black children led by Clara M.
Luper entered Katz Drugstore in downtown Oklahoma City, sat down at
the food counter, and waited to be served. They waited in vain. The group
returned the next day but received the same treatment.[1] White customers
who watched this confrontation perhaps failed to realize that they were
witnessing the start of a six-year campaign of sit-ins, picketing, store
boycotts, arrests, and legal disputes. Also, the waitresses presumably failed·
to foresee that the blacks would keep coming back until all of the city's
lunch counters were integrated. The demonstrators themselves no doubt
had little idea of the long struggle that lay ahead of them. Unlike later
sit-ins in the South, their campaign would be marked by relative peaceful-
ness and in many ways would become a typical example of the border state
sit-ins of the 1950s.

It was not surprising that the young blacks faced discrimination in the
capital city's eating facilities; segregation had been the rule in Oklahoma
for the major part of its history. Since the early 1900s all public accommodations in Oklahoma City outside the black community were closed to
blacks. Although there were no city ordinances demanding segregated
public facilities, white owners could use simple trespass laws to evict any
black who entered.[2]

In the late 1940s an attack was launched on Oklahoma's segregation laws
and practices; in 1955 the Oklahoma City School Board officially desegregated all public schools.[3] Despite such progress, blacks in Oklahoma City
were still systematically excluded from most of its theaters, restaurants,
barber and beauty shops, and amusements.[4] Thus the demonstrations can
be seen as part of a general campaign to end Jim Crow practices in the
Sooner State, a campaign which was already well underway. Yet one might
ask: Why did the demonstrations take place here and why so early? There
was lunch counter segregation elsewhere in Oklahoma. The answer is found
in the actions of the city's NAACP Youth Council and its adult advisor,
Clara Luper.

Downtown Oklahoma City during the late 1950s and early 1960s became the scene of numerous sit-ins by young blacks protesting segregation in eating establishments (Oklahoma County Metropolitan Library).

She had taught history at Dunjee High School in the city area since 1951.[5] Deeply influenced by Dr. Martin Luther King, Jr., she had written a play about him which the Youth Council was asked to perform in New York City. She and the Council players went there by way of a northern route, along which they received lunch counter service on an equal basis with whites. Enjoying a hamburger at an integrated restaurant was a new experience for most of the youngsters. On the return trip they traveled a southern route, where they faced discrimination once again. After returning the Youth Council voted to integrate the city's downtown eating establishments. The experience of being served was fresh in their minds, and they were aware of the peaceful integration that had already taken place in Oklahoma's schools, buses, and theaters.[6]

They first tried negotiation. A committee began unpublicized talks in May, 1957, with the individual managers and owners of each city eating establishment to persuade them to serve blacks on an equal basis. Youth Council members aided Clara Luper and others who were on the committee.[7] Going downtown in groups of two or three, they tried to convince the owners, but the latter explained that they would not serve

Black youths in Katz Department Store occupied every seat at the lunch counter to protest segregation (Courtesy Clara Luper).

blacks for fear of losing their white customers. After more than a year of unsuccessful talks, the Youth Council decided to stage its first sit-in.[8] Phase one of the struggle to be served (August 19–September 1, 1958) was at hand.

The Youth Council spent over fifteen months planning the sit-ins. They chose the five major downtown lunch counters—John A. Brown's, Veazey's Drug, Katz Drug, Kress', and Green's Variety Store. The Green's management cordially gave the demonstrators service, making a sit-in unnecessary there. Veazey's was also integrated without a sit-in.[9] It was a different story elsewhere.

Katz Drug was the scene of sit-ins from August 19 until August 21, when the children were finally served. The youths occupied most of the soda fountain seats and patiently waited to be served. Police remained close by to prevent disorders but there were none.[10]

The day after the group was served at Katz they went to Kress', where they won service—after a fashion. Although served refreshments, the youngsters had to stand up to eat because the management had removed the counter stools. [11] This incident bore a striking similarity to what Southern newspaper editor Harry Golden once called the phenomenon of the "vertical Negro."[12] Nevertheless the Youth Council had successfully desegregated another lunch counter.

Brown's management put up far more resistance. One day the protesters found no seats because all had been taken (before the store opened) by white youths, who yielded their places only to other white customers. [13] There were other incidents, the most serious being the arrest of a white youth after he struck a black youngster. Fortunately such incidents were rare due in part to preventive action by police, who were on hand during all demonstrations and who were ordered to remain impartial while warning or arresting anyone creating a disturbance. [14]

286

Yet the sit-ins were losing momentum. Brown's remained adamant, and school was approaching, which meant that most protesters might have to be replaced with older blacks. The Youth Council finally suspended the sit-ins on September 1. Luper called it a tactical maneuver. Barbara Posey, fifteen-year-old spokeswoman for the Council, explained that the moratorium was ordered so that members of such city groups as the United Church Women, which had contacted the youths and pledged their support, could use their influence on the business owners. [15]

At first glance the suspension seemed a tacit admission of defeat. But the young blacks had opened four of the five downtown stores on their list, and Posey claimed that over a dozen other eating places had either opened their doors or had pledged to do so at a later date. This amazing group of youngsters had also attracted the attention of reporters from *The New York Times,* which printed five separate stories about the Oklahoma City demonstrations. [16]

More striking than the publicity was the relatively tranquil atmosphere during the protests. Oklahoma City stood in contrast to Montgomery, Alabama, where a few days after the Oklahoma sit-in suspension, Dr. Martin Luther King, Jr., was arrested, jailed, and kicked by city police. Similarly in Miami, Florida, in 1959 several sit-in leaders were either beaten or threatened. [17]

The presentation of a plan for integrating all the city's eating facilities represented the first event of any significance after the September moratorium. It was written by a citizens' group representing churches, educational leaders, and other agencies. The plan called upon the public to patronize restaurants that served blacks. Although it was submitted to the Oklahoma City Council of Churches, the group gave it only indirect support. But the second stage of the civil rights campaign had begun. It was to last twenty-three months and would be marked by negotiations and more demonstrations.[18]

While talks proceeded, the Youth Council constantly reminded restaurant owners of their desire for service. They did this either through "popcorn sit-ins,"—small, brief student protests during school lunch hours—or through telephone calls to lunch counters. The blacks would simply ask: "May we eat today?"[19] The answer was usually no. According to Youth Council files, only ten establishments were desegregated by the year's end.[20]

In contrast to the last three months of 1958, Youth Council members in 1959 were back on the street testing eating facilities, although they staged few formal sit-ins. Four Council members were refused service at Adair's Cafeteria in February. Its owner, Ralph Adair, told a group of NAACP leaders that he was for blacks and had voted to integrate eating facilities at the county courthouse but would not serve them at his establishments: "I cannot make money serving Negroes because I will lose my white ...omers."[21] Manager J. B. Masoner of Katz, a recently integrated drug store, stated that serving black people had not hurt his business, but Adair's argument was repeated by the vast majority of store owners whenever they tried to justify their policies.[22]

287

Judging by the newspaper accounts of unsuccessful demonstrations, the Youth Council did not make significant headway in 1959. For example, members of the Youth Council were refused service at Brown's in June, July, September, and December. Also discouraging were the first few months of 1960, the year which marked the start of the involvement of the city council and the governor in the lunch counter controversy. E. C. Moon of the NAACP and Wayne B. Snow of the Oklahoma City Council of Churches urged the city council at the March 1 meeting to pass an ordinance outlawing segregation in places of public accommodation. But the city council agreed with Municipal Counselor E. H. Moler, who stated in a legal opinion that the council lacked such power.[23]

In protest the black community laid plans for a massive downtown sit-in, but local NAACP leaders called it off at the request of Governor J. Howard Edmondson. He issued a statement which mildly criticized the recalcitrant restaurant owners and announced the creation of a Governor's Committee on Human Relations. In place of the downtown sit-in, blacks staged a "goodwill march" to the state capitol. March leaders said they would end token sit-ins (the type that had been going on at Brown's) to allow the governor's group time to act. Meeting several times, the Governor's Committee tried unsuccessfully to reach agreement with restaurant owners.[24]

Nearly two years had passed since the first wave of sit-ins had been cancelled. Many eating establishments refused to serve black people in spite of the efforts of various groups to negotiate a settlement. The time had come for a new action—the boycott. On August 10, 1960, black city physician Dr. Charles N. Atkins announced that a boycott of downtown stores would take place if blacks were not permitted lunch counter service within five days. Because black youths failed to gain service, there was a mass meeting of members of the black community, who decided to begin the downtown boycott. The action was to be a general, not selective, boycott of downtown stores, but protest leaders exempted nine places which had previously opened their doors to blacks.[25]

288

Behind the scenes, important activities were in progress. Over the radio Luper and others informed the black community about the boycott; volunteers with cameras took pictures of black people who still shopped downtown. Telephone committees would identify these people and call them up to discourage them from patronizing downtown stores. The picketing and similar tactics had their effect on restaurant owners. The NAACP Youth Council files reveal that by the end of 1960, the number of food service facilities open to blacks had risen to 100—an increase of over 100 percent from the year before.[26]

During the boycott black demonstrators were the target of the first legal action taken against them since the campaign's onset in 1958. Nine were arrested for disorderly conduct at the Cravens Building, the halls of which they had blocked while trying to obtain service at Anna Maude's Cafeteria in January of 1961. Two months later a request for a court injunction was filed to prevent further demonstrations at the Cravens Building, but by the time the judge made a ruling, which allowed some protests to occur, the boycott was over. On July 6, 1961, Harvey Everest of the Governor's Committee on Human Relations had announced the lowering of racial barriers at three major downtown eating facilities, including Brown's. As a result black leaders announced an end to the boycott.[27]

The role of the boycott in the overall struggle to be served is a matter of controversy, with some people claiming it was effective while others asserting the opposite conclusion. A city police lieutenant present at almost all of the sit-ins claimed monetary pressure was not the major reason many owners ended their resistance. He said they feared that some of the black children might be hurt, which could cause a violent confrontation. The monetary effect of the boycott remains uncertain because store owners have died, moved away, or are reluctant to give information from their records. During the boycott merchants claimed that they saw no drop in black customers and total sales.[28] But one high official at Brown's, when reached in 1972, admitted, "It had a depressing effect on business."[29] And Luper, who maintained that the resulting economic pinch was instrumental in opening eating facilities, said that serious talks with owners did not really begin until the boycott. As evidence she claimed that hundreds of city blacks who had charge accounts at downtown stores gave them up and shopped elsewhere. Her statements are indirectly supported by an October, 1960, Youth Council survey, which found that most blacks shopping downtown were from outside Oklahoma City.[30]

The eleven month boycott had been accompanied by the absence of violence. This was in sharp contrast to many Southern cities. For example, a series of sit-ins in Jacksonville, Florida, around the onset of Oklahoma City's boycott, led to a race riot. But three long years of protest lay between the NAACP Youth Council and total victory. The last phase of the demonstrations, which lasted from July, 1961, to July, 1964, would be marked by surges of direct action followed by periods of inactivity. During these latter times the protesters would try more negotiations, and if they failed, rebuild support for further demonstrations.[31]

During the remainder of 1961 Luper led demonstrations at a restaurant called the Pink Kitchen. In this instance the protests led to the arrest of several demonstrators and the filing of an injunction suit which halted further protests there. But negotiations with other Oklahoma City eating places led to the opening of some of them; according to the Youth Council's desegregation progress report, 115 eating establishments were open to blacks as of December, 1961.[32]

During 1962 and the first five months of 1963 the Youth Council conducted almost no sit-ins, presumably devoting their main energies to rebuilding their morale and talking to more store owners. City government was aware, however, that the lull would not last indefinitely. At Mayor Jack Wilkes' request, the city council created a Community Relations Committee in May to help solve the city's racial problems and head off the renewal of sit-ins by acting as mediators for both sides in a dispute. The committee did not, however, prevent new protests.[33]

There were sit-ins every day from May 31 to June 4 at such places as Bishops and the Skirvin Hotel, resulting in a quick series of victories. More than twenty businesses began to serve blacks as a result of these protests. Mayor Wilkes played an important role in the talks during this time by serving as an arbiter between restaurant owners and blacks. Other people involved in the talks were the NAACP's Jimmie Stewart and Frank Carey of the recently formed city human relations committee.[34]

The black community was jubilant over the string of sit-in successes. Clara Luper commented that the agreements "pretty well complete" the downtown integration goals and that outlying segregated eating places

289

Holding placards proclaiming "We are Americans too" and "Is Democracy for whites only," these young civil rights protestors were seen frequently in Oklahoma City from 1958 to 1964 (Oklahoma Publishing Company).

would be among future targets. But there was to be another year of protests and legal squabbles before the city's eating facilities would be fully integrated.[35]

For nearly six months there were no sit-ins. Then in November Calvin Luper (Clara Luper's son) of the Youth Council issued a call to action at the state NAACP convention. He said that blacks should "demonstrate, demonstrate, and demonstrate with sit-ins, lay-ins, or smoke-ins to end segregation of public accommodations."[36] That same day pickets from the city chapter of the Congress of Racial Equality (CORE), later joined by the veteran Youth Council members, began demonstrations at Ralph's Drug Store.[37]

Then followed a period of moves and countermoves. Ralph's owners obtained an injunction halting sit-ins, though a visiting judge dismissed the order in early 1964. The black protesters chose to negotiate rather than renew the sit-ins at Ralph's. Meanwhile in March, the Community Relations Committee recommended that a public accommodations ordinance be passed, but the city council voted to table the motion. In May Clara Luper

291

By the early 1960s sit-ins and peaceful demonstrations had effectively ended segregation in the city's restaurants (Oklahoma Publishing Company).

led forty blacks in a sit-in at the Split-T Restaurant, but the management obtained an injunction and forced the young blacks to leave. Action once again shifted to the conference table as the Mayor's Human Relations Committee sponsored a series of hearings on the proposed public accommodations law. To underscore their continued determination, the Youth Council held another sit-in, this time at Ned's Steak House. As with so many other demonstrations in the past six years, "there was no violence and police made no arrests."[38]

The demonstrators' resolve, plus the likelihood of changes in national racial policy, pushed the city council to action. On June 2 it passed a public accommodations ordinance forbidding operators of such establishments from refusing to serve anyone because of race, religion, or color. The law included restaurants, swimming pools, and theaters. Its wording was similar to the 1964 Civil Rights Act, which went into effect on July 2, 1964, only two days before Oklahoma City's ordinance did. On July 4 two groups of Oklahoma City blacks tested four eating facilities which had previously refused them service. They were served at all four locations. The struggle to be served had ended successfully.[39]

With the passage of time and the cooling of tempers, the task of analyzing the demonstrations has become easier. Two questions can be answered with some degree of accuracy. First, what did the young blacks accomplish? By staging these protests, Clara Luper and the NAACP Youth Council successfully integrated Oklahoma City's lunch counters, providing another defeat for Jim Crow. The Youth Council also became a civil rights information center; its efforts stimulated a wave of sit-ins that integrated lunch counters across the state. Clara Luper mentioned another important result of the protests: "They proved that change could come non-violently under the present form of government."[40]

Second, why did they succeed and why were they so peaceful? The reasons are many. The age of the protesters, for example, was very important. Unlike adults, the black youths—many of whom were elementary school students—seemed much less threatening to whites; in addition, violent action against children would be more likely open to censure by whites as well as blacks.[41] Second, the discipline of the demonstrators was a factor. They were so committed to non-violence that when sporadic confrontations did occur, they did not retaliate. Of course also important was the restraint of the police, who did not harass the demonstrators, watched closely to make sure white hecklers were warned or arrested, and arrested civil rights protesters only when they were instructed to do so—usually when a court order was involved. Certainly the generally sympathetic attitudes of such city and state officials as Mayor Wilkes and Governor Edmondson was a factor, as was the persistence of the Youth Council, which stubbornly pursued its objectives for many years. Also important was the absence of segregation laws; for the most part the Youth Council had to change customary policies, not statutes. Another reason for success was the boycott, which demonstrated to owners that blacks did indeed possess the economic power to back up their demands.

Important though these factors may be, the social change which had been going on in the state and nation for over a decade was also significant. The sit-ins were but a part of changes in racial policy—such as school desegregation—which convinced many whites that future changes were inevitable. The editorial cartoons of *The Daily Oklahoman* reflect the shift in white attitudes. In 1958 one cartoon portrays a white city lunch counter owner saying "Sorry" to a demonstrator and pointing to a sign on his counter wall that says, "I reserve the right to refuse service!" In contrast to this is the cartoon of June 9, 1963, after the Youth Council opened up several restaurants. The picture is of "Jim Crow" flying down a shadowy path toward a sign marked "Extinction."[42]

The Oklahoma City sit-ins must be put in proper historical perspective. They were not the first black-led civil rights sit-ins in America. Indeed they were preceded by a number of protests which began during World War II. In 1942 and 1943 various chapters of the newly formed CORE held sit-ins in Chicago, Detroit, and Denver which opened up movie theaters and restaurants to blacks. In addition the Howard University NAACP sponsored similar demonstrations in Washington, D.C. Shortly after the war, CORE representatives led protests in such towns as Lawrence, Kansas, and Columbia, Missouri.[43]

Oklahoma City's protests are worth noting because in many respects they were typical of the border state sit-ins of the 1950s which took place in such cities as Baltimore and St. Louis. They were black-led, non-violent direct action campaigns to eliminate Jim Crow practices by dramatizing their undemocratic nature. The protesters used negotiations before resorting to -ins, and they had some success in persuading owners to change their policies without use of demonstrations. The sit-in campaigns continued on and off for a long time; those in St. Louis and Oklahoma City, for example, lasted approximately six years, and they finally led to the desegregation of amusement parks, swimming pools, and theaters, as well as lunch counters. In contrast to Southern sit-ins, those in the border states were marked by a minimum of violence, and they were in part so successful in speeding up changes in race relations because of the absence of discriminatory laws.[44]

In some ways the Oklahoma City protests were unusual. The leading organization involved was the NAACP, not CORE, even though their tactics were similar. The boycott played a larger role in the Sooner State sit-ins than elsewhere. The age of the demonstrators was another distinctive feature. Youth Council participants were elementary and high school students, while in St. Louis most protesters were adults. These differences should not be exaggerated, however. The tactics were the same, the Oklahoma City CORE chapter later joined the protests, and in Baltimore, at least, it was the young people (in that case college students) who deserved major credit for the victories, even though they sometimes exasperated the adult leadership in the process.[45]

Besides being typical examples of border state protests of the 1950s, the Oklahoma sit-ins are useful in another way. They are another reminder to historians that the so-called Civil Rights Revolution did not suddenly arise in 1960. Typical of older historical viewpoints is John Hope Franklin, who begins his chapter on the "Black Revolution" by stating that student sit-ins in Greensboro, North Carolina, February, 1960, were "the beginning of

293

the sit-in movement which spread through the South and to numerous places in the North."[46] Although technically correct, Franklin is misleading because he fails to mention the importance of the sit-ins of the 1940s and 1950s. Even historian Richard Dalfiume, who rightfully stresses that the March on Washington Movement (MOWM) of the 1940s was a precursor of the modern Civil Rights Movement, does not mention an equally important phenomenon—the sit-ins.[47]

More accurate statements on the role of sit-ins are found in August Meier and Elliott Rudwick's book, *From Plantation to Ghetto*. They at least briefly mention CORE and the border state sit-ins of the 1950s. There is some indication that recent American history scholars as well as students of black history are beginning to realize the extent and significance of such protests. Richard Polenberg's work on domestic America during World War II, for example, mentions the sit-ins as well as the MOWM. And with the publication in 1973 of Meier and Rudwick's study of CORE, historians now have at their disposal the most complete account to date of sit-ins during the 1940s and 1950s. They give further proof that the Southern college student demonstrations of the early 1960s were but larger manifestations of two earlier decades of black protest.[48]

The Oklahoma City demonstrations raise one question, however, to which few of these and other recent historical studies have addressed themselves. Why did these sit-ins, or those in St. Louis or Baltimore, fail to spread as did those in Greensboro? It is easy to see why a nation in the midst of total war would not be captivated by the protests of the early 1940s. But it is not so obvious why many black and white Americans responded in 1960 and not in the 1950s. Perhaps black Americans, especially those in the South, had not yet reached the level of militancy necessary for the protests to catch on. Or perhaps the American public paid little attention to the border states, since they expected black-white confrontations to come only from the Deep South. Perhaps the reason is something completely different. These are hypotheses which historians might profitably explore in their future studies of the black American's struggle for equality in the twentieth century.

ENDNOTES

* Dr. Carl Graves is a visiting assistant professor at the University of Kansas in Lawrence, Kansas.
[1] *The Daily Oklahoman* (Oklahoma City), August 21, 1958, p. 17. This newspaper, including the Sunday edition, will hereafter be cited as *Oklahoman*.
[2] Alan Saxe, "Protest and Reform: The Desegregation of Oklahoma City" (Ph.D. dissertation, University of Oklahoma, 1969), pp. 16–19, 49, 162.

[3] *Ibid.*, p. 136; Peter M. Bergman and Mort N. Bergman, *The Chronological History of the Negro in America* (New York: A Mentor Book, 1969), pp. 516–517, 524.

[4] Saxe, "Protest and Reform," p. 158.

[5] She is a graduate of Langston University (a predominantly black Oklahoma college) with a math major and history minor who received a Master of Arts degree in secondary education at the University of Oklahoma. In 1968 she became an instructor of American and Oklahoma history at Oklahoma City's Northwest Classen High School. This "long-time Oklahoma City civil rights leader" was to receive her greatest fame for her role in the sit-ins, but she has remained active, directing the NAACP Youth Council, leading demonstrations during the 1969 city garbage workers' strike and editing the black-oriented, state-based magazine, *Black Voices. Oklahoman,* August 14, 1968, p. 1, August 16, 1969, p. 1.

[6] Mrs. Clara M. Luper, private interview, July 17, 1972; *The Black Dispatch* (Oklahoma City), September 26, 1958, p.2. This newspaper will hereafter be cited as *Dispatch.*

[7] Kaye M. Teall, *Black History in Oklahoma: A Resource Book* (Oklahoma City: Oklahoma City Public Schools, 1971), p. 241.

[8] Luper interview; Barbara Posey and Gwendolyn Fuller, "Protest Drug Counter Discrimination," *Crisis,* December, 1958, p. 612.

[9] *Dispatch,* August 29, 1958, p. 1, *Oklahoman,* August 25, 1958, p. 2.

[10] *Oklahoman,* August 21, 1958, p. 17, August 22, p. 5.

[11] *Oklahoman,* August 23, 1958, p. 1.

[12] He observed that "vertical segregation" has almost been eliminated: Blacks and whites now stood at the same grocery counters and shopped in the same department stores. "The fur begins to fly" quipped Golden, only when blacks sit down next to whites. He jokingly suggested that the way to solve the problem was to remove the seats. Little did the editor of the North Carolina *Israelite* know that someone would actually try such a thing. *Only in America* (Cleveland: World Publishing Company, 1958), pp. 121–122.

[13] *Oklahoman,* August 25, 1958, p. 2.

[14] *Oklahoman,* September 2, 1958, p. 1, August 24, pp. 1–2, August 27, p. 6; Lieutenant Don Rogers, private interview, July 19, 1972.

[15] *Oklahoman,* August 30, 1958, p. 5, August 31, p. 8A; Luper interview; *Dispatch,* September 5, 1958, p. 1.

[16] *Dispatch,* September 5, 1958, p. 1; *New York Times,* August 22, 1958, p. 11, August 23, p. 16, August 24, p. 24, August 26, p. 18, August 28, p. 25.

[17] Congress of Racial Equality, *Cracking the Color Line* (Pamphlet; New York: CORE, 1962), pp. 18–20; *Dispatch,* September 5, 1958, p. 1.

[18] *Oklahoman,* September 10, 1958, p. 7, September 16, p. 13.

[19] Luper interview.

[20] Saxe, "Protest and Reform," p. 168.

[21] *Dispatch,* February 6, 1959, p. 1.

[22] *New York Times,* September 12, 1958, p. 12.

[23] *Dispatch,* June 19, 1959, p. 1, July 31, p. 1; Luper interview; *Oklahoman,* September 20, 1959, p. 12A; *Dispatch,* January 1, 1960, p. 5; Oklahoma City *Council Journal,* Vol. 34-A, pp. 401–403, 429–434; *Dispatch,* March 4, 1960, p. 1, *Oklahoman,* March 9, 1960, p. 13.

[24] *Dispatch,* April 1, 1960, p. 1, August 19, p. 1; *Oklahoman,* April 1, 1960, p. 20, April 3, p. 1, Aligist 19, p. 1.

[25] Atkins later became the city's first black city councilman in 1966. *Oklahoman,* October 4, 1966, p. N4, December 31, p. 1, August 7, 1960, p. 1A, August 20, p. 1, August 11, p. 2, August 13, p. 7.

[26] Luper interview; Saxe, "Protest and Reform," pp. 168–169; the Youth Council files

295

were destroyed in 1968 when a fire bomb gutted the Freedom Center in which they were stored. But Saxe had seen the files before the fire and included yearly figures, quoted here, from them in his dissertation.

[27] *Oklahoman.* January 15, 1961, p. 1, February 5, p. 4A, March 19, p. 1A, March 12, p. 1A, July 7, p. 1; *Dispatch.* November 10, 1961, p. 1, March 24, p. 1.

[28] Rogers Interview; *Oklahoman.* August 24, 1960, p. 1.

[29] Interview with unnamed employee of Brown's Department Store, December 16, 1972; this official knew the daily sales figures during the boycott; he asked that his name and position be kept confidential.

[30] Luper interview; *Dispatch.* August 26, 1960, p. 1, October 14, p. 6.

[31] Bergman and Bergman, *Chronological History.* p. 570; August Meier suggests that the alternating periods of action and inaction in Oklahoma City were similar to those occurring in Southern civil rights protests of the early 1960s. He contends that the summer, 1963, "revival of direct action in Oklahoma City came in the wake of the Birmingham demonstration that same spring." August Meier to the author, February 1, 1974.

[32] *Dispatch.* November 3, 1961, p. 1; November 10, p. 1; Saxe, "Protest and Reform," p. 168.

[33] *Dispatch.* September 7, 1962, p. 1; Oklahoma City *Council Journal.* Vol. 37-B, pp. 979–980; *Oklahoman.* May 29, 1963, p. 13; *Dispatch.* May 31, 1963, p. 1.

[34] *Oklahoman.* June 1, 1963, p. 1, June 2, pp. 1–2, June 3, pp. 1–2, June 4, pp. 1–2, June 5, p. 11; *Dispatch.* June 7, 1963, p. 1.

[35] *Dispatch.* June 7, 1963, p. 1.

[36] *Oklahoman.* November 17, 1963, p. 1.

[37] *Oklahoman.* November 19, 1963, p. 13.

[38] Oklahoma City *Council Journal.* Vol. 38-A, p. 327; *Oklahoman.* November 21, 1963, p. 1; *Dispatch.* January 24, 1964, p. 4, May 15, p. 1, June 5, p. 1, *Oklahoman.* May 7, 1964, p. 5, May 19, p. 2.

[39] Oklahoma City *Council Journal.* Vol. 38-A, pp. 698–699; Bergman and Bergman, *Chronological History.* p. 583; *Oklahoman.* July 5, 1964, p. A13.

[40] Luper interview.

[41] One black man, who was 18 in 1958 when he began his participation in the sit-ins, estimated that the protesters averaged 10 years of age. Though some of the youngest demonstrators did not completely understand the protests in which they took part, he felt that the vast majority knew what they were doing and were dedicated to their cause. Mr. Willard C. Pitts, private interview, June 8, 1977. Thus the Oklahoma City sit-ins were not a case of adults using children for tactical advantage, but of activist youths—such as Barbara Posey—taking most of the initiative. Clara Luper's inspirational role, however, should not be forgotten.

[42] *Oklahoman.* September 12, 1958, p. 10, June 9, 1963, p. 16A.

[43] CORE, *Cracking the Color Line,* pp. 1–4; Richard Polenberg, *War and Society: The United States, 1941–1945* (Philadelphia: J. P. Lippincott Company, 1972), p. 107; August Meier, Elliott Rudwick, and Francis L. Broderick, eds., *Black Protest Thought in the Twentieth Century* (2nd ed; Indianapolis: Bobbs-Merrill Company, 1971), p. 246; August Meier and Elliott Rudwick, *CORE: A Study of the Civil Rights Movement* (New York: Oxford University Press, 1973), pp. 56–57.

[44] CORE, *Cracking the Color Line.* pp. 5–12; an account of one phase of the Baltimore sit-ins which provides many comparisons to the Oklahoma City protests is August Meier's, "The Successful Sit-Ins in a Border City: A Study in Social Causation," *Journal of Intergroup Relations.* II (Summer, 1961), pp. 231–237.

[45] *Ibid.*

[46] John Hope Franklin, *From Slavery to Freedom: A History of Negro Americans* (4th ed; New York: Alfred A. Knopf, 1974), p. 476.

[47] Richard M. Dalfiume, "The 'Forgotten Years' of the Negro Revolution," *Journal of American History*, Vol. LV (June, 1968), pp. 90–116.

[48] August Meier and Elliott Rudwick, *From Plantation to Ghetto* (Revised ed., New York: Hill and Wang, 1970), pp. 252–254; Polenberg, *War and Society*, pp. 102–107; Meier and Rudwick, *CORE*, pp. 3–100.

297

BLACK RADICALIZATION AND THE FUNDING OF CIVIL RIGHTS: 1957-1970*

HERBERT H. HAINES
Western New England College

A neglected topic in social movement theory is the effect of factionalism within movements, particularly the role of "radical" activists in shaping responses to
"moderates." This paper investigates the effect of black radicalization during the
1960s on the ability of moderate civil rights organizations to attract financial contributions from outside supporters. Trends in donations to seven major black organizations are analyzed. It is concluded that the activities of relatively radical black organizations, along with the urban riots, stimulated increased financial support by white
groups of more moderate black organizations, especially during the late 1960s. This
finding partially contradicts the widely-held belief that black militants only brought on
a white "backlash." On the contrary, the task of fundraising by moderate civil rights
organizations was apparently made easier, not more difficult, by the racial turmoil of
the 1960s.

299

Nearly all social movements divide into "moderate" and "radical" factions at some point in
their development, although the meaning of these labels is continually changing. Bifurcation has
occurred, for example, in the U.S. labor movement (Rayback, 1966), the women's movement
(Freeman, 1975), the anti-nuclear movement (Barkan, 1979), and the black revolt in the United
States (Allen, 1969; Killian, 1972). Analysts of social movements have largely neglected how
radical groups alter the context in which moderate groups operate. In other words, what happens
to moderates when radicals appear? Does a backlash ensue? Or do policymakers and other
important audiences become more receptive to moderate claims? In the face of militant
challenges, do moderates find it easier or more difficult to pursue their goals?

These questions are complex, and they touch upon an issue which is crucial to understanding
social movements and social issues: the relationships between factionalism and responses to
competing varieties of collective action. Though theoretically important, this issue has received
little attention from sociologists and political scientists. This paper addresses these topics by
examining changes in the funding of civil rights organizations in the United States during the late
1950s and the 1960s — a period when portions of the black movement were becoming increasingly
militant in both their goals and their tactics. The paper begins with a discussion of the sparse
literature dealing with the effects of radical factions on moderate groups. Following this brief
review, I will describe the escalation of the goals and tactics of organized black activists during
the twentieth century. I will then present and discuss data on the funding of civil rights organizations during the period from 1957 through 1970. Although white reactions to black collective
action during those turbulent times were diverse, these data will show that radicalization of
segments of the black community had the net effect of improving the resource bases of more
moderate civil rights organizations by stimulating previously uninvolved parties to contribute ever
increasing amounts of financial support.

* An earlier version of this paper was presented at the annual meetings of the Society for the Study of Social
Problems, Detroit, Michigan, in August, 1983. The research was supported in part by a grant from the
National Science Foundation (#SES-8205299). The author thanks Joane Nagel, Doug McAdam, the staff of
the Martin Luther King Library and Archives, and Minnie Clayton of the Trevor Arnett Library and Archives,
Atlanta University, for their help. Correspondence to: Herbert H. Haines, School of Arts and Sciences,
Western New England College, Springfield, MA 01119.

THEORETICAL BACKGROUND

Activists and scholars alike have suggested that the activities of radicals in a social movement can undermine the position of moderates by discrediting movement activities and goals, and by threatening the ability of moderates to take advantage of the resources available from supportive third parties. I refer to this general backlash as the *negative radical flank effect*. The history of social movements in the United States provides several examples of the fear of such negative effects among movement participants. Moderate abolitionists of the early 19th century worried that anti-slavery extremists would discredit their cause and delay the emancipation of black slaves (Nye, 1963). Groups opposed to nuclear power plants have expressed the fear that violent or obstructionist tactics and efforts to expand the movement to embrace nuclear disarmament and anti-corporatism will hurt the immediate goal of stopping nuclear power development (Barkan, 1979). Some scholars have suggested that black radicalization and rioting during the 1960s weakened the position of such mainstream civil rights groups as the National Association for the Advancement of Colored People (Masotti *et al.*, 1969; Muse, 1968; Powledge, 1967). Others have blamed the failure of the Equal Rights Amendment on the statements and actions of militant feminists (Felsenthal, 1982).

Conversely, a *positive radical flank effect* can occur when the bargaining position of moderates is strengthened by the presence of more radical groups. This happens in either (or both) of two ways. The radicals can provide a militant foil against which moderate strategies and demands are redefined and normalized — in other words, treated as "reasonable." Or, the radicals can create crises which are resolved to the moderates' advantage. Freeman (1975) has argued that mainstream reformist women's organizations would have been dismissed as "too far out" during the late 1960s and the early 1970s had it not been for more radical groups: lesbian feminists and socialist feminists appear to have improved the bargaining position of such moderate groups as the National Organization for Women. Ewen (1976) and Ramirez (1978) have suggested that demands by the labor movement for an eight-hour day and collective bargaining became negotiable only after the emergence of serious socialist threats in the early 20th century. Others have argued that the emergence of black militants in the 1960s helped to increase white acceptance of nonviolent tactics and integrationist goals (Elinson, 1966; Killian, 1972).

An understanding of radical flank effects would greatly enhance current social movement theory.[1] The literature on social and political movements abounds with more or less casual references to these effects, and they have been frequently debated by movement activists; but they have received almost no systematic attention. Gamson's (1975) research represents the most direct investigation of the effects of factionalism on protest outcomes. He examined the conditions under which groups came to represent a set of constituents and managed to gain "new advantages" for those constituents. Among the many conditions Gamson examined was the existence of moderate and radical groups championing the same broad issues. He tested — and rejected — the hypothesis that the existence of more militant organizations enhanced the success of less militant organizations. Gamson's test is less than conclusive for several reasons. There were measur-

---

1. Radical flank effects are relevant, for example, to the debate between the resource mobilization model of protest and that of Piven and Cloward (1977, 1978). The resource mobilization perspective stresses the dependence of protest groups on the resources available from third parties (Jenkins and Perrow, 1977; Lipsky, 1968). Implicit in this model is the notion that protest groups must refrain from tactics and statements which would alienate prospective supporters. Piven and Cloward, on the other hand, suggest that reliance on such resources only undermines protest goals and that protest groups can succeed by tactics of mass disruption. Positive radical flank effects in protest movements provide a link between the two; under certain circumstances, moderate groups might well be able to maintain good relations with supporting groups by distancing themselves from the disruptive activities of radicals while at the same time profiting from the crises that they create.

ment and coding problems (Goldstone, 1980). He examined only 30 groups. Labor unions were over-represented in the sample. And, most important, he focused upon only two dimensions of reactions to moderate organizations: (1) the designation of a group as a legitimate representative for a group of constituents; and (2) the group's success in winning significant benefits for its constituents. While these dimensions are important, a number of others remain to be examined. Radical groups might, for example, increase or decrease the level of public *awareness* of moderate groups. They might alter public *definitions* of moderates as more or less "extreme," "reasonable," or "dangerous." Radicals might increase or decrease moderates' *access to decisionmakers*. And, finally, radical flank effects might influence the capacity of moderate groups to *attract resources* from supporters who are not members of the moderate groups themselves. This paper focuses upon the last of these dimensions.

THE BLACK REVOLT IN THE UNITED STATES

The black revolt in the United States after the Second World War is well-suited for studying radical flank effects because it involved a variety of organizations, ideologies, and strategies, and has experienced rapid tactical and rhetorical escalation, especially during the 1960s. This section briefly traces the escalation of black insurgency, highlighting those movement transformations upon which radical flank effects were based.

301

The National Association for the Advancement of Colored People (NAACP) was the preeminent organizational representative of black interests in the United States from its incorporation in 1910 to the Supreme Court's landmark school desegregation decision in 1954. Other organizations existed, such as the National Urban League, the Commission on Interracial Cooperation (renamed the Southern Regional Council in 1944), and Marcus Garvey's Universal Negro Improvement Association. But none of these matched the NAACP in long-term influence. The NAACP functioned mainly as a legal group; its primary tactic was litigation. Initially, the NAACP did not challenge legalized racial segregation and discrimination. Well into the 1930s it aimed to ensure equality of rights and facilities under the "separate but equal" doctrine established in *Plessy v. Ferguson* (1896), rather than to attack the doctrine outright. During the 1930s, however, this goal changed. The NAACP launched a protracted campaign of litigation, culminating in *Brown v. Board of Education of Topeka* (1954), in which the Supreme Court invalidated segregation in public schools. Thereafter, the nature of the black revolt was fundamentally transformed.

Prior to 1954, many groups in the United States periodically defined and attacked the NAACP as a radical organization. This was especially true in the southern states, where many blacks also regarded the NAACP's approach to racial justice as militant. The NAACP's integrationist philosophy and program of aggressive litigation *was* rather "radical" in those times.

When white resistance prevented the kinds of sweeping changes that many blacks expected the Supreme Court's desegration ruling to produce, the movement changed. So did the characteristics of what was called "militancy." Ideologically, the radicals of the late 1950s remained dedicated to racial integration and close to the spirit of U.S. political philosophy—i.e., they sought assimilation and reform, not "revolution." Tactically, however, they were very different. Organizations such as the Southern Christian Leadership Conference (SCLC) and the Congress of Racial Equality (CORE) called for nonviolent direct action—marches, picket lines, boycotts, and the like—to challenge discrimination. Ostensibly, nonviolent direct action worked by appealing to an opponent's latent sense of right and wrong. In practice, however, direct action was usually successful only when it created crises that the white community could not afford to ignore. Direct action was infrequent during the late 1950s but, beginning with the student sit-ins of 1960, it became a popular and widespread tactic in the first half of the 1960s. The Student Nonviolent Coordinating Committee (SNCC) joined the SCLC and CORE as major proponents of nonviolence. Then SNCC quickly drifted into militant voter registration and community organizing activities. These three organizations occupied positions on the radical end of the black political spectrum during the early 1960s. The NAACP and the Legal Defense and Educational Fund (LDEF), whose tactics continued to be limited largely to litigation, were by this time better classified as middle-of-the-road or moderate. The National Urban League was the most conservative of the national black organizations.

During the mid 1960s the predominance of nonviolent integrationism broke down, and militancy was transformed once again. As violence erupted in the black ghettos of northern cities and as many black activists began questioning the assimilationist orientation of the civil rights movement, leaders such as Martin Luther King and organizations such as the SCLC were increasingly defined as moderate or, at the very least, as "responsible" militants (Meier, 1965:55). *Real* militancy came to imply a separatist or nationalist outlook and an acceptance of retaliatory violence against an intransigent white power structure. One should not overgeneralize, for there were indeed several different types of black radicalism during the mid 1960s (Allen, 1969). Nevertheless, most black radicals rejected racial integration and strict nonviolence to some degree. Major proponents of the "new" black radicalism after 1966 were the Student Nonviolent Coordinating Committee, the Black Panther Party, the Revolutionary Action Movement, the Republic of New Africa, and, to a far lesser extent, the Congress of Racial Equality.

While it is clear that black moderation and radicalism evolved during the 1950s and 1960s, students of black collective action are divided over its effects on the civil rights mainstream. Masotti *et al.* (1969:174), Muse (1968), and Powledge (1967), among others, contend that the escalation of black radicalism damaged the position of black moderates by strengthening white resistance to black claims and undermining black-white coalitions. Others have suggested that black radicalization not only failed to weaken moderates but actually enhanced the respectibility of established leaders and organizations, thus increasing their ability to bargain for gradual reform (Elinson, 1966:371; Hough, 1968:224; Meier, 1965; Oberschall, 1973:230).

It is probably impossible to settle this debate in any conclusive manner; it relates to a multi-dimensional issue, and both positions undoubtedly contain at least a grain of truth. No scholar, however, has yet examined organizational funding patterns in light of radical flank effects.

THE IMPORTANCE OF OUTSIDE RESOURCES

Prior to the 1970s, most scholars tried to explain the emergence of collective action in terms of participants' motives. But as theoretical and empirical problems have emerged in such explanations (Gurney and Tierney, 1982; Jenkins and Perrow, 1977; McAdam, 1982), scholars began focusing on the organizational needs of social movements — especially the need to mobilize material and non-material resources (Jenkins and Perrow, 1977; Lipsky, 1968; McCarthy and Zald, 1973, 1977). Since many aggrieved populations lack the resources necessary to wage large-scale collective challenges, resources obtained from outside supporters are frequently essential. The utility of the resource mobilization perspective is still being debated (McAdam, 1982:23), but it has been rather firmly established that organized conflict cannot operate for long on shared discontent and moral commitment alone. Thus, an understanding of processes which affect a movement organization's ability to mobilize resources would be useful. Unfortunately, resource mobilization theorists have had rather little to say on this subject (McAdam, 1982:21).

Resources may include such material things as money, land, labor (Tilly, 1978:69), or facilities (McCarthy and Zald, 1977:1220). But less concrete resources — including "authority, moral commitment, trust, friendship, skills, habits of industry" (Oberschall, 1973:28) — may also be valuable resources for collective action.

While it would be a mistake to equate resources solely with money, I believe money can serve as a convenient index of radical flank effects. I assume that outside supporters contribute money or other resources only to those movement organizations which they consider acceptable. Supporters need not totally approve of the organization to contribute to it. Rather, they need only have a perceived interest in supporting the cause and they need only define the movement organization as an acceptable beneficiary. I also assume that acceptability is a *relative* thing. A movement organization's acceptability may be largely a function of the relative acceptability/unacceptability of *other* movement organizations. I use the levels of outside financial support obtained by a given social movement organization as rough indicators of the organization's acceptability to financial supporters.

Bearing all of this in mind, one can conceive of several hypothetical effects of radical groups on resource mobilization by moderate groups. Each would be expected to produce a distinct pattern in outside contributions to moderate organizations. We would expect *negative* radical flank effects — backlashes caused by radicals — to produce *declines* in the outside incomes of moderate groups (or a leveling of prior patterns of increasing moderate incomes) following significant ideological or tactical escalations by more radical groups. We would expect *positive* radical flank effects, on the other hand, to produce *increases* in the outside incomes of moderate groups (or a leveling of prior patterns of decreasing moderate incomes) following such escalations. The absence of significant changes in the outside incomes of moderate organizations during periods of radical escalation would indicate an absence of radical flank effects or a balancing of positive and negative effects.[2]

There are two subtypes of positive radical flank effects. One of these occurs when the radicalization of an established organization — such as the Congress of Racial Equality or the Student Nonviolent Coordinating Committee — causes some of its outside supporters to defect to less extreme organizations. If this were to occur, increases in outside income to moderate groups would match decreases in outside income to radical groups. In other words, a fixed sum of total movement income would be redistributed. The second subtype, and the one which is more significant in theory, involves moderate income gains *in excess* of radical group losses. Here we have not merely a redistribution of a fixed sum of resources but also the infusion of new resources into moderate coffers in response to radicalization. My data indicate that this in fact occurred among civil rights organizations during the 1960s.

DATA

To examine the relationship between radical flank effects and financial support, I set out to gather detailed information on resource mobilization by major black movement organizations during the 1950s and the 1960s. The ideal data would include total income broken down by its sources for each year and each organization. No such data have been compiled by students of the civil rights movement. The authors of organizational histories (Carson, 1981; Meier and Rudwick, 1973; Parris and Brooks, 1971; St. James, 1958) and of more general works on the movement (Brisbane, 1974; Muse, 1968) have provided limited information on the funding of particular organizations. None of these sources, however, contains data that are sufficiently systematic, detailed, and complete for an examination of radical flank effects.

I have used McAdam's (1980, 1982) data on movement income, which he compiled, not to study radical flank effects, but to determine the usefulness of resource mobilization theory as an explanation of the civil rights movement. McAdam was unable to obtain much information from

---

2. Obviously, radical flank effects are not the only factor which might affect rates of resource mobilization. Decisions to contribute funds for collective action are complex, and a more complicated multivariate research design would be necessary in order to make truly confident propositions about radical flank effects on resource mobilization. Factors such as the state of the economy and the competition from other movements also need to be considered.

TABLE 1

Total Outside Income of Major Movement Organizations, 1952-1970

Year	NUL	NAACP	LDEF	SRC[a]	SCLC	CORE[k]	SNCC	Total Movement Income
1952	NA	NA	210,624[c]	27,495		4,604		
1953	NA	16,436	224,321[c]	35,735		5,989		
1954	NA	30,944	200,021	59,403		5,600		
1955	NA	40,606	NA	79,308		6,911		
1956	265,000[b]	NA	346,947	31,369		10,115[l]		
1957	265,000[b]	103,907	319,537	109,062	10,000[d]	15,506		823,012
1958	265,000[b]	90,679	315,081	138,274	10,000[d]	22,936		841,970
1959	265,000[b]	93,703	357,988	126,285	25,000[e]	55,324		923,000
1960	265,000[b]	103,838	489,540	139,106	54,756	130,609	5,000[o]	1,187,849
1961	257,000	96,936	560,808	NA[f]	193,168	213,248	14,000[o]	1,475,160
1962	572,000	81,547	669,427	168,247	197,565	244,034	71,927[p]	2,004,747
1963	1,221,000	251,579	1,197,204	161,311	728,172	437,043	302,894	4,299,203
1964	1,539,000	292,738	1,425,321	180,005	578,787	694,588	631,439[q]	5,341,848
1965	1,824,000	388,077	1,661,793	101,105	1,643,000[g]	677,785	637,736[q]	6,933,496
1966	2,201,000	597,425	1,695,718	NA[r]	932,000	400,000[m]	397,237[s]	6,324,485
1967	2,812,000	1,294,909	2,046,356	138,670	932,000[h]	280,000[n]	250,000[o]	7,753,935
1968	3,921,000	1,904,512	2,535,430	269,112	1,000,000[i]	250,000[n]	150,000[o]	10,030,054
1969	8,619,000	2,418,000	2,811,825	204,591	500,000[j]	670,000[n]	50,000[o]	15,273,416
1970	14,542,000	2,665,373	2,980,998	174,321	400,000[j]	210,000[n]	25,000[o]	20,997,692

Notes:

a. Data on the Southern Regional Council relate to the organization's general fund only. Surviving financial reports prior to 1964 do not list information on special projects. I have excluded special projects income from the figures for 1964 through 1970 to permit trend analyses. It should be kept in mind that this seriously deflates SRC income during the mid and late 1960s.

b. I could not find any information for the National Urban League prior to 1961. According to Parris and Brooks (1971:394), NUL income during the mid and late 1950s fluctuated between $209,000 and $315,000. In order to compute movement totals for those years, I have adopted the rather inelegant procedure of estimating yearly income midway between these two figures. The figure of $265,000 is a gross estimate only and should not be taken to mean that there were no changes in NUL income between 1956 and 1960.

c. This represents net income after fundraising expenses were deducted. LDEF financial reports for 1952 and 1953 do not list either fundraising expenses or gross income.

d. This is an impressionistic estimate of the SCLC's outside income derived from various primary and secondary materials.

e. This figure is an estimate based upon receipts for organizational contributions to the SCLC during 1959. The total rests upon my estimate that no more than $4,500 in individual contributions were received. During its early years, the SCLC received hundreds of individual contributions, most of which ranged from $2 to $5.

f. In order to derive a total movement income, I arbitrarily set SRC's outside income for 1961 at $140,000. This is probably somewhat lower than the actual figure, given the trend of preceding years.

g. This figure is an estimate. The SCLC's income data for fiscal year 1964-1965 are available only for the first ten months (83.3 percent) of that year. I reduced the total income for the year as reported in the final audit by 9.8 percent, which was the proportion of the previous year's total income which came from outside sources. This yielded an amended fiscal year 1965 estimated income of $1,409,335.40. This figure, in turn, was increased by 16.6 percent (the estimated income for the two remaining months) to produce the estimated figure shown.

h. This figure is an estimate which was derived from various partial financial reports. It may exclude a limited amount of income from benefit concerts, etc.

i. This figure is an estimate.

j. SCLC income estimates for 1969 and 1970 are adapted from McAdam (1982), by permission of the author.

k. CORE's fiscal year ran from June 1 to May 31. My examination of monthly and quarterly CORE financial reports yielded no reliable manner in which to adjust these figures to a calendar year basis.

l. This figure is an estimate based upon a percentage of total CORE income for 1956 of $12,000 as reported by Meier and Rudwick (1973:78). The percentage, 82 percent, is taken from the internal/external ratio of the previous year.

m. See Meier and Rudwick (1973).

n. CORE income figures for 1967 through 1970 are based upon estimates by McAdam (1982). Each, however, includes foundation grants located in my search through *Foundation News* (Haines, 1983). Consequently, the numbers are somewhat higher than McAdam's estimates, especially for 1969.

o. McAdam (1982:253).

p. The SNCC income for 1962 is taken from Student Nonviolent Coordinating Committee (N.d.).

q. These figures are estimates. I divided external income for 10 months of each year (which is all that has survived) by 10 to yield an estimated monthly average income. This is interpolated to yield the estimated yearly income.

r. SRC outside income for 1966 is missing. For purposes of producing a movement total, I arbitrarily set it at $101,105, the income of the previous year.

s. This estimate is based upon the same procedure used for 1964 and 1965, except that 1966 financial data are available for only seven months of that year. Actual income for the first seven months is $231,721.32. It is quite possible that the interpolating procedure inflates the total SNCC income for 1966, since the black power slogan was born in the summer of that year.

primary sources such as organizational files and records. Consequently, he relied upon estimation and interpolation from incomplete secondary sources. In an effort to improve upon his data, I obtained financial information on major civil rights organizations during the period from 1952 through 1970, including two that he did not examine: the National Urban League and the Southern Regional Council.[3] I sought data for each of the following major black organizations active during the 1950s and the 1960s: Congress of Racial Equality (CORE); NAACP Legal Defense and Educational Fund, Inc. (LDEF); National Association for the Advancement of Colored People (NAACP); National Urban League (NUL); Southern Christian Leadership Conference (SCLC); Southern Regional Council (SRC); and Student Nonviolent Coordinating Committee (SNCC).

In 1981 I wrote to each of the organizations which still existed — all of them except SNCC, which had disappeared by 1972 — requesting the necessary information. Only the National Urban and the Southern Regional Council provided the data. I subsequently examined the financial records of the NAACP and the Legal Defense and Eduational Fund at their respective headquarters in New York City. I obtained partial funding data on the Southern Christian Leadership Conference, the Congress of Racial Equality, and the Student Nonviolent Coordinating Committee at the Martin Luther King Library and Archives in Atlanta, Georgia.

My attempt to improve upon McAdam's data yielded mixed results. I was unable to obtain even total outside income from some organizations during certain years — for the National Urban League before 1961, for the NAACP in 1956, for the Legal Defense and Educational Fund in 1955, and for the Southern Regional Council in 1966. The Southern Christian Leadership Conference and the Congress of Racial Equality refused to divulge their financial records, thus forcing me to rely upon sometimes incomplete archival material.[4] In general, I obtained the best data from those organizations most commonly designated as moderate: the NUL, the LDEF, the NAACP, and the SRC. Fortunately, these are the organizations whose incomes comprise the dependent variable for this research.

FINDINGS

Table 1 shows the total outside incomes of the major black organizations from 1952 to 1970.[5] The organizations are arranged from left to right according to their moderation/militancy over

---

3. For purposes extending beyond the topic of this paper, I also made a concerted effort to obtain figures that were broken down by the following donor categories: (1) government agencies; (2) corporations and other business firms; (3) charitable foundations; (4) labor organizations; (5) churches and religious organizations; (6) other types of organizations; (7) members, chapters, or branches (i.e., internal sources); and (8) non-member individual contributors (Haines, 1983).

4. The otherwise excellent collections of original SCLC and SNCC materials which are maintained at the Martin Luther King Library and Archives contain only incomplete financial information. Surviving materials of the Congress of Racial Equality are somewhat better, but post-1967 information is missing. Even those existing organizations which have generally maintained the most complete and detailed financial records have lost older material. The National Urban League is unable to locate financial reports for years prior to 1961. The SRC, the NAACP, and the LDEF have also lost financial records for a few years of the 1950–1970 period.

5. I used different approaches to determining outside income for each organization. The *National Urban League* provided yearly income totals derived from several categories of donors, including "affiliates dues," "special events," and "other." I eliminated these three categories, leaving only income derived from strictly external sources. Income for the *Southern Regional Council* was taken directly from financial reports supplied by the SRC and the Atlanta University Archives. SRC figures appearing in Table 1 include "contributions from SRC members and friends" but do not include "members dues," fees, sales, subscriptions, and the like. Miscellaneous outside income, such as honoraria and overhead from grants, is included. In calculating the *NAACP's* outside income, McAdam (1980:52) merely subtracted regular branch memberships from total organizational income. I used a more conservative approach, excluding all receipts from branches and miscellaneous income such as interest and dividends. For the *Legal Defense and Educational Fund*, I subtracted interest and dividends as well as the proceeds from the sale of securities. The *Southern Christian Leadership Conference* is not a membership organization, and from what little I could find out about the group's

305

the years; e.g., the National Urban League has long been the most moderate of the groups, while SNCC was the most militant. The Southern Christian Leadership Conference and SNCC were founded in 1957 and 1960, respectively. Data for the National Urban League (1952 through 1955) and the NAACP (1956) were not available. Therefore, I restrict my discussion and analysis to the years 1957 through 1970.

Two characteristics of the data in Table 1 deserve attention. First, the older, more established, and generally more moderate organizations—the National Urban League, the NAACP, and the Legal Defense and Educational Fund—received more outside income than other groups which were younger and more militant. Secondly, the incomes of the NUL, the NAACP, and the LDEF grew steadily during the 1960s. The incomes of the SCLC, CORE, and SNCC, on the other hand, grew rapidly during the early 1960s and then rapidly declined during the second half of the decade. Total movement income, however, increased steadily after 1957. (Combined totals for 1952 through 1956 are unavailable due to the lack of National Urban League figures for those years). With the exception of 1966, total movement income never failed to increase. During the 1950s, total income remained relatively constant.[6] During the early 1960s, and especially in 1963, it began to grow rapidly. Spectacular leaps occurred in 1963, 1969, and 1970.

Table 2 shows the relative magnitude of income growth for each of the seven organizations and for the movement as a whole. The greatest increase, 114.5 percent, occurred in 1963. Aside from that year, the greatest proportionate increases occurred at the end of the 1960s.

Table 3 shows the distribution of the total movement's outside income among the seven organizations. The National Urban League and the Legal Defense and Educational Fund received the largest shares of outside income during the late 1950s and the early 1960s. The LDEF received the most outside funding in 1957. By 1970, its share had declined considerably, but its raw income had not (Table 1). The NAACP's share of outside income declined during the late 1950s and early 1960s but recovered somewhat during the middle part of the 1960s. Most astonishing of all, however, is the National Urban League's staggering increase, especially during the late 1960s, when it became the financial giant of black collective action. All of the more militant organizations—the Southern Christian Leadership Conference, the Congress of Racial Equality, and the Student Nonviolent Coordinating Committee—increased their shares of total movement income during the early 1960s, then entered a period of decline.

These changes in organizational shares of total movement income may be understood largely in terms of shifts in major sources of funding which took place during the 1960s. Unpublished analyses I have made of the data on which this paper is based (Haines, 1983, 1984) suggest that *elite* contributors became vastly more important money sources for moderate black organizations during the second half of the decade. Among these elite contributors were corporations, foundations, and the federal government.

306

---

methods of fundraising, I think I can safely assume that little error results from treating all of its income as exogenous. I have done so for the most part, although funds of a clearly internal nature have been eliminated from the data when identified. The *Congress of Racial Equality's* financial records make it difficult to distinguish accurately between income from internal and external sources. In most cases, for example, local CORE chapters were not set apart from other, non-CORE organizations, and their meager contributions to national CORE's coffers were simply lumped into the "organizations" category. Nevertheless, CORE chapters were notorious for their reluctance to contribute to the national office, so little is lost, I believe, in subtracting convention income, sales, and the like from outside income. *Student Nonviolent Coordinating Committee* records are even less specific than those of CORE, and I used a nearly identical procedure to determine SNCC's outside income.

6. The characterization of the 1950s trend as relatively constant suffers, of course, from my lack of an absolute baseline. While I lack estimates of the incomes of the National Urban League and the NAACP for 1952, I believe it is reasonable to estimate total movement outside income for that year is not more than $450,000 (Table 1). Assuming that this were true, the proportionate increase between 1952 and 1957 would have been nearly 83 percent. Such a growth rate over six years is not inconsiderable, yet the total amounts are so small in comparison to later years that the increases seem unspectacular.

TABLE 2

Annual Rate of Growth in Outside Income, As A Percentage of Preceding Year[a]

Year	NUL	NAACP	LDEF	SRC[b]	SCLC	CORE	SNCC	Total Movement
1952								NA
1953	NA	NA	6.5	30.0		30.1		NA
1954	NA	88.2	NA	66.2		-6.5		NA
1955	NA	31.2	NA	33.5		23.4		NA
1956	NA	NA	NA	-60.5		46.4		NA
1957	NA	NA	-7.9	247.7	NA	53.3		NA
1958	NA	-12.7	-1.4	26.8	0.0	47.9		2.3
1959	NA	3.3	13.6	-8.7	150.0	141.2		9.7
1960	NA	10.8	36.7	10.2	119.0	136.1		28.7
1961	-3.0	-6.6	14.6	NA	252.8	63.3	180.0	24.2
1962	122.6	-15.9	19.4	NA	2.3	14.4	414.6	35.9
1963	113.5	208.5	78.8	-4.1	268.6	79.1	321.1	114.5
1964	26.0	16.4	19.1	11.6	-20.5	58.9	108.5	24.3
1965	18.5	32.6	16.6	-43.8	183.9	-2.4	1.0	29.8
1966	20.7	53.9	2.0	NA	-43.3	-41.0	-37.7	-8.8
1967	27.8	116.7	20.8	NA	0.0	-30.0	-37.1	22.6
1968	39.4	47.0	23.9	94.1	7.3	-10.7	-40.0	29.4
1969	119.8	27.0	10.9	-24.0	-50.0	168.0	-66.7	52.3
1970	68.7	10.2	6.0	-14.8	-20.0	-68.7	-50.0	37.5

Notes:

a. Based on data in Table 1.

b. General fund only.

307

TABLE 3

Distribution of Outside Income As A Percentage of Total Movement Income[a]

Year	NUL	NAACP	LDEF	SRC	SCLC	CORE	SNCC	Total
1957	32.2	12.6	38.8	13.3	1.2	1.9		100
1958	31.5	10.8	37.4	16.4	1.2	2.7		100
1959	28.7	10.1	38.8	13.7	2.7	6.0		100
1960	22.3	8.7	41.2	11.7	4.6	11.0	0.4	100
1961	17.4	6.6	38.0	9.5[b]	13.1	14.5	0.9	100
1962	28.5	4.1	33.4	8.4	9.9	12.2	3.6	100
1963	28.4	5.9	27.8	3.8	16.9	10.2	7.0	100
1964	28.8	5.5	26.7	3.4	10.8	13.0	11.8	100
1965	26.3	5.6	24.0	1.5	23.7	9.8	9.2	100
1966	34.8	9.4	26.8	1.6[b]	14.7	6.3	6.3	100
1967	36.3	16.7	26.4	1.8	12.0	3.6	3.2	100
1968	39.1	19.0	25.3	2.7	10.0	2.5	1.5	100
1969	56.4	15.8	18.4	1.3	3.3	4.4	0.3	100
1970	69.2	12.7	14.2	0.8	1.9	1.0	0.1	100

Notes:

a. Derived from the data in Table 1.

b. Based on estimated outside income.

Corporations were rather slow in becoming supporters of black collective action, but their involvement grew as the movement entered its nonviolent collective action phase around 1960. But business contributions became truly large only after successive summers of urban rioting

(Cohn, 1970). While several black organizations benefitted from corporate donations after 1967 (Cohn, 1970:73), the National Urban League provides perhaps the best illustration. In 1962, such contributions amounted to only $153,000. By 1970, they had risen to $1,973,000 (Haines, 1984:18). Similarly, Cohn (1970) reports that the NAACP received considerable amounts from corporate sources after 1967, but I can provide no independent verification of this due to the lack of such information in its Annual Reports.

Foundations also played an increased role in funding black organizations during the 1960s. As the black struggles of the 1960s progressed and as the militancy of the black population grew, foundation contributions became major sources of income for the National Urban League, the Southern Regional Council, and the Legal Defense and Educational Fund — all moderate organizations. In 1970, these three received an estimated total of $7,143,534 in foundation gifts, up from $1,461,264 in 1964 (Haines, 1984:23). Not only was more money directed by foundations to moderate black groups as the decade wore on, but more foundations became involved and a much higher number of individual grants were made. On all of these dimensions, the increases in foundation involvement in funding black collective action and related activities far outpaced the *overall* expansion of foundation activity which occurred during the same time span (Haines, 1984:30–32).

308

One of the moderate organizations, the National Urban League, became the recipient of large amounts of federal government money during the late 1960s. While these funds were for NUL-run programs for the disadvantaged, not "contributions" in the conventional sense of the word, they were nevertheless unique among the seven major organizations and deserve to be mentioned. No federal money was channeled through the NUL until 1965. During that year, the League received $294,000 from the U.S. government. By 1970, the total had risen to $6,913,000, and it topped $13,000,000 in 1970.

DISCUSSION

The most significant finding of the study is the dramatic increase in the level of outside funding for the civil rights movement as a whole during the 1960s (Table 1). Little increase in outside funding took place during the 1950s, when black radicalism was largely equated with litigation aimed at integration and when nonviolent protest was rare. But as nonviolent action became more frequent and intense during the early 1960s, outside funding accelerated. The year during which nonviolent direct action seems to have reached its dramatic zenith, 1963 (Burstein, 1979:169; Carson, 1981:90), was also the year of the steepest climb in outside income (Table 2). Outside supporters, it seems, were "discovering" civil rights. Income continued to climb until 1966, when it dropped for the first time. This was the year during which Stokely Carmichael of SNCC popularized the black power slogan. Ghetto rioting continued during the summer, drawing media attention. The income slump of 1966 probably reflected a decline in white support due to controversy surrounding the movement. It was, however, only a temporary setback for the movement as a whole. Total outside income resumed its upward spiral during the late 1960s. In fact, yearly proportionate increases for 1969 and 1970 surpassed all other years except 1963 (Table 2). In dollar amounts, these increases were unprecedented. Thus, it was clear that urban violence and black power did not have a negative radical flank effect, at least when measured by outside funding. On the contrary, the data suggest that there was a positive radical flank effect.

During the 1960s, and especially after 1966, three moderate organizations — the National Urban League, the Legal Defense and Educational Fund, and the NAACP — received increasingly greater shares of the movement's total outside funding. Not only did these three organizations suffer no financial backlash in the turbulent years of rioting and black nationalism, but their outside incomes rose more rapidly than ever before. The most moderate of the groups, the National Urban League, received a late-1960s windfall that was nothing less than astounding. Together, the

NUL, the LDEF, and the NAACP accounted for all of the aggregate increases in combined movement income by the end of the 1960s. The radical organizations, on the other hand, received rapid increases in outside income during the early 1960s followed by equally rapid declines during the era of the new militancy.

McAdam (1982:208) argues that the level of outside funding for the civil rights movement depended heavily upon the relative acceptability of the organizations involved in the struggle. This, of course, is what I have suggested and is quite consistent with the notion of positive radical flank effects. McAdam suggests that, as movement goals and tactics became more radical around 1965 and 1966, outside support groups came to see the NAACP as virtually the only acceptable recipient of funding. Consequently, the NAACP's outside income rose rapidly. While my procedures for distinguishing between the NAACP's outside and internal income differ from those employed by McAdam, my data bear out his conclusions about the NAACP's enhanced respectability. My data do suggest, however, that McAdam is wrong to conclude that the NAACP emerged from the fray of the mid 1960s as the *only* acceptable recipient of funding. To McAdam, the National Urban League did not qualify as "civil rights organization" and consequently he did not examine its income trends. Regardless of how sociologists classify the NUL, it clearly fit the bill as well as or better than the NAACP did in the eyes of many outside donors.

309

The shift in outside funding from 1965 to 1970 was more than a zero-sum shift within the community of movement organizations, as McAdam's discussion (1982:208) might be taken to imply. That is, it was not merely a case of a fixed amount of outside money being reallocated among a fixed number of recipients. On the contrary, there was a vast increase in total outside funding as well as a greater concentration of resources in the coffers of two moderate organizations. This is vitally important. Had such moderate organizations as the National Urban League, the NAACP, and the LDEF done no more than pick up the funds that CORE and SNCC (and, to a lesser degree, the SCLC) had forfeited by virtue of their militancy, we would not have a true positive radical flank effect as I have conceived it. Rather, we would simply have a case of an intra-movement shuffling of resources, consistent with the fixed-total subtype. My data suggests that the radicalization of some factions of the civil rights movement increased the total amount of outside financial contributions in a variable-total manner. This is precisely what we would expect a positive radical flank effect to do to the financial support structure of a movement.

CONCLUSION

I have analyzed trends in resource mobilization by major civil rights organizations in order to test the hypothesis of radical flank effects. Admittedly, the approach which I have used lacks many of the essential characteristics of a controlled investigation. But rather than formally testing an hypothesis, I have sought to examine how the data fit the models of positive and negative radical flank effects. This analysis yields three findings:

1. The total amounts of money contributed to the seven organizations by outsiders increased dramatically during the late 1950s and the 1960s. It peaked during the turbulent late 1960s.
2. The increases in total movement income, especially during the late 1960s, primarily reflected vast increases in the incomes of moderate groups.
3. The increased income of the moderate groups did not result from a mere reallocation of a fixed sum of resources within the movement. Rather, it involved the injection of large amounts of new money into the moderate groups. Most of this new money came from elite white groups, which became increasingly important sponsors of moderate civil rights activity.

These findings suggest that positive radical flank effects contributed significantly to increases in the outside funding of moderate civil rights organizations in the 1960s. The increasing importance of corporations, foundations, and the federal government, moreover, suggests that a portion of the nation's corporate elite recognized that it had a crucial interest in pacifying the black population, particularly in the volatile cities, and in accommodating certain manageable black demands. It also suggests that many previously uninvolved groups were "enlightened" by the glow of burning cities, after years of indifference to nonviolent cajoling by the National Urban League and the NAACP. Some whites came to realize that the integration of blacks into the U.S. mainstream was not such a bad idea after all, that it was in their own best interests given the more radical alternatives, and that it was something they ought to be encouraging with their resources. The prime beneficiaries of such changes of heart were the big moderate groups, the very organizations that had become most concerned with an impending white backlash. Certainly, a white backlash did occur. But the data presented in this paper suggest that, beneath it all, there was occurring an important acceptance and facilitation of "reasonable" black activism and that the effort would not have been made without the progressive radicalization of large numbers of blacks in the United States.

310

This conclusion suggests a new question: are radical flank effects unique features of the black revolt, or might they be overlooked but critical factors in numerous social movements? I strongly suspect that they affected the course of the U.S. labor movement, and they may have been involved in the ill-fated campaign for the Equal Rights Amendment. The difficulties in identifying positive and negative radical flank effects with confidence are considerable. Financial data, which serves as a measure of only one limited dimension, may be difficult to find for other movements. But these difficulties are not insurmountable, and if we are to understand collective action more completely, we need to carry on the search for evidence of radical flank effects.

REFERENCES

Allen, Robert L.
1969   Black Awakening in Capitalist America: An Analytic History. Garden City, NY: Anchor Books.
Barkan, Steven E.
1979   "Strategic, tactical, and organizational dilemmas of the protest movement against nuclear power." Social Problems 27(1): 19–37.
Brisbane, Robert H.
1974   Black Activism: Racial Revolution in the United States, 1954–1970. Valley Forge, PA: Judson Press.
Burstein, Paul
1979   "Public opinion, demonstrations, and the passage of anti-discrimination legislation." Public Opinion Quarterly 43(2):157–162.
Carson, Clayborne
1981   In Struggle: SNCC and the Black Awakening of the 1960s. Cambridge, MA: Harvard University Press.
Cohn, Jules
1970   "Is business meeting the challenge of urban affairs?." Harvard Business Review 48(2):68–82.
Elinson, Howard
1966   "Radicalism and the Negro movement." Pp. 355–375 in Raymond J. Murphy and Howard Elinson (eds.), Problems and Prospects of the Negro Movement. Belmont, CA: Wadsworth.
Ewen Stuart
1976   Captains of Consciousness: Advertising and the Social Roots of the Consumer Culture. New York: McGraw-Hill.
Felsenthal, Carol
1982   "What went wrong in the ERA fight." Kansas City Star. July 4: sec. A, pp. 29, 32.
Freeman, Jo
1975   The Politics of Women's Liberation. New York: McKay.
Gamson, William A.
1975   The Strategy of Social Protest. Homewood, IL: Dorsey.
Goldstone, Jack A.
1980   "The weakness of organization: A new look at Gamson's *The Strategy of Social Protest*." American Journal of Sociology 85(5):1017–1060.
Gurney, Joan M., and Kathleen J. Tierney
1982   "Relative deprivation and social movements: A critical look at twenty years of theory and research." The Sociological Quarterly 23(1):33–47.

Haines, Herbert H.
1983 "Radical flank effects and black collective action, 1954–1970." Unpublished Ph.D. dissertation, University of Kansas, Lawrence.
1984 "Crisis and elite support of social movements: The case of civil rights." Paper presented at the annual meetings of the Midwest Sociological Society, Chicago, Illinois, April 18.
Hough, J.C.
1968 Black Power and White Protestants: A Christian Response to the New Negro Pluralism. New York: Oxford.
Jenkins, J. Craig, and Charles Perrow
1977 "Insurgency of the powerless: Farm worker's movements (1946–1972)." American Sociological Review 42(2):249–268.
Killian, Lewis M.
1972 "The significance of extremism in the black revolution." Social Problems 20(1):41–48.
Lipsky, Michael
1968 "Protest as a political resource." American Political Science Review 62(4):1144–1158.
McAdam, Doug
1980 "The generation of insurgency and the black movement." Paper presented at the annual meetings of the American Sociological Association, New York, August.
1982 Political Process and the Development of Black Insurgency, 1930–1970. Chicago: University of Chicago Press.
McCarthy, John D., and Mayer N. Zald
1973 "The trend of social movements in America: Professionalization and resource mobilization." Morristown, NJ: General Learning Press.
1977 "Resource mobilization and social movements: A partial theory." American Journal of Sociology 82(6):1212–1241.
Masotti, Louis H., Jeffrey K. Hadden, Kenneth F. Seminatore, and Jerome R. Corsi
1969 A Time to Burn? An Evaluation of the Present Crisis in Race Relations. Chicago: Rand-McNally.
Meier, August
1965 "On the role of Martin Luther King." New Politics 4(Winter):52–59.
Meier, August, and Elliot Rudwick
1973 C.O.R.E.: A Study in the Civil Rights Movement, 1942–1968. New York: Oxford.
Muse, Benjamin
1968 The American Negro Revolution: From Nonviolence to Black Power. Bloomington: Indiana University Press.
Nye, Russel B.
1963 Fettered Freedom: Civil Liberties and the Slavery Question, 1830–1860. Lansing: Michigan State University Press.
Oberschall, Anthony
1973 Social Conflict and Social Movements. Englewood Cliffs, NJ: Prentice-Hall.
Parris, Guichard, and Lester Brooks
1971 Blacks in the City: A History of the National Urban League. Boston: Little, Brown.
Piven, Frances, and Richard A. Cloward
1977 Poor People's Movements: Why They Succeed, How They Fail. New York: Vintage.
1978 "Social movements and societal conditions: A response to Roach and Roach." Social Problems 26(2):172–178.
Powledge, Fred
1967 Black Power, White Resistance: Notes on the New Civil War. Cleveland: World.
Ramirez, Bruno
1978 When Workers Fight: The Politics of Industrial Relations in the Progressive Era, 1898–1916. Westport, CT: Greenwood.
Rayback, Joseph G.
1966 A History of American Labor. New York: Free Press.
St. James, Warren D.
1958 The National Association for the Advancement of Colored People: A Case Study in Pressure Groups. New York: Exposition Press.
Student Nonviolent Coordinating Committee
N.d. "You can help support programs for SNCC." Mimeographed pamphlet. Martin Luther King Library and Archives, Atlanta, GA.
Tilly, Charles
1978 From Mobilization to Revolution. Reading, MA: Addison-Wesley.

Cases Cited

Brown v. Board of Education, 347 U.S. 483, 1984.
Plessy v. Ferguson, 163 U.S. 537, 1896.

Albany, Georgia

By Vincent Harding and Staughton Lynd

AT this writing, certain things seem clear about the situation in Albany, Ga. The federal government has miserably and disgracefully failed in its duty of protecting the elementary civil rights of the Negro citizens of Albany. After its dramatic attempt to secure total freedom all at once by mass marches on City Hall, the Albany Movement has reverted to more conventional tactics: legal suits for desegregation of schools and public facilities, and voter registration. Although the Movement has thus far failed to achieve any of its tangible goals, the spirit of the Negro community in Albany has been transformed and morale is high.

These big facts are made up many

VINCENT HARDING is directing community service activities for the Mennonite Church in Atlanta, Georgia, while completing his Ph. D. dissertation. He has spent at least one week a month in Albany since December 1961, including four days spent in the city jail.

STAUGHTON LYND teaches history at Spelman College in Atlanta. His article, "Freedom Riders to the Polls," appeared in *The Nation*, July 28, 1962.

of "little" facts: facts about bullets fired into homes which missed sleeping children by inches; about white men (including public officials) who assaulted Albany Negroes, tell F.B.I. agents and reporters "I'll do it again," but are permitted to remain at large; about students of the Student Non-Violent Coordinating Committee living, like the early Christians, on the free-will offerings of the families they are helping; facts about songs; facts about jails; facts about jobs.

What do the facts mean? As the Albany Movement moves into a quieter phase, many people lie awake at nights wondering, with anguish, what the last twelve months in Albany have meant. What have they meant to the Negro community, so many of whose families have lost jobs and savings in the course of the Movement? What have these months meant to the white community: how much are they disturbed by business losses, and by the destruction of Albany's image as a forward-looking town congenial to new industry?[1] What has Albany meant to the individuals and organizations from other parts of the nation who have attempted to provide support and counsel for the local Movement?

313

What has the Movement meant to the Negro population of the counties surrounding the Albany trading center: "terrible" Terrell County, "bad" Baker County, and the rest?

It is probably too early to answer these questions with confidence. But it is not too soon to draw some pointed conclusions about the failure of the federal government, as our friend and colleague Dr. Howard Zinn has done in his report for the Southern Regional Council.[2] Perhaps, too, it is time to make some tentative evaluations of the different forms of protest that have been used at Albany. Life in the midst of the broad sweep of a revolution is most dangerous for the historian, especially if he senses within himself a calling beyond that of recording and interpreting events. Such a life is dangerous because it catches him up in the temptation to make generalizations at least as large and as broad as the movement itself. With this caveat and confession, we offer our view of the meaning of the Albany protest for the larger civil rights movement.

The word "protest" comes from the Latin root *protestari*, to declare publicly. The Albany Movement has expressed itself through ten forms of protest or public witness: freedom rides; marches; jail-ins; boycotts; picketing; prayer vigils; sit-ins; legal action; voter registration; and mass meetings. Obviously, the full inventory of protest techniques developed by the civil rights movement has been brought to bear in this one Deep South locality.

The *freedom ride* was not a major form of protest in Albany. Rather, the arrest of freedom riders at the Albany railroad depot in December 1961 served as a spark to ignite the growing dissatisfaction within the Negro community over the stringent segregation in their city, and over the adamant refusal of the city commissioners to take action on apparently reasonable requests from Negro representatives. But in demonstrating that Albany's police force and city government were actually obstructing the right of Negroes to make use of the bus teminal, thereby disobeying the ruling of the Federal Interstate Commerce Commission, the freedom riders exposed the illegality and hypocrisy of the entire segregation policy of the Albany city fathers.

CRITICIZED ASPECT

The most criticized aspect of this form of protest is that freedom riders blaze into a town, upset its peace and tranquility, throw it into confusion, and then leave, sharing none of the long range burdens, experiencing none of the permanent scars. It was different in Albany. The first tests of the I.C.C. ruling, in November, were by students from local Albany State College, and two Albany State students were among the eleven riders arrested on December 10. The other riders were mainly S.N.V.C.C. workers, active in Albany voter registration before the rides and still at it today. In fact, the Negro community had been sensitized, and the freedom ride proved to be just what they needed to begin a major campaign for freedom. One of Albany's most vituperative attackers of "outside agitators" finally confided to an author of this article

314

that it was likely the city would not have made any move towards change if the so-called outsiders had not ridden into town. Here then was a case in which the local Negro leadership was able to make use of creative tension and to capitalize on the shattering of the old "peace and tranquility."

This unique situation does not, of course, destroy the force of the basic criticism that the freedom rides have an element of irresponsibility about them. Nor does it begin to answer what seems to us at least as important a question: How justified are men and women in leaving their own brand of segregation behind, untouched and unchallenged, and going to challenge their neighbors' variety? (This is not to suggest, of course, that such a charge can be brought against all the persons who participate in the freedom rides.) Finally, it appears that a key problem of freedom ride activity is that it is necessarily a vanguard movement, usually involving persons who do not ordinarily use the facilities in question. Therefore, it is often the case that when the right to full use has been established, sometimes at the cost of no little blood and pain, the larger Negro community is not at all prepared to make use of the dearly-won prize, largely because they themselves did not take part in the particular struggle.

By contrast, the *mass marches* drew a far larger group into a protest activity which demanded the giving of their whole selves. At the same time that the young people of Albany State College and S.N.V.C.C. were beginning to protest through freedom rides, the adult Albany Movement was forming. It was a coalition of previously-existing groups, one of them a neighborhood association which had pressed for the paving of streets in Albany's "Harlem." The leaders were for the most part young, college-trained professionals. By the time the riders came to trial in mid-December, the appropriate action had been agreed upon. On the day of the trial, some thirty persons came to City Hall to kneel and pray on the steps of this building where the court room was located. They were arrested. The next day more than 150 persons marched around City Hall in further protest. They too were arrested. After another day of marching and arrests, there were close to 400 persons in jail.

PUBLIC DEMONSTRATIONS

Then Dr. William Anderson, Albany osteopath and president of the Movement, called upon Martin Luther King, his personal friend, to come down from Atlanta and bring his worldwide leadership and prestige to the cause. King decided to come, but before he arrived, another hundred or so persons had marched. Finally, Martin King and Ralph Abernathy led 200 persons, singing "We Shall Overcome" across Oglethorpe Ave. and into jail. By December 18, when an agreement was reached (or seemed to have been reached) with the white power structure, Chief of Police Laurie Pritchett had made more than 700 arrests to stop the marches.

Marching gave the Negro people of Albany an alternative to the self-defeating ways of fearful acquie-

315

scence and bitter, underhanded revenge. Now they were able to offer a public demonstration of those deeply-felt longings within them, those groans that could not earlier be uttered. The first (approximately) 300 marchers did not know they would be jailed. Those who came after did know it: more and more they believed themselves as they walked down the street toward the police singing "we are not afraid, we are not afraid today." The marchers included children as young as nine and adults as old as seventy. All observers agree that the outlook of the Albany Negro community can never be again as it was before December 1961, and the decision of hundreds of ordinary citizens to march and to endure jail is without question the fundamental reason for this new dignity and courage.

The marches in Albany also served the purpose of addressing an open letter to the white citizens of the town. The marches were an attempt to let the whites know that Negroes were not as satisfied as some of the maids and yardmen led them to believe, and that Albany's Negro citizens were seeking not for revenge but for that mutual respect which must precede all reconciliation.

Of course, it was not to the local white community alone that the marches were directed. Martin Luther King told a mass meeting one night before a march that they had seen justice denied in a local court, and now they must raise their case before the court of world opinion. Like the freedom rides, the marches dramatized the situation, and brought international publicity. The need for this world-wide attention must not be denied, of course, for Albany is not an island and Georgia (despite campaign speeches to the contrary) is not a sovereign state. However, in Albany there were more than a few times when the presence of thirty or forty newsmen induced too great a concern for press deadlines, and too eager a practice of calling the press to inform them of each move. Inquisitive reporters left the Negro leaders inadequate time for the reflecton and planning which the situation demanded. Moreover, the understandable concern for national and world-wide publicity tended to push aside one of the basic understandings of non-violence: that in the struggle against an evil system, one must always assume that the proponents and supporters of the system are in possession of conscience and so capable of change. Instead, Albany's leaders seemed at times to pay little attention to the local white community, with which, in the end, the Negro people of Albany would have to find a way to live.

PURPOSE OF JAIL-INS

The *jail-ins*, too, were both inner —and outer—directed. Going to jail served the obvious utilitarian purpose of concentrating public attention on the situation, especially since hundreds were willing to go and since Martin Luther King was one of their cellmates. In the case of Albany, "public attention" often meant the attention of Washington, D.C., or the attention of persons who could bring pressure to bear on Washington, which might in turn lead to pressure on Albany. One cannot deny the efficiency of this aspect of the jail-in, particularly in view of the regular phone calls that passed between Washington and · Albany while Dr. King was there, and especially while he was in jail.

However, this willingness on the part of Negroes to participate in protest activities which were certain to lead to jail, produced certain inner effects no less important. In a middle-class-minded society, which looks on jail as an evil to be avoided, the willingness to go to jail for cause tells an important story. There were times in Albany when the stanza "we shall go to jail today" was added to "We Shall Overcome". Here was an expression of the new spirit which the sit-ins had announced. Negroes were learning to go to jail, sometimes with gladness, for conscience's sake. Jailing was one of the ultimate threats which the Albany police could bring against Albany Negroes in the effort to maintain segregation, and now hundreds of Albany's Negroes were not cringing in the face of that terror. This was one of the most disquieting things to the police in the whole Albany situation. One of the writers will never forget the strange, thoughtfully troubled look that came to the face of a policeman as a group of young Negroes sat calmly behind bars one evening and sang with assurance, "no more segregation, no more segregation, no more segregation over me." The act of going to jail became not only a means of exhibiting the Negroes' determination, but also a method of building up that resolve within them. Moreover, the experience of jail itself — sometimes with sixteen or more persons in a call made for four — helped many persons to experience the sense of a joyful, suffering *koinonoia*' that they had never known in any church.

The jail-in, like every other form of protest, presented characteristic problems. One was the tendency for jail-going to degenerate from a creative form of courageous protest to a means of spiteful defiance. Secondly, many — perhaps most — of the persons who went to jail in Albany were not prepared for the rigors of a prolonged stay, and in some cases their enthusiasm was actually lost as a result of having to undergo much more discomfort or even suffering than they had expected. Finally, one of the most subtle problems of the whole jail-going movement is the constant temptation to measure a man's courage and worth by the number of times he has gone to jail. This "martyr measurement" leads people to forget that not everyone is called to this particular way of witness, and can trap persons into what T. S. Eliot calls "the greatest treason: doing the right thing for the wrong reason."

FUNCTION OF BOYCOTTS

Although the marches and jail-ins attracted hundreds of Albany's Negroes, the most broadly-based part of their protest consisted of various *boycotts*. The boycott on the city buses was begun when the verbal agreement of December 18 between the city commissioners and those leaders of the Albany Movement still out of jail — the agreement which brought the marches and jail-ins to an end until the following July —

317

broke down. The bus boycott (like its famous Montgomery predecessor) grew out of the Negroes' dissatisfaction with segregated seating and with the bus company's failure to provide jobs for Negro drivers, in spite of the fact that at least 90 per cent of its passengers were Negroes. By the end of December the basic justification for the boycott ended when the bus company agreed to desegregate its seating and to hire at least one Negro driver. Then the Albany Movement tried to get a written agreement from the city that it would not interefere with bus desegregation. The city commissioners balked at this. The bus company's offer was then rejected and the boycott continued, becoming essentially a secondary boycott in its attempt to get the company to bring pressure on the commissioners. Finally the company stopped operation.

During December, a boycott was placed on downtown stores. This was a secondary boycott from the outset. Moreover, there was no sustained attempt to speak to the business people before the boycott was initiated, or while it was going on. Today, after twelve months, the boycott is estimated to be 50-75 per cent effective. But the Negro trade is not quite important enough to constitute real economic leverage, and the retail merchants are in any case not so influential in the city's power structure as the Movement at first supposed. On the whole, the boycott has failed in its actual purpose of influencing the city commissioners. The white community of Albany regards the boycott as an unexplained, unprovoked attempt to hurt the city's economy.

In Albany, *picketing* and *sit-ins* were used primarily to supply material for an omnibus suit against segregation of public facilities. Since one of the fundamental strategic mistakes of the Albany Movement was its delay in launching such a suit, picketing and sit-ins were not prominent until the summer. There were sporadic sit-ins during the six-month lull between December and July, a period which Albany students remember as a time when a white policeman killed a Negro and white hoodlums laughed at the funeral, and as a time when young Negroes wore blue jeans to Easter services as a token of solidarity with the boycott.

The *prayer vigil* has more often been used in the peace movement than in the civil rights movement. In Albany, the prayer vigil was one of the first forms of public protest, but was not used again until this summer, when three or four groups followed Dr. King's example in praying in front of city hall for an opening of negotiations. In all but one instance they were arrested. A dramatic variation of the prayer vigil occurred on the night of July 21, when in defiance of a federal injunction the Rev. Samuel Wells led over 150 persons toward city hall and, when commanded by Chief Pritchett to go back, dropped on his knees in prayer.

Here was a way in which the deep resources of non-violent declaration and the ritual of the Christian church could be brought together. Here was a means by which the worship of the sanctuary could be brought boldly into the midst of the world. Indeed on one occasion when such a vigil was held in front of City Hall, one of the older sisters "got happy," as they say, and responded to the spirit just as if she were praying in the aisle of the Shiloh Baptist Church. For others it was difficult to pray genuinely with a policeman at one's elbow, and the prayer vigil was ever in danger of becoming simply a coercive technique or a publicity measure. At is best, though, the prayer vigil demonstrated a tremendous potential. The police found it most difficult to deal with such a form of protest, especially when the group knelt on the sidewalk with some persons refusing to rise even after arrest. They were praying and would not be moved.

LEGAL ACTION

To turn from the prayer vigil to *legal action* is seemingly to enter an entirely different sphere. The tension between church-centered and court-centered activity is the deepest tension within the civil rights movement. It is a real tension, not (as so often declared on public occasions) merely a clash of organizations, generations or personalities, or an artificial creation of the segregationists. For the coercion which underlies any legal system *is* essentially alien to a Christian philosophy of moral conversion and long-suffering love. We do not pretend to have an answer for this fundamental dilemma. Indeed, the observer of Albany is forced to the perplexing conclusion that the Movement's initial reliance on direct action alone (as exemplified by Dr. King's statement that "we will wear them down with our suffering") led to over-long

delay in resorting to the courts; but that, at the same time, a persistent weakness of the Albany Movement has been its failure to confront the whites of Albany directly and personally. (Dr. Anderson's appearance in July over a local television network was a happy exception to this generalization, but was not adequately followed up.)

From the outset, the white politicians of Albany have said that the Negroes should go through the courts rather than engaging in direct action. This may be a plea simply to take the city out of the limelight and off the spot: to give segregation more time to live. Albany's failure to act on the Supreme Court's school desegregation decision of 1954 and on the I.C.C.'s bus desegregation ruling of 1961 lend strong support to such an interpretation. On the other hand, Albany officials may be asking for the courts to force them to do what they know they must do eventually: one commissioner in Albany has come so far as to praise N.A.A.C.P. for believing in "due process as opposed to those direct action groups who want, he said, "to short-cut everything." Perhaps the critical factor in evaluating the role of legal action is the assumption one makes about what happens when individuals or groups are forced by outside power to do what they know to be right. Many studies of compulsory desegregation in the Army, in public housing projects, and in the National Maritime Union seem to show that when discrimination is forcibly halted, prejudice in time dies away. The argument on the other side is that the efficacy of law

319

in Albany depends on general acceptance from the community, and that both historical experiences like Reconstruction (as C. Vann Woodward, the most eminent historian of the South, argues) and the teaching of Jesus (as the philosophers of nonviolence emphasize) go to show that such acceptance cannot be forced.

There is yet another problem. involvled in reliance on the courts. Such legal action as an omnibus suit involves relatively few persons in direct participation. Out of this lack of participation there can grow the phenomenon mentioned in connection with the freedom rides: a lack of broad, community- based response to the opportunities made available by the courts. The whole movement is thrown open to the charge, You see the Negroes really didn't want desegregation.

NEED FOR PROTEST

Perhaps these ambiguities surrounding legal action simply underline the need for protest to go on at every level, involving as many persons as possible, and using whatever openings are available. Dr. King has written that while in jail in Albany last July he became convinced of the need for such a "four-pronged approach" to the city's problems: the four prongs are legal action, direct action, economic boycott and voter registration.[5]

Of the four, as Dr. King stressed in a September 18 talk to the Southern Christian Leadership Conference, *voter registration* now seems the most important. S.C.L.C. asserts that the registered Negro vote in Al-

bany has doubled during 1962. It believes that the larger Negro vote had much to do with moderate Carl Sanders' victory in Dougherty County in the September 12 Georgia Democratic primary. Dr. King and S.C.L.C. believe further that the increased Negro vote in Albany has already produced some softening in the city's attitude, and that this trend will continue.

One of us has discussed elsewhere the double-edged sword which the new emphasis on voter registration and political action presents to the civil rights movement.[6] It is beyond question that the mere existence of a sizeable block of registered Negro voters tends to restrain police brutality, as Myrdal long ago pointed out.[7] There also appears to be a definite correlation between the size of the Negro vote and the degree to which desegregation can be carried out smoothly and peacefully.

Yet the lasting significance of Albany may be that there a Deep South Negro community glimpsed the possibility of a truly free America, of what *The Crisis* had recently called "Final victory";[8] and from this standpoint, voter registration must be viewed as only the preliminary to a creative and comprehensive *use* of the vote. Using the ballot merely to hold the balance between two inadequate candidates, to settle for a perennial choice between the lesser of two evils, to go no farther than "rewarding one's friends and punishing one's enemies," is not enough. Even running independent Negro candidates is not enough. The civil rights movement must begin to envision the use of the vote to produce the comprehensive social changes—including not only civil rights but also, for example, the creation of more jobs—which are required to produce real freedom for all citizens.

The witness of Albany is to the necessity of final victory and total freedom. When Albany leaders rejected the possibility of bus desegregation they may have made a tactical blunder, but in another viewpoint they were saying: Montgomery is no longer enough for us. "If you ever want freedom, now is the time," speakers told the crowds in the packed churches in early July. However much the movement at large may differ from the Albany Movement in tactics, it must keep faith with Albany by hewing steadfastly to the goal of total freedom, right now. (For in the words of the Talmud: If not now, when?)

This freedom, this community, this brotherhood unconscious of skin color, has already existed in Albany in that form of protesting which throbs at the very heart of the Albany Movement: the *mass meeting*. One young Negro minister has characterized the weekly mass meeting in Albany as the gathering of the true church. For here men and women from the various denominations (and some with no formal affiliation) come to deal with the really burning issues of life. A prayer meeting led by some of the older women and men often forms the preliminary, and petitions are offered for mayor and police chief, for leaders and opposition, for the coming Kingdom of God. By the time the meeting really gets going anywhere from 500 to 1,000 persons have gathered, depending on the size of the church and the space available around the doors and windows outside. Then the singing begins in earnest. This is a form of protest in which all can participate: regardless of their fears, regardless of their economic vulnerability, they can sing. The singing must be experienced to be known.

Much is told in the words themselves as they rend the evening air. The main theme of freedom is set by the popular "Woke up this morning with my mind set on freedom." This firm resolve is reinforced when they almost shout out the words to a relatively new favorite, "Ain't gonna let nobody turn me around, keep on walking, keep on talking, marching to the freedom land." The new insights and new courage are seen in "This little light of mine," especially when they sing, "right in front of the City Hall I'm gonna let it shine," "all in the jail house I'm gonna let it shine."

Interspersed through the singing are several announcements, reports on the present status of the struggle, the collection for the movement, and always there is a main address, most often a sermon. Sometimes, if this is a special night or day, the mass meeting provides the occasion for the miracle of the Word become flesh. For there has been more than one mass meeting in which the preacher has exhorted the soldiers of freedom, calling them to march for the cause of justice and truth, and they have answered, "We are able." Then in that very moment, instead of a closing organ postlude and the polite shaking of hands, both preacher and a goodly part of the

321

flock have taken up the marching song and streamed out of the church doors into the midst of the world, marching to jail for their freedom, and for the liberation of all their brothers, black and white.

As one sees the band of dark pilgrims marching out of the church doors singing, "We shall overcome," it is almost impossible not to believe them.

REFERENCES

1. It is significant that in the Georgia Democratic primary on Sept. 12, Dougherty County (in which Albany is located) voted for "moderate" Carl Sanders over segregationist Marvin Griffin, although all the counties adjoining Dougherty went for Griffin. The Sanders vote in Dougherty was twice as large as the number of registered Negro voters in the county.
2. Dr. Zinn's reports may be obtained from the Southern Regional Council, 41 Exchange Place, Atlanta, Ga.
3. *Koinonoia* is the word used in the Greek New Testament for "congregation" or "church." Near Americus, Georgia, an hour's drive north of Albany, is an interracial co-operative community which calls itself Koinonoia. In the mid-1950's the Koinonoia Cooperative Community was subjected to bombing and shooting, just as the Albany Movement is today, and Koinonoia has been virtually ruined financially by a white economic boycott which has lasted over six years.
4. For accounts of these studies, see, for example, Gordon W. Allport, *The Nature of Prejudice*, abridged ed. (New York, 1958), Chapter XVI; M. Collins and M. Deutsch, *Interracial housing: a psychological evaluation of a social experiment* (Minneapolis, 1951); S. W. Cook *et al.*, *Human relations in interracial housing: a study of the contact hypothesis* (Minneapolis, 1955); George E. Simpson and J. Milton Yinger, *Racial and Cultural Minorities: An Analysis of Prejudice and Discrimination*, second edition (New York, 1952), pp. 752, 780: Edward Suchman *et al., Desegregation: Some Propositions and Research Suggestions* (New York, 1958), 90, 107.
5. Entry for July 30, "Reverend M. L. King's Diary in Jail," *Jet*, Aug. 23, 1962, p. 18.
6. Staughton Lynd, "Freedom Riders to the Polls," *The Nation*, July 28, 1962.
7. Gunnar Myrdal. *An American Dilemma* (New York, 1944), 498-499.
8. Gloster B. Current, "53d Annual Convention," *The Crisis*, August-September 1962, p. 378: "final victory . . . will mean the wiping out of every vestige of second-class citizenship, tokenism, quotas, and percentages; abolition of the ghetto and all of its damaging ramifications into education, public accomodations and travel; erasure of the color line in employment and the substitution of competence; the destruction of government by color."

Dr. Harding, chairman of the Department of History and Social Science at Spelman College in Atlanta, was for several years southern representative of the Mennonite Service Committee, working in Atlanta. He is the author of MUST WALLS DIVIDE? published by Friendship Press, and articles on the southern scene in THE REPORTER, THE CHRISTIAN CENTURY, and other magazines.

WHERE HAVE ALL THE LOVERS GONE?

BY VINCENT HARDING

Reflections on the Nonviolent Movement in America

> *I speak Americans for your good. We must and shall be free I say, in spite of you. . . . And wo, wo, will be to you if we have to obtain our freedom by fighting.*
> —*David Walker (Boston Negro), in his APPEAL, 1829.*
> *Do to us what you will and we will still love you. . . . We will soon wear you down by our capacity to suffer.*
> —*Martin Luther King, Jr., STRIDE TOWARD FREEDOM, 1958.*
> *A black man has the right to do whatever is necessary to get his freedom. We will never get it by nonviolence.*
> —*Malcolm X, 1964, quoted in LIBERATION, February, 1965.*

Prologue: Will They Learn?

Sometimes it seems far more than a decade and sometimes it seems no longer than a fiercely stretched and searing day since a young, frightened and eloquent black preacher stood in the churches of Montgomery, Alabama and urgently called a determined Negro populace to fight evil with love. As those tens of thousands began their long walk of protest against the deeply entrenched injustice and humiliation of segregated buses, they were challenged with these words:

> Our actions must be guided by the deepest principles of our Christian faith. Love must be our regulating ideal. Once again we must hear the words of Jesus echoing across the centuries: "Love your enemies, bless them that curse you, and pray for them that despitefully use you. . . ." In spite of the mistreatment that we have confronted we must not become

bitter, and end up by hating our white brothers. . . . If we fail to do
this our protest will end up as a meaningless drama on the stage of history, and its memory will be shrouded with the ugly garments of shame.[1]

In these ardent, moving words were the convictions that had been delivered
up out of the man's own dark and solitary nights of turmoil and search. They
were the words that struck responsive chords in the minds and spirits of his Negro
listeners, and as he spoke, his words repeatedly brought forth impassioned outbursts of hope from trembling lives. Soon each intonation, each line was heard
throughout the wounded and broken communities of the South. Soon they seeped
into the weary ghettos of the North, finally pouring out to a world half cynical,
half wondering if this might indeed be the way.

In the minds of black and white men alike grim visions and somber dreams
were thrown against these words of hope. Memories of Nat Turner, images of the
carnage at Shilo and Antietam, sounds of hateful, fearful mobs, pictures of black
bodies swaying in the winds on lonely country roads or above exultant, guilt-torn
crowds—all these seemed too much to forget, to forgive, to overcome.

Still the black preacher preached on, and the people marched, and the court
finally ruled on their behalf. And when the deaths continued, when the oppression
seemed more devious but no less unrelenting, the young man born in the South
adopted the Indian saint as his own and cried out,

We will match your capacity to inflict suffering with our capacity to
endure suffering. We will meet your physical force with soul force. We
will not hate you, but we cannot . . . obey your unjust laws. Do to us
what you will and we will still love you. Bomb our homes and threaten
our children; send your hooded perpetrators of violence into our communities and drag us out on some wayside road, beating us and leaving
us half dead, and we will still love you. But we will soon wear you down
by our capacity to suffer. And in winning our freedom we will so appeal
to your heart and conscience that we will win you in the process.[2]

Soon a generation even younger than his own heard the call and moved into
the battle. Their language and convictions were not as outwardly Christian as
the prophet of Montgomery, but their personal commitment was no less complete.
As they sat at the counters and rode the buses, as they fell beneath the billy clubs
and sang in the jails, they too were hoping that this preacher of love was right
and they were willing to risk their lives on the gamble—at least for a time. A
new society might be worth a man's life.

Then in the midst of the tumult, among the community of white, hoping
wondering men—especially in the leader's own Southland—a question was raised
a haunting, agonizing question: "Will they learn to hate before we learn to love?"
The image of "they" was legion and yet one, and almost impossible to define
smiling, patient, loyal, devious, annoyingly shrewd, lazy, unctuous, happy, sad
fearful, and black. All of these, but not hateful, not yet. And the "we"? "We"
were ruling, cringing, domineering, fearful, superior, confused, patronizing, con
servative, and white. All these, but not loving, not yet.

It was a self-protective, anxious question, but it was also a question tha
revealed a painful courtship of hope. For it was surely true that some of th
questioners dreamed of a day when their unclaimed Montgomery brother woul
be proved right, when the crushing shell of their whiteness and their customs an
their possessions would be penetrated by the piercing shafts of love, and the

---

[1]Martin Luther King, Jr., *Stride Toward Freedom.* New York: Ballantine Books, 1958, p. 5!
[2]*Ibid.*, pp. 177-178.

would be "won" indeed. Passively, most often too passively, they waited, asking, almost fearing the answer, "Will they learn to hate? Will they?"

Now at the end of a decade of deaths and burnings, of victories and scarring overturnings, now with the echoes of Malcolm still in our ears and the flames of Watts dancing in the recesses of our minds, now the answer seems to be in. They have learned to hate and we have not learned to love; and the only real question seems to be, when will the ghettos of Atlanta and Birmingham hear the cries, "Burn, Whitey, Burn!"

After a ten year walk on the brink of hope is this our final answer? Has nonviolence lost its way in the American racial revolution? This essay pretends to no definitive answers, but represents rather a series of reflections which might provide a path toward some truth. Reflections are first in order on nonviolence in the Freedom Movement. Reflections are no less fitting on the anguished question concerning "we" and "they." Finally, reflections have no meaning without some attention to the grounds for future hope, resignation or despair.

325

Reflections, I: The Paradox of Success

As it began to be organized in Montgomery, this latest phase of American nonviolence grew up in paradox, no fertile ground for firm answers. (Among the first of paradoxes, of course, was the blooming of such a flower in the Cradle of the Confederacy, at the heart of the most militant section of the nation.) Only a moment's reflection on Montgomery suffices to force to the surface some of those fretful dilemmas that continued with the movement. For instance, all of the rhetoric and many of the convictions of those early days were framed against the background of that sublime fanaticism: "Love your enemies." When these words were originally spoken to the long aching hearts of an oppressed and noble people there were only two promises connected with them. One was acceptance as a son of God. The other was the cross. Through the life of the first Galilean speaker the two promises became coterminal.

In Montgomery, different promises were often made, promises of "victory" of "winning" the enemy, of achieving desegregation, of creating "the beloved community." Ghandi was joined to Christ for social relevance, and nonviolence became a "tool" in the civil rights campaign. In the minds of many men it was seen as one means of achieving some very tangible and necessary goals. It was an experiment with struggle, even in Montgomery, and it was clear that a majority of those who tried it were ready to turn to other means if it did not work.

For a time in the South it "worked." But even where tangible successes came forth they too were hedged in by paradox, and Montgomery was again a classic example. One aspect of the paradox of success there was partially resolved in advance by Martin Luther King when he spoke not of a boycott against the bus company, but of non-cooperation with evil. He said this was an imperative. No such delicate distinctions were made, however, by the walkers on the city's streets. Most of them had read neither Thoreau nor Ghandi (and they did not understand their Christ to have spoken of bus companies). They knew only America and its profit-oriented world. "Hit them where it hurts," some said, "in the pocketbook." Somehow, though they hoped for a different reality, they often believed that the withholding of money was a surer weapon than sacrificial love. It was the cash register that changed men, not the heart. The tension between the hope of love and the trust in economics was painful, and whenever it was relaxed it was most often love that lost. What else could one expect in a society so fearfully proud of its material possessions?

Even more difficult, perhaps, was the fact that when the busses were finally desegregated the action did not come through the initiative of a converted white community, nor even through the power of the dollar. It came rather by the fiat of a federal court, with its ultimate appeal to the coercive, destructive power of the government's armed might. (More will be said later about this strange ally in the cause of love.)

What would have happened if the courts had not come to the people's aid after a year of non-cooperation? King himself remembers that it was near the end of the protest, when the legal harassment of the city grew serious, when the car-pool was threatened with disarray, when the length of the struggle seemed interminable—it was then he says that he was able "to feel the cold wind of pessimism passing through" his followers. What would have happened without the courts? Would the winds have extinguished even the guarded hope in love? Experiences elsewhere strongly support such a guess.

Is this the natural fate of nonviolence when faced with a prolonged struggle? Is it possible that a mass, nonviolent movement cannot be maintained in America? Are thousands (to say nothing of millions) of men and women and children too many, too variegate, too individualistic to submit to the self-discipline and group discipline required by nonviolence? Both Ghandi and King believed that a dedicated core of true believers could serve as the spine for the fluid crowds when times of disappointments came. And with sharp intuitions King knew that many discouraging times would come, for he realized how different were the tasks of winning independence from a society and integration into one. (How much easier it is to demand land and control in the nebulous West or in the all too specific heart of Harlem than to break down every steel-bound, fear-bound wall through the power of creative, disciplined loving.)

Where then was the solid center of believers in the North, in the South? Could it be that the movement was never prepared to "experiment" with nonviolence for the long years that might be required before a truly new and united community of respect and love could be built? Could it be that the necessary dedication to truth and to poverty that Ghandi assumed was hard to imagine among black men who had been forced for centuries to use a mask as a way of life, who lived in an image-oriented, public relations-dominated society, and who had tasted the tempting affluence of America? Or was it simply that the hope for the "beloved community" was an impossible one from the beginning, no less chimerical than the Marxist dream of the New Society? And even if it is more than a dream, can love be used as a tool, even for good ends? Can its results ever be predicted, be guaranteed?

Perhaps Martin Luther King was involved in an unresolvable dilemma when he first called men to follow the commands of Christ as a means of achieving integration. It may be that the Negro boy sitting in the debris of Watts saw more clearly than he knew when he said, "I'm tired of hearing about the good old Jesus Christ . . . The cross is a sign of death, that's all there is to it. Jesus Christ hung from it." What is the future of nonviolence in America or in the world without a cadre of those who will face the cross—and its equivalents—as a beginning and not as the end?

326

Reflections, II: God is Nice, But . . .

Among the strange and paradoxical elements of the attempt at nonviolent resistance in our midsts few are more perplexing than the activities of the federal government, especially in its role as the *deus ex machina* for many men. After Montgomery, against the background of a relatively sympathetic Supreme Court, the Movement turned again and again to the hope of federal power. President Eisenhower was castigated for moral neutrality and apparent unconcern. Men wept as he waited until troops seemed the only alternative in Little Rock. The late John F. Kennedy was repeatedly taken to task for playing too shrewd a game with his narrowly won power and his great popularity. Criticism was widespread against his failure to speak out with clarity and precision until after Birmingham. And from the outset of Lyndon Johnson's assumption of presidential power the pressure was on him to use that massive weight on the side of civil rights and integration. Meanwhile Congress was being constantly assailed for its staunch refusal to deliver national legislation that would help to secure the rights of black men and their allies to life, liberty and the pursuit of power.

327

Throughout the cities of the South nonviolent demonstrations often seemed more precisely aimed at Pennsylvania Avenue and Capitol Hill than at the Albanys, Greenwoods or Shreveports where they were taking place. At times it appeared that the demonstrators and their leaders did not really live in the hope their non-violent rhetoric proclaimed. Decades of disappointment, duplicity and suffering seemed to have produced a certain skein of hopelessness in their attitudes toward the local white citizens, officials and police.

There were exceptions of course, but by and large the approach seemed to be a short-circuited one that leaped quickly and brilliantly beyond the seemingly impenetrable consciences of a segregationist, fear-ridden populace to the power inherent in the national government. The placards were to be read in the White House. The marches were timed for Huntley-Brinkley and Telestar. The assistant attorney general—after the first hard grueling months—was often on call to deliver the prisoners if jail got too long or too hard.

All this was understandable when hope was discounted. When little but repression was really expected of "the white man" then other allies were needed. The consciences of influential northern liberals seemed less impervious, and their complaints seemed helpful upon reaching the White House or various congressional offices. All of this fitted into a pattern of pressure and dependence upon the federal power, but it may have compromised the integrity of the power of non-violence. It may have by-passed the stubborn, frightened southern opponents in the understandable search for quicker, less painful results. Meanwhile, an enemy who might have been waiting in terrified, flailing anticipation of love was left to laugh and cry alone in his fear.

In 1964 the results of such strategy began to come in. Apparently the pressure on Washington and the appeal to the world had worked. Suddenly the movement was beseiged by a president who operated with as great a flair for publicity as any civil rights lieutenant; who made and carried his own placards, who moved quickly and often ruthlessly with great power whenever it pleased him, or so it seemed. The marchers and field workers were overwhelmed by money, by registrars, by national legislation, by a war on poverty, by a chief executive who seemed ready to burst out with the music as well as the words to *We Shall Overcome.* A repentant white Southerner had seen the light. What more could be desired? Here was federal power, often with a vengeance. If some persons felt that the appearances and the labels were often more impressive than the actuality they still could not deny the seemingly ubiquitous reality of the federal presence. Here were the "results" that the Movement had so long sought.

The great majority of television-prone barriers that were such obvious targets for nonviolent demonstrations and protests now seem to have been broken down by the actuality or the threat of federal force. In the minds of many financial contributors the battle is done and money flows into the civil rights coffers far more slowly than at any time in the last five years. Young heroes of the Movement are drifting back into school, moving reluctantly toward the army, or simply wandering, like the remnants of a victorious but forgotten crusade. Officials are turning to the service of the Great Society. Is that the natural resting place for a movement that began as an experiment with Christian love, became a syncretistic appeal to "all men of good will" and then a tool in the struggle for power? Is it natural that it should have been lured into the national consensus to sing the paeans of a greatness created by fiat, television and money?

The results are in, and in many ways they are impressive, but at the same moment a strange, almost inexplicable malaise has settled down like a spangled shroud over the Movement. Somehow it all seems so overwhelming. The heavy-breathing octopus of government initiative seems to have sucked the life out of so many protests and creative actions. Is this the end of the nonviolent aspects of the Movement? Could it be that nonviolence has passed and we are left no nearer to the beloved community than we were ten years ago? Segregation remains at the core of the American Way of Life. Unemployment figures arouse little compassion and are countered by contracts for ammunition, helicopters and napalm. "Desegregated" schools are shields for the continued alienation that both Negroes and whites endure, and the churches remain the last public—but increasingly irrelevant—bastion of fear.

Is this what was bargained for? Is it possible that dependence on Federal power, a conservative, manipulative power, has actually sapped the *elan vital* of nonviolence? Could it be that the movement that began with a promise to match "physical force with soul force" may well have found too easy a way out in matching instead the physical force of the federal government against the terror of Al Lingo's state troopers? Could it be that the movement that promised to encounter the "enemy" with tough, protesting, forgiving love may have escaped the hard and costly encounter by appealing to Washington in the showdown? Is it possible that the movement that sang "God is on our side" was really more happy with the national guard around it, and thus may have chosen the lesser part? In the process many a strategic battle has surely been won, but no one seriously speaks any longer of "redeeming the soul of the South" or of America. Has the task been given up as hopeless or have the victories been confused with redemption?

Dare we even raise such questions? Do they suggest unbelief? Who is to say that there was not a spirit at work among us, created by the truly nonviolent minority, a spirit which accounts for victories yet unseen? Who is to say that all is known when we describe laws and cash registers and troops? Was there no tortuous movement of conscience beneath the surface of expediency? Did the gallant songs from Parchman jail, the blood on Birmingham's street, the death of William Moore and his brothers—did these produce no fervent tumult in the lonely nights among judges, police and presidents? Perhaps our myopic bondage to the perspectiveless present bars us from the vision of miracles such as these.

Nevertheless we *are* bound ànd the appearances are what they are. And they seem to suggest that the task of redemption through suffering and dogged loving has been given up without sufficient effort. Perhaps the marchers and the singers have now accepted the chilling conclusions of the black poet, LeRoi Jones, when he speaks with evident conviction of "the rotting and destruction of America." Or, do they look with less despair (but no more hope) to Bayard Rustin, that veteran of the struggle, as he says:

> Hearts are not relevant to the issue; neither racial affinities nor racial hostilities are rooted there. It is institutions—social, political, and economic institutions—which are the ultimate molders of collective sentiments. Let these institutions be reconstructed *today,* and let the ineluctable gradualism of history govern the formation of a new psychology.[3]

329

Reflections, III: Farewell, White Brothers, Farewell

Such questions lead to reflections upon the future of a movement once called nonviolent, now often nameless, indescribable—like some rage. What is its direction, what are its goals? In a sense it is Rustin who has articulated what many persons believe to be the newest (yet very old) goals of the Movement. Through this attack on institutions Bayard and Malcolm's heirs, Martin and Muhammed's followers would all see a common greater vision: to bring to America's Negroes a sense of manhood, a conviction of true human dignity.

How, specifically, shall that be achieved? Is there possibly a role for nonviolence here yet? In a society that so often equates manhood with the capacity to use physical, destructive force against animals and men, this is a difficult matter. For many Negroes believe that America will recognize their manhood and their dignity more quickly through the sniper's sights of Watts than through the prison bars in Jackson. (Thus one reputable Negro professional will soon produce a book that goes beyond the Deacons for Defense in its call for the formation of a Mafialike protective police force among Negroes to face the federal government with a grim alternative.) Only if Negroes—and whites—in America find some more transcendent standards of manhood could the situation be different. Under such conditions of thought nonviolence is surely passe and has no role in the new phase of the Movement. For it suggests another standard by which to measure a man. The vision of nonviolence suggests that it is a man's commitment to truth, to love, to life that makes him truly man and not his readiness to "defend" himself. It affirms that manhood is to be found in the ever deepening and interdependent life of the loving community rather than in the traditional violence and personal isolation of romantic frontier individualism. Whether nonviolence can ever deeply dent the American image of manhood is a moot question.

And what of dignity? It is not surprising that the means of achieving dignity are now equated with political and economic power. It is not surprising, but it is so very disappointing in the light of history's verdict on power. Still even the voice that once spoke of winning the enemy through enduring love now says "political power may well . . . be the most effective new tool of the Negro's liberation"; and one wonders what struggles against the hardness of our hearts led to this new path

---

[3]*Commentary.* February, 1965, p. 28.

for him. One wonders if his words reflect a loss of hope for any deeper way to
dignity in the midst of a society of men and women whose capacity to coil themselves around power and privilege seems greater than any capacity to receive the
sword of love.

Clearly power has become the theme. Even though we have been greatly disillusioned by the uses of federal power, even though a library of volumes and unknown graves mark the exploitations of private power, still there is an infatuation
with political and economic force. "We must have jobs and income, not simply for
what they mean to our families and our spirits but for the lever they give us." So
goes the cry. "We must have the capacity to influence those political decisions that
concern us. We need the power of self-determination in the ghettos of Harlem and
Chicago and Detroit no less than the black men of Africa and the nonwhites of the
rest of the world. The white man is the same the world over and we do not trust
him. Power alone can change our situation, can bring us the dignity of real men."

This is the new theme in the Movement. (And those who are waiting yet to be
loved by "them" need to recognize the current preoccupation. It is a direction that
no longer offers any significant attention to the needs of "our white brothers" for
redemption, but rather focuses on the needs of "our black brothers" for dignity.
It has evidently appeared that both cannot be done at once. In some ways the new
fascination appears racist and in some ways it is. As such it may simply indicate
another way in which we have "succeeded," another way in which the Negro has
broken into the mainstream of American thought.) But here again the question
must be raised: Are these really the things that bring dignity to a man, important
though they may be otherwise? Do the spokesmen for such goals consider the members of the "power structures" in our cities and nation, the wheelers and dealers, to
be persons of dignity and true manhood? Do the worshipers of power assume that
Negroes would use economic and political levers in a more humane and compas-
sionate way than others? How can this happen unless at the same time something
is changed within the human spirit?

The continuing problems of socialist nations reveal to us the human factor at the
heart of the issue. New institutions and control over them—no matter how benevo-
lent their intent—do not produce either humanity nor dignity. The greatness and
awesomeness of nonviolence was that it promised to reform not only the evil system
and the men who ran that system, but it essayed a change in the nonviolent resister
himself. Is such a hope in vain? Or is it too much a threat, too frightening to realize
that we might have to experience change no less radical than the society and the
men we face on the line? Perhaps the devotees of nonviolent change desired more
of the pie-as-is than anyone knew. Perhaps the burning ship wasn't so bad at all
if you could travel first class and dance with anyone you please.

Perhaps it was not their fault. Perhaps there simply is not present in America
any philosophical, moral or religious grounds for an understanding of new men or
new society. Could it be that bad?

Reflections IV: In the American Style

Whatever the causes, there now appears solid reason to believe that "they"
have at least forgotten about loving, and at most may have learned to hate. If this
is true then it may be that there is no hope for us at all save a possibly slower "rotting and destruction" than Jones expects.

Have "they" really learned to hate? How hard it is to hear such words. How terrifying to live under such a cloud. Have they? While Martin King once spoke of enduring and wearing down the whites with love, now a different set of voices can be heard in every section of the land, sections where even the brave warrior of southern streets dares not walk when the "next time" becomes now and fire burns the land. In such places Malcolm is still echoed and revered for saying "I'm against anyone who tells black people to be nonviolent while nobody is telling white people to be nonviolent . . . Let the Klan know we can do it, tit for tat, tit for tat." In Los Angeles a young man reflects on the experiences of Watts' riot and says:

> It was the best thing that ever happened. You come to the Man and try to tell him, over and over, but he never listens. Why, the Man has always been killing. He first drove the Indians out. Now my arm's almost been bit off. I've got to bite back. The riot? There'll be more of the same until the Man opens up his eyes and says "We're going to give it to you because we're tired."[4]

331

Thus the capacity to endure suffering is exchanged for the bitter resolve to wear out the deaf and blind "Man" with the capacity to inflict violence.

Why is it that such voices seem more dominant in America today? Have "they" really learned to hate? Perhaps they knew all along. Perhaps they were waiting too, to see if consciences would truly be moved, to see if deep changes in the society would be made voluntarily, to see if love might well prevail. Perhaps they knew their hate too well, knew its fearful debilitating consequences, and waited, hidden from us, at the other end of the brink of hope. Perhaps they did not try hard enough, perhaps they did not wait long enough, perhaps they should have entered the nonviolent movement more deeply, perhaps there should have been a movement for their concrete jails.

However much we yearn for it to be different, they are waiting no longer. They are rising up, and it must be known and it must be affirmed that their response is no new hatred, learned at our feet. It is as old as man, old as the first slaveship rebellion, old as Walker's *Appeal* and Nat Turner's rusty sword, old as the Deacons for Defense and *Negroes With Guns*. It is a response more human than black, a reaction to humiliation, exploitation and fear. So it is not that "they" have learned to hate, rather they were human all along, just as "we" are, and they knew the arts of hate, knew them well. They were only waiting with cool, masked hope to see if Martin King would make any significant change in the American Way of Life.

In their eyes he did not. If there were changed consciences they could not see them. What they saw was force and pressure and the power of law, of money and of guns. Meanwhile they were still unemployed, still given atrocious schooling, still kept out of the Man's communities, still humiliated by social workers and coerced by police — in spite of all the highly praised laws. Periodically they were still being swept off the streets into the patronizing, isolated job corps camps or into the burning jungles of Vietnam. They had neither the words nor the concepts but they knew the truth was being spoken by the man who said:

> The unintegrated Negro is the symbol of our democratic failure and the unemployed Negro is the most conspicuous evidence we have of the breaking down of the economic machinery. I do not believe there is any chance that the private, self-adjusting economy can provide today's unemployed Negro with a job, the traditional means to dignity and self-respect. Tax cuts and war on poverty notwithstanding, most Negroes

---

[4] *Christianity and Crisis*. October 4, 1965, p. 201.

now without work are not likely to be taken up into the private economy again.[5]

When the hopelessness within them seemed to give a vivid witness to such statements about their society and their future, then they gave vent to their anguish in the American way. (Perhaps they do not hate us. Perhaps more than anything else they despise us. Perhaps they are blind in their rage because we did not learn in time, and if we did learn, then did not resolve to act in ways radical enough to save them from decay. Did they not want us to love? Is this the madness of it all? Is this why the heat, the seeming hate is so intense? Are we like lovers in some limbo, acting out the urgings of death, repressing the surgings towards life and never never reaching far enough and long enough to touch the fevered hand, the atrophied heart on the other side? And where other broken seekers in other kinds of worlds would then take to the long silence of meditative night and slow dying, is it that we turn instead to violence and shall at least burn together?) Is this the anguish imbedded deep within the meaning of the young black man's soliloquy in Watts?

332

If it is, then what more than failure could we have expected of nonviolence in such a land as ours, when faced with such terrible pain and humiliation? What could we expect of non-violence in a nation that had come to being in the midst of armed revolution? What could we expect of nonviolence in a nation that had realized its Manifest Destiny over the unburied bodies of the natives of this land? What could we expect when the savagery of Civil War seemed required to bring freedom to four million men in the land we believed chosen by God as the world's last best hope?

What could we expect of nonviolence in a nation that had bombed some enemies into submission, atomized others out of existence and now lives easily with the threat of complete annihilation of all who would seek seriously to oppose or dominate us? What could we expect of nonviolence in neighborhoods where frightened policemen recorded their fear in fierce words and quick guns? What could we expect of a society that defines manhood as the state of being willing to "fight for your rights?"

Violence to the enemy is built into the American grain far more deeply than nonviolence. Negroes in Chicago and Los Angeles and Atlanta consider the Man to be their enemy. They have seen the economic, educational and residential walls being built stouter and higher against the majority of them. They attribute this either to the malignant purpose or the careless disdain of the Man. Why should they not turn to violence if they believe that he will listen to nothing else?

(When will the violence come south? If some observers are right it has begun in the North because the cities of that promised land were once considered pinpoints of hope in a racist society. Something more than despair was expected where hundreds of laws were on the books and where newspapers daily and fully condemned the white South. Now the moment of truth has come and many Negroes have discovered that their hopes are being dashed more cruelly because they had hoped for more. Northern residential segregation is more humiliating because it is denied. Northern unemployment is more difficult because the food-producing land has been left behind and the signs of other men's affluence are even more obvious. Northern schools are more offensive because they have been "desegregated" in some places for a long, long time. The North claimed to offer more,

---

[5]W. H. Ferry. *"Toward a Moral Economy."* Unpublished mimeographed copy of a speech delivered in Atlanta, Georgia, December 11, 1965.

partly because it just wasn't the South. So its frustrations are greater, and TV simply helps to make all of it breathlessly vivid. Thus the argument goes.

(If this is true then we need wait only long enough in the South for our city officials, newspaper editors, and chambers of commerce to announce to the world our new image. Soon we too will claim to be fully liberal, desegregated and great havens of economic opportunity for all men. We too will no longer have any racial problems. We will have gathered all our Negroes from their Diaspora throughout the cities and placed them in concentrated enclaves. Then we will chide the rural areas of the South and ask for federal action on behalf of those wonderful Negroes. When that day comes we can expect our own explosions, explosions that will make us long for Birmingham and Albany. For as long as Negroes expected us to act like Southerners, clinging to official segregation, practicing informal desegregation, waiting for "them" to love, we could escape. Once we claim to be as good as the North, our nakedness will be seen. For in the eyes of black, sensitized men we shall be as bad, as frustrating and as provocative as Chicago or New York. Then the burning will begin. Such seems to be the price of progress in our America.)

333

We say it is madness for them to choose violence. Their minority status in a hostile nation would make their destruction certain. But they find it hard to hear us when any night's newscast brings to them glimpses of the American style in the world. Is their madness any greater than ours when the nation attempts the same approach in a world where "we" are in a minority? Is our destruction any less certain? The voice of conscience from Montgomery once proclaimed to Negroes that the use of violence to achieve justice would cause their "memory to be shrouded with the ugly garments of shame." The nation seems little concerned about the way future generations will judge its dress. Why should the Negroes care more?

Reflections, V: Shall We Overcome?

Perhaps such harsh reflections can lead us to one of the deepest insights for the present moment. It may well be that in a society of violence it is no longer a matter of our learning to love the Negro, but our learning to love. Perhaps we shall find no solution for the explosive problem in our own midst until we eschew violence as a way of life in international affairs or keep the Negroes out of the army and away from TV sets. For who can tell the black, indignant men that violent solutions are no real solutions while he has television or can join the military forces? Who can speak of the need to love those who are hating him when our national policy is at least to frighten and at most to destroy those who hate us?

Can the American Negro — so very American — change his heart before the rest of us? Once Martin King and a host of other men deeply hoped for this. Once they thought the Negro might bear some Messianic possibilities for our nuclear-ringed world, but the evidence is not with them now. We have not learned to love soon enough, and Negroes have not chosen to be the suffering servants of the society on a long-term basis (most of them had no desire for this on even the briefest terms). Now we must do our own loving and it may be too much to require, for now it must include Negro and Chinese and Castroite Cuban and a variety of intermediates. Indeed the "we" must now be expanded to encompass both the black and white non-lovers and haters. Perhaps this is what it really means to overcome, to overcome even our we-ness and our they-ness on a scale no less than the measurements of the globe. Have we given up all hope that such a day could possibly begin to appear?

So we return again to hope. Perhaps the problem is lodged deeply in that direction. Is it possible that our capacity to hope is now as far from us in America as our sense of moral absolutes? The conquest of nonviolence depends both on hope and upon truth. It speaks of love and goodness, of evil and wrong as if such things were real, as if amoral meant immoral. Could it be then that the failure (how sad a word!) of nonviolence in our own generation is a sign of our multiple loss: loss of hope, loss of nerve and loss of any truth outside our own small, quaking lives? The ultimate vision of nonviolence is the beloved community. Where shall we find our model in the midst of America's age of personal isolation and corporate fear? Where shall we find it in the midst of our non-families? Where shall we find it when we protect ourselves against the majority of the human community with never sleeping silos of concentrated hell?

334

Perhaps it was all too wild a dream in the first place, this hope of redemption. Perhaps it was a child's fantasy in the sleep of night, or another Negro folk tale dredged up from the long dead age of faith. But if it was, then who shall preserve us from the day, from this age, from the sudden blaze of fiery light?

Epilogue: Speak to Us of Love, But not Much

In the midst of our endless, almost involuntary, hopeless search for "them," for the black brothers who once held hope for us all, there is something raging within that turns us instinctively to glance toward the man who preached the tender words so very long ago.

Now ten years older, a thousand years sadder, the wounds of evil upon him, he still seems to search for grounds of hope — sometimes desperately. As he moves — such burdened moving — from East to West, from ghetto to cotton field, searching for his followers, we cannot stifle a sudden, urgent call, a call to him.

"Speak to us of love; speak of hope; speak of brotherhood," we say. And all we hear is the anguish of his troubled words describing, protesting napalm and gas and death in Vietnam.

We are angry; and in our anger's rigid, fearful strength we push to keep him in his place, his place of civil rights, his place of nonviolence, his place of love for us.

"Speak to us of love, not of fighting for our freedom against 'them,' "we say. What must he think as a billion of the humiliated "them" gather in watchfulness under the strange darkness of his visage? What ranges of almost bitter sadness and weighted laughter must the somber shades of flesh and blood conceal?

What must he think?

Who will save us from the breaking in of fire, of light?

Black Radicalism: The Road from Montgomery

VINCENT HARDING

O Americans! Americans!! I call God—I call angels—I call men, to witness that your DESTRUCTION *is at hand*, and will be speedily consummated unless you *REPENT*.

—David Walker's *Appeal*, 1829

Is white America really sorry for her crimes against the black people? Does white America have the capacity to repent—and to atone? . . . What atonement would the God of Justice demand for the robbery of the black people's labor, their lives, their true identities, their culture, their history—and even their human dignity?

—Malcolm X, *Autobiography*, 1965

America, you'd better repent and straighten up or we'll burn you down.

—H. Rap Brown, 1967

The living annals of oppressed and troubled peoples abound in wry, unanswerable comments; it is said among black people here that when Lenin was told there were black conservatives in America, he raised his eyebrows and exclaimed: "Oh! And what precisely do they have to conserve?"[1] In an age when instantaneous global communications were only beginning to be exploited, this was a natural question for an outsider to ask, and especially for a stranger who dealt in revolution. At a time when lynchings and emasculations of Negroes were public celebrations, when urban riots meant that white mobs were raging for the lives of defenseless Negroes, who could fault such a question from afar? For anyone who was close to the black communities of the United States, however, there was an answer: They had their *lives* to conserve.

Throughout most of their strange black pilgrimage in this often threatening land, the struggle to stay alive—to conserve their lives and the lives of their children—has been the dominant concern of Afro-Americans. The bravado cry of "Liberty or Death!" has sprung from their lips no more readily than from the lips of other men. Their shaping of revolutionary institutions has not been a significant activity. Neither radical words nor deeds have surged easily from black people in America. They have, instead, survived within the realities of Claude McKay's poignant lines:

> . . . I was born, far from my native clime,
> Under the white man's menace, out of time.[2]

For most of those who live as an indelibly marked minority in the heart of such a menace, conservatism—at least in public—comes as naturally as breathing. (And, like breathing, it often seems a necessary condition for staying alive.) Indeed, even the special black breed that has courageously dared to raise voices of protest in the midst of such a hostile situation has had to come to terms with their distance from "home," and their darkly obvious status as the outnumbered ones. So for those who have been at once black, angry, and wise, protest has never moved easily over into radicalism. Even when protest has made this leap, most of its actions and energies have been defensive. Black radicalism, therefore, has been focused largely on the means for realizing "the American promise" rather than on shaping new, dissenting goals.

One facet of the dilemma was described a decade ago by one of the most famous black radicals, Paul Robeson. In his autobiographical statement, *Here I Stand*, Robeson delineated what he called "a

338

certain protective tactic of Negro life in America." Speaking from bitter experience, this politically sensitive artist said:

> Even while demonstrating that he is really an equal . . . the Negro must never appear to be challenging white superiority. Climb up if you can—but don't act "uppity." Always show that you are *grateful*. (Even if what you have gained has been wrested from unwilling powers, be sure to be grateful lest "they" take it all away.) Above all, *do nothing to give them cause to fear you*, for then the oppressing hand, which might at times ease up a little, will surely become a fist to knock you down again! [3]

Robeson's conclusions are confirmed by Lerone Bennett, another perceptive recorder of the black experience, in *The Negro Mood*. "The history of the Negro in America . . . has been a quest for a revolt that was not a revolt . . . a revolt . . . that did not seem to the white power structure to be an open revolt." [4]

If in one sense these analyses are being outstripped by the pace of current events in the nation's black communities, they nonetheless describe much that has happened up to now (and the death of Martin Luther King appeared to many persons as additional proof of their validity). Such insights, moreover, suggest a set of guidelines for understanding the nature of black radicalism in America.

At what point does black radicalism begin? Perhaps it begins when black men lose or repress their fear of the descending white fist and carry Negro protest to one of its logical conclusions, regardless of the consequences. Perhaps it begins when sensitive, restive souls lose faith in "the myth of Negro progress" within the American system.[5] Perhaps we may speak of black radicalism when men are pressed by our society to seek alternatives (even though chimerical and "unrealistic") to the American way of life for Afro-Americans. Even now, black radicalism is more a reaction than a calculated strategy, more an agonized thrust than a body of thought; and this is one of its weaknesses.

Inchoate though they may be, as one sorts out the elements of the Afro-American experience with radicalism, several themes can be identified. First of all, it becomes clear that the classic, primarily European terms of "left" and "right" or "communist" and "capitalist" usually provide insufficient contexts for a discussion of American

339

black radicalism. Even the sometimes helpful separation into social, political, economic, and racial radicalism at last becomes a tiresome burden in probing the subject. This radicalism, which grows out of a situation as emotionally weighted and psychologically distorted as the black-white encounter in America, cannot adequately be described in terms that are largely intellectual and theoretical. For such "irrational" reasons (among others), those classic "radicals," the Communists, found American black revolutionaries a very difficult brood to cultivate.

Another thematic reality is that in every generation there has been a group of black radicals (marked with the blood that always accompanies new births and violent deaths) that has moved far beyond the acceptable or customary lines of protest and revolt. Sometimes this has been simply a personal groping with the menace; sometimes it has been organized. At various times the emphasis of the radical approach has been on armed self-defense; and occasionally it has urged armed uprisings against the status quo. In each generation the "radical edge" has reached a different point in the overall experience, but it has always been present—marked by despair, alienation, fierce anger, and sometimes even by hope.

A third continuity is found in the constantly recurring, religiously oriented themes of apocalyptic messianism and atonement. Basically this has implied the conviction that there could be no ultimate deliverance for blacks (or whites) without a black-led rebellious movement, which would involve levels of anguish and blood-letting surpassing those of the Civil War. From the first attempts to capture their slave ships to the current talk of "taking over the ghettos," the black radical impulse has been informed by a vision of blood, a vision often understood as being of divine origin.

Usually, however, the goal of black radicalism has appeared to be the simplistic, "moderate" goal of assimilation into American society; but many radicals have realized there is nothing simple or moderate about such an aim. They knew that the American nation would have to be drastically transformed before it would fully open itself to the native-yet-alien presence in its midst. This was what a black leader of the Communist Party meant when she said, in the 1930's, "It is impossible to take one step in the direction of winning for the Negro people their elementary rights that is not revolutionary." [6] Nevertheless, other radicals eventually became convinced that such a transformation is impossible. Thus black nationalism and black zionism also have sought to chart a course in the endless search. Their path, of course, has not been towards assimilation.

Against such a background it becomes clear that the transformation of black radicals from the singing, integration-directed marchers of Montgomery, Alabama, in 1955 into the avowed guerrilla fighters and alienated rebels of the late 1960's was in keeping with historical precedents.[7]

I

In 1955 Martin Luther King and the black community in Montgomery faced a situation that contained much that was new as well as much that was brutally old. Social, political, and economic injustices to Negro citizens were evident on every hand; the South was considered the major bastion of enforced second-class citizenship; and segregation in public facilities seemed the most blatant example of racial humiliation. But there was something new as well. The previous spring the Bandung Conference in Southeast Asia had reminded the world how much World War II had done to intensify the struggles of formerly colonized people in wrenching themselves free of Western domination. In New York City the United Nations was an expanding forum for the views of the formerly silent peoples of the earth. The United States was deeply engaged in ideological—and occasionally military—struggles with powers that were quick to exploit this nation's poor record as a protector of its own oppressed. Younger, better-educated black people and their families were moving from rural to urban areas and were determined to play a new role in American society.

In this context, and under the prodding of the National Association for the Advancement of Colored People, the Supreme Court in 1954 had declared that racial segregation in public schools was unconstitutional. Concern about school segregation focused on the South, for it was recognized that the decision, if firmly enforced, also could signal the end of many other institutionalized forms of segregation. Some blacks who saw this possibility now moved forward with a conviction that, for the first time, the nation's highest tribunal was on their side. At the same moment, the Court's decision was a call to fierce resistance for many white persons.[8]

It was at this point that Martin Luther King entered the scene.

The decision of a gentle black lady to retain her disputed seat on a segregated bus, then the decision of Montgomery's Negro community that her subsequent arrest be protested—these and other events helped press the twenty-six-year-old Baptist minister into the radical path.[9] Neither his somewhat sheltered middle-class Atlanta background nor his rather conventional education had prepared him for such a mission, but he accepted it. Martin Luther King's brand of radicalism can be traced to a number of sources: the lives and the teachings of Christ and Gandhi, the thinking of Thoreau, the aborted hopes of James Farmer and A. Philip Randolph,[10] the tough strategy talks of Bayard Rustin, and the exigencies of the situation. From these and other sources King shaped his old-new hope, catalyzed by his own creative impulses.

342

Love was the answer. Not sentimentality, but the tough and resolute love that refused bitterness and hatred but stood firmly against every shred of injustice. Few brands of black radicalism had ever required so much. Men were not only urged to stand and face the menace, they were called upon to be true to themselves and to reject the very weapons that had destroyed them for so long. They were called upon to transform American life by substituting moral and spiritual courage for its traditional dependence upon violence and coercion. This new (and untried) weapon could easily be distributed to—eventually—the overwhelming majority of ordinary black people. To the confused and often fearful white faces behind the menacing fists Dr. King addressed these words:

> We will match your capacity to inflict suffering with our capacity to endure suffering. We will meet your physical force with soul force. We will not hate you, but we cannnot . . . obey your unjust laws. Do to us what you will and we will still love you. Bomb our homes and threaten our children; send your hooded perpetrators of violence into our communities and drag us out on some wayside road, beating us and leaving us half dead, and we will still love you. But we will soon wear you down by our capacity to suffer. And in winning our freedom we will so appeal to your heart and conscience that we will win you in the process.[11]

After the victory against segregation in public buses in Montgomery (which many persons explained away in legal terms), King sought to institutionalize his vision in the Southern Christian Leadership Conference. King and the SCLC still harbored David Walker's messianic hope that black people would lead the way to a redeemed America, but they would not use Walker's method. The new radical hope (is it not always radical to think of redemption for America?) was expressed in an SCLC document:

> Creatively used, the philosophy of nonviolence can restore the broken community in America. SCLC is convinced that nonviolence is the most potent force available to an oppressed people in their struggle for freedom and dignity.[12]

In uniting the broken community King and the SCLC sought to build what they called "the beloved community," in which black and white Americans of every social and economic level would recognize their bonds of human unity.

343

The power of nonviolence, however, was temporarily vitiated in the attempt to apply the tactic to its immense task. SCLC could not maintain the dynamic level of Montgomery in the new challenges it faced. Perhaps this was partly because SCLC was made up not of black radicals but for the most part of Negro Baptist ministers, but, whatever the reasons, it was not until 1960 that the vision King projected was snatched up by an even younger generation of southern Negro students; and the sit-in movement was born. Black southern students had not been noted for their radicalism, but this generation had grown up as witnesses of the successful struggles of other non-white peoples for freedom. Although they had seen white resistance to legal desegregation solidify in their own section, they had less to lose than Baptist ministers.

Beginning in Greensboro, North Carolina, they went beyond the marches and sermons of Montgomery; they walked through the "white only" doors, stood and sat where blacks had never dared go before, and confronted the protectors of the status quo with their insistent black presence. In all of this the students were aided by television and other mass media, which carried their crusading image to other students and persons all over the world.

As the movement spread across the southland and even into the Deep South, and to many places in the North, it was clear that this public defiance of all the institutions of the fist was a most radical move for that place and hour. There had been scattered precedents, but never a campaign that involved thousands of persons in hundreds of cities. In a revolutionary generation, however, the radical actions of the preceding year may appear moderate or even acceptable the next year, especially in America, where the domesticating of radical impulses seems to take place with ease and rapidity. In some ways this was what happened to the nonviolent (actually un-violent) attempts to desegregate public facilities in the South.[13]

II

As the sit-ins, freedom rides, and other demonstrations moved across the South, white resistance stiffened, and some black radicals were not convinced that nonviolence was their most effective weapon. They saw little evidence of the pliable "hearts and consciences" to which King had addressed his appeal; rather, they saw mobs, heard bombs, felt the impact of heavy clubs. Thereupon they chose Denmark Vesey, David Walker, and Nat Turner as the fathers of their black radicalism. Indeed, it was in North Carolina, the state in which the mass sit-in movement was born, that the newest call to armed Negro self-defense was sounded.

In 1959 Robert F. Williams, a Marine Corps veteran, drew attention to himself and to his branch of the NAACP in Monroe, North Carolina. Williams had changed the usual middle-class makeup of the association's branches by forming a group from laborers and other persons whose thoughts and inclinations were closer to his own. He had already begun to talk of Negroes' arming themselves when, in 1959, a white man was acquitted of charges of physical assault and attempted rape of a black woman, despite the testimony of a number of Negro witnesses.

> This . . . shows [Williams said] that the Negro in the South cannot expect justice in the courts. He must convict his attackers on the spot. He must meet violence with violence, lynching with lynching.

The NAACP's national office immediately disassociated itself from Williams' statement and attempted to remove him from his position. Eventually, however, the local and state officials took care of this matter; they hounded the burly, outspoken black radical from the city and the state. But Williams was not silenced. In 1962, when nonviolence was still in its ascendancy, he maintained that

> any struggle for liberation should be a flexible struggle. We must

use non-violence as a means as long as this is feasible, but the day will come when conditions become so pronounced that non-violence will be suicidal. . . . The day is surely coming when we will see more violence on the same American scene. The day is surely coming when some of the same Negroes who have denounced our using weapons for self-defense will be arming themselves.[14]

Events made Williams a prophet; but the question that continues to rise from such thinking is whether the call to armed self-defense is a conservative or a radical move? It can be argued that Williams—and others like him—simply become part of the violent pattern of American life and promise no more than its continuation. Can a nation that is built on violence be constructively transformed by violence? On the other hand one faces the perennial, inherent ambiguity in black radicalism: in the minds of some persons nothing could have been more radical, even in the 1960's, than the decision of Negroes to arm themselves. Williams' group, in arming itself, determined to defy both the southern mob and the southern police, who seemed ready to expose them to the mob's fury. On one such occasion a "very old . . . white man . . . started screaming and crying like a baby, [while saying:]

345

> 'God damn, God damn, what is this God damn country coming to that niggers have got guns, the niggers are armed and the police can't even arrest them.' [15]

Whatever the accuracy of definitions of black radicalism from the lips of very old southern white men, Williams soon would follow a familiar black radical path as he moved from Cuba to Moscow to Peking. Later, his call for armed self-defense would be accepted by a black revolutionary liberation struggle in America, and by 1968 he would be elected Provisional President of a separatist black nation in American exile.[16]

Behind the most militant words and deepest commitments to black radicalism of all who have spoken of black revolution in America, whatever the variety, has been a battery of unresolved but realistic questions. How does an easily identifiable minority carry out such a revolution? Where does it find allies in a hostile and threatened nation? Against whom will the revolution be directed, and what are its goals? These were the questions of the early sixties, when nonviolence was counterposed against armed and militant self-defense.

After 1954 it was generally assumed that the enemy was the system of segregation in the South and that the major allies were the federal government, the liberals of the North, and the conscience of the nation. But step by step this assumption was transformed. More and more black persons began to ask whether segregation properly could be isolated in the South merely because it was supported by law only in that region. Others wondered how a "federal government" could be separate from the pervasive prejudice and discrimination black men had always found in the nation as a whole. Was the United States Congress really more liberal than the homeowners, real estate dealers, and corporations it represented? Was it not obvious that, when serious attempts were made to direct action into the North, there was a noticeable cooling of ardor among erstwhile allies, especially when issues of compensatory hiring, suburban housing, and integrated education were raised? [17]

Moreover, as the nation became more deeply enmeshed in Vietnam, who was willing to approve the scores-of-billions-of-dollars price tag for the rehabilitation of the black communities? And what kind of radicalism was needed to force a complacent nation to confront the need to rehabilitate the black community? What kind of a "revolution" depended on federal troops to protect and advance it? These were some of the vexing questions of the post-Montgomery decade. In Birmingham, Alabama, in the spring of 1963, SCLC activists attempted tentative answers to some of those questions.[18] More black people than ever before were called into the streets to face the prospect of jail. Larger numbers of children and young people were involved in SCLC-directed civil disobedience. At the same time, King's group raised its sights beyond the integration of public facilities: jobs for black people became part of the broader demands. But broader demands meant the willingness to launch in Birmingham a long seige of direct action, and SCLC did not seem prepared for such a trial. Besides, more and more young people of the city became involved in the protest, and their susceptibility to violent radicalism was not easy to control. Therefore the city's business leaders (forever concerned with images), the federal administration, and parts of the SCLC leadership seemed ready to bring the Birmingham campaign to a halt sooner than the results might have indicated. Thus the expanded agenda did not bring the predicted results, but some observers thought they saw the direction nonviolent action must take if it was

346

to remain on the constantly moving forward edge of black radicalism.

One of the insights that emerged from the Birmingham demonstrations was the need for even larger attempts at civil disobedience, aimed at Washington, D.C., and utilizing the pent-up energies of thousands of black young people. A civil rights bill had finally been introduced in Congress, in response to Birmingham, but some SCLC staff members and others were determined to push the nation even beyond such legalities. It was proposed that A. Philip Randolph's old idea for a march on Washington be revived and that thousands of black people be brought to the capital for a massive act of nonviolent civil disobedience. The objective was to paralyze the life of the nation's capital until Congress and the country were willing to move much more meaningfully toward equality. But because of opposition within the civil rights establishment—from financial benefactors and from the highest level of the federal government—this massive nonviolent "attack" on the nation's capital became the "polite" March on Washington.[19]

347

America had domesticated another radical movement. The militant speeches were censored, the taverns were closed for the day. Radicalism that sought to reach the heart of the black condition in America also sought to remain on good terms with the President and the Attorney General. It had been easily seduced, but the lesson was not lost on some of the younger militants. The words that had been censored from one of the speeches had questioned whether the federal government was truly an ally of the black movement, and some of these perceptive young people soon answered this question in the negative.[20] Other radicals continued to urge that the nonviolent movement engage in massive civil disobedience or lose its relevance to the condition of black America.

At a SCLC convention soon after the Washington march, Wyatt Tee Walker, the conference's executive director, said:

> The question is, whether we want to continue local guerrilla battles against discrimination and segregation or go to all-out war. . . . has the moment come in the development of the non-violent revolution that we are forced . . . on some appointed day . . . literally [to] immobilize the nation until she acts on our pleas for justice and morality? . . . Is the day far-off that major transportation centers would be deluged with mass acts of civil disobedience; air-

ports, train stations, bus terminals, the traffic of large cities, interstate commerce, would be halted by the bodies of witnesses non-
violently insisting on "Freedom Now"? I suppose a nationwide work
stoppage might attract enough attention to persuade someone to do
something to get this monkey of segregation and discrimination off
our backs, once, now and forever. Will it take one or all of
these? [21]

Because Walker was known to be given to flights of rhetoric, it
was difficult to ascertain how serious he was, but he seemed to sense
the new mood. The nonviolent movement would die if it did not become more radical—to a degree that would shock most civil rights
leaders and more radical than its chief financial backers would approve. Part of the familiar frustration was symbolized by Walker's
vague reference to the need "to persuade someone to do something":
Who should they try to persuade, with even the most radical action,
and *what* should they be persuaded to do? Walker's organization did
not support him, nor was there support for a proposed large cadre of
nonviolent demonstrators who would commit themselves for at least
a year of continuous action before they returned to their homes, jobs,
or school. In the North, attempts at school boycotts, traffic disruption,
and other forms of civil disobedience met with indifferent success.
None of the major organizations was ready to move in the direction of
large-scale civil disobedience. With court-enforced desegregation depriving the black movement of easily articulated goals for the struggle,
momentum could not be built. Meanwhile, however, another kind of
black momentum built fiercely.

III

In the summer of 1967 the transportation, commerce, commuting,
and other schedules of more than one American city were totally disrupted by "witnessing" blacks, but not in the way that Walker had
considered four years earlier. The young people who were to have
been the core of the rejected nonviolent campaigns stormed angrily
through the cities, witnessing with bricks, Molotov cocktails, and
rifles. Much of their violence was a reaction to the callousness of
American society at large, but it was certainly aggravated by the
lack of meaningful alternatives, the result of the nonviolent movement's failure to move with the urgency the situation demanded.

What had happened between Walker's speech in 1963 and the immobilization of the cities by fear and fire in 1967? What turns black minds upon the path of alienation and armed violence? One of the crucial events was the bombing in Birmingham, less than a month after the March on Washington. The exhausted civil rights movement was mesmerized before the spectacle of the death of four black children in Birmingham, the result of a bomb that had been planted in the Sixteenth Street Baptist Church. Negro radicals saw this atrocity as a typical white American response to increasingly cautious, impotent, religiously oriented nonviolence. One of the younger black radicals wrote:

> What was needed that Sunday [of the bombing] was ol' John Brown to come riding into Birmingham as he had ridden into Lawrence, Kansas, burning every building that stood and killing every man, woman and child that ran from his onslaught. Killing, killing, killing, turning men into fountains of blood, . . . until Heaven itself drew back before the frothing red ocean.
>
> But the Liberal and his Negro sycophants would've cried, Vengeance accomplishes nothing. You are only acting like your oppressor and such an act makes you no better than him. John Brown, his hands and wrists slick with blood, would've said, oh so softly and so quietly, Mere Vengeance is folly. Purgation is necessary.[22]

Atonement by blood is a persistent motif in the minds of black radicals.

Other youths were utterly embittered by the refusal of "liberal" northern political leaders even to admit that psychological violence and destruction was wreaked daily upon the lives of black ghetto-dwellers. Nothing was getting better for the submerged black people despite all the talk of "Negro progress" and "going too fast." Their schools were progressively miseducating more black children. Their houses were still decaying. Their incomes relative to whites' were decreasing. No one—radical or otherwise—seemed to be creating meaningful programs to deal with the immense problems, to challenge the widening alienation.

Equally significant, perhaps, was the growing perception that political leaders did not intend to take chances with their white constituencies by enforcing the civil rights legislation that had been enacted in 1964. When tough choices had to be made, they still

349

seemed to favor the whites. In this "reconstruction," as in the first, the key to basic change for Negroes seemed to be in the hands of the white North, which in the mid-1960's appeared no more committed to full equality and restitution for black men than it had been a century before. Perhaps now, as then, politicians and people intuitively recognized that the social, economic, and political changes that were necessary for the rehabilitation of black America would constitute a revolution. What majority has ever presented a minority with a legislated revolution?

Therefore, as he had predicted, Robert Williams—in Cuba—spoke for more and more black persons when he said: "What is integration when the law says yes, but the police and howling mobs say no? Our only logical and successful answer is to meet organized and massive violence with massive and organized violence. Our people must prepare to wage an urban guerrilla war of self-defense." [23] In Williams' opinion, racism had become so intrinsic a part of the nation's life that it could be exorcised only with "shock treatment." Only in this way, he said, could America be saved.

Other conclusions also were drawn from Williams' premise. By 1963 America's attention had been called to Elijah Muhammad's Nation of Islam, largely through the work of the group's outstanding spokesman, Malcolm X. The Nation, which claimed a tie to the Islamic peoples of the world, had its organizational roots in the broken black hopes of the 1930's. Focusing on the black lower classes and teaching a version of religious black nationalism, the group successfully attempted to rehabilitate some of society's most alienated black rejects, and Malcolm X was one of these. He had heard the teachings of the "messenger," Elijah Muhammad while serving a term in prison for his activities as "Detroit Red," a pimp and a narcotics pusher.[24]

Speaking for his group, Minister Malcolm said: "We don't think that it is possible for the American white man in sincerity to take the action necessary to correct the unjust conditions that 20 million black people here are made to suffer morning, noon, and night." From such a premise there followed a logical conclusion, one also derived from a long history of black radicalism. Malcolm continued,

> Because we don't have any hope or confidence or faith in the
> American white man's ability to bring about a change in the in-

justices that exist, instead of asking or seeking to integrate into the American society we want to face the facts of the problem the way they are, and separate ourselves. . . .

. . . This doesn't mean that we are anti-white or anti-American, or anti-anything. We feel, that if integration all these years hasn't solved the problem yet, then we want to try something new, something different and something that is in accord with the conditions as they actually exist.[25]

Elijah Muhummad's people were moved by what was surely to come, by Malcolm's conviction that "we are living at the end of time," when "the earth will become all . . . Islam," and when those who reject the Prophet's teachings will be destroyed by Allah. They were separatists, therefore, because "we don't want to be wiped out with the American white man." What other conclusions were logical for those who had lost all faith in American whites but had gained a faith in a just and all-conquering God? Except for "Allah," of course, the script had been written in America many times over since 1800.[26]

351

By 1964 this remarkable young radical had rejected Elijah Muhammad's version of the old script, apparently having decided against separatism, and therefore he was faced with the dilemma Frederick Douglass and others had faced before him. In a speech before an integrated group in New York that same year, Malcolm X demonstrated his ambivalence. First he predicted that

1964 will see the Negro revolt evolve and merge into the worldwide black revolution that has been taking place on this earth since 1945. The so-called revolt will become a real black revolution. . . . Revolutions are never . . . based upon . . . begging a corrupt society or a corrupt system to accept us into it. Revolutions overturn systems. And there is no system on this earth which has proved itself more corrupt, more criminal, than this system that in 1964 still colonizes 22 million . . . Afro-Americans.

But instead of describing the terrors of the coming revolution, he seemed to backtrack: "America is the only country in history in a position to bring about a revolution without violence and bloodshed by granting the suffrage to all black people." Like Douglass, however, he had to admit: "But America is not morally equipped to do so." [27] Malcolm seemed to be caught in a painful ambivalence similar to that which had dogged the earlier radicals.

In an anguished display of mixed emotions and convictions, Malcolm nevertheless predicted that blacks' use of the franchise would "sweep all of the racists and the segregationists out of office." This, in his opinion, would "wipe out the Southern segregationism that now controls America's foreign policy, as well as America's domestic policy." More and more frequently Malcolm X proclaimed that, for the Negroes, it had to be "either ballots or bullets," either a revolution of votes or guerrilla warfare. How he expected to gain the franchise in a totally corrupt system was never made clear. (This, of course, is one of the basic dilemmas for all black leaders who have tried to help their people through a reformist ballot method. Who will vote with this minority, with those who are at once powerless and most in need of the help that can come only from a transformed society? Who will vote with them when giving that help may mean the loss of a significant share of power? In light of this conundrum, what shall black radicals do if they are determined to remain loyal to the way of life that has been blessed as most truly democratic by the rest of the society?)

Struggling with the problems of tactics and strategy, Malcolm X formed his own group, the Organization of Afro-American Unity. Avowedly black nationalist, he saw no other position for those who would work for, with, and in the black ghettos. As he traveled in various parts of the world his religious commitment deepened and was transformed. He also became more convinced of the classic black nationalist vision of the need for internationalizing the struggle of American Negroes, and with this in mind he began to seek aid from African leaders in bringing the plight of Afro-Americans before the United Nations. "Our African . . . Asian . . . [and] Latin-American brothers can throw their weight on our side, and . . . 800 million Chinamen are . . . waiting to throw their weight on our side.[28] A troubled spirit, Malcolm moved through the ghettos and college campuses trying to construct a way where so many other brilliant black radicals before him had failed.

On self-defense he was positive and clear. Black men must exercise their right, he said, especially "in areas where the government has proven itself either unwilling or unable to defend the lives and the property of Negroes." On other issues he moved from guerrilla warfare to the ballot, but he never seemed to believe that the vote could be gained without the shedding of much blood, and perhaps not even then. On economic issues he took the predictable path of espousing socialism, partly because "almost every one of the countries that has gotten independence has devised some kind of socialistic system." Besides, he said, "you can't operate a capitalistic system unless you are vulturistic; you have to have someone else's blood to suck to be a capitalist. You show me a capitalist, I'll show you a bloodsucker." [29]

Up to the time of his death, however, Malcolm had had no vision of the path to final liberation. Near the end of his life, and before a predominantly black audience, he succumbed to the natural temptation to oversimplify the problem and its solution. In late 1964 he said: "What we need in this country is the same type of Mau Mau here that they had over there in Kenya. . . . If they were over here, they'd get this problem straightened up just like that." [30] But such loose words were testimony more to the desperation he felt before a host of enemies and an unfeeling nation than to the real level of his searching. His seeking was profound, burdened by all the agony that radical black integrity must carry, and it was complicated by his new vision of Islam and its commitment to an all-inclusive brotherhood of many-colored men. How could this be achieved in a country whose seeds of racism were embedded so deep? Perhaps all that one can, tentatively, say of him was compressed into the lines of Robert Hayden:

353

> He fell upon his face before
> Allah the raceless in whose blazing Oneness all . . . .
>
> Were one. He rose renewed, renamed, became
> much more than there was time for him to be.[31]

First among the black rebels to be cut down in the classic American style—by gunfire at a public meeting—Malcolm X had become a martyr and a saint even before his last breath escaped his body. He had helped bring modernity and a new respectability to black nationalism among the younger militants of his day. Even before he died the integrity of his life and his obvious identification with the masses among whom he had hustled and been reborn had deeply impressed the angry young men. Just before and just after his death a new flowering of militant black nationalist organizations testified to his impact on the ghettos.

IV

If one group inherited the time that had been denied Malcolm it was the Student Nonviolent Coordinating Committee, which earlier had served as the shock troops of the nonviolent movement. Organized in 1960, soon after the sit-in movement began and committed to radical nonviolent direct action, these high school and college-age young people invaded the worst hard-core racist sections of the Deep South: southwest Georgia, black belt Alabama, and Mississippi's rural areas. They had paid more of the dues of the movement than any other group. In 1962 and 1963 sncc leaders had agreed (for complicated and fascinating reasons) to switch from conventional direct action to voter-registration campaigns. Although such campaigns would be considered a defiant form of action in many of the most resistant parts of the South, by the 1960's they could certainly not be called radical action. Nevertheless the sncc corps seemed to founder, physically and psychologically, and became increasingly impatient with southern resistance and increasingly disillusioned by temporizing and northern evasion. They had been influenced, moreover, by Malcolm X, a man who was "up tight" and "knew what was happening." Then, in 1964, several developments drove sncc into a more radical national-ist direction.[32]

After having decided to organize a new black-led nonsegregated Democratic party in Mississippi, sncc and other groups sponsored the "Mississippi Summer." [33] During these months hundreds of white persons, especially college students, moved into the state to help with various kinds of community organization and voter-registration tasks among black people (few were willing to try their skills on Mississippi whites). Forthrightly, sncc admitted that the white newcomers had been invited as hostages to a white world that did not seem to care as much about black deaths as it did about white deaths. But the young white crowd brought something more than their willing bodies. Often, despite great personal bravery and compassion, they were insensitive to the kind of development that had to take place in the black persons with whom they worked. Too often they tended to take over tasks, conversations, meetings, and publicity that should have been handled by Negroes. Sexual competition and jealousy was another divisive issue. Many of the less articulate but no less sensitive Mississippi Negroes who worked in the summer project grew restive

354

and resentful; and by the time the summer was over it was clear that all this would force SNCC to examine its much-publicized interraciality more closely. Could black people really grow and develop under the tutelage of white allies? "Black Power" became one of the basic responses to this basic question.

The summer of 1964 also saw the failure of the Mississippi Freedom Democratic Party to win official recognition and the state's delegate votes at the Democratic National Convention. The maneuvering and attempts at political compromise that met this challenge only strengthened the conviction of young radicals that allies were not to be found in any of the traditional sources that the civil rights movement had heretofore taken for granted. Of even more significance was the increased disillusionment with the black civil rights establishment that resulted from the Atlantic City experience.[34]

355

Finally, 1964 was the summer in which the black ghettos exploded, after which black leaders everywhere were forced to ask what effect their programs thus far had had in the ghettos. Among the radicals, only Malcolm X seemed to have even a tenuous claim to leadership in a dissenting, explosive world. His "thing" had been blackness; and other radicals now saw that this also would have to be their "thing" if they were to learn to speak with and for the Negro masses. SNCC heard the message.

In 1965 the impulse to a new version of black radicalism was intensified when Malcolm X was cut down by bullets. Almost none of the black radicals believed the story that the Muslims were responsible. Why, they asked, had the French government refused Malcolm permission to visit that country just before his death? What did the French know of Malcolm's enemies? Had the CIA somehow been involved? It seemed to them that America had destroyed another black man who had refused to cower before the fist and who had threatened to bring its shame fully before the world. The alienation deepened; this was not a nation that listened to moral appeals, they said. In the month after Malcolm's death the last major attempt at tactical nonviolence in the South reached a cruel climax in Selma, Alabama, one of the areas in which SNCC had conducted a voter-registration campaign. State troopers, "performing" on foot and horseback before television cameras, waded into marchers and scattered broken bodies and broken hopes before them. Understandably, many persons asked if a march in support of the right to vote was worth all of that.[35]

The summer of 1965 was the summer of Watts, of burning, of a hostile, fearful response from a nation that for many generations had prepared the tinder and matches. The event was followed by the usual investigation, the usual recommendations, and the usual inaction. Meanwhile, urban school segregation went on unchecked in the North. In South Vietnam, another American war for the right of self-determination of other men was absorbing more energies, more money, and the best of the black "rejects."

So the score was in for the new breed of black radicals, grouped organizationally in SNCC and CORE but spread throughout the ghettos of America. It seemed to them that nonviolence and integration were not only failures but probably a betrayal: "The only thing non-violence proved was how savage whites were." [36] Other radicals claimed that integration meant only a constant drain of the best-trained black brains into a white-oriented world, leaving the ghettos as exploited, colonized infernos. Holding such convictions, the younger radicals turned ever more sharply from the path of Martin Luther King, not only because they could not believe in his weapon but because they no longer believed in his dream of integration. King's eloquent vision seemed irrelevant to the conditions of the black masses, who, like Malcolm X, began to assail the dream of middle-class integration as the substitute for the nightmare all around them. Like other radicals before them, they questioned the ultimate value of a way of life that permitted so much suffering and injustice in the most affluent nation in the world. They turned their backs on the respectable and secure ideology of assimilation to such a society, and they trumpeted their refusal to take up arms to fight such a society's overseas wars.

Like Malcolm X, their hero, these radicals are often tossed on uncertain waves of ideology. Sometimes they search for new weapons, new programs, new issues that might lead to black freedom; at other times they are given to despair, and occasionally to blind rage. Sometimes, in sheer frustration, they break down and weep. Almost always, they look only to the black communities.

Much of the feeling of this new generation of Afro-American rebels was gathered up by Julius Lester, a gifted writer:

> America has had chance after chance to show that it really meant that "all men are endowed with certain inalienable rights." America has had precious chances in this decade to make it come true. Now

it is ovef. The days of singing freedom songs and the days of combating bullets and billy clubs with Love. "We Shall Overcome" (and we have overcome our blindness) sounds old, out-dated and can enter the pantheon of the greats along with the iww songs and the union songs. As one sncc veteran put it after the Mississippi March, "Man, the people are too busy getting ready to fight to bother with singing anymore." And as for Love? That's always been better done in bed than on the picket lines and marches. Love is fragile and gentle and seeks a like response. They used to sing "I Love Everybody" as they ducked bricks and bottles. Now they sing

> "Too much love,
> Too much love,
> Nothing kills a nigger like
> Too much love."

357

They know, because they still get headaches from the beatings they took while love, love, loving. They know, because they died on those highways and in those jail cells, died from trying to change the hearts of men who had none. They know, the ones who have bleeding ulcers when they're twenty-three and the ones who have to have the eye operations. They know that nothing kills a nigger like too much love.[37]

Perhaps because the hopes had been so immense, rarely had a movement of black radicalism turned so fully from its former dreams.

> At one time [Lester wrote], black people desperately wanted to be American, to communicate with whites, to live in the Beloved Community. Now that is irrelevant. They know that it can't be until whites want it to be and it is obvious now that the whites don't want it.

As Lester saw it, while some black radicals would now like all whites who so deeply disappointed them to be destroyed, he was personally convinced that "the white man is simply to be ignored, because the time has come for the black man to control the things which affect his life." According to this view the black man must no longer live his life in reaction to whites. And, Lester continues:

> Now he will live it only within the framework of his own blackness and his blackness links him with the Indians of Peru, the miner in Bolivia, the African and the freedom fighters of Vietnam. What they

fight for is what the American black man fights for—the right to govern his own life. If the white man interprets that to mean hatred, it is only a reflection of his own fears and anxieties and black people leave him to deal with it. There is too much to do to waste time and energy hating white people.[38]

v

With the new ideology fermenting, it was not long before the nation's news media sensationalized the situation through their vast image-creating (and image-destroying) techniques. At the same time, ironically, when the occasion came, one of the most articulate new voices had two of the most honored black prophets of the earlier radicalism as his foils. James Meredith, the black Mississippian who had caused a riot when he attempted to enter his state university in 1962, returned to Mississippi in June of 1966 to walk the length of the state on foot as a witness against black fear. After he was shot from ambush and hospitalized, the march was continued by leaders of what still was called the civil rights movement, among whom were Dr. King and Stokely Carmichael, the self-possessed new chairman of SNCC. In the course of the rejuvenated march there were many open as well as private debates among the leaders about the need for a renewed emphasis on "blackness" in the movement. The debates were not really settled at that time but SNCC and Carmichael were the obvious victors in the jousting for publicity from the mass media, and King's international prestige served to bring public attention to the phrase that had been germinating for a long time.[39]

"We shall overcome" already was tame enough for a Texas-born president to quote in a national address, but the young radicals had moved on. Thus the press corps and a people, both of them constantly in search of fearful sensations, found them in "Black Power" and Stokely Carmichael. Only the term, however, and the violent response of the public media and the nation, were new; its concepts were old. "Black Power" merely expressed the radicalism of Afro-Americans who had decided there was no physical escape from this land and who saw no future in an integration that demanded the giving up of blackness. "Black Power" therefore meant turning away from assimilation and emphasizing the existence and beauty of an authentic Afro-American culture. "Black Power" meant a movement of and for the masses that honored the memory of Marcus Garvey and Malcolm X and the early Adam Clayton Powell. It also meant a proud association with Africa and pan-Africanism and a connection with oppressed and colonized people all over the world. Who could not hear W. E. B. Du Bois' impeccable language paraphrased in Harlem slang?

Again it was the radicalism of those who had tried white allies and had found them wanting in the tasks of building the black community. Black power sent such allies away, some with less ceremony than others. It told them to work with the white menace and to transform it into something healthy and new. It sometimes indicated that one day there might be a meeting, after the work had been done on both sides of the wall, but only blacks could now move effectively among their teeming, disaffected masses. As in an earlier day, Black Power meant armed self-defense for many adherents, who later would advance the rhetoric and the reality of the positive benefits of violence. Its emphasis was on self-determination for black people in their communities, which included political, educational, and cultural self-determination.

As the idioms of a colonialized people began to be used, the maxims of Frantz Fanon became more clear; a century-old phrase was frequently heard: "We are a nation within a nation." [40] (How can one account for the resilience of this concept? How do we explain the fact that today it is more widely accepted among Negroes than it was in the nineteenth-century day of Martin Delany—more readily heard today than it was forty years ago, when the Third Communist International appropriated black nationality as a major organizing theme for America?) [41] The words came readily but the new programs were not yet clear, and radicals who saw Black Power as more than rhetoric attempted to fill that vacuum. To those who had no response to the new version of black radicalism save an accusation of riot instigation, Stokely Carmichael gave this answer:

> As long as people in the ghettos . . . feel that they are victims of the misuse of white power without any way to have their needs represented . . . we will continue to have riots. These are not the products of "black power" but the absence of any organization capable of giving the community the power, the black power, to deal with its problems.
>
> . . . Without the power to control their lives and their commu-

359

nities . . . these communities will exist in a constant state of insurrection. This is a choice that the country will have to make.[42]

The voices of black alienation and black wisdom were again, combined this time in a group whose politics clearly were counter to almost everything America considered was in its self-interest on the international scene. Adherents of Black Power were among the earliest black critics of the war in Vietnam, on the grounds that it was racist, anti-revolutionary, and diverted critically needed men and money from the ghettos.

By the end of 1966 Carmichael was suggesting that SNCC change its name to the Student Liberation Movement, thereby identifying themselves with anti-colonial national liberation movements throughout the non-white world. Before 1967 was over, he would be in Havana—at a conference of Latin-American revolutionaries—echoing the calls of Robert Williams for a black guerrilla-type liberation struggle in the ghettos of America. And later he would visit Hanoi. Thus he became the most recent leader in the long procession of black aliens ("alien" is used in its broadest sense) who have lost faith in the promises of the American way. At the same time, however, like so many of these aliens, he has found it almost impossible to break completely with American myths and formulate a constructive radical program that, in the last analysis, does not depend upon the grudging largesse and enlightened self-interest of the white American society.[43]

360

VI

SNCC was only the clearest manifestation of a black radicalism that had many indigenous ghetto roots as, was shown when a National Conference on Black Power met in July, 1967, in Newark, New Jersey. Although various radicals seriously questioned the motivation of the conveners and would not attend, a thousand Afro-Americans came from scores of different communities (the Newark uprising earlier in the month was a spectacular spur to attendance).[44]

The speeches, clothing, and variety of visions and commitments showed that every strain of black radicalism was represented at this meeting. Indeed, there was an awesome terror in the fact that—more than a century after the Civil War—these strains should still be so obvious in the North and often so strong: separatism, radical black nonviolence, armed struggle, the Harlem Mau Mau. And a telegram was received from Robert Williams, in Peking, urging a long guerrilla struggle. The entire scene was filled with a sense of angry, outraged determination, and sometimes one could sense an air of millennarian expectation.

White members of the press corps tasted black anger at some of the four-day sessions; indeed, their bodily eviction from one of the meeting places was symptomatic of the intensity and hostility of some of the younger radicals. Members of this group urged a march through the streets, in direct confrontation with the police riot forces that patrolled the area, to protest the fact that hundreds of blacks still were in jail as a result of the recent uprising. At the highly charged plenary session where this call was issued, more than at any other time, this group resembled conventional revolutionary elements. Rap Brown and others, however, reminded the activists that violent action alone did not make radicals or revolutionaries; Brown suggested that persons who would lead unarmed men to face the guns of the frightened Newark policemen were either irresponsible fools or *agents provocateurs.* "First go and get your guns," he counseled; "then lead the march."

There was no march, partly because there were few guns, but also because black radicalism had not yet found a leader who could challenge the romanticized memory of Malcolm X and rally the forces for such a desperate move. It is much more likely, however, that there was no march because black radicalism had not yet created a program sufficiently clear and compelling to demand the rational allegiance of those who must march and perhaps die. It was obvious to many participants at Newark that such an ideology and its accompanying program would not spring from so large and disparate a group of persons and organizations.

But it was equally evident that such a gathering, if only for purposes of initial contact, could be most important. The lack of a leader and a clearly articulated framework of thought did not negate the significance of the meeting. The African costumes of explosive color, the proudly "natural" hair styles, the many persons who had adopted African and Islamic names in exchange for their "slave names," the impassioned and sometimes dangerously fiery debate—all this testified to vitality in the radical edges of the black movement.

Although the dominant idiom of the conference was the language of the ghetto, how serious was the talk of beginning a national debate

361

on possible partition? This is yet to be seen, especially when one reflects on the fact that the delegates were housed in two of Newark's most expensive, white-owned hotels and when one recalls the black action at the New Politics convention in Chicago one month later.[45] (The luxurious housing reminded many persons of the continued dependence upon white benevolence, and the appearance in Chicago seems a strange prelude to black partition.) How significant was the constant discussion of black revolution? One of its foremost exponents, Ron Karenga, said: "We are the last revolutionaries in America. If we fail to leave a legacy of revolution for our children we have failed our mission and should be dismissed as unimportant." Although Karenga, like others, believes the cultural revolution of black consciousness is most important at the present time, he has vividly pictured the next stage:

> When the word is given we'll see how tough you are. When it's "burn," let's see how much you burn. When it's "kill," let's see how much you kill. When it's "blow up," let's see how much you blow up. And when it's "take that white girl's head too," we'll really see how tough you are.[46]

After the Newark Conference Rap Brown, SNCC's chairman, added his cry: "Straighten up America, or we'll burn you down."

Had revolt come out of hiding, no longer fearful of white men's thoughts or fists? If it had come out of hiding, what were the implications of revolution, of threats to wage war by fire? As a collective black *cri de coeur* the threats and implications were completely understandable. As radical programs, as proposals to change America by guns and flames, they were at least open to question, especially because so many of the front-line ghetto guerrillas are so young, impressionable, and desperate for a self-affirming role in life. Would the advocates of guerrilla warfare miss the point that paratroopers were brought into Detroit, some of them veterans of guerrilla struggles in Vietnam? Did they misjudge America's military capacity to crush troublesome revolutionaries, or had they overestimated their own strength? Were they responsible for the young black dead in those calls for guns? Had they felt that death was preferable to the stunted, broken lives that would be forced upon those teen-age boys? Did they deem death in Newark and Detroit more honorable than death in Vietnam? At Newark, and especially after the Detroit riot, many less publi-

362

cized black radicals began to evaluate the military assets of America much more carefully and to speak less frequently of urban warfare. For some of them this coming to realistic terms with American power led (as it had often led in the past) from black radicalism to despair and total cynicism. Others felt that "liberty or death" was still a meaningful cry, regardless of paratroopers. But they knew that both liberty and meaningful struggles to the death required far more planning and discipline than had yet evolved in the black movement.

Shortly after the Newark Conference, with the sounds of Detroit's dyings still hanging in the air, it became clear that the nation's resistance to basic change was pushing relatively moderate black leaders into more radical positions. This was especially true of Martin Luther King, Jr. who had already become a major critic of American foreign policy and the war in Vietnam. At the end of August, 1967, in another SCLC convention, King called for a level of central economic planning that could have been easily labelled as socialism. Of even more immediate importance for the black movement, the SCLC leader went on to announce plans for his organization's entry into the kind of radical, massive civil disobedience which had been urged by Wyatt T. Walker and others four years before.

Soon it became clear that King intended to expand the struggle of black people in America to take in other oppressed minorities in the land: Indians, Mexican-Americans, Puerto Ricans, and poor whites. He promised to mobilize these forces and move on Washington, D.C. in a "last chance" for nonviolent direct action. There was even talk of "dislocating" the city until Congress and the nation acted on the needs and demands of the poor. The obvious revolutionary potentials of such a class-oriented mobilization were not lost on the minds of many persons. In his plans for a "Poor People's Campaign," King was now going in a direction which seemed far removed from Montgomery in 1955 and Washington in 1963—but was it?

Whatever the meaning of his actions, his mood was indicated late in 1967 when he faced an Atlanta, Georgia audience, pressed his hands up to his eyes and said, "My God, the dream I once had for America seems to be turning into a nightmare." On April 4, 1968, in Memphis, Tennessee, the nightmare was momentarily extended to the world when a sniper's bullet blasted the life from Martin Luther King who was standing on a motel balcony. Another insistent black seeker after justice had been cut down in America. For countless thousands

363

of Afro-Americans the message seemed clearer than ever before now, and it was articulated by a young speaker in Atlanta on the night of King's death: "O.K., America, Nonviolence is dead. You just killed your last chance for peaceful revolution. We won't forget." The radical black edge had been moved even further out into the bleakness of alienation, and the eventual essential failure of the Poor People's Campaign served to accelerate its motion.

VII

In light of even so cursory an historical survey it is essential to question some of the interpretations of black radicalism in America. John P. Roche, in his introduction to Wilson Record's *Race and Radicalism,* agrees with that book's thesis that

> the "radicalism" of the American Negro today is nothing more than a radical Americanism. Despite subjection to slavery and discrimination, the Negro has never massively responded to gospels of alienation but has persistently and with incredible patience fought for his rightful membership in the American community.[47]

Because these lines were published in 1964, and probably were written at the apex of the nonviolent movement, Mr. Roche might be forgiven for some of his myopia. However, if we have established the fact that radicalism is never measured by "massive" responses, we must add an insistent question mark to such an evaluation of the black radical past. Alienation has often been at its heart, and alienation was its dominant hallmark in the past decade.

In many ways a much more sensitive appreciation of black radicalism is suggested by a European radical. Victor Serge's *"Memoirs of a Revolutionary, 1901–1941"* opens with lines that are strongly reminiscent of some of the men we have met in these pages.

> Even before I emerged from childhood, I seem to have experienced, deeply at heart, that paradoxical feeling which was to dominate me all through the first part of my life: that of living in a world without any possible escape, in which there was nothing . . . but to fight for an impossible escape. I felt repugnance mingled with wrath and indignation, toward people whom I saw settled comfortably in this world. How could they not be conscious of their captivity, of their unrighteousness?

364

Irving Howe wrote, in response to this remarkably sensitive opening of the heart: "Few Americans could, in good faith, say as much: perhaps none but a handful of jail-hardened militants at the outer edge of the Negro movement who have chosen alienation from American society as a badge of honor." [48]

Howe is only partly right. The number of alienated black militants greatly exceeds "a handful," and they are not on the "outer edge" of the Negro movement in America; indeed, the center of the movement draws closer to them each day. And they discovered their "badge of honor" buried deep within their breasts almost as soon as they came to know themselves.

What is the future of this black radicalism that claims no desire for membership in the American community? Will sensitive, justice-starved black aliens be condemned to an endless search for "an impossible escape"? Are they damned to move, like burning, cursing wraiths, in the midst of unending darkness? Of if they find, from some now unknown source, the strength to do the task, will their most noble vocation be to "tear this building down"? [49] It may be that the growing number of radically engaged black intellectuals will avoid the pitfalls of despair, accommodation, and empty rhetoric and will, instead propose acceptable alternatives to the society they increasingly scorn. Therefore,—if theory does indeed follow practice, if ideologies are most often worked out in the midst of fiery social transformation —the whole or partial tearing down may yet come, as a beginning rather than as an end.

Are there still grounds for radical hope? Perhaps some statements of the "shining black prince" of this generation's black radicals will help illuminate the enigmatic answers to this question. In one of his most thoughtful moments Malcolm X entered into the black radical religious tradition to speak of judgment and atonement:

> I believe that God now is giving the world's so-called 'Christian' white society its last opportunity to repent and atone for the crimes of exploiting and enslaving the world's non-white peoples, but is white America really sorry for her crimes against the black people? Does white America have the capacity to repent—and to atone? Does the capacity to repent, to atone, exist in a majority, in one-half, in even one-third of American white society? Indeed, how *can* white society atone for enslaving, for raping, for unmanning, for

365

otherwise brutalizing *millions* of human beings, for centuries? What atonement would the God of Justice demand for the robbery of the black people's labor, their lives, their true identities, their culture, their history—and even their human dignity? [50]

The former "Detroit Red" knew the ghettos well enough to be clear on what was *not* the answer: "A desegregated cup of coffee, a theater, public toilets—the whole range of hypocritical 'integration'— these are not atonement." Malcolm X was never given a clear answer nor did he provide one, but the man who saw life in America "like it is" also knew that it must get much better or much worse. "Only such real, meaningful actions as those which are sincerely motivated from a deep sense of humanism and moral responsibility can get at the basic causes that produce the racial explosions in America today." Without such actions, "the racial explosions are only going to grow worse." [51]

This was written in 1964, a few months before the man who struggled to grow under the menace from Detroit Red to El-Hajj Malik El-Shabazz was given a personal reply to the questions he had so insistently raised. Nor was Martin King allowed to come any closer to the "Promised Land" of true freedom which he constantly spoke of. Would it really materialize in America as he desperately hoped to the end, or would there come instead some brutal fulfillment of the tragic nightmares both he and Malcolm had foreseen? Whether their deaths were an answer or only another question is not certain, but this much seems sure: Unless America becomes as different from the rest of the world as its most blind lovers already believe it is, the necessary radical social movement toward black liberation (and therefore toward the liberation of all) will not take place without the acute suffering and the shedding of blood that has long been predicted by black radicals. The hundreds of billions of dollars, the unfeigned national commitment, the transformation of priorities and energies will not be produced without stark agony, if they come at all.

There is still a minority among black radicals who view themselves not only as major architects of the new ways and seers of the new visions but also as suffering servants who must pay the price for the change. But there is a larger group, the young and rising black tide, which, despite its alienation, has been "too American" to accept (or understand) such a role. They see blood and they know it probably will be theirs. They hear the voices of police chiefs and other officials who promise to respond to their black rebellions and to riot commission reports with increased firepower. They realize that one police commissioner most likely speaks for many others when he says "We're in a war, and law enforcement is going to win." When they heard the President of the United States define "crime in the streets" as the major domestic problem, they knew he was speaking of them. These black young men see blood, but they are determined it shall not be theirs alone. Whatever they seek in life, they seek no separate death, and the words of Malcolm X are often on their lips: "It takes two to tango. If I go, you go"—a despairing invitation to the dance of death. Surely it is not an intellectual's radical program, but for black men (especially the young and cast-off) who consider themselves "under the white man's menace, out of time," it is understandable—in the absence of other programs.

Can the menace be lifted and the times set right? Or will the forces of law and order—and death—again prevail over radical black visions of justice and hope? Will every Martin Luther King have to be buried in his native land before he can really be "free at last"? Historians can deftly refer such questions to various prophets, and walk away, but it may be that the prophets of long ago who spoke of sowing and reaping will have the last, the final, word.

[1] It has not been possible to trace this comment to its source; perhaps it is only part of the black mythology.

[2] "Outcast," in Selected Poems (New York, 1953), p. 41.

[3] Here I Stand (New York, 1958), p. 28 (emphasis in original). In my history of the development of black radicalism since 1800, Black Radicalism in America (Indianapolis, 1969), I deal with Robeson at some length. One of the most interesting evaluations of his role in the Negro protest movement is Harold Cruse's The Crisis of the Negro Intellectual (New York, 1967), pp. 285–301.

[4] Lerone Bennett, Jr., The Negro Mood (Chicago, 1964), p. 10.

[5] Idem, Confrontation: Black and White (Baltimore, 1966), p. 169: "The Myth of Negro Progress . . . is the only thing that stands between the Negro and revolt."

[6] Louise Thompson, "Southern Terror," Crisis, 41 (November, 1934): 328.

[7] For a brief and perhaps more philosophically oriented examination of the path from Montgomery to the ghetto explosions, see my "Where

367

Have All the Lovers Gone?" in Alan D. Austin, ed., *The Revolutionary Imperative* (Nashville, 1966), pp. 110–27.

[8] Few works deal adequately with the historical developments of the 1945–55 preparatory period, but two lively and valuable accounts are Bennett's *Confrontation*, pp. 169–91, and Langston Hughes' *Fight for Freedom* (New York, 1962), pp. 90–139.

[9] The story of Montgomery is covered adequately (but not critically) in Martin Luther King, Jr., *Stride toward Freedom* (New York, 1958), and Lerone Bennett, *What Manner of Man?* (Chicago, 1965), pp. 55–105.

[10] Some of the earlier ideas of Farmer and Randolph on nonviolent direct action are recorded in Bennett's *Confrontation* (pp. 145–54) and James Farmer's "Memorandum to A. J. Muste" in Francis L. Broderick and August Meier, eds., *Negro Protest Thought in the Twentieth Century* (Indianapolis, 1965), pp. 210–21.

[11] King, *Stride toward Freedom*, pp. 177–78.

[12] In "This Is SCLC," in Broderick and Meier, eds., *Negro Protest Thought*, pp. 269–70.

[13] A general treatment of the student movement up to 1963 is Howard Zinn's *SNCC, The New Abolitionists* (Boston, 1964).

[14] Robert F. Williams, *Negroes with Guns* (New York, 1962), p. 63. Harold Cruse's *Crisis of the Negro Intellectual* (esp. pp. 347–419) raises important questions about the meaning of Williams' call for armed self-defense and about the current popularity of the urban guerrilla-warfare concept among black radicals.

[15] Williams, *Negroes with Guns*, p. 46.

[16] See *idem*, "U.S.A.: The Potential of a Minority Revolution," in Broderick and Meier, eds., *Negro Protest Thought*, pp. 321–33 (published originally in *The Crusader Monthly Newsletter*, vol. 5 [May–June, 1964]).

[17] It is not possible to give proper attention to concurrent developments in the black communities of the North in this essay, but they will be discussed in the aforementioned work on *Black Radicalism*.

[18] Much of the material that follows is based on my own participation in the events in Birmingham. See also Bennett's treatment in *Confrontation*, pp. 235–44, and *The Negro Mood*, pp. 3–23. (Randolph's March on Washington Movement developed in the 1940's.)

[19] This section is based on my recollections of conversations I heard in Birmingham and elsewhere at that time.

[20] This is based on my conversation during the fall of 1963 with John Lewis, whose speech was censored. The unabridged version of the speech is available in Staughton Lynd, ed., *Nonviolence in America* (Indianapolis, 1966), pp. 482–85. See also Julius Lester, "The Angry Children of Malcolm X," *Sing Out* (November, 1966), p. 22, for his knowledgeable ac-

count of the circumstances of the March on Washington. It was from the speakers' platform in Washington that the nation first heard of the death of W. E. B. Du Bois in Ghana, announced by Roy Wilkins.

²¹ In Bennett, *Confrontation*, p. 244. The Poor People's Campaign of 1968 was meant to realize much of Walker's hope for massive civil disobedience. See below, pp. 41–42.

²² Lester, "The Angry Children of Malcolm X," pp. 24–25.

²³ Williams, "U.S.A.," in Broderick and Meier, eds., *Negro Protest Thought*, p. 330.

²⁴ The most fascinating account of Malcolm X's conversion to the Nation of Islam cause is in his *Autobiography* (New York, 1966), pp. 151–210. The first edition of the *Autobiography* was published in 1965.

²⁵ In Malcolm X and James Farmer, "Separation or Integration: A Debate," in Broderick and Meier, eds., *Negro Protest Thought*, p. 363 (published originally in *Dialogue Magazine*, vol. 2 (May, 1962).

²⁶ *Ibid.*, p. 365. Unfortunately, it is not possible for this essay to develop the ironic theme of the "Americanness"—and therefore innate conservatism—of the Nation of Islam.

²⁷ In George Breitman, ed., *Malcolm X Speaks* (New York, 1965), pp. 49–50, 56–57.

²⁸ *Ibid.*, p. 35. Of course Malcolm X knew that mainland China was not a member of the United Nations. Rather he was being pointedly precise when he referred to that country as "waiting" to throw its weight on the side of the black cause.

²⁹ *Ibid.*, pp. 43, 128–29.

³⁰ *Ibid.*, pp. 141–42.

³¹ Quoted in Dudley Randall and Margaret G. Burroughs, eds., *For Malcolm X* (Detroit, 1967), p. 16. Hayden's lines are part of a longer poem, "El-Hajj Malik El-Shabazz."

³² For the background of SNCC's participation in the Voter Education Project, see Pat Watters and Reese Cleghorn, *Climbing Jacob's Ladder* (New York, 1967), pp. 41–74.

³³ Again, much of the material that follows is based on my experience in Mississippi and my relationships with many persons who were involved in the 1964 experiment. For an independently formulated corroboration of my views, see Alvin F. Poussaint, "How the 'White Problem' Spawned 'Black Power,'" *Ebony*, August, 1967, pp. 88–94.

³⁴ This paragraph is based partly on my conversations with SNCC staff members who helped formulate the strategy for the MFDP challenge and who were present in Atlantic City (especially Charlie Cobb, James Foreman, and Robert Moses). See also Len Holt, *The Summer That Didn't End* (New York, 1965), pp. 149–183.

[35] The Selma episode is treated in Bennett, *Confrontation*, p. 252.

[36] In Clyde Halisi and James Mtume, eds., *The Quotable Karenga* (Los Angeles, 1967), p. 13.

[37] Lester, "The Angry Children of Malcolm X," p. 25.

[38] *Ibid.*

[39] Dr. King's account of the Mississippi discussions can be found in his *Where Do We Go from Here?* (New York, 1967), pp. 23–32.

[40] Fanon's work, *The Wretched of the Earth* (New York, 1965), has often—and rightly—been mandatory reading material for would-be revolutionaries of the non-white world.

[41] One of the most fascinating aspects of the entire situation is the fact that the American Communist Party jettisoned the self-determination theme when the hope for integration had been paramount, in 1959 and 1960. Partly as a result of this move, they often find they are ideologically outflanked in their efforts to make contact with the newest black movements. Instead they must watch—no doubt in doubled vexation—as Peking-oriented Marxists enter the black nationalist mood with what seems to be much greater ease. For the story of the American Communists' change, see Joseph C. Mouledous, "From Browderism to Peaceful Co-Existence," *Phylon*, 25, 1 (Spring, 1964): 79–90. James Farmer, the national chairman of CORE, offers a terse but intriguing comment on some of the Mao–black nationalist relationships in his *Freedom When?* (New York, 1965), pp. 102–3.

[42] "Towards Black Liberation," *Massachusetts Review* (Autumn, 1966), pp. 648–51.

[43] This problem is evidenced throughout Carmichael's book (co-authored with Charles Hamilton), *Black Power* (New York, 1967).

[44] The statements concerning the Newark Conference are based almost entirely on my own notes and reflections as a participant.

[45] The relationship of the New Politics convention to the development of black radicalism will be discussed in my aforementioned essay, on *Black Radicalism.*

[46] In Halisi and Mtume, *The Quotable Karenga*, pp. 11, 10.

[47] In Wilson Record, *Race and Radicalism: The NAACP and the Communist Party in Conflict* (Ithaca, N.Y., 1964), p. vi.

[48] In Irving Howe, ed., *Steady Work: Essays in the Politics of Democratic Radicalism, 1953–1966* (New York, 1966), pp. 258, 258–59.

[49] A nineteenth-century Afro-American spiritual constantly repeats these words: "If I had-a my way, I'd tear this building down." See one version of the song in Sterling A. Brown *et al.*, eds., *The Negro Caravan* (New York, 1941), p. 443.

[50] Malcolm X, *Autobiography*, p. 370.

[51] *Ibid.*, pp. 370, 377.

1. THE RELIGION OF BLACK POWER

by *Vincent Harding*

For scholars and ordinary citizens standing near the edges of the latest stage of America's perennial racial crisis, certain conclusions are easy to come by, especially when they are formed against the glare of burning buildings, the staccato reports of weapons, and a certain malaise verging on fear. To the observers who are at all concerned with what might be called religious phenomena, there is an especially deceptive set of circumstances and deductions surrounding the newest expression of Black Power as a force within the ancient struggle. For if movements are judged primarily by their public rhetoric and other obvious manifestations, it seems abrasively apparent that the time of singing, of preaching, and of nonviolent concern for the redemption of American society is rapidly passing, if not gone. More black love for whites evidently burns in every ghetto-shaped inferno. By certain standards, the religious elements of the struggle are to be studied only as historical manifestations from a recent and lamented past.

Such an interpretation of the present black moment is encouraged by the words of an anonymous spokesman for the current mood: "Man, the people are too busy getting ready to fight to bother with singing any more." When a song does burst forth it often proclaims,

> Too much love,
> Too much love,
> Nothing kills a nigger like
> Too much love [13:25].

Even in the presence of such compelling testimony against the adequacy of the older, more comforting religious symbols, rituals, and words, it would be myopic to miss the central issues of

3

human life and destiny which course through the current expression of blackness. Issues of anthropology, incarnation, the nature of the universe and of God, issues of hope and faith, questions of eschatology and of the nature of the Kingdom, problems concerning love and its functions — all these and more are at stake in the present situation. That they are usually disguised, often submerged, and sometimes denied does not lessen the power of their reality. Indeed the inherent power of the issues may be heightened by such camouflaging pressures. (One may even conjecture that the current black mood is in surprising harmony with much of the American trend towards a secular religion or a religionless church which, though it often overreacts to older explicit orthodox formulations, is shaped unmistakably by the life of the streets.)

BLACK POWER AND THE NEW MAN

In spite of the tendency among Black Power advocates to repress any reference to the earlier Afro-American religious expressions — especially as they were found in the nonviolent movement — the most familiar word from the past remains available to set the stage for an exploration of the religious implications of the current themes. At a forum on Black Power in Atlanta during the fall of 1966, while discussing "love," a spokesman for Black Power was heard to say, "Martin King was trying to get us to love white folks before we learned to love ourselves, and that ain't no good."

When there is serious reflection upon these words, a meaningful examination of the religious elements of Black Power may properly begin, for here is an issue which, if not the heart of the affair, is certainly very near the center of things. In spite of some public images to the contrary, it is likely that no element is so constant in the gospel of Blackness — at least as it is encountered in its native communities — as the necessity of self-love. One writer tells much that is crucial to the story when she refers to

372

4

"the inner power that comes with self-esteem, the power to develop to full stature as human beings" [4:29].

Healthy self-esteem has been seen in many traditions as a prerequisite to the establishment of community — whether with a spouse, a society, or a God. It has most often been the bedrock of love. It is surely this that comes through in the teaching of Jesus to love the neighbor as oneself. Black Power is a calling for black self-love, but it is not an unambiguous summons. Its clearest implications on this level are suggested by John Oliver Killens, one of the major literary spokesmen for the movement, when he writes,

373

> [Black Power] does not teach hatred; it teaches love. But it teaches us that love, like charity, must begin at home; that it must begin with ourselves, our beautiful black selves [11:36].

Stokely Carmichael has put this love in the context of the building of a black society "in which the spirit of community and humanistic love prevail" [2:8]. So in spite of "too much love" and in spite of the fact that Carmichael also admitted that the word was "suspect," no writer in the newest black stage fails to refer to a need for this love among black people.

Such an emphasis grows partly out of historical necessity, for all who make it are actively aware of the crushing psychological effects American life has had on the self-image of black men and women. However it may also rise out of an intuitive recognition that a call to love cuts across the deepest grain of man's being when it is addressed to an individual who is without some clear ground of self-respect.

It is precisely at this point that the ambiguity of the new black love becomes most evident, especially as it is exemplified in the writing of Killens. In the essay cited above he goes on to say that the love taught by Black Power is

> so powerful that it will settle for nothing short of love in return. Therefore, it does not advocate unrequited love, which is a sick bit under any guise or circumstance. Most black folk have no need to love those who would spit on them or practice

5

genocide against them. . . . Profound love can only exist between equals [11].

Killens' point of view represents much of the thinking on this
subject in Black Power circles, and it is obviously a retort to
what is understood to be nonviolence and to what is thought to
be the teaching of Christian churches, especially black ones.
However, it may be an overreaction, for, while one is eminently
wise to realize that love flows out of self-esteem, one may be less
than wise in demanding a predetermined response to black love.
In a sense this is an interesting variation on one of the basic pitfalls of the rhetoric of nonviolence. For while the nonviolent
movement promised that black love would bring predictable,
favorable white responses, Killens says that, unless whites respond as they ought, love will stop. Much of the world's religion
teaches that love demands nothing more than the freedom of the
other to respond. Perhaps it takes the strongest love of all to continue in the path while realizing that such freedom can never
be coerced.

374

Perhaps, however, it is even more pertinent to note that Killens
speaks of love and hate as being totally irrelevant until black and
white men are equals. This is the even stronger frame of mind in
the ghettos today. Love for Black Power is, as Carmichael puts
it, a love "within the black community, the only American community where men call each other 'brother' when they meet. We
can build a community of love," he says, "only where we have
the ability and power to do so: among blacks" [2:8]. At this
juncture white persons are simply not considered as valid objects
of black love. Such love (or, more accurately, its outward appearance) has been forced from blacks for too long; now, as one
of the movement's most sensitive authors puts it, for many of the
present black generation,

> the white man no longer exists. He is not to be lived with and
> he is not to be destroyed. He is simply to be ignored. . . .

If whites consider this relegation to nonexistence as hatred, Julius
Lester says, such an interpretation "is only a reflection of [their]
own fears and anxieties. . . ." As for blacks, he says, "There

6

is too much to do to waste time and energy hating white people" [13:24].

This powerful strand of Black Power thinking raises a long series of religiously oriented issues. First among many is the recurring issue regarding the control and direction of love. If it is assumed — as it surely must be — that black love must begin among black people and find its nurture there, can it be quarantined? What shall be said of a love that is willed towards some men and not towards others? Is this goal in any way related to the deadly disease that has afflicted so much of American life for so many generations?

375

An interim goal is now to make white men "invisible" while black men are brought into the light. Can it be brought off by blacks with any less poisoning of the spirit than occurred in whites who invented "tuning out"? If it is true that white men dream long dreams of the dark brothers they have rejected, what are the dreams in black beds? Such an exploration must also ask whether it is enough not to hate. Does our recent experience suggest that hatred might well be preferable to the creation of a new breed of nonexistent nonblack men?

The answers do not come with ease. Perhaps refusal to hate is enough to begin with when one considers the deep sources of human justification for black hatred and revenge against whites. Perhaps those who can rise out of such carefully poisoned wells of human experience with the strength not to hate their oppressors have made a major beginning, whatever their dreams may be. Of course, if anyone should dare to press on and raise the most disturbing religious issue of even loving enemies, there may be two initial responses. It must first be acknowledged that the American religious communities have offered no consistent examples of this love for enemies, especially in times of war. (Black people consider themselves at war, and they have imbibed more of American religion than they know.) Secondly it is essential that all questioners should examine the possibility that men may need the freedom to hate their enemies before love can become an authentic response. It may be that black freedom offers no less dangerous a path than any other variety.

7

BLACK POWER AND THE NEW COMMUNITY

In part, an answer to our questions must await the further development of the black pilgrimage in this hostile land. Now it is sufficient to note another major thrust of the Black Power movement that has deep religious moorings, a sharing in man's constant search for community. As black exiles search in an often alien world for the ground of their being, the movement is increasingly towards the building of community. Love is recognized as a necessary foundation for this structure — whatever its form.

There was a time when the vision of the community to be built was as large as America, but that is no longer the case. At least that seems no longer a task that black men can set themselves to. Julius Lester put it this way:

> At one time black people desperately wanted to be American, to communicate with whites, to live in the Beloved Community. Now that is irrelevant. They know that it can't be until whites want it to be, and it is obvious now that whites don't want it [13:25].

Now black men must build their own beloved black community, Lester concludes. Does such a statement indicate a recoil from the religious search for the fully inclusive community, or is it a more sober and therefore a more faithful estimate of the world and of the power of race?

Those persons who think of such a withdrawal into blackness as a racist or nationalist retreat from universalism would likely find comfort in the thoughts of one of the Afro-American leaders who said, "The fact that we are Black is our ultimate reality. We were black before we were born" [8:3]. When one considers some of the basic "realities" of American life, there is a certain soundness in this view, and it is supplemented by Lester's call for black men to recognize and celebrate "those things uniquely theirs which separate them from the white man."

Those who see goals of black community as falling short of the goal of universal community must recognize the fact that black men in America have long been encouraged to disdain their community no less than themselves. Therefore, such a call may be the beginning of true corporate health and integrity for black people. It is surely a significant change from the major direction of Afro-American movement toward the larger society during the past generation, for that has been largely a movement away from the ghettos, away from the ground out of which we sprang. "Integration" has most often been the call to escape. (At least it was so interpreted until hard white rocks made clear the nature of its siren sounds.) Now a Karenga teaches that "Our purpose in life should be to leave the Black Community more beautiful than we inherited it" [8:27]. Now Carmichael and others like him plead with black college students to train themselves not to be siphoned out of the ghettos, but to pour themselves back into it. This direction of Black Power is one of its surest words of judgment upon the black churches of the Afro-American communities. It is the same judgment that the Nation of Islam and Malcolm X brought, for it speaks to congregations and pastors who usually have no more use for the black depths than their white Christian counterparts.

377

The call for communal identification among the black outcasts of America has had observable impact and will probably increase in force. It is the closest thing to a sense of religious vocation that some of the current black college and graduate students know. It is surely significant that one of them spoke in the image of John Donne's human land mass when he voiced the response of a growing proportion of his generation. In a recent article in *Ebony* magazine, Stanley Saunders, a Rhodes Scholar now in Yale's law school, confessed his former attempts to hide from his white friends the truth of his origins in the blackness of Watts. Saunders said this attempt was for him a means of gaining acceptance and assimilation into the American society. Now, with the coming of the new black consciousness, that has changed. He can say instead,

> If there is no future for the black ghetto, the future of all Negroes is diminished. What affects it, affects me, for I am a child of the ghetto. When they do it to Watts, they do it to me,

9

too. I'll never escape from the ghetto. I have staked my all on its future. Watts is my home [17:36].

There is probably a message in these words for all who see the call for solidarity with the black community as a call away from universalism. For it is quite possible that the earlier liberal invitations to highly selected black men — calls into the Party or into the Church, or into some other wing of the idol of Integration — were really deceptive, or at least premature. Perhaps we were urged towards an identification with mankind-at-large (often meaning white mankind) before we had learned to identify with our black neighbors. It is likely that our humanity really begins in the black ghetto and cannot be rejected there for an easier, sentimental, white-oriented acceptance elsewhere. So it may be that the question of "who is my neighbor?" is answered for us.

Of paramount importance is the fact that these questions are being answered for persons in the ghettos who will never see Yale. Many of the burgeoning black-oriented groups — organized in varying degrees of structural sophistication — are manned primarily by young men who have been cast out of the restless bowels of a technological society. Now in their teens and early twenties, with little prospect of any meaningful work in the larger society as it now stands, these black youths have begun to find themselves as members of groups dedicated to the protection and development of the ghetto that has so long been their prison. The new vision that Black Power has brought to them may be one of the most important of all its consequences. These were the rejected stones of integration. They had neither the skills nor the graces demanded. They may well become the cornerstones of a renewed black community.

Such a transformation may suggest that if black men are ever to achieve to the larger universal calling, we must, like Paul, clearly apprehend the things which are a part of our own racial and cultural heritage. Perhaps we must be able to glory in that past as a gift of God before we will be prepared to count it as garbage for the sake of the new family of man [16]. For if we begin with a conception of our ancestral community as garbage, of our heritage as worthless, we shall be guilty of irresponsible

378

10

escapism and not growth when we move to transcend them. Isn't it taught in some circles that Jesus of Nazareth had first to explore the most profound levels of his own culture — both physically and spiritually — before he was eligible to transcend it?

So Black Power holds a healthy possibility for the coming of true religious community. It suggests the destruction of ugly and ironic caste distinctions within the Afro-American community. It encourages the discovery of roots long buried and rejected. It insists that men be true to themselves. It calls a broken people to see its own black section of the mainland. It reveals the gifts of those who were once the scorned members of the black body. Karenga may therefore be most accurate when he writes, "Until Blacks develop themselves, they can do nothing for humanity" [8:2]. Obviously, what is being suggested is that men must not only love themselves in order to love their neighbor, but they must love their communities in order to love the world.

379

Actually, many sections of the world are already included in the concerns of Black Power, and one has the feeling that there is intimated in these concerns a universalism that is at least as broad as that known by most western religious traditions. Black Power calls for an identification between black people here and all the wretched nonwhites of the earth. (Some leaders, like Carmichael, now expand this to the poor and oppressed of every color.) This is certainly the meaning of Lester's statement that, while a black man must now live his life in the United States

> only within the framework of his own blackness [that] blackness links him with the Indians of Peru, the miner in Bolivia, the African and the freedom fighters of Vietnam. What they fight for is what the American black man fights' for — the right to govern his own life [13:25].

(Is it possible that a universalism based on suffering, struggle, and hope is more vital than some vague identification based on common links to a possibly dead Creator-Father?)

Such breadth of concern for "the broken victims" in their struggle to be free is surely another of Black Power's judgments upon American religion, especially the faith of those persons who

II

claim a great tradition of prophetic concern for social justice, and those who claim a Master who came to set all broken victims free. For while such religious respectables stand silently or march weakly protesting, the devotees of Black Power identify themselves unambiguously with the oppressed and with the revolutions made by the oppressed. So if only by sheer numbers – the numbers of the earth's humiliated people – such identification actually brings Black Power into the orbit of a universality more authentic than the largely parochial sentiments of a "Judeo-Christian" western commitment.

380

Nor are the righteous delivered by pointing accurately to the fact that Black Power makes no effort to identify with the oppressors who, according to the teachings of many traditions, are also theoretically eligible for concern. The example of American religion has been poor (perhaps it will eventually prove poisonous), for its identification has been largely with the exploiters or with those who live comfortably because of the action of exploitation. Therefore black men may well sense a need to redress this imbalance, this "crookedness" that is prevalent throughout the western world – no matter how many times *The Messiah* is sung, which refers to making the crooked become straight (Isaiah 40:3–4, e.g.).

Perhaps, too, black rebels remember the example of Jesus, the focus of much of western religion. For while he evidently was filled with ultimate concern for both oppressed and oppressor, he reserved his sharpest words of judgment for the politico-religious leaders and oppressors within the Jewish community, and his death came outside the gates of respectability. Black Power may well suggest that religious concern for both sides does not mean neutrality in the face of injustice. Indeed, it reminds us that the world most often will not permit that questionable luxury, even should it be desirable.

(This identification with the wretched of the earth is especially significant for the incipient struggle for leadership between Black Power adherents and the traditional spokesmen of the Negro masses – their ministers. For though there have been important exceptions, the public stance of most of the respectable pastors has been in accord with the dominant American attitudes towards

modern, radical revolution. By and large, the black church hierarchy has been no more Christian than its white counterpart on
such issues, except where the accident of race has forced it to
certain stances. Should the sense of solidarity with the exploited
peoples grow to major proportions in the Afro-American communities, it may well prove impossible for such religious leaders
to hold on to their already shaky grounds.)

BLACK MESSIAHS AND MARCHING SAINTS

381

The qualified universalism of Black Power is also streaked with
vivid suggestions of Messianism at many points. Indeed, Afro-
American intellectual history has long been filled with images
of Black Messiahs, either individually or en masse, rising up to
deliver Black America from its bondage and White America
from its lethal folly. Though the first event was always guaranteed, the second did not necessarily follow from it in every case
[9]. In our own century the theme was first voiced fully in the
fascinating and significant movement led by Marcus Garvey.
It was this audacious black genius who sent a Messianic promise
to the black world from his cell in the Atlanta Federal Peni-
tentiary. In 1925, Garvey said,

> If I die in Atlanta my work shall then only begin, but I shall
> live, in the physical or spiritual to see the day of Africa's glory.
> When I am dead wrap the mantle of the Red, Black, and Green
> around me, for in the new life I shall rise with God's grace and
> blessing to lead the millions up the heights of triumph with the
> colors that you well know. Look for me in the whirlwind or
> the storm, look for me all around you, for, with God's grace, I
> shall come and bring with me countless millions of black slaves
> who have died in America and the West Indies and the millions
> in Africa to aid you in the fight for Liberty, Freedom and Life
> [7:136–137].

There are still Afro-Americans in this country, the West Indies,
and Africa who attribute every movement towards black liberation to the living, vibrant spirit of Marcus Garvey.

It was so, too, with Malcolm X, and after his death there came

13

a resurgence of the Messianic theme. The visions of an anointed leader and a Messianic people have been most recently joined in the work of a black novelist, Ronald Fair. Writing in *Negro Digest* about the meaning of Black Power, Fair moved quickly to the issue of ultimate hope, and said,

> we are the ones who will right all the wrongs perpetrated against us and our ancestors and we are the ones who will save the world and bring a new day, a brilliantly alive society that swings and sings and rings out the world over for decency and honesty and sincerity and understanding and beauty and love. . . . [5:30, 94].

Again the chosen people are black and promise a new day out of the matrix of their sufferings. Fair was not specific about the means by which the newness would come, but he said, "we fight on and we spread the love we have been told we cannot feel for ourselves to each and every black man we meet."

Finally the novelist tied the Messianic people to its leader and invoked the revered name when he said,

> We look about us and wait because somewhere, somewhere in the tenements in Harlem, or from the west side of Chicago, or from Watts, there *will* be another Malcolm and this one won't be murdered.

As Ronald Fair read the moment, "every black man in this country is aware that our time has come" [5:94].

Now is the fullness of time in many black minds; and though traditional religion is often denied, the deeper symbols and myths are appropriated to express the sense of expectation that stirs within the black communities, focused now in the ideology of Black Power. As might be predicted, the black Messianic hope expands beyond America's shores, and this aspect of it was also expressed by Killens. He wrote,

> we black Americans are no longer a "minority" but a part of that vast majority of humanity yearning to be free and struggling with every ounce of their strength to throw off the black-man's burden and the yoke of white supremacy. We are a part of that fellowship of the disinherited which will surely inherit the earth in this century [11:37].

382

The ambiguities of Fair's "fight" are largely discarded in Killens' vision of the way ahead. It is those who were forced to be meek (as some count meekness) who now enter into armed struggle to inherit the earth.

Another spokesman for Black Power is even less ambiguous, for Nathan Hare speaks of a "Black Judgment Day around the corner" for America. He envisions it as a possible "black *blitzkrieg* . . . making America a giant, mushrooming Watts, in which this country will either solve its problems or get the destruction it deserves" [10:01]. It is surely not presumptuous to suggest that elements of the same vision impel an H. Rap Brown to demand from the nation that it either "straighten up" or face the fire of judgment.

383

Within the heart of Black Power stands the perennial tension between a salvation leading to swinging and singing and love, and a day of destruction demanded by a just God. Throughout the history of black American radicalism run the themes of repentance and atonement or judgment [18:62–147]. Always there is the memory of bloodshed being connected to the remission of sins. But when the chosen, sinned-against people become both armed and anointed, when the saints march with guns, then the issues are mooted, and the day of the Lord is clouded indeed. For it may be that armed and marching black saints in Harlem are not likely to conceive of their task any differently than those who killed infidel Indians in New England, cut off unrepentant heads in old England, or now burn "suspected" children in Vietnam. Is it given to black men any more than to whites to be self-commissioned executors of Divine judgment on evil-doers? Easy replies must not suffice, for what if the Divine Judge has retired from his bench, leaving all things in the hands of men? What then? Does evil for evil become mandatory?

BLACK RESURRECTION: THE POWER AND THE GLORY

What are the means to be used in building new black men, new black communities and a renewed, black-oriented world? Already certain pathways have been suggested. The new men must come partly from a new vision of themselves. Indeed the image

15

that has been constantly used in this century involves more than new self-image, it presumes resurrection. Ever since Marcus Garvey preached an Easter sermon on "The Resurrection of the Negro" in 1922, the theme has been constantly renewed. For Garvey, self-knowledge was a key to this resurrection.

On the occasion of his sermon he said, "We are about to live a new life — a risen life — a life of knowing ourselves" [6:88]. His central passage in the discourse was an anticipation of so much that was to come on the black scene that it merits another temporary movement back into the first quarter of the century. Continuing the crucial image of resurrection, Garvey said,

> I trust there will be a spiritual and material resurrection among Negroes everywhere; that you will lift yourselves from the doubts of the past; that you will lift yourselves from the slumbers of the past; that you will lift yourselves from the lethargy of the past, and strike out in this new life — in this resurrected life — to see things as they are [6:90].

The theme was continued faithfully in the Nation of Islam where Elijah Muhammad constantly spoke of "dead, so-called Negroes" who needed to be resurrected to their true life as black men [14]. At the current juncture the same concept finds various expressions among those who seek to build new black men. Thus Ron Karenga insists that "We must not be so busy calling the Negro dead that we can't work out methods to resurrect him" [8:17]. One of the methods is obviously the love and concern that other black men show for the "dead" brother. Another, related, path to new life is suggested by Carmichael who speaks of "the necessity to reclaim our history and our identity from the cultural terrorism and depredation of self-justifying white guilt" [3:639]. The process of teaching becomes crucial. History becomes a balm for healing and a hope for new beginnings.

The pages of recent black history are thus filled with testimonies of Afro-Americans who saw themselves as "dead" or "sick" before their contact with the healing and resurrecting power of black concern and black self-knowledge. One of Karenga's own disciples (and the word is used intentionally) recently wrote,

16

I can remember myself before Maulana ["Great Leader," the title assumed by Karenga] showed me the "Path of Blackness." I was so sick no one but Maulana could have saved me. Running around with no identity, purpose or direction. Maulana gave me an alternative to this white system. . . . I say, "all praises due to Maulana" . . . [8:iii].

Such dependence upon new or previously hidden knowledge for salvation is at least as old as Gnosticism and most of the mystery religions, and perhaps one also hardly needs to comment about the significance of love as a conqueror of death. Nevertheless it might be well to note that in a world where God's absence is more evident than his presence to large numbers of men, an individual's worth may no longer be sufficiently affirmed in terms of his worthiness before a Divine being. Or could one say that black love and resurrection are simply ways of speaking about and discovering incarnation where it is most needed today?

385

Some persons are nevertheless disturbed by what they consider a "glorification of blackness" in the healing process under discussion. In a significant sense, this is exactly what is involved in the relationship of Black Power to black and broken men who have been made ashamed of their blackness. It is indeed glorified; and a perceptive theological interpreter of this aspect of the issue offers a most helpful understanding of the action when he writes,

> The glorification of blackness implicit in the term Black Power is a conscious or unconscious effort to stake a claim for the worth of those in our nation who are termed nonwhite. Essentially it is a clarification. The root meaning of the term "glorify" is to clarify, to make clear and plain and straight [19:139].

Nor does Nathan Wright confine the issue to the human sphere with this highly suggestive description of black glorification. He goes on to say,

> All of life must be clarified in this sense. It must be given and seen in that dimension which sets it forth in terms of glory — now and forever. To see life as it truly is means to see it as God sees it, in its eternal dimension, in the glory appropriate to its involvement with and in the life of God [19:139–140].

17

If one follows this invaluable line of thought, it is obvious
that Black Power has within it the possibility of setting black
men in an entirely new light — the light of their Creator. They
are called upon to see themselves as they were meant to be. This
glorification has the potential of setting them at peace with themselves and with the creative purposes of the universe; they no
longer need to curse God and die. For their blackness is now —
like the rest of their createdness — a sign of His love and not
His anger.

At its best, such glorification sets black men at peace whether
or not the white world recognizes the reality of their dark bless-
edness; such clarity makes it unnecessary for them to prove to
whites the facts of that glory or even to demand that they be
recognized. For men at peace with the universe are at once profoundly at peace with themselves and with all others who participate in that universe. Unfortunately, such a time is not yet
with us, and black men have been forced to live in shameful
dependency and self-negation for too long. So the process of
resurrection may well be more like three generations than three
days for some of the black dead. But it is also possible that the
coming forth may be unlike the quiet stories of the Gospels and
more like the volcanic eruptions of the Old Testament or the
fire-framed bursting of the graves in the vision of John.

One difficult aspect of the rebuilding task urged by Black
Power is the break with white leadership. This has long been a
subject of furious discussion among blacks, and in this century
it began when several Negro members of W. E. B. DuBois' radical, black Niagara Movement, refused in 1909 to join the newly
created white-dominated National Association for the Advancement of Colored People [1: vol 2, 927]. In our own time the
issue was perhaps raised most sharply by SNCC, partly as a result of its Mississippi Summer experience of 1964. Even before
the experiment of bringing large numbers of whites into the state
had begun, it was reported that some black staff members of the
organization "felt that it would destroy everything which they
had accomplished." According to Julius Lester's account, the
objectors were convinced that

18

Whites, no matter how well meaning, could not relate to the Negro community. A Negro would follow a white person to the courthouse, not because he'd been convinced he should register to vote, but simply because he had been trained to say Yes to whatever a white person wanted [13:23].

Therefore it was determined that the resurrection of black people required decisive breaks with the old patterns of life, patterns of constant dependence on whites which had been begun in slavery and then encouraged ever since. By 1966, Stokely Carmichael had put the new dictum into words, using "psychological equality" as a synonym for black mental resurrection. He wrote, "The need for psychological equality is the reason why SNCC today believes that blacks must organize in the black community. Only black people can convey the revolutionary idea that black people are able to do things themselves" [2:6].

387

While this decision on the part of Black Power advocates has been one of the most difficult for well-intentioned whites to abide, there is much logic in its direction if one is primarily concerned with the building of men and communities which have long been shattered, threatened, or used by forces with white faces. It is difficult for white men and women to be told to go and organize in white communities "where the racism really is," but such words are certainly worthy of serious consideration, especially if one's deepest concern is with the healing of shattered black egos more than with the bolstering of relatively intact white ones.

Even though the logic is powerful, the implications of the movement towards separation and the questions it raises are no less significant. How shall the black and white victims of American racism best find their healing before the last night settles in? What is the nature of the binding process and under what conditions shall it best take place? One wonders, for instance, if the restoration of broken, embittered spirits can take place apart from the presence — at some point — of the offending, denying, guilt-dominated brother. Or is it impossible for black men to build the necessary strength to love themselves — which must precede all else — except through studied alienation from their

19

former oppressors, even the truly repentant ones? Perhaps an even more sobering and "practical" question is whether or not a white community without inner quietness will allow the black workers time and space to build a unique (and thereby threatening) set of structures and beings.

The models for guidance are difficult to discover, but it is evident that the ancient issue of means and ends is involved in the discussion, if one takes seriously the stated goals of some of the Black Power advocates. For instance, few members of the younger, enraged generation have any program of separate states or of Zionism on another continent. Therefore most seek to find some *modus vivendi* on the American scene. At the heart of the matter under discussion is the issue of how we can prepare black people to live with integrity on the scene of our former enslavement and our present estrangement. In examining this matter, Karenga says, "We're not for isolation but interdependence — but we can't become interdependent unless we have something to offer." In other words, he says, "We can live with whites interdependently once we have Black Power" [8:3]. So the summary response to the central question seems to be that it is only a temporary withdrawing of the black community into itself which will prepare it for interdependence, and therefore the end appears threatened by the seemingly unavoidable means.

(Somehow the black-white dilemma is often suggestive of an unhealthy and mutually destructive marriage which may require at least a period of separation for the mutual benefit of the two partners. At other times America seems to be the forever unfaithful lover of the Blues, the lover who is always lamented but never left — until the last, inevitably bloody scene. The same unclarity that marks the religious response to unhealthy love affairs and destructive marriages is likely present when one searches for guidance here. Is divorce preferable to the kitchen knife? But what would divorce mean?)

A question no less difficult arises in another step that Black Power takes towards the building of black men and the black community — the emphasis on self-defense. Speaking for his organization in 1966, Carmichael set the most obvious theme: "SNCC reaffirms the right of black men everywhere to defend themselves when threatened or attacked" [2:5]. Moving the idea from a right to an authentication of black freedom, Killens wrote, "Men are not free unless they affirm the right to defend themselves" [11:33]. But for those who would intelligently explore Black Power, even these explanations are insufficient. It was Killens who set out — largely by implication — the fuller and more profound psychological significance of self-defense for black men. He wrote in the same revealing article,

> We black folk have a deep need to defend ourselves. Indeed we have an obligation. We must teach the brutalizers how it feels to be brutalized. We must teach them that it hurts. They'll never know unless we teach them [11:34].

389

The issues raised by this series of statements are worthy of thoughtful consideration, for they eventually move to a level of profound moment. On the surface they seem to be nothing more than an affirmation of the somewhat disreputable "American right" to self-defense. (A right, incidentally, which most Americans have no sound moral grounds for questioning when it suddenly appears among angry black men.)

In some ways this affirmation of self-defense is an obvious response to a situation in which black people find that neither separation, respect, nor love is forthcoming from the dominant portion of the society. On another, related, level it is a repetition of the earlier theme of judgment at the hands of the injured. As we have mentioned, in a world in which God is at least obscure, and where no one else seems a dependable agent of justice for black people, black men should stand firmly on their reponsibility to do the necessary work. There is, however, an even more profound issue involved in what Killens describes so sensitively as "a deep need" for black men to defend themselves. What he seems to be implying is this: when men have long been forced to accept the wanton attacks of their oppressors, when they have had to stand by and watch their women prostituted, it is crucial to their own sense of self-esteem that they affirm and be able to implement their affirmation of a right to strike back.

The basic human search for a definition of manhood is here set out in significant black lineaments. Does manhood indeed depend upon the capacity to defend one's life? Is this American shibboleth really the source of freedom for men? Is it possible that a man simply becomes a slave to another man's initiative when he feels obliged to answer his opponent on the opponent's terms? Is there perhaps a certain kind of bondage involved when men are so anxious about keeping themselves alive that they are ready to take the lives of others to prevent that occurrence? The question is really one of the image man was meant to reflect; what is it? Certain ways of looking at the world would suggest that such questions are pointless before they come from the lips. Other religious perspectives might suggest that manhood can be discussed, but only in terms of the capacity to create new grounds for response to danger, and in the act of bringing new life into being, rather than in the animal capacity to strike back.

In his characteristically vivid way, Karenga allows no circumventing of the issue. He writes, "If we fight we might be killed. But it is better to die as a man than to live like a slave" [8:19]. In the midst of a hostile, threatening environment the Zealot pathway is often chosen by those who are in honest search of their manhood, by those who seek to protect and avenge their oppressed community. Most persons who claim to be followers of the Man who introduced Zealots to a new way of response have chosen not to follow him at this point. And here is one of the most telling witnesses to the possibility that Black Power may be more fully bound to the traditions of the western Christian world than its proponents would ever dare believe.

Now, if it is possible that the fullest stature of man was found in one who honestly and sharply opposed his enemies but finally faced them with his cross, then Black Power may have chosen far less than the best available way. If it has chosen a bondage to death, the mistake is completely understandable. It is understandable not only because retaliatory violence is deeply etched into the American grain, but also because men who have been forced up against crosses all of their lives find it difficult to take one up when the choice is fully theirs. It is understandable, too, because western society now seems unable to offer any normative response to the question, "What is man?" Moreover it appears

22

totally without courage to experiment with possibilities beyond the old, "heroic," destructive replies.

Perhaps one possibility yet stands in the future, and Black Power's immediate choice must not be counted as its last. For who knows where the inner quest will lead black men if they are honestly in search of true manhood, true community, and true humanity? Are there not grounds for hope wherever men are soberly and devotedly engaged in the quest for new light?

OLD WHITE MODELS AND NEW BLACK HOPES   391

If the relationship of self-defense to the building of black manhood is crucial on the personal level, then it is likely that the kinds of "power" sought by the black community is the focal question on the broader scale. Not only is it crucial, but it faces us with another set of religious issues of considerable force. Initially one must ask: what is the power necessary to build the new black community? Perhaps Stokely Carmichael best summarized the normative Black Power response when he wrote,

> Almost from its beginning, SNCC sought to [build] a program aimed at winning political power for impoverished Southern blacks. We had to begin with politics because black Americans are a propertyless people in a country where property is valued above all. We had to work for power, because this country does not function by morality, love, and nonviolence, but by power [2:5].

Political, economic and social power, with a final recourse to armed self-defense are at the heart of the black search, even though Carmichael has since gone on to espouse aggressive guerrilla warfare. Ron Karenga, who feels the movement is not yet ready for such warfare, put the issues of power for the black community more colorfully, but no less directly when he said,

> Like it or not, we don't live in a spiritual or moral world and the white boys got enough H-bombs, missiles, T.V.'s, firehoses and dogs to prove it.

23

Therefore, he concluded, "we must move not spiritually but politically, i.e., with power" [8:19].

In some ways it is understandable to hear the avowed revolutionaries among Black Power forces refer to political, economic, and military realities as the ultimate forces in life. It is even more interesting to note that same direction in the forceful statement of an impressive group of black churchmen who wrote on the subject of black and white power in 1966. In the midst of the national furor over the newly discovered term, the churchmen published a full page advertisement in *The New York Times* which said, in part, "The fundamental distortion facing us in the controversy about 'black power' is rooted in a gross imbalance of power and conscience between Negroes and white Americans." After setting out this basic introduction to their thesis, the statement continued,

> It is this distortion, mainly, which is responsible for the widespread, though often inarticulate, assumption that white people are justified in getting what they want through the use of power, but that Negro Americans must, either by nature or by circumstances, make their appeal only through conscience. As a result, the power of white men and the conscience of black men have both been corrupted. The power of white men is corrupted because it meets little meaningful resistance from Negroes to temper it and keep white men from aping God.

Tracing the corruption of the black conscience, the churchmen attributed it to a condition in which,

> having no power to implement the demands of conscience, the concern for justice is transmuted into a distorted form of love, which, in the absence of justice, becomes chaotic self-surrender. Powerlessness breeds a race of beggars. We are faced now with a situation where conscienceless power meets powerless conscience, threatening the very foundations of our nation [15:187].

It was evident that the churchmen were convinced that "conscience," or "love" as they later referred to it, was "powerless" without the coercive forces of the society. They appeared no less disturbed than John Killens about "unrequited love," and in a

392

sophisticated adumbration, the group simply gave religious expression to the political views of Carmichael, Karenga and a host of other black spokesmen. Though it is not fully stated they seem to be saying that the ultimate weapons necessary for the building of the new black community are those now monopolized by white power leaders. Blacks have to get their hands on some of these weapons and perhaps depend upon their own consciences to "temper" black uses of the same instruments whites had used for such destructive purposes. But when blacks begin getting their proper share of the power, it would appear that they might be less dependent upon the development of "conscience" — unless it was theirs in large supplies "by nature" rather than "by circumstance." How then would black power be tempered?

393

A question at least as compelling is this: Does the theological position implicit in the churchmen's statement carry a doctrine of two kingdoms with it? Do these leaders seek the Kingdom of the weaponless, defenseless, homeless King at certain times, and the Kingdom of the armed, propertied, politically powerful, American, white (soon to be technicolored) King at another time? Where do the kingdoms meet? Are the guidelines to the nature of human community as blurred as those for the nature of man? On issues of ultimate power, are the insights of Christian ministers only accidentally the same as Stokely Carmichael's and Ron Karenga's?

The implications of the churchmen's statement are numerous and provocative, but it is important to supplement that statement with an even more theologically astute brief for Black Power by one of the individual signators, Nathan Wright. Dr. Wright, who is also chairman of the National Conference on Black Power, recently wrote of the image of God and its relationship to power among black men. He said,

> In religious terms, a God of power, of majesty and of might, who has made men to be in His own image and likeness, must will that His creation reflect in the immediacies of life His power, His majesty and His might. Black Power raises . . . the far too long overlooked need for power, if life is to become what in the mind of its Creator it is destined to be [15:136].

In a fascinating way Karenga, one of the best trained and most thoughtful of the Black Power leaders, picks up the precise line set down by Wright. In all likelihood he does it independently, so it is even more significant and illuminating that his definition of Black Power should also find its basis in a powerful deity. He writes, "God is God who moves in power; God is God who moves in change and creates something out of nothing. If you want to be God just think about that" [8:26]. (Karenga's last sentence is not random rhetoric. Evidently he has so imbibed the homocentric orientation of the American society that he upstages the Mormons by telling men that they become Gods now by entering into Godlike action. Indeed, the emphasis on autonomous black action is another of the hallmarks of Black Power ideology, a hallmark that leaves little room for any dependence on what might be called grace — a hallmark that would stamp it as far more Protestant than one might desire.)

394

The difficulty with the analogy evoked by Wright and Karenga is its failure to recognize another aspect of the power of God within the biblical tradition. If Wright and the other black churchmen put any serious stock in the life and teachings of Jesus of Nazareth as the clearest possible window to the face of God, then one must at least examine another way of power. That is, one must see the power of God demonstrated in weakness and in humiliation. Is it not possible that the God who dies for his enemies, who rejects their terms and their weapons — and their kind of power — is also worthy of consideration as a model for the empowerment of the black community?

Though it is difficult to propound, it would appear that such a question may have some possible validity when one remembers some of the goals of Black Power. May not one properly ask if a new black community will be created by the appropriation of the old American weapons of power? More specifically, what of Karenga's insight into the nature of racism? He said at one point,

> Racist minds created racist institutions. Therefore you must move against racism, not institutions. For even if you tear down the institutions that same mind will build them up again [8:14].

How does one "move against racism"? Surely not with "H-bombs, missiles, T.V.'s, firehoses . . . dogs" and all the other institutions of political power now possessed by "the white boy." And what of Stokely Carmichael's strangely religious metaphor: "For racism to die, a totally different America must be born" [2:6]? Will a black community in search of a new society really participate in the process of new birth by a reactionary fixation on all the kinds of power which have helped to corrupt the nation? How does new birth come?

Talk of weakness and death, quests for new birth, all tend to be at once sources of fascination and anathema for the current black breed. It is likely that the apparently contradictory references to such matters in their writings are largely unconscious, and that the conscious stance is one of opposition to Gods who die on crosses. As we have seen, black men have been chained to weakness for so long that any talk of voluntarily choosing a way that the society counts as weak is considered sheer madness.

Is this the scandal of the cross for the present black moment? Or is it all foolishness in the most irrelevant sense of the word? Perhaps Karenga was most true to himself and to the universe when he said, "We don't live in a spiritual or moral world." Somehow it sounds like the old black deacons who constantly joked behind the minister's back: "Praying is fine in a prayer meeting, but it ain't no good in a bear meeting."

If the world is primarily a bear meeting, and if the only way to survive in such a gathering is by becoming a bear, then the way of Black Power is evident. (Even the preachers seem to agree with elements of Black Bear Power.) Nevertheless, in such a situation, the way of human beings remains cloudy.

BLACK POWER AND RELIGION: BEYOND IMPLICATIONS

Reference to a black prayer meeting serves as a reminder that the discussion of religious issues in this essay has generally grown out of the intimations, suggestions, and tendencies one finds in the words and deeds of Black Power advocates. There has been al-

395

most no attempt to address the subject of the precise, institution-alized religious manifestations of Black Power, largely because such an attempt would be somewhat premature. It is evident, however, that if the ideology does institutionalize itself, a more clearly articulated religious message and ritual will likely develop, or rather a set of such phenomena will emerge.

Anticipation of this is present already throughout the black ghettos. Ever since the days of Garvey's African Orthodox Church, Black Nationalist groups have found religion to be one of their major modes of expression. The Nation of Islam's success is the best known indication of the power inherent in this direction. Recently — especially since Malcolm X's appearance on the national scene — there have been many Black Nationalist attempts to reestablish variations of African religious practices, and one can only speculate on the mutual transformations such attempts may bring about.

None of these developments should be surprising, of course. For instance, when the strongly nationalist Bandung Conference of Afro-Asian peoples gathered in 1955 a resolution was passed "to resurrect their old religions and cultures and modernize them. . . ." Similarly at the world conference of black writers, artists, and intellectuals held in Paris in the following year, one of the participants said that "the main and only resolution called for the rehabilitation of their ancient cultures and religions" [20:22]. These were significant international prefigurings of Black Power in America, and they probably suggest the way that the Afro-American movements will increasingly take.

Besides the plethora of Black Nationalist religious experiments in the ghettos of the land, it is likely that Karenga's west coast organization, US, has so far articulated the most clearly structured and self-consciously religious manifestos of all the Black Power groups. It is representative of much of the movement's concerns both in its rather humanistic, secular (in the most recent religious sense of that word) orientation and in its obvious reaction to the black Christian churches. Thus Karenga teaches that "We must concern ourselves more with the plans for this life, rather than the next life which has its own problems. For the next life across Jordan is much further away than the grawl [sic] of dogs and policemen and the pains of hunger and disease" [8:26].

In spite of the familiar reference to Jordan, groups like Karenga's tend to believe that men live on only through the lives of their children, and there is among them a strong emphasis on the rebuilding of the shattered black home. In such a home the role of the woman follows almost strictly Pauline lines, and some female believers in Black Power find it difficult to adjust their western indoctrination of equality to the old-new emphasis on the supremacy of the black man.

397

The New Testament stream that flows through their doctrine of the relationship of husband to wife does not prevent Black Power groups from engaging in constant attacks on the Christian churches. For instance, Karenga — in keeping with many other similar leaders who preceded him — says that "Christians do good because they fear — we do good because we love. They do good because God says so — we do good . . . in response to need" [8].

The issue of religion is constantly before many of the young persons who are drawn back into the ghettos by the urgent logic of Black Power. As they return — from college or from prison — to struggle against what can be reasonably described as "principalities and powers" which seem anonymously but fiercely to control the life of their people, they find themselves often insufficient as autonomous sources of inner strength. They cannot return to the Christian churches they once knew, because these churches have so often appeared irrelevant to the real needs of the community, and most often they are controlled by older men and women who seem unprepared for the competition from radical black youth. In here, strangely enough, a few black Christian churches have responded fully to the call of Black Power. In Detroit, the pastor of one such congregation, the Reverend Albert B. Cleague, Jr, of the Central United Church of Christ, preaches of a black revolutionary Jesus who came to set the nonwhite peoples free. A Black Madonna is the focal point of worship, and the church has probably attracted more persons committed to Black Power than any other single institution still connected to the Christian churches.

Even when they cannot find such havens, there is nevertheless something in the black religious tradition that continues to attract many racially conscious young people. For instance, it is most moving and revealing to watch a group of them respond totally with clapping and dancing to the Gospel songs that continue to shape the tradition that spawned them. They are at home for a time. Ideologies aside, this is still "Soul."

On what may or may not be another level of their being, some of the group also sense a strange sense of attraction to Jesus of Nazareth. They are convinced that an encounter with the historical Jesus would likely be a meeting with a revolutionary, but they have been turned off by the whiteness infused into this Jesus by the western Christian tradition. They are also able and often accurate cataloguers of the unfaithfulness of the churches — black and white. Sometimes they consider these churches as irrelevant as white persons are. A few of the seekers turn to Judaism, but often meet the reality of the Jewish middleman in the ghettos and find it an obstacle to faith. Others move towards Islamic variations of belief, often giving up their western, Christian names. This is partly another declaration of independence from slavery and its postreconstruction variations, but it is in some situations simply part of the ancient practice of men taking on new names when they find new faiths.

In the light of their search for the lineaments of a new societal order, it is surely significant that some black groups have now moved towards various forms of communitarianism. In locations like Los Angeles and Philadelphia attempts are made to find this style of life in the urban context. In upper New York state real estate has been set aside for such an experiment; while in Brooklyn a group of some sixty men and women now plan for moving back to the south, to the land. Is it likely that such actions represent more than exercises in anguished flight? Is it possible that they are really a challenge to the two settings which have been most destructive to black life — the city and the south? Are they expressions of hope in the power of resurrected black lives to conquer even these ancient foes?

398

30

There is a sense of religious ferment on the path to Black Power, a sense that is not easy to document. Mixtures of old and new approaches to the essential issues of life are being attempted. Allah and other gods of Africa enter into competition with Yaweh, Jesus, and Buddha. It is a joyously difficult time, but part of the affirmation of Black Power is "We are a spiritual people." The institutional manifestations of that affirmation are still being tested. A people separated from their past now attempt to build bridges, create new realities, or search among the ruins for whatever remains of value there may be.

So Afro-Americans enter the experience that many peoples have known before them, peoples who in time of national crisis have turned to the gods they knew before the coming of Christian missionaries, seeking for what seemed a more solid ground. Nor should it be forgotten that such searches have taken place in this century no less significantly in Ireland and Germany than in Kenya and the Congo.

As for the possible results here, one can only begin to speculate, for instance, on the impact of some African religions on a Black Power movement that is still more western oriented and Protestant than it can possibly admit. Will these religions which seek unity and harmony with the forces of God in the universe transform an ideology that is still determined to change the world around it? Can one accept the Yoruba dreams and dress without falling sway to its world view? Only the questions are available now.

Meanwhile, few adherents of Black Power deny their need for religious moorings, and, though no clear pattern has yet emerged, it must be evident by now that for many persons this movement is likely to become as fully a "church" as the earlier phase was for others. Not only does it begin to fill the need for personal commitment and a sense of fellowship with other similarly committed black persons; it also embodies impressive social concern, a call for ultimate justice, and a search to be present with the sufferers of the society. Gladly identifying with the oppressed beyond national borders, this church increasingly seeks to glorify at least that part of God which may reside in black folk.

In the midst of such developments, one central question cries out for an answer, the kind of answer that is perhaps to be found most fully in the insight of true religion. Though often articulated only in parts, if put into words by Black Power adherents, it would be, "How shall we deal with an enemy who has more power than we do, who has long controlled and destroyed our lives that are even now more fully dependent upon him than we dare confess?" Whatever religion arises from the heart of Black Power will need to address itself to such a dilemma with more honesty than most black religion has ever done before. (One of the generally unrecognized religious blessings of this movement is the honesty it has already forced into the black-white dialogue in America. It has not produced hate; it has rather revealed hate and called upon both whites and blacks to admit its sorrowful depths. There are, of course, large segments of the society who still fear this radical honesty, but it is likely that they also fear true religion.)

400

EPILOGUE: MARTIN LUTHER KING AND BLACK POWER

No discussion of black religion in America today can ignore the immensely important figure of Martin Luther King. In spite of statements to the contrary, he remains an individual of critical importance for anyone who would gain insights into the black experience here. Therefore it is crucial to examine King's response to a movement that has seemed to push him off the stage. The encounter may well provide unexpected illumination for some summary views.

In his most recent work, *Where Do We Go From Here?* [12] King attempts an assessment of Black Power that is significant and revealing, not for its originality or its challenge, but for the basic weakness of his response to the realities evoked and addressed by the ideology. There is in one chapter a favorable interpretation of the "positive" aspects of Black Power as a psychological healing force. Then as King attempts to define the elements which will bring the "necessary" power to the black community, he refers to power as "the strength required to bring about social, political or economic changes," and identifies this power in many of the same ways as the churchmen and the leading Black Power advocates. When the words come from Martin Luther King, however, they bear somewhat more powerful implications. He writes,

> There is nothing essentially wrong with power. The problem is that in America power is unequally distributed. This has led Negro Americans in the past to seek their goals through love and moral suasion devoid of power and white Americans to seek their goals through power devoid of love and conscience. . . . It is precisely this collision of immoral power with powerless morality which constitutes the major crisis of our times [12:37].

401

In religious (as well as political) terms, King's words constitute something of a crisis in themselves and raise many difficult issues. They tempt us, most importantly, to ask whether Martin Luther King was describing his own movement when he spoke of Negroes in the past who sought goals "through love and moral suasion" because no other way was available to them. If this identification is precise, then one must surely question the nature of such love and the motives of the moral suasion. And if the love was "powerless" why were so many past references made to "the power of love and nonviolence" — references found even in King's current work?

Surely the talk of love and suasion that was a kind of last resort is not in keeping with the insights of the great teachers of nonviolence, who set out this way for men who were not cowards, who had other weapons available, but who chose to put them aside for the sake of a better way. King's statements cause one to ask if there was really a nonviolent movement at any point. Was "too much love" really the problem? Could it be that nonviolence was simply impossible for a people who had never had an opportunity to affirm their manhood or to choose violence as a way of response on a widespread scale? Perhaps the late, lamented nonviolent movement can really come only after the Malcolms, Stokelys, and Raps have offered another real choice to millions of black folk.

Even more significant for the present discussion is King's failure to deal clearly and precisely with the central black radical conviction concerning America. Its advocates believe (and they have a growing company of fellow believers) that this nation will not allow black men the freedom, opportunity, and restitution needful for meaningful lives without a total, violent disruption of the society. Like revolutionaries before them, they believe that the national fabric must be rent before white people will believe in the validity of black demands for life. Here is the price of three centuries of racism, they say. King does not really respond to this assumption. He warns against cynicism, but fails to set out in clarity his response to a situation in which even massive, disciplined nonviolent resistance will continue to meet increasingly violent (and/or sophisticated) repression.

Somehow the night of that terror seems too dark for King to enter. His only real attempt at an answer to the Black Power conviction is a vague statement of faith, but the object of the faith also remains vague. King writes,

> Our most fruitful course is to stand firm, move forward nonviolently, accept disappointments and cling to hope. Our determined refusal not to be stopped will eventually open the door to fulfillment. By recognizing the necessity of suffering in a righteous cause, we may achieve our humanity's full stature. To guard ourselves from bitterness, we need the vision to see in this generation's ordeals the opportunity to transfigure both ourselves and American society [12:46–47].

There are missing links and false notes apparent in any religiously focused examination of this central statement. Nowhere is there any explanation of why King believes that the door "will eventually open." Is it faith in American goodness, in the power of a nonviolent movement that he hardly discusses, or faith in an abstract justice in the universe? (King's God often seems no less dead than anyone else's — at least if one judges life by appearance in the printed pages.) Without such clarification, his call could be dismissed as a Pollyanna voice attempting to challenge the whirlwind.

Even more important is his failure to discuss the possible rea-

402

34

sons for an amorphous, variously motivated group of black people to suffer without retaliation the continued scorn and injury of people they consider at least fools and at most devils. When King referred to "powerless morality" and identified authentic power for black people with economic and political power, he was then likely obligated to ask who would be willing to live without such power once it became possible either to kill for it or to kill to protest its denial.

It would appear that, unless King is ready to face black men with the need to suffer without retaliation and also to live without the power he considered "necessary," much of his argument against violence falls apart. For the violence of revolutionaries comes not from "hatred," as he says, but from the insistence of the oppressed that they must have at least a proportionate share of the power which the oppressor insists upon keeping and defending by violent means. Leaders like Karenga say such power is absolutely necessary for black men. So does King. Black Power leaders are convinced that the country will not make such power available without armed struggle of one kind or another. What does a believer in religious nonviolence have to say to such a situation? Is it enough not to face it squarely? And if he does, must King eventually choose between armed struggle and a powerless future for black people in the United States?

403

In a sense this dilemma is a reminder of how much the present black situation — especially in its religious dimensions — is a microcosmic expression of the main lines of the development of American Christian ethics in this century. Within the microcosm King stands for the liberal tradition, continuing to maintain faith in American goodness, in reason, in the ordered nature of the world. Such a stance seems to require his refusing to look directly into chaos, seems to demand that he fail to trace the deepest lineaments of the nation's racist core. In a sense King appears to hope that dark "principalities and powers" in massive array are only figments of overexercised religious imagination. In their place he substitutes an eloquent dream.

On the other hand stand the proponents of Black Power, like some dark blossoms of "realism" gone beyond control. They look with cynical but not dishonest eyes at the forces of evil in the society, at their depth and their extent. They see without flinching the possibility that power will not be shared voluntarily, that atonement cannot come without the shedding of blood, and they are determined that as little of the blood as possible will flow from them. They see the night and prepare men for its terror. They refuse to dream. But like much of the realist position, they also fail to acknowledge sufficiently (perhaps because of insensitivity on certain levels of their being) the reality of creative, healing forces in the situation. Somehow the power of resurrection is totally irrelevant to the struggles they outline, except in the most personal applications to individual "dead" black men.

404

Moved out of the metaphorical microcosm, these two perspectives are badly in need of each other for the mutual sharing and the possible mutual growth which may well be the nation's only visible hope in the racial crisis. The necessary, relentless determination of Black Power to look fully on the evil of American life must be informed by some hope even more solid than King's, some expectation of creative possibilities (even of Messiahs), some determination not to succumb to the enemy's disease. Even more soberly put, it may be that all who speak with any seriousness about addressing the profound social and psychological distortions wrought by American racism must be prepared to experiment with totally new weapons, and be ready (how hard the words!) for complete defeat — at least as it is commonly counted.

For if racism rages as deep into American life as it appears and if violence is its closest brother, then a black revolution will no more solve the problem than a civil war did (even if Rap Brown gets his atomic bomb). So it may be most responsible to ask if it is more than despair to speak of a long, grueling battle with no victory — and no illusions — this side of the grave? Has it been important and necessary simply to learn that there are no large citizen armies of white deliverers? Was it not absolutely necessary that all trust in courts and troops and presidents be shattered? Is this part of a black coming of age, a coming which will eventually reveal that even the black God of the ghetto is dead?

Perhaps, though, he is not dead. Perhaps this new God has not lived long enough to die. Perhaps there is still a Beloved Community ahead. But if it is, it must be seen as the Kingdom whose realization does not depend upon whether whites (or anyone else around) really want it or not. If it comes, it may come only for those who seek it for its own sake and for the sake of its Lord, recognizing that even if He is black, the final glory is not the glory of blackness, but a setting straight of all the broken men and communities of the earth. In some strange ways Black Power may be headed in that way, but it probably needs some new and stripped-down coming of Martin King's most fervent hopes to accompany its path.

405

On the other hand, if the night is already too dark for the way to be found, or if society should make it impossible for these two black tendencies to live and find each other, then there seems little to expect that is not apocalyptic. This has always been a religious implication of life, especially black life. It is certainly one of the deepest implications of a wishful liberalism and an inescapable possibility for a Black Power that finally accepts not only America's weapons but also its ultimate definitions of manhood, power, majesty, and might.

Was it for this that we have come so painfully far together — and yet apart — in this strange land? Was it only for this? Is there no saving message from the drums of our homeland, or did all gods die at once?

REFERENCES

1. Aptheker, Herbert, ed: *A Documentary History of the Negro People in the United States*, 2 vol (Citadel Press, New York, New York) 1965.
2. Carmichael, Stokely: What We Want, *New York Review of Books*, vol 7, no 4, Sept 22, 1966.
3. Carmichael, Stokely: Towards Black Liberation, *Massachusetts Review*, Autumn 1966.
4. Cornwell, Anita: Symposium on Black Power, *Negro Digest*, vol 16, no 1, Nov 1966.

37

5. Fair, Ronald: Symposium on Black Power, *Negro Digest*, vol 16, no 1, Nov 1966.

6. Garvey, Amy Jacques, ed: *Philosophy and Opinions of Marcus Garvey* (Universal Publishing House, New York, New York) 1923.

7. Garvey, Marcus: in Cronon, Edmund D: *Black Moses* (University of Wisconsin Press, Madison, Wisconsin) 1964.

8. Halisi, Clyde and Mtume, James, ed: *The Quotable Karenga* (US, Los Angeles, California) 1967.

9. Harding, Vincent: Religion and Resistance among Antebellum Negroes, 1800–1860, in the volume by August Meier and Elliot Rudwick, ed (Atheneum Publishers, New York, New York) forthcoming.

10. Hare, Nathan: Symposium on Black Power, *Negro Digest*, vol 16, no 1, Nov 1966.

11. Killens, John Oliver: Symposium on Black Power, *Negro Digest*, vol 16, no 1, Nov 1966.

12. King, Martin Luther: *Where Do We Go From Here?* (Harper & Row, Publishers, New York, New York) 1967.

13. Lester, Julius: The Angry Children of Malcolm X, *Sing Out*, vol 16, no 5, Nov 1966, an important and eloquent contribution to our understanding of the coming of Black Power.

14. Muhammad, Elijah: *Message to the Black Man*.

15. National Committee of Negro Churchmen: "Black Power," A Statement, in Wright, reference 19.

16. Philippians 3.

17. Saunders, Stanley: I'll Never Leave the Ghetto, *Ebony*, vol 20, no 10, Aug 1967.

18. Walker, David: *Appeal* (1829) in Herbert Aptheker, ed, *One Continual Cry* (Humanities Press, Inc, New York, New York) 1965.

19. Wright, Nathan, Jr: *Black Power and Urban Unrest* (Hawthorn Books, Inc, New York, New York) 1967.

20. Wright, Richard: *White Man, Listen!* (Anchor Books, Doubleday & Company, Inc, Garden City, New York) 1964.